EMBATTLED NATION

BY THE SAME AUTHORS

Patrice Dutil and David MacKenzie,
Canada, 1911: The Decisive Election that Shaped the Country
(Dundurn Press, 2011)

Patrice Dutil and Roger Hall (eds.),
Macdonald at 200: New Reflections and Legacies
(Dundurn Press, 2014)

PATRICE DUTIL
DAVID MACKENZIE

EMBATTLED NATION

Canada's Wartime
Election of 1917

DUNDURN
TORONTO

Cover image: Wikimedia Commons
Printer: Webcom

Library and Archives Canada Cataloguing in Publication
Dutil, Patrice A., 1960-, author
     Embattled nation : Canada's wartime election of 1917 / Patrice Dutil, David MacKenzie.

Includes bibliographical references and index.
Issued in print and electronic formats.
ISBN 978-1-4597-3726-6 (softcover).--ISBN 978-1-4597-3727-3 (PDF).--ISBN 978-1-4597-3728-0 (EPUB)

     1. Borden, Robert Laird, Sir, 1854-1937. 2. Laurier, Wilfrid, Sir, 1841-1919. 3. Canada. Parliament--Elections, 1917. 4. Draft--Canada--History--20th century. 5. Political campaigns--Canada--History--20th century. 6. World War, 1914-1918--Political aspects--Canada.   7. Canada--Politics and government--1911-1921.   I. MacKenzie, David, 1953-, author II. Title.

FC557.5.D88 2017   971.061'2   C2017-904458-3
                                             C2017-904459-1

1   2   3   4   5   21   20   19   18   17

   Conseil des Arts   Canada Council    Canadä    ONTARIO ARTS COUNCIL
       du Canada   for the Arts   CONSEIL DES ARTS DE L'ONTARIO
                                                                              an Ontario government agency
                                                                              un organisme du gouvernement de l'Ontario

We acknowledge the support of the **Canada Council for the Arts,** which last year invested $153 million to bring the arts to Canadians throughout the country, and the **Ontario Arts Council** for our publishing program. We also acknowledge the financial support of the **Government of Ontario,** through the **Ontario Book Publishing Tax Credit** and the **Ontario Media Development Corporation,** and the **Government of Canada.**

Nous remercions le **Conseil des arts du Canada** de son soutien. L'an dernier, le Conseil a investi 153 millions de dollars pour mettre de l'art dans la vie des Canadiennes et des Canadiens de tout le pays.

Care has been taken to trace the ownership of copyright material used in this book. The author and the publisher welcome any information enabling them to rectify any references or credits in subsequent editions.
— *J. Kirk Howard, President*

The publisher is not responsible for websites or their content unless they are owned by the publisher.

Printed and bound in Canada.

VISIT US AT

 dundurn.com |  @dundurnpress | dundurnpress | dundurnpress

Dundurn
3 Church Street, Suite 500
Toronto, Ontario, Canada
M5E 1M2

For our daughters, Nicole, Natalie, Isabelle, Claire, and Elizabeth,
and granddaughters Norah and Margot:
May they and their country never live through
an election like that of 1917

This election is a referendum. The issue is: Shall we put the whole force of this country behind the war in munitions and men; or shall we put further contributions to the war on the Prussian basis: talk, accompanied by a furious scramble for office?

There are individuals who get purple in the face when told that this is the choice; they insist that there are other important issues which will determine the casting of their votes.

An elector in this frame of mind can give any reason he chooses to his neighbors and his conscience for the ballot he casts; but when it is cast it will be for

Going on with the war, or getting out of the war;

Remembering our troops in the field, or forgetting them;

Keeping faith with the living, or deserting the living and dishonoring the dead.

— *Manitoba Free Press*, November 23, 1917

There is no longer any reason why the whole truth should not be spoken about Quebec. The people of that Province have been rank quitters throughout the whole war. They have been prolific in excuses and evasions and in nothing else....

In short, they have done nothing in the war as yet and they hope to do nothing for the remainder of the war.... The general election of Dec. 17 is to decide whether or not they are to take charge of Canada for the remainder of the war. The man who votes against the Union Government votes for Bolsheviki rule in Canada.

— *Manitoba Free Press*, November 28, 1917

CONTENTS

PREFACE

"December 17 will be Domesday. This contest is not an election but a destiny. Beyond all reasonable doubt it is a conflict for the soul of this nation."

— *Manitoba Free Press*, December 13, 1917

Canada's wartime election of 1917 took place in the worst year of the country's history. It was a time marked by unprecedented numbers of battlefield deaths in places like Vimy Ridge, Hill 70, and Passchendaele, inconsolable sorrow, sad returns home for injured soldiers, endless tears, broken promises, and broken politics. Embroiled in a world conflict, Canadians debated the issues with all their hearts and marched to the voting polls at a rate never seen before or again equalled in the history of this nation. In its time, this election was interpreted as both the justified victory of a bipartisan effort to transcend politics and as a perversion of democracy. Since then it has been recast as an object lesson that in politics the ends do not always justify the means. Sir Robert Borden, the hero of the day, was seen as an arch-Canadian, a patriot, and a supreme defender of the Empire. Today, he ranks low on the scale of those prime ministers who held office for more than one term and he has been largely forgotten, even by some members of the party that he led for almost twenty years.[1] Sir Wilfrid Laurier was dejected after losing the election and passed away fourteen months later with the conviction that his entire political life had been a failure; that his work to bring together English and French, Catholic and Protestant, patriot and imperialist, had come to nothing. He died in melancholy, with little hope that a return to "sunny ways" in Canadian politics could again be possible. Today, he is revered by Liberals and held in high esteem by historians.[2]

The plain fact is that the 1917 election was so central to the shaping of Canada's view of the world that in many ways it still has not entirely passed from politics into history. Some excellent scholarship has been devoted to various aspects of this epic confrontation and we stand on the shoulders of those who have preceded us in imagining and reconstructing the issues and debates, the controversies and tensions, and the smoke-filled backrooms seething with gossip, dire predictions, and speculation.

Remarkably, this is the first book devoted exclusively to the "khaki" election of 1917, and it joins a short shelf of other studies of Canadian elections. Based on standard secondary authorities, published documents, official papers, and newspapers available in print and on the Internet, it also draws on diaries and private letters held in various archives in Ottawa, Toronto, Montreal, Kingston, Washington, D.C., and London (U.K.). Our aim is to flesh out the realities of this extraordinary campaign by documenting the intentions of the central characters and the unique context in which they lived and, in so doing, we have assumed the responsibility for translating all the original French-language sources. We have also followed a chronological sequence to document the ebb and flow of the passions of the day, mindful that the actors in this drama did not, and could not, know how the story would unfold. The book considers military, cultural, social, and economic factors, which have received so much attention from historians over the years, but we have deliberately chosen to emphasize political developments. We have concerned ourselves particularly with what we consider to be the central themes of this electoral campaign — nationalism and imperialism, compulsion and volunteerism, ambition and resistance, war and peace.

The key actors in this story had battled each other for more than a decade. Sir Wilfrid, the leader of the Liberals since 1887, had won four consecutive majorities starting in 1896 — a record still unbroken. The Liberal victory in 1900 was a devastating blow to the old Conservative Party and the Confederation-generation that had led it. In defeat, the party turned to Robert Borden. If Laurier was charm and wit incarnate,

Borden was plain-spoken and straight-as-an-arrow. His attempts to unseat Laurier in 1904 and 1908 failed, but in 1911 he seized on the dual issues of military support to the United Kingdom and reciprocity with the United States to finally win power. Victory was his in two key areas: Ontario, where Conservatism was wildly popular, and Quebec, thanks to an unusual alliance with journalist Henri Bourassa and his *nationaliste* followers. Laurier, for his part, seriously thought of resigning his position and abandoning politics. Instead, he clung to his seat in Parliament; it was, as Borden later remembered, his "workbench." In June 1914, Borden was knighted by George V; he would fight the next election as "Sir" Robert.

The 1917 election was fought at a time that is almost impossible to imagine today. The Bolshevik revolution was unfolding in Russia and it seemed as if the days of European royalty were coming to an end. Canada had already lost at least forty thousand soldiers by December of that year and the epic battle at Passchendaele, which brought tragedy to thousands of Canadian families, had been fought only weeks before. During the campaign itself, Halifax was almost completely destroyed by the explosion triggered by the collision of two ships in its harbour. Canada, more than at any time in its history, was an embattled nation, divided almost as much as the Europe it hoped to assist. The country was challenged physically, morally, and intellectually as never before, and it was in this context that Canadian voters were obliged to perform their democratic duty. While Canadian troops bravely marched in Europe, Canadian voters marched to the polls with the conviction that, in this brave new world, their votes would make a difference and set the country on a better path to the future.

This book begins by examining Sir Robert Borden's government at war's outset and chronicles the politics around the decision to call an election. The second chapter focuses on French Canada and more specifically on Henri Bourassa, the editor of *Le Devoir*, and how he twinned the issue of Canada's participation in the war with the schools question in Ontario. For him, it was simply incompatible for English Canada to demand a greater war effort from Quebec and French Canada while suppressing the language rights of its most important minority. The politics over the nature of Canada's war effort spilled into 1917, when Borden finally had to face the electorate. The book discusses how he created a coalition around the issue of conscription and then legislated regulations that might have the chance of winning him, the Conservatives, and the new Liberals who joined them in a Union government, a mandate to govern. Three chapters are devoted to the campaign itself. Finally, we scrutinize the results and measure to what degree Borden and his team were able to forge a winning vote.

Our final chapter considers the fallout of this turning point in the politics of an embattled Canada. Since then it has been said and repeated that Canada asserted itself in this conflict; that it emerged from the war as a true country. This is the story of how the country was almost lost by politicians blinded by ambition, lacking in imagination, and often paralyzed by incompetence and dithering. Unable to create consensus, they brought their embattled nation to the brink of disaster. This is their story.

ACKNOWLEDGEMENTS

W e are grateful to those who have helped us complete this book. Our wives, Maha Dutil and Teresa Lemieux, know all too well the moodiness that comes with spouses confronting the confusion of past events. Our families also take primary rank as they inevitably are the first to bear the brunt of new ideas being formulated. We are also grateful to Kirk Howard, president and publisher of Dundurn, who once again generously lent his support to a work that represents a sequel to the first book we published with the same firm on the election of 1911, which also appeared on the centennial of that conflict. Also at Dundurn, we thank Kathryn Lane, the managing editor, Carrie Gleason, the editorial director, Dominic Farrell, the developmental editor, and Elena Radic, the project editor, for their efforts in turning our manuscript into a book. We also extend our appreciation to Laurie Miller for copyediting the manuscript, to Courtney Horner for designing the cover, and to Dr. Alyson Brickey for preparing the index.

We are grateful to our institutional home, Ryerson University, and its Office of the Vice-President for Research. First, it provided the funding to hire Mr. Nicholas Vani and Ms. Brianna Hutchinson, two dedicated research assistants from the Ryerson student body. We are thankful for their able, cheerful, and patient assistance with this project. Mr. Vani helped us with our research in newspapers. Ms. Hutchinson created electronic scans of the ridings that were formed in the 1914 redistricting exercise and contained in J.E. Chalifour's giant book, the *Electoral Atlas of the Dominion of Canada, According to the Redistribution act of 1914 and the Amending act of 1915* (Ottawa, 1916). These images were then geo-referenced and traced precisely in ArcMap, thus creating a file that traced all the constituency boundaries in Canada; the first of its kind. She then produced the precisely drawn electoral maps that are found in the appendix. She filled a spreadsheet with all the voting data and matched it to its corresponding polygon. Her skills in geographic analysis yielded even more than an invaluable resource for the study and illustration of the outcome of the 1917 election: she also created a base on which political historians can continue to demonstrate political trends in Canada. This mapping exercise would not have been conceivable without the able assistance of Mr. Marcel Fortin, Map Librarian at the Robarts Reference Library, University of Toronto. He allowed us to scan the Chalifour book and we are grateful to him for this.

Second, our appreciations go to Dr. Janet Lum, Associate Dean (Research) of the Faculty of Arts, for her unwavering support. The Office of the Dean of Arts again came through with a grant that allowed us to create an index.

We would also like to thank Ms. Dominique Nantel Bergeron for drawing our attention to the Nantel family papers and for allowing us to cite passages from the correspondence she possesses between members of her remarkable family. She also kindly allowed us to reproduce family pictures. Jack Granatstein kindly answered many questions regarding the military situation and thoughtfully pointed us toward resources that inevitably led to answers. Joe Martin read parts of the manuscript and also offered sound advice. Naturally, none of the above is responsible for any errors of commission or omission in our research and writing about this extraordinary electoral event.

Patrice Dutil
Department of Politics and Public Administration

David MacKenzie
Department of History

Ryerson University, Toronto, July 1, 2017

1

THE CONUNDRUM: ROBERT BORDEN, WAR, AND THE CALL FOR AN ELECTION

"The difference between a politician and a statesman is that a politician thinks about the next election while the statesman thinks about the next generation."

— Attributed to James Freeman Clarke (1810–1888), American theologian and author

Clarke's famous observation was at least two generations old in the summer of 1914, but its harsh distinction was in the back of everyone's mind in Ottawa as Canada hurriedly prepared for war. Sir Robert Borden's government was already three years old and the temptation to call an early election, as Sir Wilfrid Laurier had done in 1911, was irresistible. Was this a solemn moment to display noble leadership or one to be practical politically and take advantage of an obvious position of strength to call an election?

Borden had long suspected that war with Germany was to come. He had openly said so in the great debate on the creation of Canada's Navy in 1909 and 1910. He had taken note of the Austrian Archduke's murder in Sarajevo in late June 1914, but his mind was elsewhere. Just a few days before, he had ordered the *Komagata Maru*, a Japanese vessel carrying several hundred Indian passengers anchored in the Vancouver harbour, to be escorted back out to sea by HMCS *Rainbow*. The *Rainbow* was one of the ships that had been acquired by the Laurier government to launch the Canadian Navy in 1910.

The day he learned of Franz Ferdinand's assassination, Borden left the capital for Grand-Pré, Nova Scotia, the village where he was born, to visit his ninety-year-old mother. It was that kind of welcomed summer for most Canadians: visits with the family, lazy days in the sun, maybe a bit of baseball. In the last week of July, Borden and his wife, Laura, left for Muskoka, Ontario, for a month's holiday. Borden was exhausted and troubled by endless breakouts of carbuncles — painful and often bleeding nodules in the skin that constantly needed attention. Doctors suspected they were brought on by too much work and worry, what today would be called "uncontrolled stress." Borden agreed: he needed rest.

It did not last long. Borden played golf and delighted in some swimming for a few days, but, exactly a week later, on July 30, his secretary cabled him that events were spinning out of control and that he had to return to Ottawa. Borden arrived in the capital on the morning of Saturday, August first, and immediately set to work.[1] He ordered his vacationing cabinet ministers back to Ottawa and informed the British government that Canada stood ready.

Cabinet met the next day in the East Block on Parliament Hill — even though it was a Sunday — and set off the most frenetic week of activity Canada had ever seen. Myriad orders-in-council — executive orders — were drafted and considered in light of all sorts of eventualities. Canada had never experienced such a crisis and was unprepared for these new problems, emergencies, and tensions. The first call for army volunteers went out on the Monday. Cabinet met twice the next day, and gathered again in the evening, expecting terrible news from Europe. The telegram arrived just before 9 p.m.: Great Britain had declared war on Germany. Canada, it followed in the minds of everyone present, was also at war. Borden called for Parliament to assemble and immediately commandeered the two submarines the British Columbia government had hurriedly purchased a few days earlier from a Seattle shipyard (they had been destined for Chile) and put them at the disposal of the British government. In less than three weeks, twenty thousand men would be assembled at the new Camp Valcartier, about twenty kilometres northwest of Quebec City. The leaves had barely started to turn when the first Canadian contingent, a thirty-thousand-man division, set sail for Europe and efforts were well underway to raise the second. That only a minority of these men were

Rt. Hon. Sir Robert Laird Borden, March 1918.

actually Canadian-born, let alone French Canadian, hardly mattered. Canada was responding.

The Borden Conservatives had been elected in September 1911 and took power a few weeks later with a sense of purpose. Having not formed a government since 1896, the party was eager to manipulate the levers of power, and Borden took considerable care in assembling a cabinet that would get things done. He went outside the traditional party to fill several key cabinet positions, including bringing in Thomas White from Toronto's Bay Street as his minister of finance. Otherwise, his new cabinet comprised a mixture of the forces that had carried him to power. Many of the important posts went to Torontonians, others to stalwart Tories; there was also an odd combination of imperialists like the mercurial, insufferable Sam Hughes and the anti-imperialist *nationalistes*, who had managed to defeat Laurier in Quebec by siding with Borden's Conservatives. The negotiations with the Quebeckers had been difficult, as none of the *nationaliste* chiefs were particularly inclined toward the rigours of administration, and they did not particularly relish the idea of Borden as their boss. Frederick Debartzch Monk, a long-time Tory and *nationaliste* sympathizer, accepted, but only reluctantly, as did Louis-Philippe Pelletier and Wilfrid-Bruno Nantel. It was a weak assemblage and it fractured quickly.

For Borden the central issue in the years before the outbreak of the war was Canada's naval policy and, more generally, its relationship with the Empire. The debate over what to do about the Navy provided the starkest contrast between Borden's government and the previous Laurier administration and the differences revealed two fundamentally different perspectives on Canada's international role and responsibilities. The objective of both parties was ostensibly the same — to support and participate in the defence of Great Britain — but the means to achieve that end were approached in dramatically different ways. The great naval debate was the first in a series of controversies that led directly to the election of 1917.[2]

In 1909 the Laurier government created an independent Navy as Canada's response and contribution to the Anglo-German naval race. It was to be a small force, both an affirmation of loyalty to the Empire and a declaration that Canada could assume much of its own defence. Laurier's "tin-pot navy" was ridiculed by the Conservative opposition as, at best, an ineffective response to a serious international crisis and, at worst, tantamount to a declaration of independence from the Empire. Quebec journalist Henri Bourassa was equally critical, but for opposite reasons: he argued that Laurier's commitment to a navy was both a gesture of support for London's imperialism and a guarantee of Canadian involvement in future European conflicts. Bourassa had been Laurier's close friend and colleague, but now he used the opportunity to realize a plan he had cherished for years: the creation of a daily newspaper dedicated to articulating a particular mix of conservative Catholic ideas with increasing support for a distinct Canadian policy on international issues. In early January 1910, *Le Devoir* was published for the first time, soon making Bourassa one of the most influential and polarizing figures in Canada and a man who would be a major presence during the 1917 election.

Laurier's Naval Service Act and his government's reciprocity agreement with the United States became the central issues of the election of 1911. In Quebec, especially, the Navy was *the* issue, and during the campaign Borden fashioned the "unholy alliance" with Bourassa and his loose group of followers, the *nationalistes*, in a joint effort to defeat Laurier. It was an effective strategy, at least electorally, but soon after the election it became clear that the Tory imperialists of Ontario and the *nationalistes* of Quebec had little in common.

Once in office, Borden did what he had promised to do during the election. He suspended the Naval Service Act — Laurier's navy — and declared that any proposal coming from his government would be "submitted to the people," though it was left deliberately vague whether this would be in a referendum or a general election. These actions were acceptable to both imperialist and *nationaliste* — at first.

Borden and others in the Conservative Party had earlier advocated a direct grant to the British government to help cover the cost of building dreadnought battleships, as Canada's way of contributing to the defence of the Empire. In 1912, after a trip to Great Britain to investigate the deteriorating international situation, the prime minister was convinced that the United Kingdom needed direct financial help in the arms race with Germany.

On December 5, 1912, the Borden government announced a new naval policy and presented its own Naval Aid Bill to Parliament. The bill called for a direct contribution to Britain of $35 million, roughly the cost to build and equip three dreadnoughts. The idea was that the ships would be sent to Canada once its naval department was sufficiently developed. It was a repudiation of Laurier's independent navy and a symbolic gesture of giving help to the mother country in the most direct and efficient way.

Not unexpectedly, the Liberals' reaction was strong and direct. Laurier denounced Borden's plan and launched a bitter attack on the government in January and February 1913, first demanding a referendum on the issue and then staging a filibuster to block the bill's passage. The debate was harsh and protracted, and the bill did not pass the House until May 15, and then only after the government enforced closure on the debate — for the first time in Canadian history. The debate then moved to the Senate and there the bill was stalled by the Liberal majority, which demanded an election on the issue. Borden threatened to reform the upper chamber, but in the end the bill died.

Caught in the middle were the *nationalistes*. They had campaigned against Laurier's independent navy and in doing so had, however reluctantly, aligned themselves with the Borden Conservatives. But they now found themselves having to swallow the even more unpleasant idea of giving the British treasury a good deal of cash. Trapped in their own game in record time, seven of them voted against the government. Monk resigned. Borden was able to hold on to his other Quebec ministers, at least for the time being, but a glaring tear had appeared in the fabric of the Conservative Party.

As a result, when the war began in 1914 Canada had neither Laurier's nor Borden's navy and, when asked for a contribution to the war effort, could respond only with front-line soldiers — Canada had men willing to volunteer for service, but little military hardware. All sides were disappointed — Liberal, Conservative, and *nationaliste*. In August 1914, Borden's government was aging and facing an election in the not-too-far-distant future, and his alliance with the *nationalistes* was falling apart. The divisions revealed during the naval debates could not be patched over during the war; they lingered, never far from the surface.

* * *

In the first weeks of August 1914, Borden and the cabinet focused on six key pieces of legislation. A War Appropriations Bill would provide $50 million to carry out Canada's military effort. An Emergency War Measures Bill was drafted, essentially giving the government of Canada the right to do most anything it wanted in pursuit of the "security, defence, peace, order and welfare" of the country. It suspended *habeas corpus* and authorized the government to censor the press. The government also prepared amendments to the Naturalization Act, to guard against giving citizenship to men or women of enemy countries. A Finance Bill would allow the government to intervene in banking matters, and a Dominion Notes Bill would provide for an accelerated printing of currency. A decision was made to amend the customs tariff schedule to impose additional duties on certain articles. An act to add new taxes on internal revenues was written out. Finally, cabinet crafted a bill to incorporate a new "Canadian Patriotic Fund" that would raise money to help support soldiers' families.

As the Germans stormed through Belgium, Parliament met on August 18 and the governor general, the Duke of Connaught (properly dressed in khaki for the solemn occasion), quickly read a short Speech from the Throne that simply announced that the measures prepared by cabinet would be submitted to the legislature. He concluded by reminding MPs and senators that Canada was part of an international effort. "We may be assured," he read, "that united action to repel the common danger will not fail to strengthen the ties that bind together those vast Dominions in the possession and enjoyment of the blessings of British liberty."[3] The response from the Tory benches was strategic: First, Donald Sutherland, the farmer/MP for Oxford South, spoke in English on behalf of a dependably imperialist Ontario. There was no question that public opinion in English Canada was overwhelmingly in favour of a vigorous national effort against Germany, Austria, and any of their allies. David L'Espérance, a businessman from Montmagny, Quebec, who had been elected on the coattails of the *nationaliste* campaign in 1911, spoke second and in French, and Borden hoped that the speech might rally French Canadians. That hope would prove futile.

Borden had no intention of keeping Parliament sitting for long. "They take us for Germans out to devour the money of the country and of the capital," grumbled Senator Philippe Landry. The sixty-eight-year-old Landry was an old hand in Conservative politics, a prolific writer, a former military man, and a senator since 1892. Borden had named him speaker of the Senate in 1911. In a letter to his second wife, Amélie, Landry wrote that cabinet "won't allow us to stay in Ottawa for long, and will marvellously expedite our return home."[4] But there were growing concerns. The "news of the war this morning was disastrous," he informed Amélie the following day. "The Germans have entered Brussels. The atrocities they will commit will be terrible if we are to judge by their cruelty to this point. The poor little Belgians, who have done nothing but defend themselves, are the first victims of that pirate of a Kaiser." Then, he added: "the newspapers tell us that the Germans want to blow up Parliament. I wonder if these sinister bulletins are not being spread in order to frighten everybody so that there is no resistance among the members of Parliament and [the government will] have them vote however they want them to."[5]

Within days, a British military expedition landed in Europe. The first clash took place on Sunday, August 23, near the town of Mons, Belgium. There the British met the left flank of the advancing forces of Germany's 1st Army, constituting the tightly fisted "right hook" of the infamous Schlieffen Plan. It was a brutal first encounter. Germany had a powerful army, determined to crush its enemies. The British forces resisted and stood their ground, but the violent confrontation stunned British commanders. They ordered their troops to entrench, in hopes of defending against an anticipated second assault. The French did the same, shocked at having to dig in, both in Belgium and on their own land. The war had begun.

The news of the debacle at Mons sparked an outpouring of support and sympathy for the victims of the European conflict. Borden rose in the House and announced that "in the awful dawn of the greatest war the world has ever known, in the hour when evil confronts us such as this Empire has not faced for a hundred years, every vain or unnecessary word seems a discord." Borden spoke of duty, honour, and of liberty: "Yea, in the very name of the peace that we sought at any cost save that of dishonour, we have entered into this war; and while gravely

The opening session of the House of Commons in the Victoria Memorial Museum Building after the Parliament Buildings fire of 1916. Sir Robert Borden is seated at the desk at left. Sir Wilfrid Laurier is seated at the desk on the right.

conscious of the tremendous issues involved and of all the sacrifices that they may entail, we do not shrink from them, but with firm heart we abide the event."[6]

Borden's moving statement, however, was no match for Laurier's silver-tongued eloquence, especially when the leader of the opposition rose to a crescendo of applause. "We raise no question, we take no exception, we offer no criticism, and we shall offer no criticism so long as there is danger at the front," Laurier declared. Continuing, he added:

> It is our duty to let Great Britain know, and to let the friends and foes of Great Britain know, that there is in Canada but one mind and one heart, and that all Canadians stand behind the Mother Country, conscious and proud that she has engaged in this war, not for any selfish motive, for any purpose of aggrandizement, but to maintain untarnished the honour of her name, to fulfil

her obligations to her allies, to maintain her treaty obligations and to save civilization from the unbridled lust of conquest and domination.[7]

Borden especially liked these words from across the aisle; he could not have been happier with the outcome of the work of the first three weeks of August.

There was a remarkable unity of opinion that Germany and its allies had to be punished for their actions. All across Canada meetings were held to show support for the government. In English Canada this energy translated into a direct call to arms, a conviction that the honour of the Empire was at stake and that Canada, as its eldest and dutiful first daughter, had to respond with resolve and determination. This enthusiasm could also be felt in Quebec, but with slight variations. The Quebec press was generally supportive and most francophone newspapers spoke in support of Great Britain and France.[8] *La Presse*, the largest daily, tended to lean Liberal in the early years of the war, though it had no official party ties. It called for Canadian volunteers to sign up immediately. *Le Canada*, owned by important Montreal Liberal leaders and known as the Liberal Party's organ in Montreal, was similarly enthusiastic. *La Patrie*, which tended Conservative, could not resist the pro-war momentum, giving full rein to the government to act on behalf of all Canadians: "There are no longer French Canadians and English Canadians," it declared. "Only one race now exists, united by the closest bonds in a common cause."[9] In Quebec City, the more conservative-*bleu* paper was *L'Événement*, and it was effusive. *Le Soleil*, the large Liberal Quebec City daily, said much the same.

Demonstrations were held in Montreal and Quebec City and Rodolphe Forget, one of the richest Quebeckers (who also represented two ridings, Montmorency and Charlevoix, as a Conservative), spoke out enthusiastically in support of the war effort.[10] Montreal's mayor, Médéric Martin, announced that any city employees who were French or Belgian nationals would continue to have their salaries paid if they were mobilized by their mother country. Hamilton Gault, a wealthy thirty-two-year-old Montreal businessman, immediately launched into action by funding the creation of the Princess Patricia's Canadian Light Infantry Regiment and, within two months, he had it ready to sail for Europe. He was joined by his good friend, Talbot Mercer Papineau, a young Montreal lawyer. At the same time, the Montreal chapter of the Canadian Patriotic Fund was launched with panache, and although it was directed by the English-speaking elites of Montreal, the fund's direction and management were held as an exemplary "entente cordiale."[11]

The Catholic Church also expressed its support. Mgr. Paul Bruchési, the archbishop of Montreal and one of most influential men in the province, declared that it was the duty of the faithful to support France and Britain in their hour of need. "If troops have to be sent to the other side, our brave young men will not hesitate to face the ordeal," he said on August 8, "and I know that we will find in them the same heroism which characterized their forefathers so many years ago."[12] With his counterparts in Quebec City and Ottawa, he set out to draft a pastoral letter to the faithful that underlined the duties of citizens in the war.[13] He reminded the young men who had signed up for training at Camp Valcartier that "England has protected our liberties and our faith, under her flag we have found peace, and now in appreciation of what England has done, you go as French Canadians to do your utmost to keep the Union Jack flying with honour."[14]

The feeling of unity peaked in October at a giant rally that brought twenty thousand people to the Parc Sohmer in downtown Montreal. Laurier spoke, invoking Dollard des Ormeaux's courage in the face of military adversity. He urged the young to enlist and fight, "for this cause is just as sacred as the one for which they [Dollard and his companions] gave their lives."[15] Lomer Gouin, the Liberal premier of Quebec, sat next to Joseph-Mathias Tellier, his adversary, the leader of the Conservative Party in Quebec. People saw Liberal Rodolphe Lemieux sit next to Montreal MP Thomas Chase-Casgrain, the new Tory cabinet minister.

Senator Napoléon Belcourt, the gaunt Liberal who represented Franco-Ontarians in their struggle against the Ontario government's discriminatory educational policies, was no exception in his eloquence. "Enlist, my young compatriots!" he urged the large crowd. "If we have to send two or five or ten French-Canadian regiments, we'll know how to find them." He continued:

> Is it not because the sacred cause of freedom for all is in imminent peril that the real civilization is threatened to its very root? I know that you do not love war any more than I do. We Canadians are a pacifist race. For over one hundred years we have lived in complete peace and we appreciate its worth to the degree where we will make all the necessary sacrifices to ensure its survival here and its return elsewhere. Our pacifist spirit must not compel us to become doctrinaire pacifists.[16]

His argument was liberal. Canada had to fight to affirm the right to live, to defend liberty, honour, and the solidarity of civilized peoples; to avenge the outrages and the national insults; and to protect the weak from the brute. Canada "has no right to remain a silent witness to the terrible and barbaric drama that is being played out on the bloodied and devastated fields of Belgium and France." He then added:

> England may be next; perhaps even Canada. Hence our duty is clear. It is urgent, it is immediate, and it will only be accomplished when we will have exhausted — if we must — all our resources of men and money.... French Canadians are not going to negotiate their share of sacrifices; they never have, they never will. Their devotion to the Empire is as total as every resource at their disposal. It is clear now that the war will be long and that it will bring incalculable and terrible losses and sacrifices.[17]

Rodolphe Lemieux had competing thoughts. He was worried. He had served as minister responsible for the Navy and remained Laurier's *homme de confiance*. He was also among the first to call on French Canada to respond positively to the call for arms.[18] But even Lemieux, who had been active in politics long enough to know this particular

English-Canadian brand of imperial ambition, was unconvinced by the show of national unity and was concerned about the dark clouds he saw gathering on the horizon and what they could mean for French Canada. "Our 'colonized' Englishman [by which he meant an English Canadian], without denying his real qualities, is often disagreeable, unjust even, and his spirit of domination irritates us vividly," he wrote to Archbishop Bruchési. "On top of that, the neighbouring American republic is living a nightmare that has made it narrow-minded and kept it in the dark. To our idealism [in supporting Britain and France], it opposes an egotism. But let's be just, the Englishman from England has a completely different mentality."[19] Lemieux, who still bore the political scars of the acid 1911 election campaign, slipped a hard existentialist message into his letter: "As a race, we [French Canadians] were wrong to sink our roots so deeply in the Canadian soil."[20]

It was a time to be a statesman, but it was also a time to be a politician. On the evening when news of the Mons debacle reached Ottawa, Borden met with Robert "Bob" Rogers, Francis "Silent Frank" Cochrane, Louis-Philippe Pelletier, and Douglas Hazen to talk about election possibilities. This was no ordinary group. Rogers had been a key organizer for the Conservative Party in western Canada since the turn of the century. Pelletier, the MP for Quebec County, had been postmaster general since 1911 and was, by far, Borden's most solid French-Canadian supporter in Parliament. Cochrane was the MP for Timiskaming (Ontario) and a key organizer in that province. Hazen, whose career had brought him to the House of Commons a number of times, had been premier of New Brunswick before joining Borden's cabinet in 1911. The message for Borden that night, and from Conservatives all across the country, was that an immediate election could be won.[21]

The war had given Borden a new sense of purpose. It was a new game, with much bigger stakes, and he was determined to see it through to the end, no matter the cost. "Every effort" and "every sacrifice" would be made, he said repeatedly in the fall of 1914. He had little to show for his first three years in power, and he might well gamble that the war now gave him the opportunity to prove his leadership and his government's abilities. Perhaps support and enthusiasm for the war could be turned into support and enthusiasm for the government and for the party that had been calling for military preparedness since 1909. Perhaps now the time had come to call the election.

Borden consulted with his colleagues for most of August and September. What he heard, though, confirmed some of his own suspicions. Sir Clifford Sifton, a former Liberal who had done everything he could to bring Borden to power in 1911, cautioned that the time had not come, and that even if victory were secured "we would regret it all our life." Richard McBride, the rabidly anti-Laurier Tory premier of British Columbia, was also inclined to wait. A scan of the political landscape otherwise was not very promising, either. That summer Manitoba's Conservative government was defeated, while the state of political readiness in Ontario was in doubt because Premier Whitney, Borden's key ally, had been terribly ill all summer. He died in late September. In Quebec, Herbert Ames, a former mayor of Montreal, a long-time Tory, and now the chief organizer of the Patriotic Fund, was opposed.[22] No doubt they all suspected that, thanks to Borden's lacklustre performance, and given Laurier's continued enormous personal popularity, an election at this time could lead to disaster.

Nevertheless, Borden presented a re-election plan to cabinet on October 14. His top lieutenants, Sir George Eulas Foster (Ontario), Arthur Meighen (Manitoba), and Charles Doherty (Quebec), argued that it was not time. Borden said nothing, at first. Foster, who had served under Sir John A. Macdonald, warned that a fall election would be "a fatal party blunder and a crime against the nation and Empire." Knowing how Borden was chomping at the electoral bit, moreover, Foster reinforced his view by privately threatening to resign if an election were called. Borden had to consider and reconsider his views.

In the end, "the intense disunion and fierce controversy" that would come about during a wartime election "was not justified on patriotic grounds," Borden reasoned.[23] Having made his decision, Borden informed the governor general that there would be no election for the time being. He then accepted Laurier's offer of a "political truce" for the foreseeable future and announced that the six pending by-elections would not be contested. Each party would keep its seats by acclamation. It was a deal that, as it happened, would work disproportionately in favour of the Conservatives.* A week later, Borden left Ottawa for a three-week holiday in Hot Springs, Virginia. After almost twelve weeks of frantic activity, of twelve-hour days almost every day, he was worn out. In late September, he had been confined to bed for two days.[24] It was time to take the holiday that had eluded him in the summer.

The near unanimous support for the war in the fall of 1914 gave the government every reason to seek a new mandate, yet it did not. Was it a question of statesmanship over politics? Perhaps statesmanship won out, but there were real political calculations at work. In an era without public opinion polls, Borden's lieutenants and confidants sensed that the country was not ready to hand the government a new mandate, because it had accomplished so little in its three years in power. Most Canadians expected that the war would be over soon; it was unimaginable that the German forces could resist the combined might of the French and British armies. In that context, the Borden government could not expect the war to camouflage its undistinguished record.

The economy, for one thing, offered little positive incentive for the population to again vote Conservative. Borden took power in October 1911 in the middle of an economic boom. That year, government revenues had grown by over 17 percent, from $88,700,000 to $104,300,000. Trade was strong, immigration was plentiful, and there seemed to be a sense of promise across the land. But in 1913 an economic slowdown turned into a severe recession. When interest rates rose in the United Kingdom in 1912, the international prices for Canadian raw goods dropped dramatically. Foreign investment decreased, thanks in part to

---

* Consequently, on February 1, 1915, one Liberal seat — Westmoreland, Nova Scotia — and four Conservative ridings — London and Waterloo South (Ontario), Jacques-Cartier (Quebec), and Prince Albert (Saskatchewan) — were acclaimed. The Conservatives also kept Terrebonne, but not in the manner anticipated. The Liberals did not contest it (as promised) but a by-election was held between Gédéon Rochon, the official Conservative candidate and Joseph-Alphonse Beaulieu, an independent Conservative. Rochon won the seat. See *Le Canada*, February 9, 1915.

the Balkan wars in 1913. In an attempt to bring some control on their economy, the Americans responded with the establishment of a Federal Reserve Board; the Borden government was unconvinced of the need for such an institution.

There were other pressing things to deal with. The income produced in agriculture, for instance, had declined from $670 million 1911 to $660 million in 1913, although it was recovering in 1914. Income was stagnant in other key primary industries, such as the fisheries. Construction income had grown from 1911 to a high of $275 million in 1913, but dropped significantly in 1914 to $205 million.[25] Manufacturing income, approximately $410 million in 1911, declined to $390 million in 1914. The collapse in prices led to a downturn in railway construction in western Canada. With the declaration of war, financial markets again panicked and all of Europe's stock markets, as well as American ones, closed.[26] Economically, 1914 would turn out to be one of the worst years of the twentieth century. Stock prices fell as brokers found markets outside established exchanges. When the markets reopened in December they did so at a bottom level that would not again be seen until 1929. In the spring of 1914, riots among the unemployed broke out in Winnipeg and Edmonton. Borden himself grudgingly acknowledged that "there was disturbing unemployment in some of our cities."[27] Ottawa's total budgetary revenue in 1914 was actually lower than it had been in 1911.[28] According to one economist, Canada's national income plummeted by an estimated 10 percent in 1914 and unemployment in Ontario's manufacturing centres reached 25 percent.[29] Even more worrisome, most of Canada's railways were in danger of bankruptcy. Given these economic conditions, it was no time to call an election.

The economic downturn compounded the facts that key programs had been bungled and that on numerous policy initiatives the government had appeared both aimless and clumsy. Laurier, meanwhile, had lost none of his charm and his patriotic response in support of the war effort had the potential to enhance his reputation in English Canada, particularly in Ontario, where he had always been a potent adversary. Perhaps a year — the time remaining for a traditional four-year mandate — would provide the government with the opportunity to show that it could govern effectively.

Then there was the issue of Quebec. Two of the government's Quebec cabinet ministers had decided to resign. Even with the effusive support he expressed in the first weeks of the war, Louis-Philippe Pelletier, the postmaster general and Borden's close personal colleague, lost his enthusiasm. He tendered his resignation on October 19, allegedly for health reasons (he was not a good debater and undoubtedly was tired of being harangued in the House by Rodolphe Lemieux).[30] He was named to the Quebec Superior Court a month later. Borden wrote that this minister had become "alarmed at the development of hostile public opinion in Quebec," even though every pronouncement to that point had been positive.[31] The second resignation came from Minister of Internal Revenue Wilfrid-Bruno Nantel, the MP for Terrebonne since 1908 and scion of a Tory family that had dominated the *pays d'en haut* for decades. Nantel had also become uncomfortable over the war effort. He took his leave on the same day as Pelletier and became the chief commissioner of the Board of Railway Commissioners. Neither had been particularly effective in office or an able defender of the government, so the impact of the resignations was minor and aroused remarkably little fuss in the press.

Borden called on Thomas Chase-Casgrain and Pierre-Édouard Blondin to replace the two departing ministers, and the operation was done with little controversy. Chase-Casgrain was an old Tory hand who had sat in the Quebec legislative assembly before representing Montmorency in Ottawa on-and-off since 1896. A fluently bilingual lawyer, he was put in charge of the post office. The much younger Blondin, on the other hand, was an odd combination of *nationaliste* and fervent military enthusiast. "He is now in office," Laurier said of Blondin, "but to attain office he has travelled a very dangerous road and he has sown the seed of discord, and these appeals to passion are always sure to bring forth a crop of prejudice."[32]

The Conservative government had made little headway on other campaign promises. Borden's electoral promise had been to maintain the tariff policy and not to enter into a reciprocity agreement with the United

States. The entire policy area was neglected, however, with the government content to make a few small changes here and there. The duties on cement were reduced in 1912 and taxes on sugar imported from the West Indies were reduced in 1913. In 1914, the Borden Conservatives tried to cut some tariffs on imported agricultural machinery, in large part to assuage western farmers, but that idea was blocked by the Liberals in the Senate, who dominated there by a three-to-one margin.[33] Otherwise, the policy of the Borden government had been to maintain the status quo as it had been since 1910. In fact, on most issues, Borden simply continued Laurier's policies. The Board of Grain Commissioners, an agency designed to regulate the product, had been proposed by Laurier, and was implemented by Borden. The policy of support to a number of railway companies was also continued.[34]

Borden had long campaigned on a promise to clean up the administration of government and to rid the public service of patronage and inefficiency. From the vantage point of 1914, he had nothing to show for it. He had kept all the mandarins Laurier had appointed and had dismissed only a few hundred mostly part-time or seasonal employees in the regions, far from the Ottawa headquarters of their departments. A few months after the 1911 election, Borden appointed a commission, headed by A.B. Morine, a newly transplanted Newfoundland politician, to look into the administration of the public service. Its mission was to identify "existing defects or abuses to be remedied" and to recommend more "efficient methods" to carry out the business of government. At the same time, Albert Edward Kemp, minister without portfolio, was asked to lead a cabinet committee to investigate the purchasing habits of government departments, a task remarkably similar to Morine's. Neither Kemp nor Morine yielded helpful insights or workable solutions. Morine reported in the winter of 1912 what was obvious: that the administrative "machinery" seemed to function by habit more than design and that "no organized effort had been made to coordinate these services." Morine found no proof of wrongdoing or corruption. Instead, and without providing evidence, he pointed to a general "neglect of proper methods." Kemp's efforts went nowhere and Morine's work was ignored: he resigned a month later.[35]

Borden still felt pressure to act on his promise to bring modern management methods to Ottawa. The opportunity presented itself when Sir George Murray, who had recently retired from his post as secretary of the treasury in the United Kingdom, made himself available. He arrived in Ottawa in late September 1912, and two months later presented a report that went further than Morine. For Murray, Ottawa seemed awfully old-fashioned in its way of doing things. The ministers were overworked, and the "centre" was all too consumed with details. He made a long list of recommendations, but Borden was unimpressed. Nothing happened, and nothing would happen.

As a result, the Borden government was unprepared administratively for the taxing work of organizing a large-scale military effort. The sudden stress of organizing procurement for war supplies led to errors. Newspapers were filled with allegations of graft and favouritism in the acquisition of war supplies and there was no doubt that profiteers made impressive profits selling materiel to the government at inflated prices during the first year of the war. The Ross rifle, manufactured in Quebec City, was found to be cumbersome and unpredictable in the muddy conditions of the battlefield. It had to be abandoned, leaving the Borden government with the politically difficult option of having to acquire British weapons as substitutes. Allegations of leather boots disintegrating in the mud of Belgian and French fields became a staple of complaints.

Nevertheless, the political reality was that few of the complaints, beyond those concerning the Ross rifles, were validated. Andrew McMaster, a Montreal Liberal organizer, later complained to Laurier that he was "desperately disappointed with the Liberal Party, which has allowed the Government to remain unchallenged" on these issues. The mood had turned on the Front, he was told: "The Army here is furious, and if it could give an organized expression, would be bitterly opposed to the Government. The Liberals are losing a golden opportunity and you will find a strong movement I think to create a coalition or else a new Party."[36] Laurier was more than willing to use these arguments but his demands for evidence — hard evidence — went unanswered.

Borden, meanwhile, kept his eye on the electoral calendar. He noted in his diary on March 10, 1915, that "our men all keen for an election." A week later he wrote that "every one [sic] pressing for election."[37] Better still, a few days later he added "Grits not very aggressive."[38] In preparation for a possible election campaign, a bill was tabled in the House of Commons in late March 1915 to ensure that all soldiers in the Canadian army over the age of twenty-one be entitled to vote, no matter where they were or where they came from.[39] The law was passed later that spring, along with amendments to other electoral laws (including a new provision compelling employers to give extra time to their workers to vote on election day). The Liberals were opposed to the measure, on the account that not every soldier was actually a resident of Canada, but the bill was carried. Ballots were printed and sent aboard the *Lusitania*, bound for Britain. The ship was torpedoed by the Germans and the ballots sank with it. The election would have to wait. Nevertheless, the government had expanded the franchise to young men who could be counted on to vote in its favour.

Chomping at the bit as the fourth anniversary of his mandate approached, Borden revealed his frustrations to the governor general in the early spring of 1915, pointing to the "attacks upon the personal honour, motives, sincerity, honesty, and loyalty of the members of the government" that had become routine in the Liberal newspapers. The governor general had reservations, arguing that an election in 1915 would be divisive: "I would be glad to know in what respect you would anticipate that a political campaign during an election, if one should be held, would exceed the violence and virulence of these [Liberal] attacks. It is hardly to be expected that self-respecting men will sit with their hands tied and their lips dumb under such imputations."[40] Borden considered the political landscape. The Tories still held Ontario, but the defeat of the Conservative Roblin government in Manitoba left him unsure. The reports from Quebec could hardly feed optimism. But Borden did not seem over-worried. "We can give Grits 55 seats in Quebec and still have a working majority," he wrote.[41] The temptation to call an election was strong — but in the first week of May, with bad news from the Front and the death of his mother (which moved him greatly), Borden drew back.

The government's mandate would end officially in October 1916, and long before that Borden had a decision to make, as did Laurier. A number of ridings were now in need of by-elections and there was a possibility that they could be filled with uncontested acclamations, just as had been done earlier in the year. An election was not entirely out of the question, but Borden began to reconsider the governor general's suggestion of seeking a constitutional amendment that would allow the government to delay any election until the war ended. He learned that Laurier was open to a discussion on that, and the two leaders met on October 14, 1915. An agreement to extend the parliamentary term would require a formal constitutional change, which could be done only if the British government agreed to amend the British North America Act (the BNA Act). Borden's proposal to Laurier was to extend the term of Parliament until a year after peace returned and that no election be held until then. If any by-elections were necessary in the interim the party that had won the riding in 1911 would run their candidate unopposed.

Laurier was cool to the proposal of postponing the next general election until the war was over. He reminded Borden that, in Canada, members of Parliament called to serve in cabinet had to be reaffirmed in their seats by their electors; it was a way of giving the voters the right to ratify a cabinet choice made by the prime minister. For Laurier, the notion that seats vacated by ministerial resignations should go uncontested was also not acceptable, simply because it made too many assumptions about the legitimacy of the government. With such an arrangement the Borden government could be in power for a very long time, indeed. Laurier instead proposed a simple one-year extension. He, too, was increasingly itching for an election, but had to consider all his alternatives. He asked Borden to put the offer in writing.

The two exchanged formal correspondence in the first two weeks of November 1915, each insisting on various points.[42] Laurier raised the issue of the government's continued support for the railways — he did not want the government to take advantage of a longer mandate to reshape the industry and insisted on knowing what Borden's intentions might be on that file. Borden readily agreed to "consult" with the leader of the opposition on any assistance to the railways or on any action to nationalize them. Beyond that, the agreement reached was a limited one: the British government would be requested to amend the British North America Act to extend Parliament for one year from October 6, 1916, the date on which the government's mandate was to end (therefore, to October 1917). Laurier agreed. The Liberals would, for the moment, continue to honour the agreement that seats vacated would not be contested, nor would nominations to cabinet. Thanks to this deal, Ésioff-Léon Patenaude was acclaimed in Hochelaga in October 1915 when he was named to cabinet, as was Albert Edward Kemp in Toronto East in December 1916 when he was named minister of militia and defence. For Liberal observers the deal seemed to be a good one. "Most people I think in the country believe that they did right in agreeing to the extension" commented Montreal party activist Andrew McMaster."[43]

Robert Borden told the Canadian Club of Halifax on December 18, 1914 that "under the laws of Canada, our citizens may be called out to defend our own territory, but cannot be required to go beyond the seas except for the defence of Canada itself. There has not been, there will not be compulsion or conscription."[44] He had reason to be optimistic. By the middle of 1915, there were 101,500 men under arms stationed in Canada, in training in Britain, or at the Front. The second contingent of the Canadian Expeditionary Force, which included the 22nd Regiment, reached Britain in April 1915. A third division was in the planning stages and the government set a target for the recruitment of another 150,000 men. That goal was quickly reached and on January 1, 1916, there were 213,000 men in the Canadian forces.

Before the end of the first year of war, Borden had become frustrated by the lack of information on the larger war effort. The lack of transparency was irritating, and in an effort to learn more on the progress, cost, and consequences of the war, Borden travelled to Britain and stayed for most of the summer of 1915. British prime minister Asquith flattered him with an invitation to join a session of cabinet in mid-July, and he later met with the king for a brief conversation on the progress of the war. He crossed the channel and had dinner with President Poincaré of France and accepted the honour of the Grand Cross of the Legion of Honour. He also spent many hours visiting with the wounded, both in hospitals in England and at the Front itself. The experience steeled his resolve to fight.

"This war is most horrible," he wrote to his wife, Laura.[45] He was still not satisfied with the information he was receiving, however, and made sure to tell George Perley, Canada's high commissioner, that he needed a great deal more.[46] All the same, just as in 1912, he returned to Canada with a resolve to increase Canada's commitment. Upon his return to Ottawa, he asked that the army be raised to 250,000 men, and, by January 1916, the target was raised to 500,000 — a goal that R.B. Bennett, the Conservative MP for Calgary, and others warned was impossible to reach.[47]

2

THE RESPONSE OF FRENCH CANADA: HENRI BOURASSA, SCHOOLS, AND NATIONALITIES

"They never will have conscription in Canada, at least during our period of existence. Of course, we must get wiser as a nation or perish; but it all takes time."

— Charles Wilcox to Mabel, January 27, 1916[1]

Private Wilcox, twenty-seven, was recovering at Hill House Military Hospital near Ramsgate, Kent, in the United Kingdom, when he wrote that letter to his sister. Born in Stanstead, Quebec, he had enlisted in October 1914, serving with the 4th Battalion of the Canadian Expeditionary Force (the CEF). The new year brought a sinking feeling that the war would last a long time, and, clearly, many people were already talking about forced enlistments.

Still, eighteen months into the war, routine matters had not been entirely neglected, either by Private Wilcox writing to his sister or by the House of Commons. On the freezing evening of February 3, 1916, a few members debated the government's East Coast fishery policies. Borden was in his second office in the Centre Block, putting the final touches to another long day, reviewing correspondence, and planning to go home at 9 p.m.

The ordinary hum was punctured by screams of panic. Fire had broken out and was rapidly spreading through the building. Two days earlier, a few MPs had noticed a small fire in the reading room and quickly put it out. This time, the flames spread in a rage. The prime minister was rushed out through thick smoke and within thirty minutes the roof of the House of Commons collapsed. Borden returned to his main office in the East

Block and watched as the Victoria Tower caught fire. It would take hours of fighting the blaze before it was put out. Morning light revealed a gutted building, shorn of its proud tower, and news that seven people died in the tragedy, including two guests of House Speaker Albert Sévigny and his wife. The two unfortunate guests, unable to face the freezing night, had returned to the burning building to retrieve their fur coats. Four public servants were also killed in the blaze, as was Bowman Brown Law, the Liberal member of Parliament for Yarmouth, Nova Scotia.

While the fire still burned in the fifty-year-old building, the decision was made that Parliament would sit in the new Victoria Museum Building on McLeod Street, about a mile south of Parliament Hill. The museum's auditorium was converted into a temporary House of Commons and, that very afternoon, members of Parliament, shaken but resolved to carry out their duties, resumed their business. Many people suspected German treachery in the parliamentary fire, and that suspicion never entirely disappeared. A royal commission investigating the disaster did not dismiss the possibility, but did not dwell on it, either.

If the fire on Parliament Hill has become emblematic of an embattled Canada, the scene at the base of the burned-out Victoria Tower three

A symbol of the embattled nation: the Parliament Buildings after the fire of 1916.

weeks later showed that the battle had many dimensions. On February 24, five thousand Franco-Ontarians marched on the ghostly Parliament Hill to demand that the federal government intervene and outlaw the Ontario government's Regulation 17, which was restricting the use of French in Ontario schools. For four years, Borden had dismissed that issue as a provincial one, and yet it had now entwined itself to the issue of Canada's participation in the war. His neglect was now haunting the porch of his office in the East Block.

Borden met with the delegation and promised to get involved again, but he had no reason to hope that anything would change. In the fall of 1912, when Borden wrote to Conservative premier James P. Whitney to express his concerns, the Ontario premier had simply responded that education was a provincial jurisdiction.[2] Borden's renewed attempt in 1915 yielded nothing more. At Queen's Park, both the government and the Liberal opposition, led by Newton Rowell, strongly supported the stripping of French-Canadian rights. In responding to Borden, the Ontario premier noted that the government, which was soon to face the electorate, "would not live an hour if it made [the] slightest concession."[3]

The debate on this issue had been burning for over two years by the time war was declared.[4] In 1912, a government of Ontario commission had concluded that French schools in Ontario were of poor quality, and that the English being taught in them was especially weak. The government had a remarkable ally on its side: various Irish Catholic bishops and archbishops who had decided that "bilingual" schools — not least Catholic "bilingual" schools — should cease teaching in French. Championed by Mgr. Michael Francis Fallon, the bishop of London, Ontario, the view was apparently widespread in the province, and in other parts of Canada.[5] The province passed a rule, known infamously as "Regulation 17," a measure that basically ended French-language teaching after Grade 2 once the 1913–14 academic school year was over.[6] According to Premier James Whitney, the measure was designed to improve the instruction in French-language schools. To enforce the new rules, the government announced that the schools would be monitored by both a French-speaking and an English-speaking superintendent.

The initiative quickly assumed a far greater importance than any routine administrative adjustment. Francophones saw in it nothing less than state-ordered assimilation.[7] They had organized under the banner of the *Association canadienne-française d'éducation en Ontario* (ACFEO) in 1910 to voice their protest, but Queen's Park was not moved. In response the Ottawa Separate School Board, two-thirds of whose trustees were francophones, refused to enforce the infamous regulation and closed its French schools in protest in September 1914, just as the war was getting started. French Canadians constituted 8 percent of the population of Ontario at the time, up from 2 percent at Confederation. According to the census of 1911, there were 202,422 francophones in the province. In 1909, however, the Ecclesiastical census of the province reported 247,000 French Canadians. The net effect was that a figure of 250,000 was often cited in newspapers and speeches.[8]

With the war in Europe now fully on and Canadian politicians of all stripes pledging their support to the Triple Entente, eight thousand francophone students in Ottawa were without teachers. Led by Samuel Genest, the French majority on the Board of Education sought a city by-law allowing it to issue debentures to raise money for new schools to be operated independently of the Department of Education's rulings. R. Mackell, one of the minority anglophone school board members, asked for an injunction against the board's decision to close the schools and to prevent it from borrowing or paying staff while refusing to comply with Regulation 17. The Ontario Supreme Court heard the case and agreed with Mackell. It ordered the board to reopen its schools and to employ only qualified teachers. Premier Whitney died a few days later and was replaced by William Hearst who, that October, placed the Ottawa Separate School Board under what was effectively a trusteeship. Although the issue had been festering since 1912, there was now a legal point on which Franco-Ontarians could seek redress in the courts, since the political apparatus had completely failed to respond to their demands for justice.

It was Liberal Senator Napoléon Belcourt, who also had been named leader of the ACFEO in 1910, who leaped at the opportunity to use this case as a platform to argue against the root cause of the action, Regulation 17.[9] Representing the majority of the Ottawa Separate School Board, he launched a suit against Mackell, and argued the case in early November 1914 before Justice Lennox, an individual Belcourt later described as "an ignorant and narrow-minded fanatic."[10] The timing could hardly be worse for the war effort. English Canada was demanding a national effort to support the British Empire, while at the same time denying francophones in Ontario the right to an education in their own language. In late November 1914, the Ontario Supreme Court again found in favour of Mackell, finding the board guilty of disobeying the laws of the province.

There was another incendiary in this story, one who inflamed hearts, not buildings: Henri Bourassa. He did it by linking the schools issue in Ontario and an issue he had opposed for fifteen years, Canada's participation in Imperial Britain's war policies.[11] Bourassa, a forty-six- year-old father of six, was in fighting trim when the war started. His full head of hair was now white, but he had maintained his slender figure and was easily spotted with his deep-brown eyes and signature beard: a salt-and-pepper Vandyke that featured a sharply tipped moustache set against close-cropped cheeks. His pen was as sharp as his moustache. The two matters — the protection of the French language in English-Canadian provinces and the involvement in British war efforts — combined in his mind as an existential threat to French Canada. "The English language remains, in America especially," he wrote to a Jesuit friend in New York City, "the language of agnosticism, of materialism, of yellow journalism, of everything which tends, with too much success, to paganise [sic] the masses and destroy the spirit of Catholicity in the intellectuals."[12]

Bourassa was without a doubt the most influential journalist in French Canada when the war began. *Le Devoir*, now in its fourth year of publication, was required reading for the Quebec intellectual and political elite. Bourassa knew politics — he had been a sitting politician, first in the federal Parliament in Ottawa and then in the Quebec legislature in Quebec City, for almost twenty years — and he could speak as well as he wrote. He also spoke and wrote English with as much panache and conviction as he did his maternal tongue. The *Ottawa Citizen* described him in 1912 as "witty, brilliant, able and sincere." A journalist detailed how Bourassa held "a large audience spellbound for nearly two hours, a deed none the less remarkable in so much as probably 90 percent of those present disagreed with most of what he said." He was reported as respectful of his audience, "chivalrous" and "audacious."[13] He was described by another journalist as a "snappy leader," "dapper, witty, polite and several other things."[14]

The grandson of the famous *patriote* rebel Louis-Joseph Papineau (by his mother), he entered politics as a very young man and entered Parliament in 1896, at twenty-eight, as a Laurier Liberal. Bourassa otherwise was fairly conventional. He denounced taxes imposed on agricultural

Portrait of Henri Bourassa in July 1917 as it appeared on a mortuary card in 1952.

implements and promised to vote in favour of any laws that would encourage agriculture. He campaigned to reduce the state in terms of unnecessary expenditures and the number of public servants. Presenting himself as "proudly French and Catholic," he promised to get involved in any question where "the rivalry of race and creed become evident — questions that unfortunately, stir too often our public debates ... and that can fuel a civil discord that would be ruinous for our young country."[15] He pronounced himself the defender of minority rights — for the English in Quebec and for the French and Catholic minority in Manitoba and in other provinces.

The first break with Laurier came during the South African War in 1899, when he became very critical of Laurier's willingness to send volunteers to fight as part of an imperial military force. Laurier was re-elected in 1900, but his compromises with Anglo-imperialists stirred the embers of national identity in Quebec, particularly among younger students, including a young Armand La Vergne, his old law-partner's son. The young people gravitated to Bourassa. In 1903, young writers and activists created a Ligue nationaliste to animate discussions and within a year the movement was deemed strong enough to support a weekly, *Le Nationaliste*, edited by Olivar Asselin. In 1904, the Association catholique de la jeunesse canadienne-française was established across Quebec to discuss, and to mix, religious and political affairs, particularly where they related to the health of the French language and the place of Canada within the British Empire. They wanted much more of the former, and much less of the latter.

Bourassa left Ottawa in 1907 for a seat in the Quebec legislature following another disagreement with Laurier over the schools issue in the new provinces of Alberta and Saskatchewan. The 1909 naval debate prompted him to establish *Le Devoir* and he campaigned tirelessly against Laurier and his naval plans. He launched a *nationaliste* movement when the prime minister put the question to the public in the election of 1911. Laurier was defeated, and Bourassa had played an important role in that Liberal debacle.[16] He wasted no time in attacking the new government's plan to simply donate money to the British treasury.

Bourassa found himself visiting France and Germany when the war broke out in 1914. On his return to Canada he made his first pronouncement on the war. Canada had a duty to help and to co-operate with Britain and France and with all the aggrieved. But there were limits: "Canada's national duty [is] to contribute, within the bounds of her strength and by the means which are proper to herself, to the triumph, and especially to the endurance of the combined efforts of France and England."[17] Bourassa linked language and minority rights with the war. On October 22, he gave a speech at the Monument National (a large theatre) organized by the local chapter of the Société Saint-Jean-Baptiste and he spoke of how minority rights were being trampled and that Canada was being nothing short of hypocritical in announcing itself a defender of rights in Europe while it actively suppressed the rights of its own minorities.

Bourassa's less than enthusiastic endorsement of the war sparked outrage in both the Liberal and Conservative press in Quebec and from critics everywhere.[18] Rodolphe Lemieux, who had been the butt of some of Bourassa's sharpest criticisms from 1909 to 1911, explained in a long letter to Archbishop Bruchési that articles written by Bourassa had only one goal: "to accentuate the Anglophobia of the French Canadians."[19] Bourassa also found himself increasingly at odds with Church leaders. Where they were moderate in supporting the war effort, he was casting doubt on the entire enterprise. Where he was loudly demanding and agitating in favour of Franco-Ontarian rights, the Church was mute.[20]

In December 1914, Bourassa took the stage of Ottawa's Russell Theatre and took aim at the misguided war effort in Ottawa. Many in the audience knew his arguments already and were eager to shut him down. Far better for the government, he had said, to equip a smaller contingent with crack equipment and armaments than to rush and spend millions to send a poorly organized expeditionary force.[21] Why waste money on sending foodstuffs to rot on docks in Liverpool when they could be sent to Belgium where food was really needed? "But no," Bourassa thundered, "Canada's aid has to be noisy, puffy, and obstreperous, worthy of rich and fat parvenus who dominate the worlds of high finance, big business, and big politics of the Canadian nation. It has to help the 'boodlers,' the vampires, the bribers, the hustlers of leaky boots and made-in-Germany razors. Glory to the Empire!"[22]

Bourassa did not hesitate to raise these points again. For many in the audience, this was too much. A uniformed soldier, supported by a group of friends who occupied the front row, walked up to Bourassa while he was speaking, brandished the Union Jack, and demanded that Bourassa wave it. Keeping his cool, Bourassa took it and placed it on the table next to the podium. He then defied his hecklers: "I am always prepared to stand by the British flag," he stated. "In this regard I am second to no man, but I will not be coerced or intimidated by brute force." The audience roared its protest and Bourassa had to leave, his speech unfinished.[23] Bourassa walked across the street to the Château Laurier, and completed his remarks there in friendlier company. He had made his point of joining the issues of language and war. The Ottawa audience knew that he had stopped on his way to the capital to meet with francophones in Hawkesbury, Ontario, who were actively protesting Regulation 17.[24]

Bourassa's blasting criticism of imperialism lit a firestorm across English Canada. The *Kingston Standard* demanded that he be arrested. The *Montreal Star* started to refer to Bourassa as "von Bourassa." In the Ontario legislature, Dr. J.W. Edwards, the MPP for Kingston, urged authorities to deny Bourassa the opportunity to address the students and faculty at a meeting being planned by Queen's University. He actually demanded that Bourassa be hanged because "he is much more dangerous than the Germans or the Austrians who have been detained as prisoners of war."[25] The Canadian Club of Montreal voted to expel Bourassa. (The problem with that was that the journalist had never been a member.)

Bourassa continued his campaign over the winter. He gave a speech on "Small Nations" on January 27, 1915, and the proceeds of the evening were donated to the schools of Ontario.[26] While the 1st Canadian Division engaged the Germans and their chlorine gas at Ypres and St. Julien, Bourassa climbed podium after podium to condemn the effort. How could French Canadians be expected to fight for a country that refused to respect their civil rights? In a speech to a section of the Saint-Jean-Baptiste society on March 19, 1915, Bourassa traced the history of French on the North American continent. The question in Ontario was of "justice versus iniquity," of "liberty versus tyranny," of "constitutionalism versus arbitrarianism," and, raising the stakes even higher, of "British ways versus Prussian ways," of "civilization versus barbarism."[27]

Bourassa also lamented the "deplorable, but understandable, indifference of the province of Quebec in regard to the French minorities in the other provinces."[28] Instead of doing nothing, the province should help, he argued. First, Quebec had to defend the constitution. Second, it could help fund Ontarians — this mission was far more urgent than good works abroad. Last, he described how Quebeckers were taking the lead in keeping the language alive. He urged learning French first, in order to improve English learning afterwards. He insisted that French be spoken — even on the telephone, he said — at home. Finally, he talked about love and respect, as the scrawls at the bottom of his notes reveal.

Lomer Gouin, the Quebec premier, responded to *Le Devoir*'s incessant prodding in his opening speech in the provincial legislature a few weeks later. The Quebec government, which had kept quiet about the sister province's affairs, adopted a resolution on January 13, 1916, that unanimously deplored Regulation 17 and asserted that the Legislators of Ontario were deficient in their understanding and application of traditional British principles.

Bourassa worked long hours managing his newspaper and delivering speeches. He published four important works in the first three years of the war, including *Que devons-nous à l'Angleterre? La défense nationale, La révolution impérialiste*, and *Le tribut à l'empire*, a fully indexed 409-page book. In early January 1916 he began publicly lecturing on "*Le Devoir* et la guerre," in which he again condemned the Canadian government's rationale for involvement. The lecture was quickly turned into a pamphlet.[29]

The mood in Quebec was souring. "In the midst of all these calamities, people try to have some fun when they can," wrote Amélie Landry to her husband, a few weeks after Bourassa spoke. But, she said, the annual "black and white ball" at the Château Frontenac had been ruined by incessant rumours that the hotel would be bombed.[30]

The Liberals, on the other hand, were still confident that Bourassa was a spent force. Rodolphe Lemieux said in the House of Commons in January 1916 that Bourassa "no more expresses popular sentiment in the province of Quebec than did Mr. Bernard Shaw represent public opinion in England."[31]

It was wishful thinking. Bourassa redoubled his efforts to show how the struggles for language in Ontario and the war effort had become existential issues for French Canada. At Saint-Henri, on May 30, 1916, Bourassa expounded his idea in a speech, "La lutte pour l'existence nationale" (*The Struggle for National Existence*). He argued that there were three struggles being played out over the issue of Canada's participation in the war, going back to the revolutions in England (in the 1640s) and France (in the 1790s). The first struggle, he said, was the battle between the Christian order of societies against "Protestant" disorder, Liberal "*deliquence*," and social "atheism." The second was the struggle of thought and labour against the "brutalizing yoke" of gold and organized capital. The third and final one was between "legitimate" and "traditional" nationalists against preying imperialist states, international finance, and socialism.[32]

For Bourassa, it no longer mattered whether the Triple Alliance or the Triple Entente won the war: what was crucial was the fate of small countries. Poland, Lithuania, Finland, the Balkans, had all suffered under Russia. He counted Ireland and Canada as having suffered under the influence of Great Britain. Germany had been oppressive toward Denmark, Holland, and Belgium. The only hope of this war, he said, was that the empires would wear themselves out. "Everything is being done to hide the supreme danger that our nationality could be annihilated by British imperialism and Anglo-American paganism," he told his audience. Only French Canada was carrying out the struggle of "Catholicism versus Protestantism," of "Spiritualism versus Materialism," of "Nationalism versus British Imperialism and Anglo-American Imperialism." He considered the Anglo-Saxon civilization as the "most irreligious," most materialist, and most destructive, made all the more dangerous by its hypocrisy ("honestly," (*honnêtement*) he wrote in his speaking notes, to underline both his astonishment and his certitude). The fight against it was formidable, and incessant, he declared, because there was no counterweight. "Our leaders are blind," he told his audience. Then he linked it to the language struggle in Canada. The resistance to imperial powers was being fought on the grounds of language and faith, both in Canada and in Ireland (Bourassa was clearly mindful of the Easter revolt in Dublin just a few weeks before). All French Canadians wanted was the "right to simply live out our lives" without the "influence of an Asquith or a Bethmann-Hollweg" (the German chancellor).[33]

Sir Wilfrid Laurier, who had been fairly quiet on the issue of Regulation 17, grew impatient over the lack of action. Clearly, Bourassa's campaign had been influential. Laurier, Rodolphe Lemieux, Laurent-Olivier David, and Paul-Émile Lamarche, the *nationaliste* MP who had resigned from the Conservative caucus to protest the extension of Parliament, drafted a resolution that was introduced in Parliament by Ernest Lapointe, MP for Kamouraska, on May 9, 1916. The motion resolved "That this house especially at this time of universal sacrifice and anxiety, when all energies should be concentrated on the winning of the war, while fully recognizing the principle of provincial rights and the necessity of every child being given a thorough English education, respectfully suggest to the Legislative Assembly [of Ontario] the wisdom of making it clear that the privilege of the children of French parentage of being taught in their mother tongue be not interfered with."[34]

The Lapointe resolution — which was clear in not requesting that the federal government use its powers of disallowance — was debated for two days. Borden again insisted that the issue was strictly a provincial one and that Ottawa had to stay out of it. The government side easily defeated the motion, but the linguistic split was evident. Eleven Liberals—English Canadians — voted with the government. Although seven French-speaking members elected under the Conservative-*nationaliste* banner in 1911 voted in favour, the French-speaking ministers in Borden's cabinet voted against the motion, citing provincial rights. Canada was divided. The vote of 107 to 60 crushed Laurier. He offered to resign.

The matter of Ontario's Resolution 17 would next be challenged before the Judicial Committee of the Privy Council (JCPC) in Great Britain. The French-speaking ministers in Borden's cabinet, led by Ésioff-Léon Patenaude, drafted a memorandum asking that the federal government intervene before the JCPC, and they threatened to resign if no action was taken. Borden again refused to get involved.[35] In protest Landry quit the Speaker's chair of the Senate to dedicate himself entirely to the Franco-Ontarian battle, and immediately started a cross-Quebec campaign to raise awareness of what was happening in Ontario. Landry asked Borden repeatedly to name a French senator for Ontario.[36] It was of no use: Borden was stone deaf on the issue.

While the battle of the Somme raged, the JCPC in London rendered its decision. It found Regulation 17 was constitutional, but declared *ultra vires* the provincial government's takeover of the Ottawa Separate School Board.[37] For Belcourt, there was finally some vindication. By finding that the provincial government had no right to take over schools, the JCPC had effectively given the school board the tools to continue its fight. It was a small consolation, but nothing better came from Rome. The Holy See responded on October 27, 1916, with Benedict XV's *Commisso divinitus* announcing that it refused to take sides between the Irish and French-speaking Catholics of Ontario. Instead, it called for calm and unity.

The decisions of the JCPC and Pontifical authorities effectively ended the legal fight over Ontario's Regulation 17, but did not take away any of the bitterness. The greater significance of Regulation 17 was its effect on French Canada at large. The high points in the battle against it paralleled almost exactly the cruellest losses of life on the battlefields of Europe. As tempers flared in Canada over the citizenship rights of the French minority, the mounting casualties intensified the cry for more support of the war effort. The fight between English and French now would take place over the enlistment of soldiers for the war effort, a battle that would further bruise an already demoralized French-Canadian population.

The burned hulk of the old Parliament Buildings that Borden could see from his East Block office was a reminder that 1916 had seen many turning points in French Canada. Until that winter, the war had been good for Borden, even in Quebec. Recruits were being found. The economy was responding well. There was unease in the country by 1916, however, and one by one provincial Conservative governments were falling. Labour unrest was increasingly evident and the farmers, particularly in the West, were manifestly unhappy with the state of public affairs. Across Canada, but, again, particularly in the West, there were numerous instances of soldiers rioting (mostly about local conditions).[38] Many aspects of Borden's war management were harshly criticized. The government in Ottawa often seemed incompetent.

Enrolment in English Canada was not an issue in 1914. British-born men signed up quickly and in satisfactory numbers — the pressure to serve was intense. Far fewer enlisted in French Canada, but the numbers were acceptable. The 1st Division that had gone to France had one French-speaking company. There were other, less hopeful, signs, though. Only 1,245 (3.4 percent) of the 36,267 men were listed as "French Canadian."[39] The only senior French-Canadian officer was Lieutenant-Colonel H.A. Panet of the Royal Canadian Horse Artillery, a unit that proved its valour at the second battle of Ypres in April and May 1915.

Still, "Eureka! Eureka!" wrote Eugène Nantel to his brother Maréchal in the spring of 1915 after enlisting as a lieutenant in the 41st Battalion of the CEF. "I have finally found my way, if not my vocation. If you knew how happy I am with my new position and the bright future that can be opened in front of me …"[40]

Nantel, twenty-one, a school teacher, was a scion of a notable Saint-Jérôme Conservative family. Wilfrid-Bruno Nantel, the former minister in the Borden government, was his uncle. Eugène often wrote to his mother in Outremont, Onésime Nantel, now fifty-six years old and widowed. She had, a few years before, married Alexandre Orsali, an important grocery wholesaler who had started his firm in 1874 (it eventually became the IGA chain in Quebec). Maréchal was four years older than his brother Eugène and already established as a lawyer, working on the Place d'Armes in downtown Montreal. Both had joined the militia years before the war started. Maréchal was active as an officer with the 65th Regiment of reservists in Montreal, and was well connected, on speaking terms with Liberals, Conservatives, and *nationalistes* such as Paul-Émile Lamarche.[41] Eugène sailed for Europe at the end of June. His happy days of light training and evenings at the Château Frontenac were over.[42] Things were indeed looking up. He was told he would be commissioned as a captain in the 64th Infantry Battalion.[43]

Statistically, there should have been more people like Eugène Nantel. Put in perspective (about 30 percent of the Canadian population was French

Onésime Nantel-Orsali, circa 1911.

Canadian), the success of recruitment efforts in Quebec was limited. On a province-by-province basis, Quebec ranked at the bottom by every measure. Far fewer eligible men (15.3 percent) in Quebec volunteered for the war effort than the Canadian average (31.4 percent).[44] In terms of men who actually served overseas, Quebec had the lowest ranking at 14.4 percent (the next lowest was Saskatchewan at 21 percent). (Quebec's population at that time was 18 percent English-speaking, so the Quebec figures must not be interpreted as relevant to francophones only.) By one calculation, French-Canadian participation was at the lowest rate in the Empire.[45]

On the whole, Ottawa's recruitment policy of relying on local initiative to create military units while keeping central control on deployment did not work well in French Canada. Apart from Dr. Mignault, who had raised the famed 22nd Regiment (the "Vandoos," in English), few wealthy or entrepreneurial French Canadians were inclined to amass recruits, and civilian recruitment associations that were effective in English Canada simply did not work well either in Quebec or in French Canada generally.[46] Sam Hughes and his lieutenants consistently proved insensitive to the need for some form of homogeneity within ranks. This negligence had multiple effects. First, it clearly discouraged enlistment. What point could there be in joining the ranks with a few neighbourhood chums when chances were that one would be thrown into battle with people who did not share — or even respect — one's language and culture?

Despite the best intentions, the recruiting effort quickly stalled. Laurier campaigned that summer to help enlistment, saying that "it is the duty of Canada to give to Great Britain at this hour all the assistance that is in her power," but not enough were responding.[47] On July 23, a recruitment rally for the 41st Battalion was held at the Parc Lafontaine in Montreal and attracted 1,500 people. Maréchal Nantel was on stage, alongside Rodolphe Lemieux and other Montreal notables. It turned into a riot.[48] "What you read about the meeting at Parc Lafontaine is true," wrote Maréchal to his brother, who was now stuck in the trenches. "This opposition to recruitment only lasted a few days, and was due to a few young hare-brained *Le Devoir* activists who decided to imitate the '37 *Patriotes*, preventing Canadians from enlisting. It did not last very long; but what is more regrettable about the demonstration at the Parc Lafontaine is that Major Ranger, Lieutenant Leblanc, and I were pelted with tomatoes and rotten eggs."[49]

There already were fears of conscription, as Maréchal himself noted in another letter to his brother a few weeks later.[50] By September 1915, three new French-speaking battalions (the 41st, 57th, and 69th) had been raised at full strength and a French-Canadian company existed within the 14th Battalion ("The Royal Montreal Regiment"). But this was the high-water mark. Word spread that francophone volunteers were being assigned to English-speaking, Protestant battalions and were being denied the permission to transfer to French-speaking battalions. Much of the camp at Valcartier, in the heart of the province, was managed by anglophones: there were few French-speaking instructors and few visible French-speaking officers. Even by the summer of 1917, there was only one French-Canadian officer (H.A. Panet) among the sixty-eight listed commanders of the CEF.[51] And there was an issue of branding: one did not enlist to serve in the Canadian army — one registered to serve in a Canadian battalion of the British army.

Ottawa proved unable or unwilling to use the stories of French-Canadian courage at the Front to encourage enlistment. There had been opportunities. Joseph-Philippe Landry, a talented and trusted general (he had served under the governor general), was repeatedly refused active service at the Front because Sam Hughes blocked the posting, instead promoting an anglophone with less experience and less seniority. His father, Senator Philippe Landry, campaigned in favour of Franco-Ontarian education rights. Many thought Hughes was simply handing out retribution.[52] "He is the only French Canadian in command of a brigade and I feel humiliated, as all his friends in Quebec do, to see that he is the victim of an intrigue," Landry wrote to Borden, demanding a meeting. He finally got to see the prime minister on September 24, 1915, and was assured by Borden that he would personally look into it (Borden made no note of it in his diary, however).[53]

Another example was the treatment of the fiery *nationaliste* and francophile Olivar Asselin, who had initiated the raising of a new battalion that was ready to sail by the end of November 1915.[54] Maréchal Nantel welcomed the news that Asselin had been successful. "This, [is] I believe, one of the best acquisitions that war people have made for several months, especially from the French-Canadian point of view," he told his brother.[55] It was brought to battle-strength by May 1916, only to be sent to Bermuda. It was finally sent to Europe in November 1916, but there was broken up to provide reinforcements. Asselin would serve briefly as a platoon commander in the 22nd but he, of all people, was then redeployed to reinforce an English-speaking unit. Asselin's unmatched propaganda potential was simply squandered. The federal government's inability to identify and to capitalize on war heroes was emblematic of an overwhelming indifference to propaganda needs. Asselin was one of the most recognizable figures in Quebec and one of the very few *nationalistes* who argued for participation. That his battalion was never used as a unit, but only exploited for reinforcements, was a colossal error.[56]

According to a study of recruitment released in March 1916 by Conservative senator Mason (who also served as general), French-Canadian men barely constituted 4.5 percent — about 12,000 men — of all the recruits. Relying on the figures of the 1911 census, he calculated that there should be about 445,000 francophones between the ages of eighteen

Sir Wilfrid Laurier addressing a crowd on St. Joseph Boulevard in Montreal, encouraging them to enlist (1916).

and forty-five. He also noted that over 63 percent of recruits so far had been British-born, and that another 7 percent were foreign born. English Canada had supplied 25.5 percent. In 1916, 165,000 more men were recruited. Still, it was not enough. Eugène Nantel had just joined the 22nd and was injured in the fighting in April 1916. He was shipped to a hospital in Britain to recover from gunshot and shrapnel wounds (the incident was reported in *La Patrie*). The 22nd suffered important losses in that fighting, as did the entire 5th Brigade. To reinforce it, the other French-Canadian battalions (the 41st, 57th, 69th) were broken up and integrated into the 22nd. There were not enough men to form a brigade — which typically unites a minimum of three battalions — a symbolic imperative.

Bourassa continued to speak to audiences in Quebec, Ontario, and New Brunswick. *Hier, aujourd'hui, demain : problèmes nationaux* (178 pages) and *Le Devoir, et la guerre: le conflit des races* (a sixty-four-page pamphlet) were published in 1916. His writing was translated into English, first as *Independence or Imperial Partnership* (sixty-two pages) and then *Canadian Nationalism and the War* (forty-six pages), which came out a few months later. His message was being increasingly heard by many families, including the Nantels. Eugène's mother, Onésime Nantel-Orsali wrote to her son who was wounded and convalescing in Britain, and told him of the tensions that were mounting in Montreal. Her letter revealed a growing anger in her heart:

> What then are the British overseas doing ... they take cover and leave our beautiful Canadian youth to be mowed down. I assure you, the other day an English guy knocked on the door, saying he was with city hall. He asked me: *Who lives here, Mrs Orsali*? Always in English, he told me spell my name ... So I spelled O r s a l i. *Say it in English* he repeated.... You understand that I got angry ... So I told him there is no English for proper names, you know. Go learn your alphabet if you do not know it, and then come back. He told me *I don't understand* and wanted me to write it myself, so I pulled out my English: I said *you must go away and when you can write the names you'll come back or another man will come*. And

I closed the door in his face.... Damn English. If I could have trapped his head in the door, I would have done so wholeheartedly. Here in Montreal, it's amazing to see all the German English that are here. Just on Durocher Street there are four or six families, maybe more. You remember young O'Reilly, the friend of Lucien and Chambord Bigonesse who used to come to St. Jerôme? The poor boy left with the McGill 2nd contingent and got killed almost on arrival.[57]

Onésime grew even more bitter over the summer:

I assure you that recruitment is difficult among our brave *Canadiens* and good God I agree with them when I see all these English cowards spend their time laughing and having fun when our beautiful *Canadien* youth devotes so much for their cause and is butchered for them. Oh! I just hate those English cowards who insult us and who take pride in not speaking French and who mock us when we speak English and laugh in our face. Let them win the war, you will see that our brave *Canadien* will be ignored and it will be them, these cowards, who will claim victory and then crush us like they did in Ireland.[58]

Onésime, in her own visceral way, seemed in agreement with the thinking of Henri Bourassa.

Another debate over the war opened in the summer of 1916 when an "open letter" attacking Henri Bourassa for his positions against the war effort appeared in the *Montreal Star* and was quickly republished in newspapers in Ottawa and Toronto. The author was Talbot Mercer Papineau, a thirty-three-year-old captain in the Princess Patricia's. He was the son of Louis-Joseph Papineau and, like Henri Bourassa, grandson of the *Patriote* leader Louis-Joseph Papineau, but his upbringing could not have been more different. His mother was a Philadelphia-born heiress who insisted that her son be raised as a Protestant in English Montreal. He graduated from McGill University and then Oxford University as one

of the first Rhodes scholars from Quebec.[59] Papineau was now also seriously thinking of running for a seat in Montreal. Bourassa responded to
Papineau's attack and the two men exchanged angry letters in the press.
Bourassa pointedly noted that "in spite of his name, Captain Papineau is
utterly unqualified to judge the feelings of the French Canadians. For the
most part American, he has inherited, with a few drops of French blood,
the most denationalised instincts of his French origin."[60]

On top of everything else, election was in the air in the summer of
1916 as the five-year mandate of the Conservatives was coming to an end,
but the Liberals knew they'd have a fight on their hands, in part because
the "corruption" they constantly alluded to was never substantiated. "The
general impression is that … Laurier will be returned," Andrew McMaster
thought. [61] He had written to Laurier in the last months of 1916 urging that
the opposition call for an election as soon as possible: "While the iron is hot,"
he wrote. "We are hoping for an immediate change. Act before the situation
can be improved. If the Liberals are not prepared to assume the responsibility, then for Heaven's sake let us have a coalition government."[62]

Laurier agreed that he and the opposition were not landing punches.
"Up to the present time, whenever we made any charge, we were met
immediately with denials. When we asked for investigations we were
denied it, and when granted it was so diluted as to make discovery of
facts almost impossible. Now, however, we have enough to start, but we
cannot go very far unless evidence is supplemented."[63]

Bourassa still had an audience, but it seemed to be declining. *Le
Devoir* had 18,894 subscribers in 1915 according to one estimation, but
that number was reduced to 14,000 by 1917 — a loss of almost a quarter.[64] Nevertheless, from 1914 to the end of 1916, Bourassa had played a
central role in articulating the rationale for lukewarm participation in
the war. There is no doubt that his persistence in tying the language issue
to the war had been significant. *Le Devoir* noted with some satisfaction
in late August 1916 that recruitment rallies were increasingly contested.[65]
Bourassa hammered the war effort all through 1915 and 1916: its aims,
its contradictions, and its irrational pursuit of imperialism.

Bourassa became the *bête noire* not just of imperialists, but of English
Canada. In the 1917 election, his figure was linked to treason, defeat, and

to the idea that Quebec was threatening the war effort. It would be diffi-cult to exaggerate the vilification of Bourassa in English Canada during the war years.[66] He was denounced as a German spy, a traitor, and a crim-inal by some of the most prominent individuals of his day. He often faced police harassment and threats to his life. Bourassa, nonetheless, never hesitated to speak in English Canada to make his views better known. His searing editorials on the Empire and against Canadian imperialists in *Le Devoir* were collected in a series of pamphlets and books, many of them published for the English-speaking market. He mattered.[67]

In September 1916, the Borden government established a National Service Board (NSB) to take stock of the manpower available in the country, with an eye to ensuring that the war effort was maximized. The NSB established a National Registry that required all Canadian men to complete a questionnaire. The prime minister got involved in selling the idea. Borden, accompanied by Charles Doherty, an Irish Catholic Montreal MP and the minister of justice, met with Archbishop Bruchési as Christmas 1916 approached to discuss how the registry would func-tion. Doherty's charms worked and the archbishop agreed to support the initiative. He wrote a pastoral letter over the holidays and it was released on January 3, 1917, to be read during mass on Sunday, January 7. In it he encouraged all Quebeckers to answer all the questions asked by the government. "Let us express an enlightened patriotism," he declared, "let us show a respectful deference to the civil authority, which acts within its rights."[68] Bruchési, who was fifty-six, also declared that he would sign his National Service card, and advised all eligible men to do the same — including priests and seminarians. Cardinal Bégin of Quebec City followed his lead.

Borden reached out to Laurier also, in the hope of perhaps making the effort a bipartisan one, but the overture was declined. This was government business, Laurier argued, the opposition could not support it. The govern-ment was undeterred, and registration began in January 1917. Canada had a standing army of 380,000 volunteers on January 1, 1917. One hundred thousand were still training, in Canada; the rest were in Europe.

R.B. Bennett, the Chair of the NSB, also travelled to Montreal to meet with Henri Bourassa in early January. Bourassa heard him out, and then asked what guarantees the government could offer that the program would not lead to conscription. "The best guarantee," responded Bennett. "I was in favour of conscription. It was Robert Borden who demonstrated to me that it was impracticable in Canada." Bourassa could not doubt the good faith of his interlocutor, but did not sign on. He did not, however, speak against the National Registry.[69]

Moderates in Quebec were willing to work with their counterparts in English Canada. For John M. Godfrey, a Toronto lawyer, and Arthur Hawkes, a journalist with the *Toronto Daily Star*, the fires that were burning between English and French had to be put out. In the midst of these events, they started the *Bonne Entente* movement to build bridges between the two communities. In August 1916, it held its first meeting in Quebec City and quickly attracted elite opinion-makers who really did want to see recruitment numbers go up. Future prime minister Louis St-Laurent, already a leading lawyer in the Quebec capital, attended and was asked to offer his views. He was "unimpressed by the flow of compliments and expressions of good will," wrote his biographer, "and delivered a heated lecture on the importance of respecting one another's views."[70] On January 8, 1917, the *Bonne Entente* movement entered a new phase with the visit of eighty-five leading Quebeckers to Toronto — the heart of "imperial Canada." It included the *crème de la crème*: Lomer Gouin, the Quebec premier; Adélard Turgeon, the speaker of Quebec's upper chamber, the legislative council; Mayor Henri-Edgar Lavigueur of Quebec City; Sir Georges Garneau, the former mayor of Quebec City; and Louis St-Laurent. The Montreal Chamber of Commerce sent five delegates. A grand dinner was held that evening by the key organizers of the movement. Toronto Mayor Thomas Langton Church talked a great deal about Toronto's military efforts. Newton Rowell and Ontario premier Hearst sat near Quebec premier Gouin. "It was a tournament of patriotism and loyalism," wrote historian Robert Rumilly, who interviewed many of the participants on the Quebec side. "Gouin tried to talk bilingualism. The Ontarians would respond with recruitment."[71]

The City of Hamilton held another superb banquet the following night in honour of the Quebec visitors. Ernest Bilodeau, the *Le Devoir* Ottawa correspondent who accompanied the delegation, noted on his return that "When an English Canadian utters the word 'patriotism' he means a love of Empire, while a French Canadian, using the same word, only thinks of Canada." Bilodeau suspected that the *Bonne Entente* movement was only preparing the ground for conscription.[72]

Borden had to reach a *bonne entente* of his own as he planned out the year 1917 and finally turned to the task of bolstering his Quebec contingent in cabinet. He chose Albert Sévigny, a thirty-six-year-old Quebec City lawyer who had been a Tory all his career. After a few failed attempts to get elected, Sévigny had succeeded in 1911, but had attracted little attention. In 1915 he had been named deputy speaker of the House of Commons and a year later graduated to become the Speaker. He seemed like a good choice: Borden chose Sévigny to become minister of inland revenue.

Before he could be formally named to cabinet, Sévigny had to seek re-election and receive the blessing of his electors in Dorchester (in the Beauce region, southeast of Quebec City). For the opposition, this was a golden opportunity to test the waters. Laurier abandoned the 1915 agreement that by-elections would be uncontested. With an election in 1917 likely, the Liberals were willing to gamble big, hoping to embarrass the government in the same way the Conservatives had famously deflated Laurier's naval proposals in 1910 by challenging the government's candidate with an unknown in the riding of Arthabaska, in the prime minister's own backyard.

The Liberals proposed Lucien Cannon as their candidate. Cannon, a highly regarded former judge, was the local provincial MP and a formidable nominee with many accomplishments. He was a bit hesitant at first, but accepted, convinced by the arguments of Ernest Lapointe, and the increasingly active president of the Jeunesse Libérale de Québec, Oscar Drouin. The by-election fight was bitter, and the cold of January 1917 was no help. The first debate took place just ten days after the *Bonne Entente* visit to Toronto and Hamilton and both candidates put on a good show. Sévigny was solid in his arguments in favour of the war effort; Cannon was merciless in recalling every administrative error and in painting the darkest images of what was being threatened with the National Registry. Sévigny's *nationaliste* credentials were not the least spared, nor was the money. According to historian Robert Rumilly, again relying on first-hand accounts, an election typically cost a party $2,000 to $3,000 in those days; this time the tally ran to $20,000.[73] The local Conservative newspaper, *L'Événement*, played a highly influential role, according to some, by repeatedly making the point that Laurier himself was in favour of conscription, something Robert Borden was not.[74] The by-election was held on January 28. Sévigny narrowly won, by 270 votes.

The Liberals had come close, but, significantly, after more than two full years of war, the Conservatives could still take a seat in Quebec — albeit in a traditionally *bleu* riding. The only good news for the Liberals at the beginning of the new year of 1917 was that Major-General François Lessard was finally put in charge of organizing recruitment in Quebec. Blondin shifted from his post in cabinet as secretary of state (it went to Patenaude) to become postmaster general and then also joined Lessard's recruitment drive to raise the 258th Regiment. Rodolphe Lemieux's son enrolled in it.

Canada was at an impasse. Inflation was skyrocketing. The winter was bitterly cold and snowy, and part of the country suffered a shortage of coal.[75] Church leaders gathered in Ottawa again to consider *Commisso divinitus,* the papal judgment on the schools questions that had been issued in September 1916, but, true to their past attempts, the bishops could not generate an acceptable compromise, and again simply pleaded for peace in the schools until a solution could be found. Worse, the government in Ontario announced that it would propose new laws to further restrict French-language education.

Borden was beginning to think of unifying the country by inviting Liberals into his cabinet, but gave up on the idea. "The attitude of Laurier on bilingualism made coalition with him almost impossible," he wrote in his diary.[76] He would need another issue. Private Wilcox had called it, from his sickbed in England in early 1916. He knew Quebec and understood that conscription would take time to come to Canada. He had, however, underestimated the prime minister's resolve.

3

THE ISSUE: CONSCRIPTION

"We get newspapers quite often so have an idea of what is going on in the outside world. I wonder if they are going to have a form of conscription in Canada, similar to that in England. I also saw something in one of the papers about giving us three months' pay after our discharge. That would be pretty good, wouldn't it?"

— Robert Gordon Brown to his mother, June 2, 1917[1]

Sir Robert Borden left for England on February 14, 1917, and arrived in Liverpool a week later. He would be in Europe for almost three months to attend the Imperial War Conference, and on his return to Canada on May 14 would set in motion the process culminating in the December federal election. Before leaving, he told the House that he would be asking for a second extension of Parliament so that a wartime election could be avoided, at least for one more year. And, as on the previous occasion, he stated that he wanted the consent of both parties and that he would not pursue an extension without the opposition's support.[2] If it rejected his request, that would put the responsibility for the holding of a wartime election on the shoulders of Sir Wilfrid Laurier and the Liberal opposition. As he boarded the *Calgarian*, he likely welcomed the thought of getting away from wartime Ottawa, if only briefly. It was his second trip to Britain since the war began, and he was less sure of what awaited him in London. He could not have known it at the time, but it was the start of a new chapter in Canada's war effort.

Borden had been summoned to the Imperial War Conference by British prime minister David Lloyd George. Lloyd George had become prime minister a few months earlier, in December 1916, and swiftly established a British War Cabinet before issuing invitations to the Dominion leaders to visit London for the conference and as members of a new imperial institution, the Imperial War Cabinet. Lloyd George was not particularly interested in imperial constitutional questions; indeed, his bigger concerns were to obtain greater help from the Dominions for the war effort, and to find ways to cement his own political position.[3] The British leader wanted more men and a greater commitment from Canada and the other Dominions and he offered more extensive consultation in return — he could provide access to information about the war situation that had not previously been available to Borden or to any of the other prime ministers.

Borden jumped at the opportunities, because he had things he wanted to discuss with the British. He knew what the problems were, even if he did not have the answers. Canada had done more for the war effort than anyone could have imagined before 1914 and had made enormous economic sacrifices, while the number of Canadian casualties was shocking and steadily rising. Throughout, the Canadian government had pursued a vigorous war effort and had received nothing in return. Requests for information were routinely dismissed and calls for more consultation over the use of Canadian forces were brushed aside even as military commanders of questionable capacity sent thousands of men to their deaths. The slaughter was unimaginable, the lack of communication unacceptable. Borden wanted the system to change.

The Imperial War Conference began on March 20 and meetings of the Imperial War Cabinet were held on alternating days. The War Cabinet was a smaller group consisting of the British War Cabinet and the Dominion leaders, and it was established to discuss important issues including war aims, the fate of Germany's colonies, and the proposed new international league for peace. Borden was a major player in both groups and he attended endless meetings, conversed with important figures, and dined with royalty. He also travelled to France and inspected the Western Front. He interviewed soldiers and their commanding officers, and visited military hospitals and consoled the wounded. For weeks he had such access to confidential information about the war that, according to his biographer, it "was almost like a dream come true."[4]

By far his greatest accomplishment was to be the driving force behind Resolution IX of the Imperial War Conference, which recognized Canada and the other Dominions as "autonomous nations" and fully equal within the Empire, and called for a process of "continuous consultation" for the Dominions and an "adequate voice in foreign policy."[5] Resolution IX has since been celebrated as the moment when the British Commonwealth began to emerge out of the old Empire and as a milestone in the long road that Canada travelled in its evolution from colony to nation. All the specific arrangements were to be ironed out at a future imperial conference, but Borden believed that he had achieved a real victory for Canadian autonomy within the Empire. Despite all the death and destruction, something good had come out of the war.

His English trip also coincided with immensely important developments in the war. In March news arrived of the Russian Revolution and the abdication of the czar. In early April, he basked in the glory of Canada's "splendid victory" at Vimy Ridge, the battlefield in France he had visited only a few weeks earlier.[6] For the first time the Canadian Corps acted together in battle; the Ridge was taken and thousands of prisoners were captured. It was a triumph, no doubt, but it came at an awful price: taking that long low ridge produced more than 10,000 casualties, including an estimated 3,500 Canadian deaths. At almost the same time came the momentous news of the American declaration of war against Germany.

For Borden, all these events led to one inescapable conclusion. The Russian Revolution was the start of Russian withdrawal from the war, which would permit the redeployment of German forces from the Eastern to the Western Front. The entrance of the United States was welcome, but he knew that it would take many months for the Americans to raise, equip, and transport a sizable force to France. In other words, the war, which was already going badly, was likely to get much worse before the Americans could help. More Canadians would be needed to hold the line until then. And there were other things to consider. He had just helped initiate one of the most important constitutional advancements

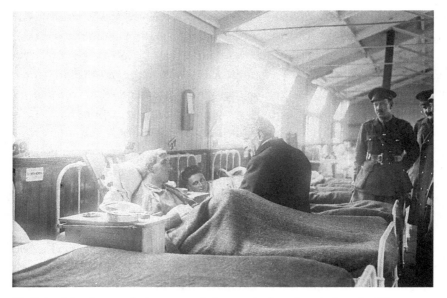

Sir Robert Borden speaks to a wounded man at a base hospital on the Western Front, March 1917.

in Canadian history: in his mind this was no time to withdraw or to diminish Canada's contribution to the war. It was more important than ever that Canadians see it through to the end, and he resolved to do whatever was needed to do that.

Borden had always said there would be no conscription, and there had been no mention of it in the Speech from the Throne a few weeks earlier, but London changed his mind. The Canadian contribution, the sacrifice, and the gains Canada had made all seemed to argue in the other direction. More and more, Borden heard English-Canadian opinion — in the newspapers, in letters sent to him, from his cabinet colleagues — calling for conscription; and the members of the Conservative caucus had been hearing it from their constituents all across the country.[7] The battle at Vimy Ridge and his meeting the sick and wounded soldiers brought matters into sharp focus. On one hand, the victory gave a great boost to Canadian pride and prestige, and the sacrifice of these thousands of Canadian soldiers only made Borden more determined not to let them down. On the other, the cost in lives was unbearable and, when compared to recent recruitment numbers, unsustainable. Casualty rates were far higher than new enlistments. Something had to give. He knew it would be a political bombshell that could deeply divide the country, but by the end of 1916 he had stopped declaring that he would never introduce conscription. Three months in Britain had changed his perspective, and his focus was increasingly on the demands of the war, and less on domestic politics. Borden was a cautious man, often criticized for being indecisive, even plodding. But once he made up his mind on a given issue he became determined. As he left Britain in the middle of spring and sailed for Canada, he knew what he had to do. Borden now had his policy; Canadians were about to get their election issue.

Borden arrived in Quebec City on Monday, May 14, took the train to Ottawa, and arrived there early Tuesday morning. He had been kept informed of political developments in the capital while he was in England, and he was briefed upon his return. He met with his cabinet several times over the following few days, reporting on the Imperial War Conference and his dealings in England. On May 17 he informed his cabinet colleagues that the voluntary method of recruitment had failed and that it was time to introduce compulsory military service. This decision launched a new voyage, as he described it in his memoirs, on "an exceedingly stormy political sea, which was swept, from time to time, by gales of varying intensity and from many quarters."[8] Later that day a "tired and worried" prime minister met with the governor general, the Duke of Devonshire, to inform him of his decision.[9]

On reflection, this decision marked the unofficial launch of the 1917 election campaign. For the next seven months the three issues of conscription, election, and coalition would be inescapably intertwined, unfolding in a complex political ballet that would not only determine Canada's government, but also have a profound impact on national unity, on Canada's war effort, on the future of the two political parties, on Borden's personal legacy, and, ultimately, on the future of the country.

Regardless of the divisions, the upheaval, and the anxieties that conscription would produce, Borden was convinced of its necessity and determined to see it through. But he had several important decisions to make concerning whether or not to form a national coalition government, as Britain had done. He might be able to do it in a way that would both introduce conscription and remove the need for an election; or, he could try to form a national government, and then trigger an election to secure a broad national mandate for it. But if the Liberals rejected a coalition and refused his request for a second extension of Parliament he then would be forced into an election along strict party lines. And what if he lost such election — how would that impact not only his policy of conscription, but also Canada's war effort and the new autonomy and international role that he had worked so hard for in England? For Borden, the one certainty was that the men and women overseas and Canada's war effort generally could not be let down; Canada's honour demanded that the war be fought to the fullest extent, to the very end.

His cabinet colleagues were the first — and easiest — to rally; they did not need much persuading, for almost all were already in favour of conscription. The lone voices of dissent came from the few remaining francophone members. Albert Sévigny, the minister of inland revenue, at first appeared willing to go along and was reported to have told the prime minister that "according to your presentation, the allies have practically been defeated. The gravity of the situation and the measures that need to be taken require a union cabinet, don't you think?"

Borden responded, "Would Mr. Laurier accept it?"

Sévigny replied, "He'll accept it if his party forces him."

All of this led Arthur Meighen, the solicitor general, to say to Sévigny as they walked out of the meeting, "You are making history, today."[10]

Ésioff-Léon Patenaude, the secretary of state, and Pierre-Édouard Blondin, the postmaster general, also initially agreed to stand — and fall, in their particular cases — with Borden and the government, but they warned that conscription would "kill them politically and the party for 25 years."[11] Patenaude, in particular, was more reserved and skeptical (his biographer calls him a sphinx), and eventually declared himself against conscription.[12] According to historian Robert Rumilly, who interviewed many of the players, Patenaude raised three points. The first was that French Canadians were completely opposed to the policy and that he, as one of their representatives, could not support it. The second was that he thought conscription would ruin the party in Quebec and he did not want to contribute to its failing. The third was that Borden had given his word — to him and to Archbishop Bruchési just a few months earlier — that there would be no conscription and that Patenaude had campaigned on that commitment. Under these circumstances he could not remain in the government for long, despite the efforts of Borden and a few other ministers to convince him to stay.[13]

Undeterred by the opposition of a few francophone ministers, Borden announced the decision to introduce conscription in a crowded and expectant Parliament at three o'clock on May 18. He began with an account of his recent experience at the Imperial War Conference; he reviewed the war situation and the great Canadian accomplishment at Vimy Ridge; he then detailed the problems facing the military effort. The Canadian divisions in Europe could not be maintained without reinforcement, he argued, and the voluntary method had been tried but failed to produce the necessary men. If anyone knew of a way to get more volunteers, he added, "I should like to know what it is." This was Canada's war and it was a question of duty. "All citizens are liable to military service for the defence of their country, and I conceive that the battle for Canadian liberty and autonomy is being fought to-day on the plains of France and of Belgium," he said. The men overseas were calling out for help, and Borden had promised that he would not let down those who had fought and died, or were wounded, or were left fighting still. "Is there not a call to us," he continued, "from those who have passed beyond the shadow into the light of perfect day, from those who have fallen in France and in Belgium, from those who have died that Canada may live — is there not a call to us that their sacrifice shall not be in vain?"[14]

The reaction to his speech was generally positive, both in Parliament and across the country. "House greatly impressed," Borden wrote. Conservatives cheered, and some Liberals applauded. He added, "women and some men wept." Liberal leader Sir Wilfrid Laurier was caught off guard by the announcement, or at least so Borden thought. "Laurier was taken entirely by surprise," he wrote, "and made a poor speech."[15] In Ontario, Premier Sir William Hearst voiced his support.

In Toronto, the *Globe*, the *World*, and the *Mail* welcomed the announcement; "Canadians are no longer satisfied to fight the battle of human freedom by proxy," stated the *Globe*.[16] The *Toronto Daily Star* agreed, but reminded its readers that conscription was already the law of the land under the terms of the existing Militia Act, and therefore additional laws were unnecessary.[17]

In Montreal, *La Patrie* supported the measure. What mattered was that Germany be beaten, "for security and for the happiness and liberty of nations."[18] *Le Canada* called for more study and more time — and an election. For its part, *Le Soleil*, still not recovered from Sévigny's by-election victory in Dorchester discussed in chapter 2, announced that the voters had been lied to.[19] Out west, the *Manitoba Free Press* endorsed the move, and editor John W. Dafoe emphasized that it should not become a partisan issue.[20]

In the following days, letters of support arrived in Borden's office from individuals and various associations pledging personal support or reporting on group resolutions in favour of the government's move. The great majority backed the government; and a great many of those expressed their support within the context of using conscription to force Quebec to play its part in the war effort. "It is a well-known fact," one irate Ontario supporter wrote, that Quebeckers refused to enlist "because the Priests tell them not to." Make them enlist, she continued, "even if we have to take an army down to make them go. Even if they would not fight, they could at least stop a German bullet."[21]

Not everyone was so enthusiastic, however, and many questioned the need for conscription, without coming out directly in opposition to it. In Toronto, the *Globe* surveyed a group of local working men and found much less interest. "Conscription of wealth is what we're after before conscription of men," argued one member of the Plumbers' Union.[22] Several newspapers representing rural and working-class Canadians voiced their opposition, and the United Farmers of Ontario demanded that the question at least be put to the nation in a referendum. A few voters questioned the wisdom of conscripting eighteen-year-olds — whether they were physically and mentally mature enough to be soldiers. Others, such as a group of Toronto Quakers, asked that Borden ensure their exemption from military service. Still others offered support for the *idea* of conscription, but then asked for personal exemptions — for reasons of personal hardship, too many dependants, they were married, one or more son had already enlisted, their son was of age but just not ready to serve, et cetera.[23] O.D. Skelton, the Queen's University political science professor — and soon-to-be biographer of Sir Wilfrid Laurier — was certain that support for conscription was not as strong as many people thought. "Borden overshot the mark in assuming that the voice of Toronto is the voice of God," he wrote Laurier. "Quebec is not alone, though elsewhere the minority is less outspoken."[24]

But it would have been an easy mistake to make, in May 1917, to think that Quebec was indeed alone in its opposition to conscription. In English Canada, the great majority of major newspapers, provincial governments, business associations, prominent individuals, and federal, provincial, and municipal politicians — including Liberals — were lined up in support of conscription. That was made clear just days after Borden's announcement when, in Toronto on June 2, a huge rally at Queen's Park passed a resolution in support of conscription, while a group of returned soldiers broke up a socialist gathering at the Labour Temple to suppress the anti-conscription "sedition" they found there.[25]

The linguistic divide on the issue of recruitment, which had been widening since 1915, was blown wide open by Borden's announcement, leading John Foster, the American consul general, to report to Washington on the "very tense" atmosphere in Ottawa.[26] The political manifestation of the gulf between French- and English-speaking Canadians had been partly exposed by the debates over Regulation 17 and the Lapointe Resolution of the year before, but the announcement of conscription brought it into much sharper relief. There could be no more obscuring the issue, hypothetical answers, or avoidance of a decision; it was time to take a stand. Conscription was no longer just a military question concerning recruitment figures and the maintenance of the Canadian Expeditionary Force in Europe; it was now a political issue of the first rank and the greatest threat to national unity in Canada's history.

Anti-conscription posters — "*A bas la conscription!*" — had appeared around Montreal as early as mid-March[27] and coincided with several anti-conscription demonstrations, including some staged by Liberals such as Lucien Cannon and Sydney Fisher, Laurier's long-time minister of agriculture, who had been defeated in 1911. Montreal's mayor, Médéric Martin, although resolutely anti-conscription, was desperate to keep order in the city and did not hesitate to deploy the police to disrupt any such public demonstrations against the war effort. Even some city council meetings had become so inflamed over the conscription issue that he was unable to control them, banging on his desk with his hands incessantly to the point of being bloodied.[28] Elsewhere, a political meeting in Hull, across the river from Ottawa, turned violent. Fighting also broke out at a meeting at the Club Libéral de Maisonneuve organized by Liberal MP Athanase David.[29]

Even more serious, the Ontario schools question again reared up when, on May 12, members of the Ottawa separate school board were accused in provincial court of paying the salaries of unqualified teachers. The leader of the francophone section of the board, Samuel Genest, and his lawyer, Napoléon Belcourt, appeared at the Ottawa courthouse to plead their case. In addition, the conference of bishops resumed the deliberations it had started in January in an effort to find a solution to the issue, although there was still little hope for a resolution. Indeed, three of the French-Canadian bishops essential to any agreement were absent.[30] At roughly the same time, members of the *Bonne Entente* movement gathered for dinner at Montreal's Hotel Windsor. Mgr. Georges Gauthier, speaking on behalf of the Archdiocese, brought up Regulation 17 as a singular obstacle to a sound, mutual understanding. Clearly influenced by the social upheaval of the last few days, he asked his audience to imagine what would happen if Quebec's English-language minority had been treated like the Franco-Ontarians. "You'd see the flames of war rise from the hills of Westmount to the distant shores of the Pacific," he said.[31] The response from English Canada came from Anglican bishop John Farthing. There was a place to contest the actions of the government, he said, and that was the courts. But once the courts ruled, it was the duty of French Canadians to accept their decision. Sir William Mulock, Laurier's former cabinet colleague and now the Chief Justice of the Ontario court, reminded the diners that only one thing mattered: winning the war.

Violence became more common at recruitment rallies, as well. Several Quebec politicians, including Pierre-Édouard Blondin and senators Charles-Philippe Beaubien and Raoul Dandurand, helped to organize enlistment rallies, without much success. At one rally in Montreal on May 7, a young veteran of the 22nd regiment, Eugène Mackay-Papineau, declared openly that "the province of Quebec has not done its duty," drawing howls of protest so loud and so vehement that the meeting had to be ended abruptly.[32]

Major-General Lessard blamed the local priests the next day in *La Patrie*. "As for me, and I insist on saying it," he wrote, "and I want my words to carry all the weight I can give them, we expected from the clergy a generous co-operation, consistent with its great influence on our destiny."[33] For all their trouble, Blondin and Lessard recruited only ninety-two men.

It was hoped that the visit of two influential French statesmen — Joseph Joffre, who had just ended his tour as commander-in-chief on the Western Front, and René Viviani, the French premier — would stimulate more support and participation in the war effort. Viviani arrived in Ottawa on May 12, and spoke to Parliament in the Victoria Museum Building. He spoke in French, which meant that most members had no clue what he said, but "it was apparent that he was a real orator and by his voice and manner one could realize the eloquence which was his," said one MP.[34] Laurier responded to the speech and the session ended with a spirited rendering of "*La Marseillaise*" and shouts of *Vive la France!*

The next day, Joffre arrived in Montreal. A giant parade was organized, he reviewed troops, and inaugurated the new Montreal library. Onésime Nantel-Orsali observed the scene from a streetcar on her way home from visiting a friend. She was handed a small French flag and, "like everybody," waited for Joffre and his entourage to pass. "I screamed and put my flag to work," she assured her son, Eugène; there were so many people in the street it reminded her of the Eucharistic Congress that had been held in Montreal in 1910.[35]

That night, Joffre was the guest of honour at a state dinner at the Ritz Hotel attended by a who's who of the Quebec elite, including

Blondin, Archbishop Bruchési, and the premier, Sir Lomer Gouin. Prime Minister Borden, however, was absent, having not yet returned home from Europe (he landed in Quebec City the next day). It was an enormous missed opportunity, if not a colossal blunder, for Borden not to have returned a few days earlier to reap the goodwill and political benefits in Quebec that could have been his by allying himself with these popular French statesmen.

Unfortunately, the depth of anti-conscriptionist feelings was so profound that the intervention of the two Frenchmen had few tangible results. Henri Bourassa had already attacked the idea that French Canadians should enlist in the CEF as a way to defend France. "They invoke France, they make you want to believe in a French America," he wrote in *Le Devoir*, "that all that is needed is to open our veins in order to allow 'rights,' 'justice,' 'freedom,' and 'superior civilization,' payable in London, in good pounds sterling, with a fifty percent discount."[36] That had outraged the Quebec Liberal press; *Le Soleil* chastised Bourassa for easily forgetting who had started the war in the first place and expressed the hope that "those who have been duped by his sophistry, who long worshipped at his altar, finally realize the depth of the abyss where he wants to drag them."[37]

Borden's conscription announcement sparked a long, hot summer of protests across the province. On May 20, the Liberals held a big anti-conscription rally in Sainte-Anne-de-Bellevue, at the far western tip of the island of Montreal. The following day, ten thousand people gathered at Saint-Sauveur, a village about an hour north of Montreal, to hear from a group of young speakers. Oscar Drouin, the president of young Liberals in the province, and Léon Casgrain, the vice-president, were keynote speakers. Eugène Dussault, an alderman in Montreal, was named president of a *Ligue Anticonscriptioniste*, with both Drouin and a young Wilfrid Lacroix (who would go on to do the same as an MP in Ottawa during the Second World War) as vice-presidents. In Quebec City, another ten thousand demonstrated against the measure, chanting "Down with Borden" and "Shame" over the government's actions.[38] A few days later, a *Ligue patriotique des intérêts canadiens* was established to galvanize a petition-signing effort. Dr. Jean-Baptiste Prince — a guiding light of *Le Devoir* — was named president.

On May 23, a demonstration of fifteen to twenty thousand in the Parc Lafontaine, organized by young writer Tancrède Marsil, had the feel of a minor revolt. Protesters roamed from the park to the centre of town to attack and smash the windows of *La Presse* and *La Patrie*, the mouthpiece of the government.[39] More rioting erupted in Montreal on May 24 and 25, and Lachine, Trois-Rivières, Sherbrooke, Lévis, and Quebec City witnessed similar outbreaks of violence. At Quebec's Montcalm market, Eugène Dussault, Wilfrid Lacroix, and Armand La Vergne spoke. The latter even declared himself in favour of conscription, but only for Canada's territorial defence. "I will never accept conscription [for overseas service], voted or not voted, decreed by the government, or not. I'll be hung or shot but I will always demand, before we accept conscription, elections or a referendum." The French consul in Quebec City denounced La Vergne, while Joseph-Édouard Caron, the provincial minister of agriculture, declared that "Canada had done too much for the war." Fights broke out and rioters smashed the windows of the *Quebec Chronicle*, the English Tory paper. In Montreal on June 7, an anti-conscription rally was staged with speakers including Dr. Jean-Baptiste Prince, Édouard Montpetit, Athanase David, and Montreal lawyer and former Conservative-*nationaliste* MP, Paul-Émile Lamarche, a moderate in his pronouncements though deeply committed to his anti-conscriptionist message.[40] The following day, June 8, Ésioff-Léon Patenaude resigned from the cabinet.

Archbishop Paul Bruchési was livid. He wrote Borden on May 22 that the people were "much agitated. Newspaper articles alone do not fully represent the public's sentiment. In Quebec especially, we can expect uprisings. Protest rallies are being organized and riots are likely. Must we go so far as to spill blood?"[41] On May 25 he issued a pastoral letter asking for calm, but to little effect. In towns large and small, in all parts of the province, demonstrations multiplied over the next few days. Hull erupted again. In Ottawa, Senator Philippe Landry organized his own meeting, using it to denounce the attitude of the clergy over the language issue. City councils in Lachine, Sainte-Scholastique, Trois-Rivières, Sherbrooke, Saint-Joseph-de-Beauce, Quebec City, Jeune-Lorette, Saint-Grégoire-de-Montmorency, Beauport, Château-Richer, Rimouski, and

Grand-Mère passed anti-conscription resolutions.[42] Soon, practically every municipality had done the same.[43] Montreal erupted again on May 28 and June 3 as multiple assemblies were organized to debate the issue. In Waterloo, Tancrède Marsil went so far as to say that "We'd rather see two or three thousand men killed in our streets than to have two or three hundred thousand men massacred in Europe. I said it in Montreal and I'll repeat it here: before we have conscription, we'll have revolution."[44]

The depth of despair of the average Quebecker can be seen in the correspondence of the Nantel family, between Onésime and her two sons, Maréchal in Montreal and Eugène, who was serving in France. "We hear a lot of talk about conscription, everyone is opposed," Onésime reported to Eugène. "There are petitions against. It is certain that if Borden passes this law, there will be revolt in the province and the government will be rejected *en bloc*. The spirits are so raised by a group of hotheads that would rather have civil war than fight for the English, they say. Up to a point, I approve of them."[45]

Eugène had been wounded — for the second time — at Vimy Ridge, and was unsympathetic. "For me the French Canadians are just cowards," he wrote to his mother, "we are here a handful of young people trying to make a name for our country, while over there others only think about having fun, and is it not right that they in turn smell a little gunpowder; is it not?"[46]

No one in Quebec was better placed to observe and influence the situation in French Canada than Henri Bourassa. "You have countless readers among the clergy who are sympathetic to your works," wrote Mgr. Paquet from his desk in the Quebec Seminary. "I think I see that, in many places, there is a will to emancipate oneself of the political yoke that has caused us such great harm, and this beautiful outcome [is] in large part due to the actions of *Le Devoir* and of its director."[47] The idea of "emancipating" the country "from the political yoke" could be interpreted in many ways, but Bourassa responded that he took no satisfaction in seeing events he had predicted become a reality. "I'm a little disgusted in seeing people suddenly gathering around me because the winds are turning — certain people who for a decade at least were backbiters and who no less than six months ago would have been willing to pull the rope to hang me."[48]

Nevertheless, Bourassa formally denounced Borden's conscription policy in a long editorial on June 6. The government had lost all legitimacy, he proclaimed. Borden had no right to break his earlier promises, and "to decree conscription without the consent of the people would constitute appalling cynicism. It would be an act going beyond the worst tyrannical acts for which the champions of democracy criticize the 'autocrats' in Berlin, Vienna, and Constantinople." For Bourassa there was only one way out: "The present or the future Parliament must not adopt conscription. It cannot, out of justice and prudence, impose it on the country without the consent of the people and the opinion of the people can be expressed freely only by a plebiscite."[49]

Premier Gouin was more outspoken and to the point. "We are not junior partners. We are not children in this land, we are the elders. We are at home here, and we will stay here.... There is no power on earth that can impose conscription against the will of the people of Canada. Don't anyone forget it!"[50]

More than anyone else in the country Sir Wilfrid Laurier became the focus of the opposition to conscription. Joseph-Édouard Caron wrote the former prime minister that "all our friends have turned their eyes to you, Sir Wilfrid, and everyone is anxiously asking themselves what your attitude will be in the present situation."[51] Laurier was less surprised by the announcement than Borden had thought, but he was fully aware of the dangers that conscription posed for his party and his country. He remembered the linguistic split among Liberals over the Lapointe Resolution and, while sitting in Parliament listening to Borden's speech, he had observed many English members of his party applauding in support; he also was receiving daily letters and telegrams urging, warning, and pleading with him to embrace conscription.

Laurier's initial reaction was one of disenchantment and frustration; he was disappointed that Borden had come out in favour of conscription despite years of insisting that he never would; and he was frustrated at being in opposition and unable to direct the course of events. There also was concern — and a degree of astonishment — over recent events. He blamed imperialists everywhere and "Tories." "Toryism has obtained an enormous influence in Ontario," he wrote his old friend and former cabinet colleague Sir Allen Aylesworth. "In fact, Ontario is no longer Ontario: it is again the old small province of Upper Canada, and again governed from London."[52] As for the future, he was clear in his own mind; he had always been steadfast in his opposition to conscription and he could not change course now. "I cannot support conscription and will not," he wrote Ontario Liberal MPP Hartley Dewart. To do so would be wrong on principle and a disaster politically, as he "would hand over the province of Quebec to the extremists." Besides, his sharp political instincts were telling him that, despite the outpouring of support for conscription among prominent Ontario Liberals, the "rank and file" did not share those views. There was still room to manoeuvre.[53]

"The Liberals are somewhat less keen for an election than they were prior to the introduction of the new issue of conscription," noted Foster, the American consul general.[54] A week later, he reported to Robert Lansing, the secretary of state, that "the growing opinion seems to be that the Conservatives have an issue upon which they can go to the country with some prospect of success." He predicted an election in September, but conceded that "there is … so much uncertainty in the situation that it is difficult to predict what will occur." As for Laurier, he added that his "great desire is to maintain national unity and he believes that a very dangerous situation may develop in the Province of Quebec if conscription should be adopted."[55]

Laurier's most pressing immediate concern was to keep his own party from fracturing. But the cracks within the Liberal Party were already evident and a complete rupture now appeared distinctly possible. On June 9, several dozen prominent Liberals addressed a rally in Toronto's Massey Hall. With an audience of 3,500 and music from the band of the 48th Highlanders, resolutions were passed endorsing conscription and calling on others to back it.[56] Newton Rowell, the Ontario provincial Liberal leader, spoke at the meeting and two days later was present at a largely Conservative rally that also endorsed a pro-conscription resolution.[57] Rowell had given strong support for the government's recruitment campaign and had supported Borden and R.B. Bennett on their cross-country tour promoting the national registration scheme.[58] In Manitoba, members of the provincial Liberal government spoke out in favour of the conscription measure; in Owen Sound, Ontario, a pro-conscription rally was held under the auspices of the Owen Sound Women's Liberal Association.[59] Laurier's English-speaking colleagues — many of whom for decades had been his closest friends and confidants — appeared to be slipping away. Even Mackenzie King, his former minister of labour, who had been defeated in 1911, had come round to support conscription; Nova Scotian W.S. Fielding, Laurier's former minister of finance and close ally in the struggle for reciprocity, felt the same. For some, like Fielding, the best idea might be not to block the government's actions, but to call for a referendum on conscription — that way pro- and anti-conscription Liberals could remain united, even if only in the short term.[60] At least it would give the party a little time.

Time was something that the Liberals did not have much of, as the government moved swiftly with the conscription legislation. Borden entrusted the task of writing the bill to Arthur Meighen, a rising star in the Conservative Party (although not yet Borden's acknowledged heir-apparent). He was a strong voice for the West, an area where the government was relatively weak. He was also a brilliant performer in Parliament, and an unwavering and profound believer in conscription. Within a week, Meighen had a draft bill, which the cabinet discussed "section by section." Borden found the original bill "very verbose and badly drafted,"[61] and sent Meighen back to revise it. The revised bill was introduced in the House of Commons, by Borden, on June 11, 1917.

The Military Service Bill called for the raising of a conscript force of up to one hundred thousand men. Rather than relying on the existing Militia Act, which had been amended in 1904 to permit the sending of Canadian conscripts abroad and called for the selection of conscripts by a more random system of ballot, Borden, Meighen, and others believed that a more selective method was necessary, where the men would be called up not only on their eligibility, but also according to the importance of their jobs or their situations at home. The bill divided all male

British subjects in Canada between twenty and forty-five into six classes based on age, marital status, and whether they had children. There were numerous exclusions and exemptions written into the law (for essential workers, cases of serious hardship, conscientious objectors, et cetera), and it called for the establishment of a system of tribunals to consider exemptions and hear appeals.

The debate on the Military Service Bill was vigorous, heated, emotional, and protracted — closure was not introduced and it was debated on at least twenty-five occasions from June 11 to August 18.[62] On June 18, Laurier moved an amendment to the bill calling for a pause in the debate until a referendum on conscription could be held. That was the approach Bourassa had demanded during the naval debate, and it had just been used in Australia, where conscription had been voted down by the people in October 1916. Frank Oliver, who supported conscription, seconded his leader's views, and Charles Marcil and Ernest Lapointe also spoke in favour. Rodolphe Lemieux recalled Borden's firm promises to Archbishop Bruchési, and an enormous petition against conscription was tabled in the House. L.J. Gauthier capped it off by declaring that resistance in Quebec would go to the "most regrettable extremities," because French rights had been transgressed. A few francophone Conservatives also supported the resolution, including Edmond Proulx, the MP for Prescott (Ontario). Nevertheless, the idea was dismissed by Borden and Meighen and easily voted down — and some eighteen anglophone Liberals voted with Borden against Laurier's referendum proposal, while a few francophone Conservatives voted with Laurier.

Other amendments — to shelve the whole thing, or to wait until after the election was held, for example — were likewise rejected. The votes on the three readings of the bill, as well as on the various proposed amendments, varied considerably, but a couple of things became clear. First, support for conscription among Conservatives was very strong, but within that group there were only a small number of francophone supporters, and those francophone MPs who did vote with the government tended to represent francophone ridings outside Quebec. Second, on each vote a varying number of English-speaking Liberals broke party ranks to vote with the government.[63] On the vote after the second reading, for example, the bill passed 125 for, 55 against. Of those opposed, almost all were Quebec MPs; only four Liberals west of Quebec voted with Laurier.[64] Among those who voted with Borden were several very influential Liberals, including George Graham, Laurier's former minister of railways and canals and one of his most trusted advisers; Frederick F. Pardee (Lambton West), the Liberal chief whip; and Hugh Guthrie (Wellington South). "The lineup was clear," Conservative MP Sir George Foster wrote in his diary, "the French versus English. To such a pass has Laurier's early teachings and practical lessons brought us. The House rose to a man and sang 'God Save the King.'"[65] Language, more than party affiliation, was the key. The result of the final vote on the bill was never in doubt.

With the debate on the bill underway in early June, a new wave of protests swept Quebec. A few newspapers supported the government, including *L'Événement* in Quebec City and *La Patrie*, but most, such as *Le Canada* and *La Presse*, demanded a referendum.[66] On June 16, the young journalist Tancrède Marsil shouted to a large crowd in Montreal's east-end working-class Hochelaga district that "it is necessary to oppose violence with violence." He exhorted his listeners to be ready for anything, while several among the crowd called out for arms.[67] On June 20, at a second event in Hochelaga, Henri Bourassa spoke alongside Lamarche to a crowd estimated at two thousand. Bourassa spoke again the following night in Cartier Hall in working-class Saint-Henri, just southwest of downtown.[68] On both nights Bourassa emphasized that the issue was one that belonged not only to French Canadians — but to all Canadians. They had to fight conscription and, if it was introduced, they had to fight its implementation. The task was to save Canada from "ruin and suicide."[69] Sunday, June 22, saw more demonstrations. A small event took place in Sainte-Rose but it ended with demands for a conscription referendum. A much larger event was staged on June 24, the Saint-Jean-Baptiste holiday, in the Parc Lafontaine.

By Dominion Day — the fiftieth anniversary of Confederation — it appeared that the Canadian project had never been so fragile. Monster rallies were held in many parts of the province, including Quebec City, Sainte-Hénédine (in Dorchester County), Saint-Hyacinthe, and

Drummondville. In Montreal, it was an Irish demonstration against conscription, dominated by J.J. Guerin, the former mayor of Montreal, that made the news. Each Sunday in July witnessed large rallies. In Hull, on July 15, J.C. Watters, the president of the Labour Congress of Canada, spoke out against conscription. In Montreal at a similar event, Senator Landry again tied the issue of conscription to French-language schools in Ontario, while Armand La Vergne demanded that conscription be resisted "to the death." On the twenty-fourth, after the conscription bill passed its third reading, *Le Canada* declared in a bold headline that the government had "signed the death warrant of 100,000 young Canadians." Borden's photo appeared under the caption as "author of the odious law and the blood tax." On the Champ-de-Mars in Montreal, demonstrations continued. Meanwhile, the few recruitment rallies that were held in Quebec often disintegrated into mayhem and violence. In mid-July, Blondin's recruitment rally in Trois-Rivières was interrupted by protests and Blondin was assaulted.[70] Everywhere he went, Blondin was personally threatened and burned in effigy, as were Albert Sévigny and Senator Joseph Bolduc.

Two intellectuals struck back with pro-conscription tracts. Louis-Georges Desjardins, a former MP and lieutenant-colonel of the Lévis regiment, published *L'Angleterre, Le Canada et la Grande Guerre*, and Ferdinand Roy, a Laval law professor, published *L'appel aux armes et la réponse canadienne-française*. They had little impact. In Montreal, the *La Ligue patriotique des intérêts canadiens* gathered steam while a similar club, *the Ligue de la patrie canadienne*, was launched in Trois-Rivières. Likewise, Tancrède Marsil and Gordien Ménard, a Montreal alderman, launched a murky political organization, *Les Fils de la liberté*, in opposition to conscription.

Others called for more direct action. In Montreal, Élie Lalumière, a former *nationaliste* partisan who had earlier worked for a Tory minister in Borden's government, brought together a band of young activists in the backroom of his music records and electric appliances shop on Saint Laurent Boulevard. Lalumière and his friends, including Ubald Paquin, the store owner, and the journalist Marsil, started a new club — the *Ligue des Constitutionnels*. For Lalumière it wasn't enough just to protest — the club began making plans to bomb Parliament or Montreal's Windsor

Anti-conscription parade at Victoria Square, Montreal, May 24, 1917.

Hotel, where many politicians and military leaders stayed.[71] Although they never acted on their plans, Lalumière and a few accomplices were ultimately arrested and, in court, Lalumière revealed a vast plot to bomb English newspapers, the Mount-Royal Club, and Senator Beaubien's home, and to assassinate the prime minister.

Maréchal Nantel, who considered himself a Conservative, warned his brother that the province was moving into uncharted territory, writing that "no one knows where this policy imposed without popular consent will lead us. French Canadians have never been as mistreated and insulted since the beginning of the discussion of this [conscription] bill, and the few English who believe it is their duty to enslave us and who believe that they can insult us into enlisting are wrong."[72] In a second letter he added that "I must tell you that things don't look the same in Montreal as they do in London or Paris." If his brother had seen how the government had handled the situation, "you'd hardly be surprised to see the indignation and the spirit of revolt that prevails not only in

Quebec but, do not delude yourself, in all parts of the Dominion." His greatest fear was "not conscription itself but the general strike and civil war that will break out throughout the Dominion on the day conscription is enforced. And I would not be surprised, because Borden and his ministers did everything to alienate popular opinion. If a government in Europe had dared to act as they did here, it would have led to its certain downfall and complete collapse."[73]

Onésime was equally pessimistic, writing in August that "there is a cry of 'Down with Borden, long live the revolution.' Civil war is coming to Montreal. A general strike across the province will be declared. This is not funny, last night there were riots, men were wounded, windows were broken, streetcars vandalized. It is not good to go out at night."[74]

A few weeks later, Maréchal added that "before duty to allies and the Empire, the French Canadians have a duty themselves, and I do not see why we would encourage a policy whose ultimate goal is to strangle us."[75]

The unsettled situation in Quebec also caught the attention of John Foster, the American consul in Ottawa. "The sentiment of French Canadians has become very much inflamed in opposition to compulsory service for overseas," he reported to Washington. "There have been several riots during the past week in Montreal and other Quebec points and it is probable that in the event of the passing of conscription by closure through the Houses of Parliament, there will be considerable violence and some bloodshed."[76]

Near the end of August the Military Service Act received royal assent and became law, but this was merely the first step in the debate over conscription. The major election issue was now clearly established and the two political parties had carved out their respective positions. What was less clear was what effect the introduction of conscription would have on the government and opposition, and what the two parties would look like when it came time for the people to vote.

The introduction of conscription and the Military Service Act crystalized the companion issues of political coalition and national election. The 1915 extension of Parliament had postponed the need for an election until October 1917, when either another extension was required or an election had to be held. For many Canadians, it was unthinkable, at the height of the war, to hold a partisan election campaign that would only divide Canadians, weaken the subsequent government, and potentially devastate the Canadian war effort. The creation of a coalition government containing the best individuals and representing the whole country was widely considered as one way to address the problem; its formation could preclude the need for an election altogether or, at worst, simplify the choices and remove partisanship from the campaign. For an increasing number of Canadians, it was time to remove partisanship, so a truly national government could focus all its energy where it belonged — on the national war effort.

The desire for a national government was strong, particularly in urban English Canada, and the voices of support grew increasingly loud as the war progressed. Internationally, it appeared that national governments were becoming the norm, and the formation of Lloyd George's national government in Great Britain provided more ammunition for supporters of a coalition in Canada. By the beginning of 1917, thousands of individuals, newspapers, and associations and groups voiced their support for a coalition. Meetings and conventions were held across the country calling on the government to act, bipartisan organizing began, committees were created to spread the word and generate a national movement for a coalition. Resolutions in favour of national government were passed by the Canadian Club of Winnipeg, the Canadian Club of Toronto, the Vancouver Board of Trade, the Brantford Trades and Labour Council, and the Local Council of Women of Winnipeg, among others.[77] "Among the rank and file of both parties," the *Montreal Gazette* reported, "the opinion is gaining ground that the time has arrived when party warfare must cease."[78]

Two influential men who reflected the shifting national debate about national government were J.W. Dafoe, the editor of the *Manitoba Free Press*, and Sir Joseph Flavelle, the Toronto industrialist and chair of the Imperial Munitions Board, who had provided crucial behind-the-scenes support for Borden in 1911. In the West, Dafoe had backed Laurier and the Liberal Party in 1911 because of his support for reciprocity with the

United States, but after 1914 his support for a vigorous war effort inevitably drew him closer to Borden and the Conservatives. By 1916, one of his biographers wrote, "Dafoe, for the first time in his life, was a man without a party."[79] Dafoe felt strongly that neither Borden nor Laurier appeared able to rise above partisan politics to deliver the kind of government that Canadians needed. The Liberals were sitting back waiting for an election because they believed they could win, he wrote in a long letter to George Wrong, the University of Toronto historian; Borden, meanwhile, was "a well-meaning incompetent," and the Conservatives were "constitutionally unable to rise above the level of selfish political considerations." An election in this atmosphere could prove to be "an incalculable disaster" and, therefore, for Dafoe, a coalition government — for "a greater purpose" — made the most sense.[80]

In the East, Flavelle came to a similar conclusion. He had returned in December 1916 from a visit to England as a convert to national government. He had originally opposed bringing Liberals into the government but, he wrote the prime minister, he had changed his mind and believed that "a Coalition Government should be formed now." What had impressed him in England was the "absence of party spirit," and what concerned him in Canada was that without a coalition the country would face a wartime election on party lines, which would mean, in his mind, "setting the heather on fire, English versus French, with long years of bitterness to follow."[81]

Both men were former Liberal supporters who had been shifting their support to the Conservative Party, though neither was fully committed to Borden as leader. But their greater concern was that a failure to achieve a coalition would necessitate an election — an election that Laurier and the Liberals might win. The thought of turning over the government and Canada's war effort to Laurier and his French Canadians was unacceptable; they would "owe their election to the French Canadian who refused to fight, and to German and Austrian voters who will undoubtedly vote against the Government."[82]

Support for a coalition agreement varied between and within the two parties, but at first appeared stronger among English-speaking Liberals and their supporting newspapers than among Conservatives.[83] The idea of replacing the government immediately attracted some Liberal followers; western Liberals who supported the government's war effort but hoped for a change in tariff policy could also see the benefits of a coalition; the "anybody-but-Borden" factions in both parties saw the logic of the situation; and in the business community there was emerging support for replacing Borden for all the above reasons but also because his railway policy seemed to be heading toward the nationalization of the private companies. A.E. Blount, Borden's personal secretary, informed the prime minister that "the papers [were] beginning to discuss the question again. It is intimated that Laurier will make a statement to the effect that if returned to power he would form a national government. Men connected with the Bank of Commerce, the Bank of Montreal and possibly the Canadian Pacific [Railway] are backing some such movement. It has been intimated that a prominent official of the Bank of Montreal has approached one of your colleagues with a view to arriving at an understanding that he would be included in a national government and that he would retain his present portfolio."[84]

Until early in 1917, Borden had appeared rather cool to the idea of a coalition with the Liberals. When he learned that Flavelle planned to make a public speech calling for a national government, he asked him (unsuccessfully) to refrain. Borden also knew that important colleagues within his government were adamantly opposed: Sir Thomas White, his minister of finance and one of the steadiest members of his government, had earlier informed Borden that any scheme for a coalition along the lines advocated by Flavelle "would be the ruination of the Conservative Party."[85] Other colleagues might legitimately wonder where they would fit in a bigger, more crowded, government.

For Borden, there needed to be a reason for a coalition; "the term 'National Government,'" he wrote, "is one which lends itself to various interpretations. My opinion is that it will lose most of its friends as soon as they attempt to decide its composition and its policy. Until I am in receipt of further information as to its objects I should not care to express an opinion; nor do I think that others should lend themselves to the movement until its policy is definitely disclosed."[86]

At first, support for the creation of a coalition government was not linked to the introduction of conscription, but that gradually changed

early in 1917 with the crisis over national registration and falling recruitment. For Borden the two became inextricably linked. In his mind the
voluntary method of recruitment had been exhausted and compulsion
had become necessary; he also realized how controversial the decision
to introduce conscription would be, especially in Quebec. It would be
preferable to have a national government behind the introduction of
conscription, rather than have the country split on party lines, and to
burden the Conservative Party alone with the consequences of that
policy. Equally important, he needed the support of the Liberals to secure
a further extension of Parliament and avoid an election.

Even more serious for the prime minister was the growing possibility that he might lose an election if it was focused on his government's
record and conscription. Borden realized that his government — three
years into its first mandate by 1914 — had already lost considerable support before the war even started. He had also alienated many of his own
supporters with his lacklustre war policies, which were criticized for
being hesitant, disorganized, and inefficient. Borden himself was seen as
indecisive and uncharismatic, whereas Laurier appeared to have maintained his enormous personal popularity across the country. Looking
out from his Ottawa office, Borden could not be optimistic about his
party's chances in a straight party election. All but two provincial
governments (Ontario and P.E.I.) were now Liberal; the Conservative
premiers of Manitoba and British Columbia, who had backed him
energetically in 1911, had been replaced by Liberals; and, conversely,
Liberal governments in Alberta and Saskatchewan were stable and in
the process of being re-elected. In the Maritimes, he could hope for a
split at best. Moreover, Quebec, and French Canada in general, was a
wasteland for the government. The limited support he received in 1911
from his "unholy alliance" with Henri Bourassa and the *nationalistes*
was essentially a manifestation of shared anti-Laurier feelings, and that
support had all but evaporated even before the war had begun. Borden's
pre-war naval policy had been rejected by Bourassa and his supporters,
and Borden's robust support for the war had not changed things very
much. Borden had won in 1911 by winning in English Canada; by 1917
his government was a government of, by, and for English Canada and

he could count on losing virtually every French-speaking riding in any wartime election.

In addition, support for reciprocity remained very strong in the West and in much of rural Canada, and the Borden government had given no indication of changing its policy of high protective tariffs. Indeed, anti-government feelings ran fairly high across the West; the West might support the war, but there was no certainty that they would support the Conservative government with their votes. To make matters more serious for Borden and the Conservatives, there was also a concern over the vote of all those Canadians, mainly in western Canada, who originally came from Germany, the Austro-Hungarian Empire, and other enemy countries. "Our people seem fairly convinced," reported Arthur Meighen from Portage La Prairie, "that the effect of a campaign, such as the Liberals would undoubtedly wage; secretly stirring them up to revile a Government that taxes them to fight Austria, would create a situation pretty hard to meet."[87] Surely these voters would choose Laurier and a more limited war effort over Borden, conscription, and a vigorous war effort. And what about all those men who had not enlisted — the national registration had revealed that there were hundreds of thousands of suitably fit Canadian men who had resisted volunteering in the CEF for three years — would they (or their parents) be likely to vote for Borden and conscription?

For Borden, there was a cold logic to coalition and it all began with conscription. To uphold the Canadian war effort and, ultimately, to win the war, conscription was necessary; to implement conscription he needed to remain in power; to stay in office he needed either to avoid an election that he might lose, or to ensure a victory in any election that he was forced to fight; to do either of these he concluded that a coalition was necessary. But he was equally well aware of the divisions within his own party over both a coalition and an election. Many colleagues shared his view of the need for a coalition to oversee the implementation of conscription; others believed that all that was needed was a further extension of Parliament, which would postpone any election until after the war and thereby preclude the need for a coalition. Even here, though, there was division: another extension of Parliament meant the passing of a resolution asking the British government to amend the British North America Act to enable the extension. To pass such a resolution, some Conservatives believed a straight vote on party lines with a plurality of votes was all that was required; for others, given the importance of the matter, it was vital to repeat what had been done in 1915 — get the support of both parties and a substantial majority in Parliament to give the request a degree of legitimacy. During the initial cabinet discussion on the need for a coalition government Borden noted that, despite "a considerable divergence of opinion," a majority was in favour. Sir George Foster and Arthur Meighen, he believed, were strong supporters; ministers opposed included Sir Thomas White, Frank Cochrane, and Robert Rogers. Then he added that there was "great division of opinion also as to putting through extension by majority vote." Here Foster and Cochrane favoured it; Meighen and Sir Edward Kemp, the minister of militia and defence, opposed.[88]

Borden discussed coalition with other colleagues, friends, and supporters, and on May 24 the whole matter was discussed again in cabinet. It was to be the "final" discussion, and the cabinet ministers were reminded of the gravity of the situation when news of anti-conscription rioting in Quebec arrived during the meeting. "Several of my colleagues strongly favoured [coalition] while others were violently opposed," Borden later wrote in his memoirs. "The discussion was lengthy and eventually became so wearisome that I interposed, informing my colleagues that they had made me sufficiently acquainted with their views, that the duty of decision rested with me, and that I would subsequently make them acquainted with my conclusion."[89] They didn't have long to wait, because Borden's mind was already made up; later that day he called on Sir Wilfrid Laurier and invited him to meet on the morrow to discuss the whole matter.

Laurier had his own perspective on conscription, national government, and the need for an election, but he well understood Borden's problems of dealing with a divided party. The introduction of conscription had driven a wedge into the Liberals, too; a party that was already splitting along linguistic lines. Laurier's goal was to keep it from completely falling apart. "The pressure has been severe from two wings," wrote Sir George

Foster, not without a degree of sympathy. "Can he hold the leadership of a divided party? How many will follow him? One hears many things."[90]

From the start Laurier saw little to gain from joining Borden in a coalition government, especially if it came with conscription strings attached. Borden needed a coalition in order to implement conscription; for Laurier that was another matter. Earlier that year, he had written to Ontario Liberal Newton Rowell, explaining that "even in the face of your insistence, I am sure you would not expect me to join [a coalition] blindly, without first knowing what would be the programme of the next administration." He continued with his frank assessment of the present state of affairs: "The situation is simply this, that the government has been constantly losing ground, but a good many of those dissatisfied, and perhaps all, do not want to entrust the direction of affairs to a leader of French origin. Analyze the situation anyway you please, and tell me candidly if this is not at the present moment the true and only difficulty." "The very fact," he argued, "that you and so many of our friends in Toronto are looking to a coalition government is abundant proof that my usefulness is gone."[91]

Borden needed the extension of Parliament in order to avoid an election; Laurier had become more certain, however, that in any fair fight the Liberals could win that election. In April 1917, Dafoe had reported to Laurier that there was no doubt that the government "was in a bad way" and their defeat "appears to be inevitable."[92] Laurier had come to the same conclusion; word had reached him from the West that the "party has recovered much and perhaps the whole of the strength which it had lost in the election of 1911." Now, Laurier was "more and more coming to the opinion that an election is now the only course open."[93] The problem for Laurier, therefore, was not to make up his mind on the issues — for his views were fairly clear — it was to keep the recalcitrant English-speaking Liberals from bolting the party for the Conservatives or some kind of coalition arrangement. He needed time to regroup and to define a plausible alternative to keep the party united. That alternative was to call for a referendum or an election on the issue of conscription with a promise that he would support the decision of the people, presumably whichever direction they chose. This would put off conscription for the time being and enable English-speaking Liberals to remain in the party, and possibly even to run as pro-conscription Liberals.

Laurier arrived at Borden's home around 11 a.m., Friday, May 25, for the first of several meetings to discuss the formation of a national government. The prime minister began the conversation with a defence of conscription by reviewing the war situation and the reinforcement crisis and reminding Laurier that without more support the Canadian divisions in France could not be maintained. At home, he continued, present political conditions made a wartime election a recipe for disaster, "as it would involve much bitterness, would divide the nation, and would distract the effort not only of the Government but of the people from the war for several months." He also added that an election would disenfranchise about three hundred thousand Canadians serving overseas because "there would be no assurance of their opportunity to vote."[94] On these grounds Borden then offered Laurier membership in a coalition government in which, outside Borden as prime minister, the two parties would have equal representation in the cabinet.

The sticking point was, of course, conscription. Laurier and the other new members of the government would have to fall in line behind compulsory military service. Laurier reminded Borden of his opposition to conscription and declared himself in favour of an election to clear the air, adding, somewhat disingenuously, that he believed that, since his Liberal Party was so divided over conscription, Borden would win the election and that he, as leader of the opposition, would "use his influence to enjoin and maintain a respect for the conscription law if it should be enacted."[95] Laurier did not immediately say no to a coalition; he asked for more time to discuss it with his colleagues.

The two leaders met almost daily over the next ten days, but the gap between them remained. On May 30, Borden made a slightly different offer in an effort to meet Laurier's demand for either an election or a referendum on the issue of conscription. Borden proposed that Laurier and his Liberals join a coalition government that would pledge that the Military Service Act would not be enforced until after the election of a new Parliament. Parliament would be dissolved immediately and the new coalition government would then seek a mandate from the Canadian people — a mandate to enforce conscription, which they would almost certainly be given.[96] This offer was interesting in that it appeared to give Laurier what he wanted, at least on the surface: a national vote on conscription. Since Laurier had earlier said that he would respect the results of a referendum or election on the issue, in Borden's mind this was a way out of the dilemma.

For Laurier it was not so simple. He spent the first few days of June discussing the matter with Liberals across the country. In Montreal, he set up quiet quarters in Senator Raoul Dandurand's home in Outremont. There he met former premier Simon-Napoléon Parent, Premier Gouin, Rodolphe Lemieux, and the other senators with whom he was closest: Frédéric Béique, Joseph-Marcellin Wilson, and J.P.B. Casgrain. On Saturday, June 2, he met with members of his caucus, including Graham, Pardee, Frank Oliver, and E.M. "Ned" Macdonald. Back in Ottawa he had breakfast with his old, dear friend Laurent-Olivier David, who told him that he had already conceded too much, and that much of Quebec would be against him: if he agreed to a coalition, he'd likely die with a curse upon his head. Laurier even agreed to meet privately with Sir Clifford Sifton. Very deaf, Sifton was confrontational and asked his old chief if he would support conscription? "No," responded Laurier. Would you support a coalition government? Laurier was categorical: "No." Would you support another extension to Parliament? "No," was the answer.[97]

Not surprisingly, the Liberal Party proved just as divided on coalition as it was on conscription. Premier Gouin strongly counselled against any association with Borden: the party would be finished in Quebec, he warned, and the province would be delivered to Bourassa.[98] Lemieux was equally pessimistic and insisted that a coalition went against what the electors really wanted — either a referendum or an election. He saw the idea of a coalition as nothing but a trap, the ultimate "jingo" plan of the "Toronto clan" to rob Laurier of any pretense of standing for Canada. "The day you yield to the obsessions of these conspirators," he wrote Laurier, "you will lose your great prestige. The spell will be broken."[99] But in Woodstock, New Brunswick, Laurier's close colleague Frank Carvell brought together some forty Liberals and this group unanimously favoured both a coalition with the Conservatives and a referendum on conscription (on conscription itself, they divided along religious lines: Protestants for,

Catholics against).[100] Meanwhile, in Ontario, a gathering of Liberals north of Toronto came out in support of conscription and agreed that the Liberal Party could not afford to oppose it at this stage.[101]

Laurier was unable to move Ontario Liberal leader Rowell. "I have been approached to enter a coalition government," he wrote. "My friends, especially those from Ontario, have pressed me very warmly to agree to it." The idea itself was "always repugnant to me," he wrote, but even if he could put his personal feelings aside, "the basis upon which it was offered to me was innacceptable [sic]."[102] Similar letters were exchanged with John Dafoe and others, with similar results. By June 5, Laurier's mind was fairly well set: "Quite a number of people about here, on both sides, are trying to run away from the situation," he wrote O.D. Skelton. "There is only one way, however, of solving it, and it is to face it squarely from the standpoint of every one's opinion. The people, in the last resort, must decide it, as you suggest either through an election, a referendum, or both."[103]

The final meeting with Borden was held around noon on June 6, but a compromise was not to be found. Laurier reviewed his reasons for objecting to a coalition: he felt it inappropriate that the government had announced the introduction of conscription *before* inviting him to join the coalition; he felt that the voluntary method of recruitment should be given one more chance to succeed; in the proposed new government, members of the present one would still dominate it with their partisan ways; there would be in this coalition individuals that he and other members of his party did not respect and could not work with; there were still divisions over the future course of action regarding the railways; and the existing government had already, as one newspaper put it, "outlived its constitutional term."[104] But there was really only one reason for rejecting Borden's offer of a coalition: Laurier could not join a government that adopted conscription. He informed Borden of his decision, the two men agreed to exchange letters confirming their conversation, and released them to the press.[105]

In the spring and early summer of 1917 Borden and Laurier moved in opposite directions and drew opposing conclusions from the same set of facts. Borden was convinced of the necessity for conscription and sought a coalition to implement it as a way to avoid a divisive and potentially dangerous wartime election. He was equally convinced that if Laurier embraced conscription his personal prestige would bring Quebec along with him. Laurier opposed conscription and, since it was already in the process of becoming the law of the land, he believed it made a coalition unnecessary. In his view, to join a coalition would tie him to conscription, implicate him in the sins of the government, and destroy his influence in Quebec. An election was the only way out. Almost a month of sparring had drawn the lines separating the two parties a little more clearly, but the two sides were still far apart. It appeared that the election that no one claimed to want was the one thing everyone would get. On the day the negotiations collapsed, the *Toronto Globe* reported "unofficially," that "everything is in readiness for a dissolution of Parliament, perhaps within forty-eight hours."[106]

A few days later, on July 17, Borden introduced a formal resolution in Parliament calling on the British government to extend the term of his government for another year, until October 1918. The moment unfolded as expected. Laurier explained his objections. He did note the large number of vacancies in Parliament that were waiting to be filled, but, more to the point, he questioned the legitimacy of the government's intentions over conscription. If there were to be no referendum on conscription, then the people needed to have their say via an election, he argued. The vote broke on party lines — eighty-two in favour, sixty-two opposed — but there was no comfort in the win for Borden. The next day he announced that, because there was only a slim majority favouring the extension, he would pursue that issue no further.[107] An election was now inescapable.

4

THE LIBERALS IN OPPOSITION: WILFRID LAURIER'S LEADERSHIP TESTED

"Yes, I see by the papers that conscription has been passed. Seems too bad but I guess it's the only way to get the men. The fellows don't seem to realize that there is a war on. I'm not at all sorry I signed up when I did, and you may lay to that."

— Pte. George Leslie Scherer to Catherine,
June 20, 1917[1]

It was fairly clear by July that there would be no national government led by the prime minister and the former prime minister, but that did not rule out the possibility of prominent pro-conscription Liberals crossing the floor and joining the Conservative Party, and it certainly did not rule out the possible reorganization of the government, either into some quasi-coalition or through the bringing into it of prominent individuals. Both party leaders were inundated with requests, updates, suggestions, and warnings, and advice came freely.

"I have no personal interests to serve — no friends to put forward," wrote publisher John Bayne Maclean to Borden from Toronto. "All I want is a Government of the ablest Executives, with a strong advisory committee of the great National leaders — business, manufacturing, financial, agricultural, labor."[2]

There was also great uncertainty and anxiety about the future. "Liberals everywhere must be more or less in this predicament," wrote Mackenzie King, "but not more so than many of the Conservatives, for the conscription issue has caused much searching of heart in every direction."[3]

Nevertheless, whether it came from newspapers, public meetings, or prominent individuals, support for the formation of a national government — either as a coalition of Liberals and Conservatives or a completely new government under new leadership — remained strong.

Borden took Laurier's rejection of a coalition in stride and did not let up. He called for all his cabinet ministers to submit their resignations to him in advance of a government reorganization that might include a number of Liberals. He also began to put out feelers to those Liberals who had supported the conscription bill in Parliament. Borden offered two prominent Liberals — George Graham and Fred Pardee — positions in a coalition government. Both were close associates of Laurier, and their defection would have delivered a serious blow. As Laurier wrote Sir Allen Aylesworth during the conscription debate: "Yesterday it was Pardee, and today it will be Graham! Graham and Pardee as dear to me as my own brothers!"[4]

When they voted with Borden and the government, Sir George Foster wrote in his diary that Laurier "gave one the idea of a hurt and stricken leader who sees his influence gone and his strongest supporters leaving him. At his time of life there is no regaining his lost ground — the slip downward is irrevocable."[5]

Graham and Pardee supported conscription, but they rejected Borden's offer, not, as they explained later, "because they were opposed to coalition, but they did not think that individual Liberals should consider going into the present Government but that the matter should be dealt with from the standpoint of the Liberal Party."[6]

Unable to attract the federal Ontario Liberals, Borden next appealed to the Ontario leader, Newton Rowell, using Sir John Willison as intermediary. Willison was an experienced Liberal journalist who had broken with both Laurier and the Liberals over a decade before and had become, by 1911, a Conservative supporter and Borden's personal friend. The death of his son at the front in 1916 only rededicated his support for the war effort. In June 1917, he was in the process of both leaving the editorship of the financially troubled and Conservative-backed *Toronto Daily News* and soliciting (unsuccessfully) a Senate appointment from the prime minister.[7] Willison approached Rowell on June 17 and asked if he would consider entering a coalition with Borden, along lines offered earlier to Sir Wilfrid Laurier. Rowell declared that he felt a national government was a good idea for the country, but hesitated. He likely reasoned that, with Laurier, Graham, and Pardee all saying "no," he would be unable to make much of a difference or be able to attract others into a coalition government. But Rowell did not shut the door on the proposal, and stated that if called to Ottawa by the prime minister he would discuss the matter further.[8]

Rowell was formally summoned to Ottawa by the prime minister and the two men met on June 26. Borden described the situation as he saw it and explained that he was trying to form a coalition with "those elements of the Liberal Party who supported compulsory military service," and that this new government would include other groups representing the West and organized labour. The only "stipulation" was to accept the policy of conscription.[9] Rowell took a similar position to Graham's and Pardee's, stating that he was reluctant to join as an individual but supported the idea of a coalition between the two parties.[10] He later wrote Borden that "I did not believe the entrance of two or three individual Liberals, including myself, into your government, would solve, or even materially contribute to the solution of the present critical situation." Rowell added that an election would "clear the air" and presumably lead to the election of a pro-conscription Parliament.[11]

Borden later wrote to Willison that Rowell "lacked the nerve" to see his way into a coalition,[12] but Rowell had found himself in an impossible position and was, like many other English-speaking Liberals, torn between his principles and his party. This gulf between English- and French-speaking Liberals was clearly displayed in the correspondence between Laurier and Rowell in July. Rowell strongly supported conscription and national government but he was reluctant to make a sharp break with Laurier and his party, and continued to urge his party leader to accept Borden's offer of a coalition. He wrote Laurier of his surprise that "some common ground" could not be found among the political class to both prosecute the war to its fullest and preserve national unity.

Laurier agreed, but pointed to the sticking point of conscription: a common ground could be found if conscription were removed from the equation, but Rowell seemed "to look upon conscription as indispensable for Canada to move along with the other allied countries in the prosecution of the war."[13] His colleagues in Ontario, Laurier continued, "look at the situation from their own point of view" and failed to take into account the view of Quebec Liberals. From Quebec, Laurier was hearing the view that "we have to fight at once the Nationalists at one end, the English-Speaking Liberals at the other end and the Tories everywhere. The case is hopeless for us and for the ideals which we always had." Then he added, "I deplore more than I can say the desertion by the English-speaking Liberals of what have always been traditional principles of the party."[14]

Rowell responded sharply. If anyone had tried to compromise it was the English-speaking Liberals, like himself, who were willing to do anything they could to make the voluntary system work and to resort to conscription only as the very last resort. It was, he argued, the Quebec Liberals who refused to budge on the issue and refused to take into consideration the impossible situation facing English Liberals — they would have "to sacrifice what they believe to be the cause of liberty and Canada's own national honour it they were to agree that there should be no compulsion." As for deserting the traditional principles of the party, Rowell was indignant: "I am at a loss to understand what Liberal principles you have in view. I have never heard that it was a Liberal principle not to fight to preserve our own liberty and to defend our own national honour and the cause of democracy." To underline the point he referred to the present British and American governments as well as to Abraham Lincoln — all had introduced conscription in the name of democracy and freedom.[15]

The rift between the two political leaders and between the two linguistic groups was, of course, over the matter of conscription, but the roots of the problem arose from their different views of the war. For Rowell, this was "Canada's war" and Canada was fighting not to protect another country or for someone else's values but, rather, to defend Canada's values and way of life. In this context he pointed to the Militia Act, which Laurier's own government had amended to include conscription for service overseas in defence of Canada. Even Laurier had foreseen the day when it might be necessary to conscript men for overseas duty — and that time had arrived in 1917.[16]

Sir Wilfrid Laurier addressing the Members of the House of Commons in the
Victoria Museum Building.

Laurier's response reflected his different view of the war. It was completely true, he wrote, that all citizens were compelled to fight a common
enemy, including overseas if necessary, but the case in this war was different. "We are not fighting to repel an enemy — we never were threatened by an invasion — but we fight to assist in a noble cause."

In that one word — "assist" — Laurier, perhaps unintentionally, revealed
the essence of the matter, and Rowell surely must have bristled when he
read it, because for him Canada was doing far more than "assisting" Britain
in the war. English- and French-speaking Liberals, like these two political
allies and long-time friends, were moving in different directions.

"You and I are old friends," Laurier wrote, sadly, "and while it seems
to me we are drifting more and more apart, I would be sorry if anything
that was said between us at this time were to mar our actual friendship
or future relations."[17]

Rowell, like Graham and Pardee, was hesitant about joining a coalition
with Borden because he preferred that Liberals join as a party. For such
action, the Liberal Party — or large parts of it — would have to be in
agreement, and, to that end, Ontario and western Liberals came together
in July and early August in search of a consensus. The two Liberal

gatherings, first in Toronto and then in Winnipeg, were staged in a charged atmosphere. The results could hardly have been more surprising.

The lead-up to these meetings was covered in newspapers from coast to coast, and involved a flurry of pro-conscription and pro-national government rallies, culminating in a huge two-day "Win-the-War" Convention in Toronto, sponsored by the former leadership of the *Bonne Entente* movement. On August 3, some six thousand men and women, including two thousand returned soldiers, listened to anti-Quebec speeches and accusations of treason against French Canadians, and then voted a resolution for conscription, the creation of a national government, and no election.[18]

The Ontario Liberals — a mixture of forty-five federal MPs and selected candidates for the next election — met in the offices of the Ontario Reform Association at 2 p.m. on July 20.[19] It was to be an informal meeting, and, as expected, Graham, Pardee, Hugh Guthrie, and a few others led off the discussion with a review of their generally favourable positions on a coalition with Borden and the Conservatives, warning of disastrous consequences if the Liberal Party failed to accept the offer. The reaction was immediate and negative: from the first response speaker after speaker rejected the whole idea. "I am a Scotch man — a plain man — a Liberal," said Adam Thomson, the candidate for Waterloo South. "I cannot understand the attitude taken by Mr. Graham, Mr. Pardee, and others at Ottawa. The sentiment of the people is undoubtedly against the present Government, and in large measure, I believe it is against conscription. There is no question that it is against coalition and extension." Others followed in a similar vein. There were some who favoured conscription but none indicated support for joining with the Conservatives or keeping them in office any longer than necessary. And no one would speak against Sir Wilfrid.

Frederick Hogg of Ontario North interjected that, while Graham was a close friend, he would "throw him down, or throw down any other man who attempts to throw down the Old Chief." Perhaps, one candidate suggested, a national government might be formed — but after the general election, and then some "Big men" could be brought into government. He mentioned Robert Falconer, the president of the University of Toronto, as a possible minister, but was met with "cries of dissent." Someone in the back called out: "No more professors!"[20]

As Graham later put it, "[W]e met and there was an avalanche that could not be stemmed."[21] There were no formal resolutions, but he put together a review of the general consensus of the meeting that was released to the press. The Liberals agreed that everything had to be done to win the war; but there would be no extension of Parliament, no coalition with Borden, and they would stand behind their leader Sir Wilfrid Laurier. The erstwhile Liberal-conscriptionists had met and the one thing they had *not* endorsed was conscription; indeed, they agreed that a further push should be made to make the voluntary method a success.[22] "I think it is safe to say," concluded Graham in a letter to Newton Rowell, "that the feeling was not only strong, but in some instances bitter, against the action of us who have voted for Conscription."[23]

For those who supported national government and conscription, the results of this meeting were stunning and were met with disbelief. For some Liberals, the meeting itself was ill-conceived and part of a large conspiracy to replace Laurier as leader of the party; for others, the "consensus" report in the press did not accurately reflect all the views expressed at the meeting.[24] One week later, on July 26, close to a dozen Liberal newspaper editors from across Ontario came together to pass their own counter-resolutions, calling for conscription and a national government (although not under Robert Borden's leadership).[25] Rowell, who had held a meeting in his Toronto office with a few pro-conscription Liberals before the larger meeting, was surprised at the outcome because he had been told that "no formal conclusions of any kind would be reached." He now began to argue that to "save" the situation the "real" Ontario "win-the-war Liberals" needed to ally themselves with those in western Canada who shared similar views.[26]

For Borden and other Conservatives, the results were equally surprising. Sir Clifford Sifton had earlier assured Borden that there were up to twenty-eight pro-conscription Liberal MPs,[27] but when he met the prime minister the day after the Liberal meeting he was discouraged. Sifton was about to leave for Winnipeg to help organize the convention of western Liberals. Borden told him that "western Liberals should hardly let their view be obscured by the insignificant creatures who had met in that [Toronto] convention."[28] J.S. Willison, who had earlier written confidently to Borden about the "Liberal revolt in Toronto,"[29] was equally discouraged. He also now put his faith in the upcoming western convention. "If Quebec and all the 'foreign elements,'" he wrote Borden, "are consolidated behind the Liberal leaders the future of the party you lead is doubtful at best." The only hope, he concluded, was "a union of Eastern Conservatives with Western Liberals."[30]

Preliminary work on what became known as the Winnipeg Convention had begun early in July and a committee to oversee the arrangements was established, including the three Prairie premiers and various other western officials. At the same time, J.W. Dafoe and the *Manitoba Free Press* renewed their vigorous campaign for conscription and national government, while Sir Clifford Sifton toured the West, speaking in Winnipeg, Regina, and Moose Jaw in an effort to drum up support for the twin causes. "We are at a turning point of public opinion," Sifton reported. "I find that practically all the best men in Winnipeg are agreed. I never saw such complete unanimity before."[31]

Sifton had confidently informed Borden that all the Liberal provincial governments in western Canada favoured a coalition government,[32] but in the days leading up to the convention this was not a certainty. In a general way, Liberal support for a Borden-led coalition government tended to be strongest in Manitoba, while in Alberta, thanks to the organizing efforts of Frank Oliver, the former Liberal minister of the interior, support remained strong for Laurier. In fact, rather than the consensus that Sifton spoke of, the views across the West varied considerably. The *Montreal Gazette* detected four factions among the western Liberals: those who favoured a coalition with Borden, those who favoured a coalition without Borden, those who supported Laurier all the way, and those who supported the creation of a new, western-based Liberal Party.[33]

On August 7, approximately one thousand delegates arrived for the Winnipeg Convention, including premiers, ministers, aides, advisers, journalists, and a veritable who's who of western Liberalism. Also in attendance was William Main Johnson, Newton Rowell's principal secretary; he reported back to Toronto that he found the majority of delegates

and the character of the meetings intolerant, undemocratic, and lacking in leadership. Worse, he quickly learned that the "great mass of the
delegates were obviously in favor unreservedly of Sir Wilfrid Laurier
and anxious for the political advancement of the Liberal Party." Much
as at the Toronto meeting, the delegates in Winnipeg lined up behind
Laurier and the Liberal Party, and against any coalition with the Borden
Conservatives. Even Premier Norris of Manitoba, whom Johnson had
heard declare, just days earlier, his support for national government,
claimed to have been misreported and that, in fact, his support was
for a national government headed by Sir Wilfrid Laurier. "I believe the
strength of opinion is against the Borden government rather than for
Laurier," Johnson concluded.[34]

By the end of the second day of discussions, the convention had
passed several controversial resolutions, including motions denouncing
the war record of the Borden government, calling for an all-out effort to
win the war, and endorsing Laurier's leadership of the Liberal Party. Absent
from any of these resolutions was the word "conscription." In one of the
most heated debates of the convention, John G. Turriff, Liberal MP from
Assiniboia, Saskatchewan, introduced an amendment to insert in the
"win-the-war" resolution the words: "and by compulsion if necessary," but
this amendment was defeated and the resolution passed — unanimously —
without them. "The conduct of the convention," when Turriff introduced
his amendment, Johnson wrote, "was most unpleasant. There was a spirit of
intolerance and of unfairness to all the speakers in favor of the amendment
that was very disquieting." In Johnson's mind, the convention was "strongly
anti-conscriptionist," and, ultimately, a "triumph for the old guard of the
Liberal Party."[35] As for a national government, a motion was introduced by
T.A. Crerar, the president of the United Grain Growers' Company and a
leading voice for western agriculture. It called for the creation of a national
government *after* the upcoming election, "whichever party is returned to
power." It passed unanimously.[36]

In a stunning reversal, for the second time in little more than a
month, meetings arranged by largely pro-coalition and pro-conscription
Liberals had staked positions almost diametrically opposed. "The honest fair minded Grit is humiliated & ashamed," wrote Ontario premier

Hearst to his son William, who was serving overseas. "God grant that right may yet prevail and Canada be saved from the humiliation of a Laurier anti-war Government."[37]

In Ottawa, Sir George Foster wrote in his diary that "the [W]est will not stand for this negation — there will be revolt and cessation among war Liberals." Laurier was "jubilant," he added, but "rumblings of discontent are heard."[38] In the days following the convention, other meetings were held to denounce the outcome; Manitoba Liberals, including Crerar, announced their support for national government but not for Sir Wilfrid Laurier; and the *Grain Growers Guide* proclaimed that the resolutions of the convention "did not represent the best thought and opinion of the Prairie Provinces."[39]

For his part, Sifton blamed the Liberal "machine" for the turn of events and concluded that he had been able to "convince leaders but not the mass of delegates." And, given that the delegates to the convention were selected by the local riding associations rather than being selected from the "people," there was some truth in the accusation.[40] But others blamed Sifton. Although at one time he had been the voice of the West in Laurier's cabinet, by 1917 his support for Borden and his government, his continued opposition to reciprocity and lower tariffs, and his extensive eastern business activities, which often seemed inimical to western economic interests, combined to make him unpopular to westerners, Liberals in particular. It was reported that at one point it got so bad that newsboys selling a rival newspaper at the convention exits began shouting, with respect to Sifton's ownership of the *Manitoba Free Press*: "we won't sell the Sifton paper!"[41] After hearing the discouraging reports from the convention, Borden wrote in his diary: "Sifton's visit was a great mistake."[42]

The convention also discussed the unpopularity of the Borden government on a range of issues, most of which had little to do with fighting the war, including its management of the tariff, taxation, the nationalization of the railways and telegraphs, prohibition and suffrage, immigration and land settlement, among others.[43] Resolutions were passed in support of this broad range of western issues, but these were largely ignored in the press. The issues, however, were to return, with a movement for independent political action, once the war had ended.

Sir Clifford Sifton, May 1917.

Norman Lambert of the *Globe*, who also attended the convention, had a slightly different perspective. He later wrote that western skepticism of national government could be explained, in part, as a western reaction against those elements of the Liberal Party that supported it, in that these were the same "Liberals" who had deserted Laurier in 1911 over reciprocity.[44] The Toronto Liberals — like the "Toronto Eighteen" in 1911 — had turned their backs on Laurier and the West and now supported union with Borden, and they were no friends of western Liberalism.

Still others were merely exasperated: "There was something pathetic," concluded the *Toronto Daily Star*, "in the wistfulness with which the people of Canada looked to the recent Winnipeg convention to speak out and give the country the non-partisan leadership that nobody at Ottawa has furnished. The convention failed to speak out."[45] For John Foster, the American consul general, the setback in Winnipeg likely ended "all chances for a union government."[46]

Throughout the course of the summer, the governor general, the Duke of Devonshire, watched the slow progression and setbacks of national government with increasing unease. Near the end of July, he repeated to the prime minister his concerns over slow recruitment and the problems of war finance, transportation, and munition supply. He also reminded Borden of the need to be prepared for a long war. "If my appreciation of the situation in Canada today is correct," Devonshire wrote, "we find ourselves confronted with a General Election which will almost certainly raise most bitter racial issues and which may have the effect of throwing Canada back for at least a generation."[47] He still hoped, despite the recent vote in Parliament, that an agreement could be reached to extend the life of Parliament so as to avoid a wartime election. The problem, however, was that an extension needed to be confirmed by the "Imperial Parliament," as he referred to it, and there was a possibility that the British parliament would be adjourned in August or September, making it unable to approve the extension. He reminded Borden of the urgency of the situation: "we must take care that the necessary formalities are completed here in such a time as to enable the necessary act to be passed."[48] To this end he offered to host a meeting of all those involved to see if some way out of the current mess could be found.

The arrangements were made and this extraordinary meeting took place a little after noon, at Government House, on August 9. It assembled the decision-makers of Canada both in and out of government; in addition to Borden and the governor general, it included Laurier, Sifton, George Graham, Sir George Foster, Quebec premier Sir Lomer Gouin, and Lord Shaughnessy, the president of the Canadian Pacific Railway (CPR).

Devonshire opened with a review of the current situation and then left it open for discussion. It was a cordial conversation, conducted with "tact and obvious sincerity," but the serious divisions remained.[49] Borden repeated his offer of a coalition government based on a six-month suspension of the Military Service Act, a six-month extension of Parliament, and one last "united" push for the voluntary system of recruitment.[50] Laurier, with the support of Gouin, did not specifically reject the offer, but repeated his own position that an election was needed immediately before there could be any talk of a national government. Devonshire, who remained in the room, later reasoned that the recent Winnipeg Convention's solid support for Laurier "may have accounted for [his] extremely stubborn attitude."[51] By 2 p.m. it was evident that there would be no agreement. The meeting had taken less than an hour.

The final attempt had failed to bring the two party leaders together into a national government and avoid a wartime election that everyone agreed could tear the country apart. Laurier had survived, had kept his party from splitting apart over conscription, and he had skilfully managed events to ensure that Borden would shoulder the responsibility for calling the election — an election that would be fought on party lines and in which Borden would have to defend his government's record. Borden must have wondered how the aging leader, who appeared to be facing desertion on all sides, had been able to staunch the bleeding, rally his supporters, and emerge in August with a solid base in Quebec, strong support in the Maritimes, and renewed demonstrations of support from Ontario and the West. Indeed, the Liberals appeared more confident of their chances in any open contest with the Conservatives than they had been in months.

"The Winnipeg conference of Western Liberals," boasted Mackenzie King, had shown "pretty clearly that western opinion is solidly with Sir Wilfrid and that we may expect, whatever the result is in Ontario, the return of Laurier to power." As for Borden, "he knows that appealing to the people as a Conservative Prime Minister with a Tory cabinet, the lot of them will be swept out of existence in hopeless fashion."[52]

* * *

Conscription remained at the heart of the matter, of course, and for Sir Robert Borden it continued to be linked to the formation of a national government. But it was no longer an issue of trying to arrange a coalition with the Laurier Liberals as part of a larger scheme to implement conscription while simultaneously avoiding a gruelling, divisive, and costly election. Laurier had said "no" to conscription, coalition, and the extension of Parliament. Through the summer, Borden turned his attention to reconstructing his own government and to wooing Liberals from outside the federal party into a "Union" government, as it was increasingly being referred to. He had done it before; in 1911 he reached out — over the opposition of some members of his own party — to provincial Conservative premiers, Quebec *nationalistes*, and disgruntled Liberals to forge a new political arrangement and to win an election.[53] In 1917 he would try to do it again. It no longer mattered that he had not wanted to fight a wartime election; now it became vital to win it — at all costs.

There were many pro-conscription and pro-Union Liberals who might be approachable, and Borden, with the help of his two closest advisers in the party, Arthur Meighen and J.D. Reid, the minister of customs; and Sifton, Dafoe, Willison, and others outside the party, continued the process of negotiation through August. Borden knew there would be few from Quebec who might be enticed into Union, but he did appeal to Charles Ballantyne, the well-connected Montreal businessman and former mayor of Westmount. In the rest of the country it was a different story. There were still the individual federal Liberals who supported conscription or had at least appeared open to the idea of a coalition, including Pardee, Graham, Guthrie, Saskatchewan's John Turriff, and others. On the provincial level, Newton Rowell who, despite "lacking the nerve" to join, as Borden put it, remained at the top of the list of provincial politicians who had made it known that they would enter a Union government under the right conditions. In the Maritimes Premier George Murray of Nova Scotia appeared sympathetic, as did W.S. Fielding, Laurier's former minister of finance, and even New Brunswick's Frank Carvell, one of the most partisan of Liberals. Borden put out feelers in all directions.

Even more important were the westerners, for it was in the West that Borden needed support if his new government was to have "national" pretensions. And, although he failed to get the support of the federal Liberals in the West, it was clear that British Columbia and the three Prairie Liberal provincial governments were leaning toward the Union project. On August 21, for example, some two thousand Liberals met in the riding of South Winnipeg to denounce the outcome of the Winnipeg Convention, to reject Sir Wilfrid Laurier as Liberal leader, and to throw their support behind Union government and Sir Robert Borden's leadership. Included in this group was the Liberal premier, T.C. Norris.[54] Equally important, the federal political organizations were founded on the provincial bodies, so if Borden could attract provincial Liberals from the West he could bring over their ground organizations as well, and this could turn the election in his favour.

As a result, Borden looked to those western Liberals who had publicly backed conscription and national government, and there were several names on that list. First was T.A. Crerar, the United Grain Growers' Company president, who had called for a national government at the July Winnipeg Convention and already appeared to be considering a move into politics. Crerar maintained close ties to the Manitoba Liberal government and in 1917 was, in the words of historian W.L. Morton, "representative, as few, if any, others could claim to be, of both western Liberalism and the western organized farmers."[55] In Alberta, there was Arthur Sifton, the Liberal premier (and Sir Clifford's older brother), who had been rumoured since May to be interested in leaving for Ottawa.[56] Arthur Sifton was a man who, according to one historian, demonstrated a "fondness for the good things of life, cigars among them," and who did not live in the shadow of his more prominent brother.[57] Another was Henry Wise Wood, the president of the United Farmers of Alberta, who had previously supported the Liberal government in Alberta. In Saskatchewan the prize catch would be James Calder, a one-time president of the Saskatchewan Liberal Association and minister of railways in the Saskatchewan government who had taken the lead in organizing the Liberal sweep in the June 1917 provincial election.[58] In Manitoba several influential Liberals looked promising, especially two prominent Winnipeg lawyers, A.B. Hudson and Isaac Pitblado. Hudson was attorney general in the Manitoba Liberal government; Pitblado was not directly in politics but was an associate of Arthur Meighen and had signed a petition denouncing the results of the Winnipeg Convention.[59] Both men had sat on the stage with Premier Norris at the South Winnipeg meeting on August 21. Conversations were held with all of them and, on Sir Clifford's invitation, James Calder, A.B. Hudson, and Arthur Sifton had visited Ottawa earlier in the summer to discuss the possibility of a coalition.

In the Conservative Party, Union government had its supporters. Some shared Borden's view on the need for a coalition to effectively pursue the war effort, others were aware of the failing popularity of the Conservative Party and saw coalition as a way to stave off defeat in the election (and perhaps to save their own seats), still others saw Borden as their best hope for the future of the party and put their faith in his leadership. But there were serious roadblocks to coalition within the Conservative Party, too. Borden perhaps had a wider vision than many of his colleagues about the future of his party, and he may have seen in the war and his project for national government the opportunity to create a new, greater party and to forge a new national vision for the country. But many members of his party and cabinet did not share his enthusiasm for liberation from the old ways; nor could they relinquish their partisanship.[60]

For example, Sir Sam Hughes, Borden's recently knighted former minister of militia — and certainly no stranger to partisanship — was shocked by Borden's enthusiastic slide into a coalition with Liberals and others, some of whom were "not even in public life," and his apparent willingness to "forever wipe out" the old Conservative Party. These Liberals could never really be trusted to remain loyal to their new party, Hughes said, and "as soon as the conscription issue is over, these gentlemen, or a majority of them, will return to their old love on the trade issues of the day."[61] He argued that after the election the remaining Laurier Liberals could band together with the new Liberal supporters of the Union to create a new Liberal majority in the House, leaving the rump of the Conservative Party in a dangerous place. It was a bit of political arithmetic that others had added up in a similar way. In addition, all this talk of a coalition had only one certain result: endless delay in the

implementation of conscription. First it was delayed by national registration and efforts to recruit the Canada Defence Force; then more delay
over the passage of the Military Service Act; and now talk of further delay
by putting off conscription until after an election or one last recruitment
drive. For Hughes, it was asking too much and taking too long. "Surely,
you can realize that from the very outset the Chief Liberal Leaders have
been seeking to fool you; to disintegrate the Conservative Party, and to
prevent the upbuilding of the Empire Forces."[62]

Another voice in opposition came from R.B. Bennett, who likewise
saw in Union government the potential destruction of the traditional
Conservative Party. A coalition with Liberals — most of them provincial
politicians or influential private citizens — would leave *intact* the Liberal
Party under Laurier while at the same time change the Conservative
Party forever. He did not see the point. It would be better to run against
the Liberals in a straight fight — the party would lose Quebec, but sweep
the rest of the country.[63] In addition, Bennett had a personal grudge
against the Sifton brothers and the thought of sharing government with
either — especially Sir Clifford — was unacceptable. "The degradation of
public life in Western Canada," Bennett wrote his old friend Max Aitken
in London, "is directly attributable to the influence of one man, and that
man is [Clifford] Sifton."[64] Bennett was moving away from the government and, although his break with Borden still lay in the future, Borden
was losing faith in his colleague.

"His vanity," Borden wrote in his diary on August 15, "makes him
quite unbalanced."[65]

Borden was sensitive to the charge that his actions threatened to
destroy the Conservative Party. He differed from his critics in that he
would not believe that the Liberals who were discussing coalition in a
serious way were doing so in bad faith; surely they would put the interests of the country and the war effort above party? Still, he was stung
by the accusations that he was betraying his own. "A more difficult and
even tragic situation for a party leader could hardly be imagined," he
wrote in his memoirs. He maintained a strong belief that, other than the
federal Liberal leaders, "there was in the great Liberal Party throughout
the country an element of commanding strength bound to assert itself

when the test came and determined to join in creating such a National Government as would serve to the end the valiant youth who had gone beyond the seas in their country's need."[66]

The biggest roadblock for Borden, however, was Robert Rogers, his minister of public works. Rogers had been a minister in the Manitoba provincial Conservative government and gave significant help to Borden in the federal campaign in 1911. Following that victory he relocated to Ottawa, was found a seat in the House of Commons, and entered Borden's government. Rogers was a skilled political organizer — earning the nickname "minister of elections" — and partisan in the extreme: popular with the Conservative rank and file and despised by Liberals, especially those in the West. So strong was the dislike for Rogers that several of the western Liberals insisted that they could not join a coalition so long as he was a member of the government. Conversely, Rogers became an adamant opponent of Union, if only because he realized that he would not be included in any new arrangement with the Liberals. Rogers also suspected that Borden was trying to reshape the traditional Conservative Party into something different, and, like other Conservatives, after the rejection of coalition by the Liberals in Toronto and Winnipeg, he believed that a straight election based on old party lines was more necessary than ever.[67]

Rogers was implicated in a corruption scandal, dating back to his time in the Manitoba government, which removed him from the cabinet briefly in the summer of 1917. So long as suspicion of wrongdoing lingered he was little threat to Borden, but at the beginning of August his name was cleared by a Conservative-appointed commission of investigation and Rogers returned to prominence. His personal popularity in the party soared.[68] He began criticizing Borden for inaction and became the focus of anti-Union forces in the party.

On August 3, Borden learned from Sir George Foster of political "intrigue": Rogers had called for a meeting of western Conservative members, no doubt to denounce Union and Borden's leadership.[69] Rogers had become a significant threat to both Union government and Borden's leadership of the party, and the prime minister responded by threatening to resign as leader. It was not the first time that Borden had taken such an action and, as in the past, the party could produce no suitable alternative leader and, instead, rallied behind Borden. Once reconfirmed as leader, he took on Rogers's challenge directly. He met with Rogers on August 17. Rogers strongly insisted that "we should make no further effort for Union Gov't and that we are heading straight for destruction."[70] In a letter dated the following day, Rogers added that it was "quite true that I have always observed and always will observe respectful loyalty to my party, the party to which I will ever plead guilty to being devoted," but he concluded that he welcomed the time when the governor general "may be pleased to approve of my request to be relieved of my responsibilities as a Minister of the Crown."[71] Borden took him at his word, and Rogers was out of the cabinet that same day.

Rogers's resignation worked in two ways for Borden. First, it silenced his strongest Conservative critic, and, second, it removed a major stumbling block for western Liberals interested in joining the Union. The resignation "will have the effect of somewhat clearing the air," the governor general reported to London, and gave hope to those who favoured a coalition. Moreover, Borden was now completely in control of his party — if not the one indispensable leader in the country — and he was now able to pursue with greater determination his goal of Union government.[72]

The events of July–August 1917 also confirmed that there would be only one Liberal Party and that would be the party of Sir Wilfrid Laurier, making this a pivotal moment in the history of the party. As historian John English points out, Laurier avoided a split between the "old" and the "new" Liberal Party; a rupture between the former, a more conservative party of Laurier and Quebec, and the latter, a largely English-speaking party with new progressive ideas about social welfare and progress. Unexpectedly, the confrontation between the two wings occurred over the issues of conscription and coalition and, when push came to shove, the party did not break but, rather, rallied behind the old leader. It ensured a Liberal Quebec and a Liberal Party with a major Quebec component in it.[73] But the Liberals across the country were far from unanimous. Laurier had managed to keep his parliamentary caucus together, but his party was cracking under him.

Failing to achieve an agreement on Union meant two things: first, there would be no formal coalition between the federal Liberal and Conservative parties, and, second, there would be a federal election campaign in the very near future. Borden remained convinced that large parts of the Liberal Party in English Canada were with him on the central questions of the day, and if he could not have the support of Laurier and his caucus there were other Liberals, away from Parliament Hill, who would be willing to join him in his cause. Therefore, Borden redoubled his efforts to achieve a coalition or Union government. If anything, he was more determined. He had not changed his mind about the necessity of conscription or of seeing the war effort through to the end. Nor had he come to believe that a Laurier-Liberal government would be an effective war government. He was more certain than ever of the necessity of staying in power and continued to believe that a coalition would help him to achieve this end. He did not want this election, but he had to fight it. His course now was to ensure that he and his party — whatever shape it took — would win it.

5

CREATING DIVISIONS, CHOOSING SIDES: THE GREAT GERRYMANDER

"I hear there's a lot of trouble about this conscription and I think the [L]iberals with that old wop Laurier ought to be lynched. I believe it's gone through though so they can't do much. It's about time something like that happened as we can use all the men that come out."

— Pte. Howard Beverley Thorburn to Bev,
June 28, 1917[1]

In the summer of 1917 the debate over conscription became less about military requirements and more about patriotism and national identity. The poet Wilson MacDonald, who was in Vancouver to stage a musical — *In Sunny France* — wrote that conscription was the "damnation of the sweet flower of freedom."[2] In 1911 he had been a strong Toronto imperialist and ardently wished for Borden to succeed. The war had changed him.[3] In his diary, he reported fleeing to Stanley Park, where he was "glad to escape from the militant atmosphere of the streets."[4] The room for nuance and subtlety was disappearing and all Canadians were being asked to take sides and the side you chose said a lot about who you were and your feelings about the war and about the country.

The government was on edge; early in August, Archbishop Bruchési publicly declared that Canada was nearing a racial and religious war. At the same time, Lord Atholstan, the former Sir Hugh Graham and wealthy owner of the *Montreal Star*, was told that his country home in Cartierville had been damaged by a bomb. "Many people believe that there will be violence and bloodshed in the event of any effort to enforce conscription in the Province of Quebec," John Foster, the American consul general, reported to Washington, "and that for this reason that conscription so far from proving helpful toward Canada's further participation in the European war might, in fact, lessen her effectiveness."[5]

Still, the military authorities cautioned that there was "no anti-conscription organization of such a nature as to justify the sending of a military force in Quebec." Such an action, concluded Pierre-Édouard Blondin, the postmaster general and one of the very few remaining francophone members of Borden's government, would be seen as a "serious provocation."[6]

For many young Quebeckers, that meant taking to the streets to demonstrate their opposition to conscription. Rioting broke out in several parts of Montreal on August 22 as anti-conscription protesters met on the Champs-de-Mars, not far from city hall. The legal public meetings were broken up by police and the protesters dispersed to other parts of the city where rioting took place, leading to smashed windows and thousands of dollars of property damage along St. Catherine Street. Everyone had someone to blame for the riots; Montreal's mayor, Médéric Martin, accused Borden and the conscription law.[7] Across town, three thousand anti-conscription protesters gathered in Maisonneuve, in the city's east end, to demonstrate under the aegis of the Federation of Workers of Montreal. Gédéon Martel, the union president, denounced the "bandits, thieves and assassins in Ottawa."[8] The final passage of the Military Service Act at the end of the month sparked even more demonstrations; in Montreal, the *Gazette*'s windows were smashed and rioting largely destroyed downtown's Phillips Square. Anti-recruitment rioting erupted a few days later in Shawinigan.[9]

Conscription and the prospect of an election came to dominate political affairs, and the two were increasingly divorced from the actual fighting of the war. Indeed, conscription itself became something of an abstraction; as some observers pointed out at the time, throughout all the debate and controversy over conscription in 1917, not a single Canadian actually was conscripted that year. The prime minister, who had announced the policy in May with great fanfare and in response to a perceived immediate manpower crisis, appeared willing, in the summer, to delay further the implementation of that same policy.

In many of the surviving political diaries, the daily conduct of the war seems to fade into the background. It is remarkable, given that for so many of those Canadians involved in the election of 1917 the war was immediate and personal. Neither Borden nor Laurier had any children, but so many of those around them did, and both the rich and the poor considered it their duty to serve. More than two dozen MPs had personally enlisted in the military (one had died);[10] many more had children fighting overseas. It was the same across the country; Ontario Liberal leader Newton Rowell's nephew was a major in the armed services; Sir Allen Aylesworth, Lord Shaughnessy of the CPR, and Liberal Ned Macdonald each had sons in the service; Premier Hearst of Ontario had two sons in the fight, as did newspaperman John Dafoe; J.S. Willison's son Bill was killed in action in September 1916; Rodolphe Lemieux's son was killed in 1918. Letters preserved in the archives routinely begin with updates or questions about each other's sons before moving on to political business. But, even so, in the late summer and early fall of 1917 the daily events of the war seemed to take a back seat. More and more attention was focused on conscription and the election. The war was everywhere in Canadian lives; but with the approaching election the front had shifted: the war was now to be fought across political battle lines, more with ballots than with bullets.

Borden thought that the war effort was supported across Canada, but he still feared the risk of losing the election because of the unpopularity of his government. Coalition remained essential, if only to ensure that all pro-war conscriptionist support — Liberal and Conservative — rallied behind the government against Laurier, his French-Canadian supporters, and all the other anti-conscriptionists. But the numbers still added up badly for Borden: the Conservatives could hold out no hope in Quebec; support in the Maritimes was split; in the West, the government's deep unpopularity and the recent Liberal provincial election wins warned of political disaster; and even in Ontario there were questions, especially outside Toronto in the rural areas, where opposition to conscription, especially of farmers' sons, ran deep. It was a challenge to add the numbers up in any way that would produce a Conservative/Unionist victory.

For Borden, the answer was to engineer a new voting coalition and put into effect the greatest gerrymander in Canadian history. This was not a gerrymander in the traditional sense of shifting electoral district boundaries to favour one party over another, or to "hive the Grits" by stacking their voters in a select few ridings. The government instead rearranged the franchise, giving more votes to Conservative supporters and taking them away from potential Liberal voters. The great gerrymander of 1917 would be accomplished by taking advantage of two forces — one from the bright, the other from the dark side of human nature — that had become increasingly woven into the fabric of Canadian life during the war: social progress, evidenced by (limited) recognition of women's rights; and intolerance, in the form of anti-foreigner bigotry. Until 1917, voters chose their governments; in the 1917 election it was said that the government chose the voters.[11]

The government's mandate would formally run out in October, but Borden and the government still had time to prepare. Several important legislative undertakings needed to be passed before Parliament could be dissolved. The conscription-oriented Military Service Act was taking up the greatest amount of attention and time, but there were other important measures on Parliament's agenda. The government presented amendments to the Criminal Code and the Dominion Companies Act, and a bill establishing a Soldier Settlement Board. Some resolutions were introduced that failed to pass, including one to amend the BNA Act to turn the Senate into an elected body. Sir George Foster also introduced a bill to implement daylight saving time.[12]

More significantly, Minister of Finance Sir Thomas White introduced an income tax bill in July, a bill which, although "temporary," would have far more importance after the war than during it. Its purpose was electoral, to be sure — to demonstrate to Canadians that the government was conscripting wealth along with men in the summer of 1917. It was a bill that many Conservatives, including White, had argued against in the past, but by the summer of 1917 it was about more than raising revenue. It was believed that introducing an income tax would appeal to farmer and labour groups, and to many Liberals who had been demanding such a measure in Parliament for months. In this way, the income tax bill could be used as another inducement to Liberals to join a national government — or at least to remove one more obstacle to a coalition.[13]

The government also addressed the difficult situation facing Canada's private railways. Thanks to the war effort, the railway system had never been busier, and the transportation of goods was vital to the success of the war effort. The strain revealed serious problems, though, many of which predated the war. Of particular concern were the financial problems of the privately-owned Grand Trunk (and Grand Trunk Pacific) and Canadian Northern railways. When the war broke out, these railways were fragmented and already dependent on government loans, subsidies, and bond guarantees. The war failed to alleviate the situation and a frustrated Borden government began seriously considering the nationalization of all the private railways (except the financially sound Canadian Pacific, the CPR), and amalgamating them with government-owned lines such as the Intercolonial Railway into a national crown corporation. A royal commission to investigate the situation had been appointed in mid-1916, but it issued conflicting reports: the majority recommended nationalization, the minority suggested maintaining private ownership.

The Borden government was just as divided, with Borden and a few others favouring nationalization. But everyone agreed that something needed to be done. The two railways could not be allowed to collapse because of the damage it might do to the banks, especially the Toronto-based Bank of Commerce, which was heavily committed to the Canadian Northern. At the same time, no one — from western farmers and workers' organizations to the Liberal opposition critics, Conservative back-benchers, and CPR shareholders — wanted to continue showering public moneys on the railway promoters.[14] Full nationalization remained in the future, but in August 1917 the government took the first step by introducing legislation to nationalize the Canadian Northern Railway (the government already controlled 40 percent of its stock) and to provide further financial aid to the Grand Trunk.[15]

The railway situation complicated politics in the summer of 1917, and railway issues occasionally permeated discussions of coalition and the election. Sir Thomas Shaughnessy of the CPR was involved in discussions of both coalition and nationalization and it was not always possible to separate the two. He was concerned over Borden's proposed nationalization scheme because he did not want a strong government-owned competitor to the CPR, although he did offer to support nationalization if the CPR were permitted to manage the new crown corporation. His support for Borden wavered over the summer.

At the same time, the members of the "Toronto Eighteen," those Liberals who publicly broke with Laurier in 1911 to support Borden's anti-reciprocity crusade, comprised a who's who of bankers, business leaders, and board directors involved with the Canadian Northern Railway, the National Trust Company, and the Bank of Commerce. Their involvement with the government was guaranteed to raise even more suspicions in wider Liberal circles.

Mackenzie King, perhaps an extreme example, was beside himself over the machinations of these Liberal turncoats. In his diary he railed against railway promoters Sir William Mackenzie and Donald Mann. "This is where the whole rottenness lies wealth & respectability & titles. M[ackenzie] & M[ann], [Sir Edmund] Walker, [Toronto businessman, Zebulon] Lash [Sir Joseph] Flavelle, [Sir Thomas] White, Wood (?) et cetera."[16] At other times, the names were linked into one as if they represented a single — sinister — force: "Walker Flavelle White et al, the recipients of favors — titles, cash, power & what not."[17]

The irony was that the railways and banks appeared to be switching sides: the CPR and its backers in the Bank of Montreal were shifting away from the Conservative policy of nationalization, while the formerly Liberal Canadian Northern and Bank of Commerce were moving toward the Conservative Party. All these interests desired stability in government — via either a coalition or an extension — to ensure that the railway situation could be addressed, and they brought this desire for stability into their efforts to create a Union government.[18]

Finally, two important bills were introduced to pave the way to victory in the election. The first, introduced on August 20, was intended to replace the Soldiers Voting Act, passed in 1915, which was seen as insufficient given the growth and complexity of the Canadian forces at home and abroad. The goal was simple and the motive honourable: to ensure that all members of the military forces had an opportunity to vote. There were problems anticipated in accessing the soldiers in the CEF, in assigning returning officers, in ensuring the safe transport of the ballots once cast, in ensuring the fairness of the vote tallying, and, most importantly, in aligning each voter with a specific riding back home. The Military Voters Bill was meant to achieve these goals. There was also a political dimension in that reports from the Canadian military establishment in London suggested that the great majority of combatants and non-combatants in the Canadian military were supporters of the government's win-the-war policies and conscription, and therefore would be likely to vote Conservative.[19] For these same reasons the bill was guaranteed to elicit Liberal opposition.

The bill gave the vote to all British subjects enlisted (and those already honourably discharged) in all areas of the Canadian military, independent of any residency requirement, including, for the first time, three groups previously without the franchise: women, minors, and indigenous peoples. Thus, some two thousand military nurses — the "Bluebirds" — became the first Canadian women to get the federal vote. In addition, the bill extended the franchise to all British-born soldiers serving in the CEF, regardless of their length of time in Canada, as well as to any British subject ordinarily resident in Canada who was on active duty in Europe in the Canadian, British, or any other allied army. This meant that several thousand men who were either under the age of twenty-one or were British-born recruits who had come to Canada from the United States to enlist (and therefore had never lived in Canada) were granted the vote.

The bill didn't stop there. If the serviceman or servicewoman (including those serving *in* Canada) could remember his or her home riding then he or she would be able to cast their ballot in that riding; if not, then their vote could be counted in any riding where they had at one time resided. For many other voters who could not remember any electoral district or had not resided in Canada at all, their votes could be applied to any electoral district they chose, creating a kind of "floating" vote that could be applied in different ridings across the country. Finally, the bill contained a short section that appeared innocuous at first but was extremely significant: these several hundred thousand overseas votes would be counted one month after the staging of the election in Canada. And now the election would be further delayed, to make the necessary preparations for collecting the soldiers' votes. Speculation was strong that the vote would now take place in December.[20]

The Liberals were enraged by the bill and challenged several aspects of it. For one thing, it seemed unfair, if not undemocratic, to give the vote to potentially thousands of soldiers who had never lived in Canada. For another, only six scrutineers would be appointed, three from each party, and the Canadian military would not likely permit a large number of returning officers or campaigners to mix with the soldiers, which meant that the government and military establishments would be in charge of overseeing and collecting the votes. That seemed to give a great advantage to the government to influence how the soldiers voted. The bill also appeared to give the authorities unusual leeway to distribute the "floating" parts of the military vote and, given that most soldiers were understood to be supporters of conscription and the Conservatives, the bill was granting the government a remarkable and unfair advantage.[21] It was an "attempt to legislate themselves into power again," wrote one angry Liberal supporter to Laurier. "The liberty to name an electoral district in which they might want their votes to count is inviting fraud on a most comprehensive scale."[22]

As for those who were responsible for this wicked bill, the *Peterborough Review* later announced that "jails and penitentiaries are yawning for such miscreants."[23] Nevertheless, over Liberal opposition the Military Voters Act passed on August 31.

The second bill — the Wartime Elections Bill — was even more far-reaching and draconian. The essence of the bill, as with the Military Voters Act, rested on the somewhat shaky premise that because Canadians were forced to fight a wartime election on war-related issues it was fair to restrict the vote to a wartime electorate — to those Canadians who were invested in the war. From that starting point, it was argued, conversely, that those *without* a stake in the war should be deprived of their vote. Anyone with a close relative in the military naturally would be concerned about the war; those who refused to fight or came from enemy countries had — at best — a negative interest in the war. By 1917 women had won the vote in all provinces west of Quebec and there was some discussion about extending the suffrage to the federal level. But granting all women the vote federally would mean giving the vote to a great many women (especially in western Canada) who had been born in enemy countries. Giving these women the vote, argued Arthur Meighen, would be "particularly open to objection, as the percentage in that portion of our Dominion of people of alien enemy origin and parentage, is very great indeed."[24] The answer, then, was to give the vote only to "patriotic" women. Similarly, people of "enemy alien birth" were naturally suspect: they might have family in an enemy country, or relatives fighting against Canada, or harbour enemy sympathies; they could not be counted on to support the war effort to the fullest extent. The fact that they tended to vote Liberal needed to be considered as well. For many Conservatives, taking the vote away from this group made political, as well as patriotic, sense. "To shift the franchise," as Meighen explained it in a letter to Borden "from the doubtful British or anti-British of the male sex and to extend it at the same time to our patriotic women, would be in my judgement a splendid stroke."[25]

The Conservatives had been working on the bill over the summer,[26] but did not introduce it into Parliament until September 6. In the meantime, Borden had fallen ill again, so the bill was introduced by Meighen and, as was the case with the Military Service Act, he was destined to have his name linked to the measure for the rest of his life. He argued that it was possible that a great many of the soldiers overseas would not be able to cast a vote in the upcoming election and that this was not fair. To overcome this injustice the government had decided to give, for the first time, the federal vote to a segment of Canadian women, in this case all those women (including widows) who had a direct relative serving in the Canadian military — a son, husband, father, brother (living or dead) — provided they met the age, nationality, and residency requirements for electors in their respective provinces or Yukon. It did not make sense to give the vote to all women, at least at that moment in time; but the women with close relatives in the military, Meighen said, "represent in sentiment and in purpose the voice and will of those who are fighting for us."[27] What was not said was how disproportionately this would affect the country's two linguistic groups by giving the vote to thousands of English-speaking women who had relatives in the military but relatively far fewer French-speaking

Arthur Meighen: candidate for the Dominion Election, 1917.

women, thanks to the much lower number of francophone men in the CEF. The bill also conferred the right to vote on those who did not own property in accordance with prevailing provincial law but had a son or grandson in the army. (This provision affected only Quebec and Nova Scotia, as the other provinces had already abolished property- and income-based qualifications.)

What the bill gave with one hand it removed with the other: Meighen then announced that the bill would take away the vote from conscientious objectors, including Mennonites and Doukhobors, even though the federal government had exempted them officially from military service, the former in 1873 and the latter in 1898. Conscientious objectors lost the vote; anyone who voted lost all future claims to be a conscientious objector.[28] Next, the bill also disenfranchised all Canadians from enemy countries who had been naturalized after March 31, 1902. Included in this group were British subjects naturalized after 1902 whose mother tongue was that of an enemy country, whether or not the individual's country of origin was an ally of Great Britain. The same rule applied to persons found guilty of an offence under the Military Service Act, 1917. There was no evidence to suggest that any "enemy aliens" were involved in sabotage or spying; it was a matter of loyalty and support for the war effort. "War service should be the basis of war franchise," Meighen declared disingenuously, and it was "in a sense unfair to those men themselves, many whose sons and brothers are fighting in armies in Europe against us, that they should be asked to determine by their vote the vigour, or the direction which that war should take."[29] Finally, the bill stripped the provinces of the responsibility for drawing up electoral lists and gave the task to enumerators appointed by the federal government — in other words, by the Conservatives as the party in power.

That the bill would take away the vote from "enemy aliens" who tended to vote Liberal and give it to a group of women who were likely to vote Conservative was not lost on anyone. The leader of a Canadian suffrage organization hardly saw it was a great victory for women and wrote Borden of her displeasure: "[I]t would have been more direct and at the same time more honest if the bill simply stated that all who did not pledge themselves to vote Conservative would be disenfranchised."[30] While many women's organizations welcomed elements of the act, two local councils of women — in Victoria and Regina — passed resolutions in protest.[31] Laurier was equally upset: "These two measures are calculated to win the election for the government by fraud, if it cannot be done otherwise," he wrote.[32]

An upset Mackenzie King detailed the abuses of the legislation in a long letter to his old friend Violet Carruthers in London, U.K., concluding, "with all these unfair handicaps there is really no chance of a fair fight, anywhere, and I should not be surprised to see Borden returned."[33]

But the government was unmoved. Meighen was unapologetic to the accusation that the vote had been rigged by the bill. "If it is true — and apparently it is true, if hon. Gentlemen opposite are right — that the majority of women of this country whose near relatives are overseas, those who spend their days in anxiety and their nights in tears, will support us, and that those who, of all our population, are likely to favour the enemy, will reject us, then in the name of the Government which has been striving for three years to fight that enemy, I accept the compliment."[34]

It is hard not to see in these two bills — both of which would lapse once the war had ended — the determination to rearrange the electoral system to ensure the government's re-election, and there is a general consensus among historians on this point. Borden's biographer wrote of the Wartime Elections Act as "a bald, reprehensible gerrymander, designed to ensure a conscriptionist vote and to eliminate anti-conscription support in western Canada."[35]

Laurier's biographer was even more appalled: "[I]t was frankly a stacking of the cards, a gerrymander on a colossal scale, an attempt without parallel except in the tactics of Lenin and Trotsky to ensure the dominance of one party in the state."[36]

Meighen's biographer agrees that it was a gerrymander — "there can be no doubt" — but sets it in the wider context of the war effort. Borden and the Conservative Party had reached the state where they saw themselves as inextricably intertwined with the Canadian war effort; for Borden and the others a Laurier-Liberal victory in the election would weaken, if not destroy, Canada's war effort, lead to dishonour and disgrace, and damage all that had been accomplished for Canada in the war.

Such a possibility was unacceptable and thus it became imperative for the Conservatives to remain in power.[37] Borden was not the first prime minister to identify his own fate with the fate of the nation, but such thinking first justified and then led directly to the most undemocratic political manoeuvre in Canadian history.

"It is generally believed that the Conservative party has materially improved its chances in the coming elections," the American consul general reported to Washington[38] and, not surprisingly, the opposition to the bill was fierce. The government was forced to introduce closure on three occasions before the bill was passed on September 20, the day Parliament was prorogued.

Exactly why the government chose to delay the introduction of the Wartime Elections Act until so late in the parliamentary session, given that the measure had been discussed over a period of many months, has sparked considerable speculation. Historian Roger Graham offered various possibilities, including that it was just a matter of the government's full agenda that had made it impossible to introduce the bill earlier in the schedule, and that perhaps Borden waited until the very end when the Liberal opposition would be at its weakest and least likely to mount stiff resistance.

Sir Clifford Sifton, who reportedly opposed the bill, believed that it sprang from the failure to achieve a coalition. Had a Union government been created, the bill would not have been necessary; its introduction was delayed by the coalition negotiations; its use was made necessary only by the failure of those negotiations, which forced the Conservatives to gerrymander the vote in their favour to ensure victory in the election.

A better explanation might be that Borden submitted the legislation when he did as a way of prompting the reluctant Liberal-conscriptionists to make up their minds about joining with the Conservatives in a new Union government.[39] For those Liberals, especially in the West, who saw their vote crumbling and their chances of re-election evaporating, a coalition became the only alternative.

* * *

The debates over the Military Voters Act and the Wartime Elections Act interrupted but did not halt, at least at first, discussions about forming Borden's proposed Union government. A few conscriptionist Liberals had offered to ally themselves with the Conservatives, including Hugh Guthrie, Frank Carvell, and Fred Pardee, while Newton Rowell sat on the fence, waiting for others to join before plunging in himself. Late in August, several prominent western Liberals, including T.A. Crerar, James Calder, and Arthur Sifton met with Borden in Ottawa to discuss how a coalition would work and to see if a basis of agreement could be worked out. Borden repeated his offer of equal cabinet representation in any Union government. But a significant problem remained: many of the western Liberals believed that a change of leadership was required before a Union government could be created. Crerar was clearly the most adamant. He believed that a national government was necessary to win the war, but had little faith in Borden or his government. "I think without question," he wrote a Manitoban friend, "it has been the most inefficient and incapable administration we have had since the time of Confederation. It has undoubtedly applied the principle of patronage to an outrageous extent in the administration of those departments that had to do with the carrying on of the War."[40] More sinister were those lurking behind Borden. "Privately," he wrote early in September, "the man who is today chief adviser to Borden, and has been for the past two months, is Clifford Sifton. When one bears in mind that Borden, while a well-intentioned man, is sadly lacking in qualities of decision. I frankly do not like the thought of going into a Government with Clifford Sifton behind pulling the strings, unless I had the strongest colleagues possible."[41]

But the situation was critical, the Liberal Party was "unquestionably seriously split," and an election without Union could lead to a Laurier victory. That would split Canadians linguistically and religiously and could destroy the country.[42] To avoid such a disaster, Union government was the only choice. As a result, on August 26, Crerar, Calder, Sifton, and A.B. Hudson offered to join a coalition with the Conservatives; their one condition being that Borden step aside in favour of another leader. "There is no doubt whatever in my mind," wrote Crerar, "that among all the independent thinking people in the whole Dominion a Union

Government under new leadership would command a much wider popular support than it possibly could under the leadership of Borden."[43] They named four possibilities — two Conservatives (including Sir George Foster) and two Liberals — under whom they could serve.

Borden had no intention of resigning and believed that the westerners, with perhaps the exception of Crerar, were content with his leadership. Their call for a leadership change, he wrote to J.S. Willison, was a bit of a show for the folks back home who needed "some change to make their position at the Winnipeg Convention less inconsistent with their future support."[44] Nevertheless, he brought the proposal to his cabinet colleagues and then, at a meeting of the full Conservative caucus on August 29, he offered to step aside in favour of Sir George Foster. Foster was one of the most senior Conservatives, a man whose career extended back to the government of Sir John A. Macdonald; but he was not a serious alternative to Borden, and Borden knew it. Borden seriously doubted Foster's judgment — even after Foster's death Borden remained critical, writing that several of his colleagues "listened carefully to Foster for the purpose of recording their votes in the opposite sense, as they firmly and invariably relied on the unsoundness of his judgment."[45] On another occasion, Borden referred to Foster as having "no more political sense than a turnip,"[46] and the prime minister must have known that his other colleagues would refuse to serve under Foster and, instead, rally behind him as leader.

The cabinet "would not hear of the elimination of our leader," Foster, not unexpectedly, wrote in his diary on August 27. "They are quite right on all grounds." As for Borden, "no one is more necessary."[47]

It was the same with the full Conservative caucus. Borden rose to a packed room, defended his war record, and discussed his efforts to achieve a Union government. If it was necessary for him to resign in order to achieve the Union, then he was willing to do it: he offered to step aside in favour of Foster. Foster rose and rejected the idea. He "spoke strongly and eloquently, voicing his firm conviction that I must remain in the leadership."[48] The caucus agreed and swiftly issued a unanimous resolution voicing their appreciation for and confidence in Borden, and calling on him to stay as leader. Afterward, Foster told Borden that "in all his experience of twenty-five years he had never witnessed so wonderful a spirit as was shown in that gathering."

Borden added that he was "profoundly touched and toward its close when called upon to speak after the passage of the resolution I found myself for once utterly unable to say a word except with a broken and utterly inaudible voice. After a few seconds a quick witted Western Member sprang to his feet and started a familiar air "For He's a Jolly Good Fellow." This enabled me to complete a few sentences."[49]

It was a magnificent play for Borden. By threatening resignation and then rallying his party behind his leadership, his position was more secure than ever and he had turned the tables on the erstwhile Liberal-Unionists. By rejecting the conditions set out by the western Liberals, he ensured that they would enter any Union government on his terms and under his leadership. He followed the meeting by announcing that all proposals for Union would be suspended until after the proroguing of Parliament, which meant until after the passage of the Wartime Elections Act.[50] This would give all the Liberals time to consider the bill and its implications for their own political futures.

The Conservatives were buoyed by Borden's actions and as the Wartime Elections Bill wound its way through Parliament some members again began to question the need for Union at all. R.B. Bennett continued to argue against it; even Arthur Meighen, who had been a strong supporter of a coalition, raised a few questions — not so much about the idea of Union as about the possibility of bringing in so many westerners. Meighen saw himself as the cabinet's leading voice for western Canada and he had no desire to share that distinction with anyone else, especially former Liberals. Ultimately, he arranged with Borden to ensure his paramount position for the West in any subsequent Union government.[51]

J.D. Reid supported bringing in those from the East who had already said they would support the Union, but not the westerners — it would be a sign of "weakness," he wrote Borden, would "cause troubles" in the West, and would not be well received in the "older provinces."[52]

Still others argued that, thanks to the Military Voters Act and Wartime Elections Act, the Conservatives no longer needed the support of *any* Liberals to win the election and the party could win a straight fight on traditional party lines. "I have no doubt," Sifton wrote in a letter to J.W. Dafoe, "that the reactionary Tory element is moving heaven and earth to prevent the coalition."[53] Likewise, many caucus members were unsure about granting the new Liberal allies equal representation in the cabinet, as Borden had promised Laurier months earlier. It came to a head at a caucus meeting on September 19; Borden stood his ground and repeated that the offer of equal representation remained on the table.[54]

Borden was exhausted and, once Parliament was prorogued, he left for a fishing holiday in the Laurentians, north of Montreal. But any hope he had of being left undisturbed was unwarranted. On the twentieth he received a letter from Reid stating that the western Liberals (Arthur Sifton, Calder, Hudson, and Crerar) were now ready to join the government without condition. Reid's source was Sir Clifford Sifton, who "appeared terribly excited and pleased" to pass on the news. Sifton "said they were coming in, that this meant the Election won."[55]

What had happened to change their minds? "While the thing is in many ways distasteful to me," explained Crerar, "I feel as a matter of duty that in certain eventualities it might be my plain duty to join such an administration."[56]

Others were not so charitable. As one westerner wrote to Arthur Meighen, "if you had not passed the War Franchise Act, they would never have opened negotiations with you. They know now what we all know, that Laurier, or any of his crowd, has no chance to carry over ten seats west of Lake Superior."[57]

Borden was now observing from a position of strength and remained cool. "Previously we had been annoyed at their refusal and embarrassed by it," he wrote in his memoirs. "Now we were still more seriously embarrassed by their acceptance."[58]

The pieces began to fall into place early in October. Borden still wanted the westerners in; "our first duty," he wrote in his diary, "is to win at any cost the coming election in order that we may continue to do our part in winning the war and that Canada [be] not disgraced."[59] He moved first to Charles Ballantyne and Hugh Guthrie. The former was sworn in as minister of public works on October 3. Guthrie, a sitting federal Liberal, was the bigger catch and he joined the government on October 4, as solicitor general. Several more days of negotiations followed, with the westerners, Rowell, and other Liberals, including A.K. Maclean, and Conservative colleagues, including Meighen, Reid, and White. Borden grew increasingly exasperated as the discussions dragged on and complained of "frayed nerves." At one point, he was "unable to control a temper which had always been rather violent but which, throughout my life, I have kept in almost perfect discipline."[60] Finally, on October 12, the Union government was formed, as Arthur Sifton, Calder, Crerar, Rowell, and General Sydney Mewburn (both a Liberal and a veteran, who had overseen recruitment for the government's National Defence Force) were sworn into the cabinet.

Sifton became minister of customs, Crerar took over the agriculture department, Rowell was appointed President of the Privy Council, Calder became minister of immigration and colonization, and General Mewburn became minister of militia and defence. To make room in the cabinet, Sir George Perley left to become high commissioner in London, Douglas Hazen was moved out to become chief justice of the New Brunswick Supreme Court, and Sir Edward Kemp left militia and defence to take over the Overseas Ministry. Reid moved into Robert Rogers's vacant portfolio in railways and canals. Meighen became minister of the interior, the most senior post for the West, but his power was now shared with Calder and Crerar.[61]

There were only two gaps. First, there were just two francophones in the new cabinet: Pierre-Édouard Blondin remained as postmaster general and Albert Sévigny became minister of inland revenue. But Union government was not about attracting Liberal Quebeckers into the government, and no one complained about their absence. The second was the lack of a representative from British Columbia. Liberal premier H.C. Brewster was open to joining the new government but earlier had demonstrated only lukewarm support for the coalition and this was enough to raise opposition from Arthur Meighen and others. Brewster was not asked to join.[62] But even without a B.C. Liberal in the cabinet there was satisfaction with the new government. "You will see by the day's news that it has been successfully done," a joyful Sir Clifford Sifton wrote John Willison that night. "It was a very perilous task and trembled in the balance a good many times."[63]

The final act was played out by the Liberals. Early in October a small group of colleagues, including Calder, Frank Carvell, Fred Pardee, and Ned Macdonald, met with Laurier and encouraged the aging Liberal leader to resign. They told him that it was "impossible to win with a French leader" and that the party needed someone new to keep the conscriptionists in. Calder reportedly even suggested Carvell as Laurier's replacement.[64] Laurier, like Borden, repeated what he had said many times in the past — that he would step aside if the party wanted him gone, but he did not commit himself and promised only to discuss it with other members of the party. Later that day, Carvell met journalist Arthur Ford at the Château Laurier and told him that Laurier was about to resign. Ford promptly sent the news out to a number of newspapers and the story became an overnight sensation.[65]

Unfortunately for Carvell and the others, Laurier decided to stay on. He spoke with colleagues in Toronto and Montreal, and "received overwhelming assurances."[66] Sir Lomer Gouin stood by him; in Toronto he met "500 party friends" and they reconfirmed their support. In this group were several notable former ministers and MPs, including George Graham, Mackenzie King, William Pugsley, Charles Murphy, and D.D. McKenzie. Other expressions of support came in from across the country.[67] Moreover, the leak of the story "brought me a shower of representations," Laurier later wrote, and he became determined "that I should continue at my post." He would carry on: "[N]ow I am in the fight to face a murderous winter election, even if I have to die for it. This is not the time to desert the ship."[68]

The one last imponderable for Laurier would be the reaction of Henri Bourassa in Quebec. Bourassa had come out publicly in support of Laurier's call for a referendum; where the two men differed was over what to do afterwards, with Bourassa insisting that conscription was unacceptable while Laurier was clearly more willing to accept a referendum's results.[69] There was greater concern that Bourassa would take political action by reviving the *nationalistes* for one more political campaign. Bourassa had been encouraged to do so over the summer. Father Eustache Santerre, a priest from Rimouski, called on Bourassa to put together a list of candidates for the election, arguing that "it is clear that both the *bleus* and the *rouges* are being dragged, tyrannically and scandalously, towards the criminal homicide of our people and especially of our race." These were agonizing times, he wrote, noting to Bourassa that "if we get a coalition cabinet agreed to and approved by the leader of the Liberal party, your prediction regarding that poor Laurier would thus unfortunately be realized: the old chief would end

Sir Wilfrid Laurier and William Lyon Mackenzie King at Sydney Fisher's home. Brome, Quebec, August 12, 1915.

his career in the manure pile!"[70] In October, Senator Landry, the Tory senator who had turned against his party, organized a meeting at his home in Quebec City that included Paul Lamarche and Armand La Vergne, and proposed to Bourassa another *nationaliste* slate, but one loyal to the Liberal side this time.

In any case, Bourassa advised against the idea of running another third party for fear that the anti-conscription vote would be split, allowing government candidates to win.[71] On October 18, he met Laurier in Ottawa — the first time in almost ten years — and gave the Liberal leader his full support. It was a relief for Laurier not to have to face a *nationaliste* challenge in Quebec, but on the flip side there were concerns that *any* support from Bourassa would hurt Laurier and the Liberals in English Canada. Bourassa reportedly smiled at Laurier and promised that he would continue to "throw a few boots" at the old chief just for appearances. With that, Bourassa became an ally in Quebec; but, as one Laurier biographer puts it, it was in a place "where none was needed."[72]

With Laurier's determination to stay on as leader, the conscriptionist Liberals began openly negotiating terms with Borden to enter the Union government. Fred Pardee resigned as Liberal whip and declared his support.[73] Fulfilling a promise he had earlier made to Rowell, Borden also named Senator Gideon Robertson, a former official in the Trades and Labour Congress, as labour representative in the cabinet and a minister without portfolio.[74] It was expected that Premier Murray of Nova Scotia would join the new government, but after long, deliberate consideration he declined. There were three other Liberal defectors from the Maritimes: W.S. Fielding, Frank Carvell, and A.K. Maclean. Maclean was appointed minister without portfolio while Carvell became minister of public works (Ballantyne was shifted to the marine and fisheries portfolio). As for Laurier, "the old eagle had been bloodied," recorded one Quebec historian: "he had seen his feathers plucked one by one."[75]

Sir Clifford Sifton, however, seemed to relish the moment. "Everything indicates that the English speaking part of Sir Wilfrid Laurier's organization is going completely to pieces," he wrote to Willison. Regarding the defection of Fielding, one of Laurier's oldest political colleagues, Sifton added: "I imagine Sir Wilfrid will be disposed to say *et-tu Brute.*"[76]

Public reaction to the new government was generally positive, at least in English Canada. The new government "seems to be quite as competent intellectually as any Government that Canada has ever had," concluded Sir Clifford Sifton.[77] John Godfrey, head of the ostensibly non-partisan Win-the-War League, dropped all pretense of impartiality and came out fully in support of the Union government. English-language newspapers generally supported the goals of the new administration: some Quebec papers (*Le Soleil, Le Devoir*, and *La Patrie*, for example) were more skeptical.[78]

The *Toronto Daily Star* was satisfied if not enthusiastic, writing: "the new administration is as representative a coalition of the two political parties throughout Canada for war purposes as could have been formed and will meet with the approval of all who really desired to see the two political parties come together, sink their differences, and endeavor to unite their followers as one people while the war lasts."[79]

There was some Anglo opposition; Ontario Liberal (and future United Farmers of Ontario premier) E.C. Drury dismissed the new Union as "merely the old Government with a bit of window dressing."[80] One of the few outspoken Conservative critics was Sir Sam Hughes, who claimed that the whole Union government was unnecessary and, in fact, part of a plot between Sir Joseph Flavelle and Sir Thomas White, dating back to the "Toronto Eighteen" of 1911, to replace Borden with White as prime minister.[81]

The formation of the Union government was a personal victory for Borden. He had faced down the resistance in his own party and ensured that his colleagues came along, he had secured his own leadership in the process, and he had demonstrated qualities of decisiveness, persistence, intelligence, and a shrewd understanding of human nature. His own position was untouchable. Even in the new cabinet, despite his repeated offer of equal representation, he and his former colleagues dominated. Borden remained as prime minister and Conservatives outnumbered Liberals thirteen to ten; the important portfolios of finance, trade and commerce, the interior, and railways were held by former Conservatives; and, of the ten new Liberal members, only Carvell, Guthrie, and Maclean had seats in Parliament (Robertson was a member of the Senate). Rowell,

Sifton, and Calder had provincial experience, but Crerar, Ballantyne, and Mewburn were relatively new to political life.[82] Borden remained in firm control of his government.

Still, Borden had not achieved the grand coalition that he had originally wanted. He had failed to entice Laurier or any Liberal French Canadian and failed to bring in a significant portion of the federal Liberal Party. What he got was a group of prominent individual Liberals and provincial politicians who shared his view of the war effort. From May to October he was forced to scale down his ambitions from a full national government to a more austere coalition — and he needed the franchise gerrymander to achieve even that more limited goal. Following the creation of the Union government a few more federal MPs came in, but the Union government lacked unity and cohesion.

The question that remained was whether Union government would be good for the Conservative Party in the long term, and here there were a few doubters. Borden hoped that the Union would represent the advent of a new kind of politics that would reflect the new Canada that was emerging from the war. He saw a degree of permanence in this new party that would last beyond the war and into the future. Union government "may prove the herald of the destruction of patronage and the subsidence of partyism built thereon," wrote a satisfied Sir George Foster in his diary. "To my mind it marks the beginning of a new alignment of public parties in Canada."[83]

But many of the Liberals who were joining the Union government did not share this view; for them the coalition was a response to the exigencies of war, where the desire to win the election, introduce conscription, and defeat Germany overshadowed old party disputes over railways, tariffs, and patronage. After the election and the war, however, when the debate over conscription had faded, the old divisions would reassert themselves. Many Liberals could not see themselves remaining in a Union Party if it did not change in very basic ways. Crerar, for example, believed that all pro-conscription Liberals should back the government "until the war is over, but once that was done to hold themselves free to support whatever policies in a domestic sense they thought were in the best interests of Canada."[84]

Frank Carvell, who had been described as an "unrelenting and unrepentant Grit,"[85] and as a man "whose whole life had been occupied in metaphorically throwing rockets at the Conservative Party,"[86] was even blunter; speaking with his new cabinet colleague J.D. Reid, he "made it quite plain and definite this Union is only until the war ceases. Then he is out and we go back to party lines."[87]

But those were questions for the future. "As I looked outside at the cold wet sleet today," wrote a saddened Mackenzie King as he read the news about the formation of the Union government, "it seemed a fitting symbol of the present moment. War in the world, & its anxieties, change of gov't. at home with defeat of party & personal defeat virtually assured thro' the new turn of events in the coalition — my closest political friends in Toronto all against me as a consequence." This new Union government would prove to be a formidable alliance in the election that was fast approaching. "As it is," King concluded, "I shall seek to do my duty day by day & let the Future unfold itself."[88]

The cabinet of the new Union government met for the first time on October 12, not long after being sworn in. Later that night, Borden held a dinner for his new colleagues at the Rideau Club. Two new cabinet committees were also created; the first was the War Committee, which, as the name suggests, was to coordinate the war effort among the various government departments to enhance speed and efficiency; the second was the Reconstruction and Development Committee, which was given the task of overseeing all aspects of demobilization.[89] Borden chaired both committees and they consisted of a roughly equal number of Conservatives and Liberals. The new government could now boast a truly national presence in that it contained Liberal provincial leaders from Ontario, Saskatchewan, Alberta, New Brunswick, and Nova Scotia. Their provincial organizations, for the most part, came with them. In Saskatchewan, for example, the Liberal and Conservative provincial organizations merged into one, the National Government Association of Saskatchewan.[90]

Newton Rowell became one of Borden's closest colleagues in the new government and vice-chair of the new War Committee. He arrived for his first full day of work as president of the Privy Council Monday morning, October 15. It was all a little strange: "the official Liberals don't want us nor do the Conservatives," Rowell's wife wrote, "so our social circle is very limited."[91] That same day Rowell's secretary, Main Johnson, made a list of the key problems, as he saw them, facing the new government in Ontario. The first was the lack of a federal Liberal MP in the new cabinet, and although this was not precisely true, there were lingering concerns over the failure to attract the leaders of the Ontario wing of the federal party. The second, which was directly connected to the first, was the continuing devotion of the Ontario Liberals to Laurier. This would have to be confronted during the course of the election campaign. The third and more immediate concern was over the difficulties facing the new party in dividing up the constituencies for the approaching election.[92] It made sense that a sitting Conservative MP would be chosen to represent the same riding in the next election, but there were questions about what to do in Liberal-held ridings or how to determine who was a real Liberal-Unionist, and about who would pick the Union candidates.

The government's official mandate ran out and, after a hectic week of meetings, Borden met with the governor general on October 31. The general election would be held on Monday, December 17. In his announcement he explained his reasoning behind the formation of the Union government, noting how prominent individuals from different regions and backgrounds had shed their party allegiances and biases to come together into a single government united in its prosecution of the war effort. It was a clear demonstration of honour, courage, principle, and selfless sense of duty to the war and the country. And now they were asking for the support of the Canadian people.[93]

The sides were chosen; the election called. Those MPs still in Ottawa fanned out to their ridings across the country. Nominating conventions were scheduled, campaign literature written, travel arrangements and stump speeches prepared. Both parties readied for what would be a gruelling forty-seven day campaign. J.W. Dafoe welcomed the challenge. "I was not very well pleased with your services from Ottawa," he wrote, chastising one press gallery reporter. His dispatches were "too friendly to Laurier and too hostile to Borden." That had to change in the new campaign; the *Free Press* proposed to give the new government "strong independent support, particularly during the election campaign which is now at hand."[94]

Despite all the policies and promises yet to be made, there was to be a single clear election issue: the prosecution of the war effort, and its surrogate, conscription. The coalition and conscription were tightly bound together, but for Borden's government victory in the election could not have been secured without the help of a vast gerrymandering of the vote. Sir Wilfrid Laurier had good reason to be pessimistic, but remained more philosophical as he pondered the election call. "Conscription is a mere transient thing and will be over in a few months," he wrote Sir Allen Aylesworth, "but the racial chasm which is now opening at our feet may perhaps not be overcome for many generations."[95]

6

FRAMING THE CAMPAIGN

"I see by the papers that they are going to pass a measure for conscription at last in Canada, I would not like to belong to a conscript army & I'm afraid that they will not get a very good reception by the boys over here."

— Pte. Amos William Mayse to daughter Betty,
May 25, 1917[1]

On October 26, less than a week before the official start of the election campaign, the Canadian Corps launched an attack in Belgium to capture a long and important German-held ridge and the small village of Passchendaele that rested on its top. This Canadian attack at Passchendaele was part of a battle, known officially as the Third Battle of Ypres, that had begun at the end of July. By October, when the Canadians were brought in, the British Expeditionary Force had gained a meagre ten kilometres and lost over two hundred thousand men in the process. The Battle of Passchendaele has become synonymous with the horrors of the First World War — pockmarked landscape, mud and rain, poisonous gas, shell craters filled with toxic water and rotting corpses, where over one million shells had fallen and thousands had died, many by drowning when they slipped into the oozing, muck-filled craters.[2] "Everything turned into porridge," one Canadian soldier wrote, "a ghastly dreadful porridge, thigh-deep, in which if you got hit on the shoulder blade with a bullet that merely knocked you unconscious for two minutes, you drowned."[3] By the time it was over on November 10, the Canadians had achieved a great victory, but at the terrible cost of sixteen thousand casualties.

The losses at Passchendaele were part of the approximately forty thousand casualties the Canadian Expeditionary Force had suffered since April 1917; by the end of January 1918 the overall losses reached almost a hundred and fifty thousand. Enlistment numbers remained low, and one of the first acts of the new Union cabinet was to issue an Order-in-Council beginning the process of calling up the first group of conscripts under the Military Service Act. To have to fight an election in such an atmosphere of crisis only made things worse. "A new week of struggle begun. I hate this election," Sir George Foster recorded in his diary. "It was so unnecessary — it is so mischievous and dilatory as regards the war work — it seems so petty and selfish compared with the deeds and sacrifices of our soldiers at the front. The people's minds are off the war and drawn to party struggles and bickerings. Enlistment is at a standstill and Cabinet activities necessarily distracted."[4] Foster's views were shared by many Canadians, but over the course of the battle Sir Robert Borden made no mention of Passchendaele in his diary. The war situation in Europe took a back seat to the political struggle in Canada; victory in Europe could come only with victory at home.

Laurier jumped off the mark first with the release of the Liberal campaign manifesto on November 4.[5] It was a long document: a mixture of condemnation of the Borden government and promises for what a Liberal administration would do. The first point was that the entrance of the small handful of federal Liberals into the new Union government had produced no significant changes or benefits to the government, the war effort, or the lives of average Canadians. Next, Laurier attacked the government for a multitude of sins: war profiteering and corruption, bad management of the economy, and its railway legislation, which, in Liberal eyes, was little more than paying off railway investors for worthless stock. Conversely, the Liberals promised tariff reductions, including the removal of duties on agricultural implements and a rescinding of the small duties introduced by the Borden government during the war. As a way of dealing with the soaring cost of living, they also offered more economic regulation of industry to control prices. Promises were also made to clean up the corruption that was seen to be permeating the Borden government back to the days of the Ross rifle, and to end war profiteering. With respect to the latter, a Liberal government would consider nationalizing or taking over factories engaged in war work where there was evidence of blatant profiteering. Plans would also be put into motion for the demobilization of Canadian soldiers, the reconstruction of the economy, and for the revival of the immigration system.

Particular criticism was directed at the Wartime Elections Act, which Laurier described as "a blot upon every instinct of justice, honesty, and fair play."[6] It humiliated and treated with contempt thousands of Canadians; worse, it denied them basic rights as citizens. He was especially critical of its impact on Canadian women. Laurier had long wavered between support and opposition to female suffrage; unfortunately, the periods of his support did not coincide with his time in office, when he actually could have done something about it. But now, in opposition, he was outraged by the fact that the Wartime Elections Act would deny many women their right to cast their first ballots in a federal election. He based his argument on the premise that, since the federal franchise was based on the provincial franchises, women who had the provincial vote automatically qualified for the federal vote — meaning that women west of the Ottawa River should now be able to vote. But under the Wartime Elections Act, the government had restricted the franchise only to certain women (those with close relatives in the military), denying the vote to thousands of others and stripping them of a right of citizenship even before they had been able to exercise it for the first time. The act "snatches that right from them," he argued. It is "vicious" and "has for its object and for its effect to discourage and to stifle the free expression of the will of the people, and to make Parliamentary government a mere name without the reality."[7]

Not surprisingly, the Liberal document focused most of its attention on conscription and the war effort, first by attacking the government for its broken promises and for introducing conscription without national affirmation, and second by defending the Liberal platform. The Liberals promised that their government would undertake a full prosecution of the war effort; their "first object" would be "to find the men, money and resources necessary to ensure the fullest measure of support to our heroic soldiers at the Front, and to enable Canada to continue to do her splendid part to win the War."[8] But a Liberal government would rely on the voluntary method for recruitment. The Military Service Act would be suspended and the government would delay implementation of conscription until a referendum could be held on the matter. The implication was that it would be possible, therefore, to support conscription and still vote Liberal, because eventually all Canadians would be given the opportunity to express their will on the issue, in the referendum. The "supreme end" of this election, Laurier concluded, "is to assist in the tremendous struggle in which we are engaged, to maintain the unity of the nation, to avoid the divisions and discords which, for many years kept in check, are now unfortunately again looming up dangerous and threatening, to resolutely face the economic situation with the view of avoiding and lessening privations and sufferings, which should not exist in a country so richly endowed by nature as our country."[9]

On November 12, Borden responded with a broad Union manifesto listing the policies and goals of the new government. At the top of the list

What Borden Brought You: A Liberal poster from the 1917 election campaign.

was the war effort. The Union government had been created because of the war, its *raison d'être* was the war, and its goal was to pursue the Canadian war effort to the very end. The war "is the first consideration, and that to its energetic and successful prosecution union among the people is as necessary as the coalition of political leaders."[10] The parties had united as one; now it was time for the Canadian people to come together as one. "In the trenches," Borden explained, "Liberals and Conservatives fight and die for a common Canada and a common Empire. No party wall divides the wounded in the hospitals. Nor do those who minister to their wounds and ease their sufferings ask to what party the afflicted belong. Is it too much to expect that the spirit by which the Army lives and triumphs will be as active and as powerful among the people at home when they cast their ballots, and that here as there the great cause for which we contend will unify and inspire the nation?"[11]

Borden continued with other reasons to support the Union government. One of the most significant was the promise to grant women the vote. He argued that extending the franchise to women was "a measure of justice too long delayed," but he did not refer to the partial extension under the Wartime Elections Act or why he opposed granting the vote to all women immediately. "If men die, women suffer," he explained, "if they are wounded, women heal; if they are maimed, women labour, and since there can be no separation in suffering and sacrifice, there should be none in citizenship."[12] In addition, Borden again promised civil service reform and the elimination of patronage appointments, increased taxes on income and war profits, an improved land colonization and settlement scheme, and a variety of other policies to reduce government expenditures, to prevent corruption and profiteering, to enhance co-operation in the agricultural sector, to improve the railways and transportation generally, and to maintain good relations between employers and workers; promises all couched in the usual political vagueness of "effective measures," "adequate consideration," "encouragements," and "reductions." These pledges were aimed not only at traditional Tories but also at western voters who might still be wary of the new Union government.[13] But in the national emergency, winning the war was foremost. His government pledged itself "to prosecute the war with ceaseless vigour, to strive for national unity, to administer the public departments with economy and efficiency, to advise measures of taxation which will regard social justice, and to neglect nothing that may be required to sustain soldiers on service or to comfort those of their households whom they have left behind."[14]

The campaign was a lopsided affair in both English and French Canada. In French Canada, the Liberals had the upper hand from the start; in English Canada, it was the opposite, with virtually all the mainstream English-language press supporting the Union government; all the provincial premiers, save Sir Lomer Gouin in Quebec, backed the Union (albeit with varying degrees of enthusiasm); and virtually all the provincial political machines swung in behind the Union campaign. Outside Quebec, Borden and the Union government could count on well-organized events and enthusiastic welcomes, positive press coverage, and a "win-the-war" campaign message that resonated with English Canadians from coast to coast.

It is always hard to document, but it is quite likely that the Unionists also had far more money to run their campaign than the Liberals did. Liberal sources of fund raising, especially from wealthy contributors, evaporated as the Liberal political organizations swung behind the Unionist cause. Many Liberals complained of lack of funds and of having to pay their own election expenses. Still, the Unionists needed to raise more money. The *Montreal Star*'s owner, Lord Atholstan, recorded a meeting with Borden in November at which the prime minister asked Atholstan to help finance the Union campaign (the figure Borden suggested was allegedly in the $1.5–$2 million range). Borden put on him the "sole responsibility for obtaining funds," Atholstan complained that the request "was staggering and impossible of full accomplishment in Canada."[15]

An appeal was made to Britain via Lord Northcliffe, the well-connected proprietor of the *London Times*, and ultimately to Prime Minister Lloyd George, falling on the desk of Maurice Hankey, secretary of the British War Cabinet. Hankey wrote immediately that it was out of the question that the British government be seen to be funding the campaign of one party in a Canadian election, but he passed the request on to Andrew Bonar Law, the New Brunswick-born expat and former British colonial secretary. He sent it to Law "with the idea that possibly you might know privately some Canadian in England who might consider the matter."[16] That Canadian was likely Lord Beaverbrook, Borden's old friend and backer in 1911, who was already committed to helping the Unionist cause. Beaverbrook had earlier been offered a constituency if he chose to return to Canada, but he declined and instead promised to pay the expenses of the candidate who ran in his place and to make up for any losses that the Union publicity campaign in Britain might incur.[17] Another was E.R. Peacock, a Canadian businessman who had relocated to London and maintained interest in several British businesses. There are no cheque stubs to confirm, but both men helped where they could. "I think I ought to congratulate you on the very able manner in which you managed the financial side of the election campaign," Beaverbrook wrote Peacock a few days after the election. "Fifty thousand dollars may not seem a lot of money in an English election, but it is a great deal to raise in a moment for Canadian purposes over here."[18]

Most indicators — political organization, funding, press support, et cetera — favoured the Unionists. Nevertheless, pockets of Liberal support remained, even outside Quebec, and anti-conscription feelings ran deep in some parts of the country and among different groups — enough to ensure a competitive race in many ridings. Farmers' organizations, pacifist groups, organized labour, anti-Borden and anti-conscription individuals, and diehard Liberals found themselves as temporary — and not always co-operative — allies in a challenging campaign, swimming against the Unionist tide.

One of the best things going for the Liberals was the continuing admiration and respect for Sir Wilfrid Laurier. Laurier could still rally thousands of supporters virtually anywhere he visited during the campaign, and thousands of Liberals from all across the country remained loyal to the old man with his flowing "white plume" and the old causes. It had been difficult for many other Liberals to switch their allegiance to the Union government knowing that they would have to break personally with Sir Wilfrid, and it was unusual to see, at least from them, strong personal attacks on Laurier during the campaign. On the contrary, most

Liberal-Unionists spoke of him as one of the greatest living Canadians and, at worst, as a man whose time had come and gone. Far more criticism was aimed at Henri Bourassa and his *nationalistes* and what a Laurier victory would mean. Laurier might *win* the election, it was often said, but after a Laurier victory Bourassa would *rule* and destroy the war effort and all that Canada had accomplished so far.[19] The irony was that in the previous election, in 1911, it was Laurier who battled the *nationalistes* and denounced the "unholy alliance" between Borden and Bourassa — while Borden and the Conservatives remained silent; six years later it was the Unionists who denounced Bourassa as the real threat and the power behind Laurier.

These issues were articulated in the campaign literature published by the Union Government Publicity Bureau set up in Ottawa, under the direction of J.S. Willison. Posters and pamphlets were produced explaining, among other things, the creation of the Union government, doling out the "facts," listing German atrocities, and generally framing the major issues of the election campaign. Union government arose when persons of ability and dedication abandoned party politics — with its "attendant evils of rancor, unfairness, favoritism and patronage" — and came together "in the duty of service in the national interest." Together they would exert "every ounce of our power in men, munitions, provisions and wealth to help in winning the war." Conversely, to quit now, "in the middle of the fight and sneaking away from the scene of hostilities is unBritish, unCanadian, unmanly and quite unthinkable. The cry raised in some quarters that we have done enough merits only contempt." Why? Because this was Canada's war: "The war is as much as truly ours as it is that of France, Great Britain, Italy and the United States, and we would have no more right to abandon the struggle before Victory is achieved than have any of these nations."[20]

Against the forces of goodness and right stood the Liberals and those who controlled them. "Laurier gladly takes Bourassa to his bosom," declared another Union pamphlet, and "Bourassa, as every English speaking man and woman knows, or should know, is anti-British, and pro-German, and he has a bitter hatred for the English speaking people of Canada. Since this war broke out he has been guilty of utterances and

writings which are little short of treason and sedition. He is the recognized champion of the Clericals in Quebec, who, with their supporters,
have no love either for their mother country, France, or for Great Britain,
the protector of their liberties." Laurier and Bourassa were linked back to
the hanging of Louis Riel in 1885, and now the Laurier-Bourassa forces
were behind "a campaign of organized violence and intimidation to
terrorize Quebec into opposition to the Union Government." Together,
the Union memorandum continued, "the teachings of Bourassa and
the failure of Laurier to rally his race in the war, are bearing fruit in a
wave of race bigotry and desire for French-Canadian domination." And
in case the meaning wasn't clear, the sentence finished in capital letters:
"ONLY A SOLID ENGLISH SPEAKING CANADA, DETERMINED
TO MAINTAIN BRITISH IDEALS AND BRITISH TRADITIONS
IN CANADA, WILL SUCCESSFULLY COPE WITH A SITUATION
PREGNANT WITH PERIL."[21]

Indeed, as the campaign progressed the rhetoric attacking Quebec,
Bourassa, anti-conscriptionists, "enemy aliens," and Liberals everywhere
only increased and turned progressively more venomous. Laurier may
have remained popular in English Canada, but Bourassa's endorsement
of Laurier and the Liberals gave the Unionists a target that was almost
irresistible. And the outbreak of violence at a few political rallies in
Quebec only provided more ammunition. The Unionists were only trying to practice their right of free speech "in spite of Laurierites and the
provincial and municipal police authorities," reported the *Manitoba Free
Press*, as it condemned Quebec and warned that the future of the English
language in Quebec hinged on the outcome of the election.[22] The *Halifax
Herald* declared a "Laurier-Bourassa Reign of Terror," that had unleashed
the "crime" of a wartime election and warned its readers — "decent
people" — of "riots and bloodshed."[23]

The release of the first conscription numbers brought even more
attention on Quebec. The first men called up were to register by
November 10, and very quickly it became apparent that a great majority
of those called had applied for exemptions from military service. Most
of the public criticism was aimed at the apparent unwillingness of young
Quebeckers to serve, even though in the imperial stronghold of Toronto

over 90 percent of those called up sought an exemption (making it fairly clear that both young English-speaking and young French-speaking Canadians were reluctant to serve). But it seemed that virtually all Quebeckers who were drafted requested exemptions and that the great majority of them were granted. All the students in the first cohort from Laval University appeared before the military tribunal with signed letters from the university requesting an exemption.[24] The Military Service Act, which, at its deepest and darkest roots, was created as a way of forcing Quebec to do its share in the war, appeared to be failing. It was another blow to the war effort, and for many English Canadians the situation was intolerable; for the Unionists it brought the essence of the campaign into sharp relief. Quebec could not be ignored as a wasteland for the Union government; it could play a central role as a foil for all that was going wrong in the war effort, all that was preventing Canada from playing its full part, and all that might lead to the return of Laurier and ultimate disaster for the cause. On November 26, Borden recorded in his diary that he, Rowell, and Sir Thomas White, "agreed that we should attack in press and on public platform the attitude of Quebec."[25] The next day, in Lindsay, Ontario, Sir Sam Hughes hinted at treason, suggesting that it was "German gold" behind Laurier's opposition to conscription.[26]

The Liberals responded by arguing that the election was about more than the war — Borden's record, his railway policy, tariffs, corruption, and patronage. Vote Liberal and it still meant that you supported the war but it also meant that you were a democrat and favoured the right of the people to decide — through a referendum — on the key issue of the war. You would also get more, including lower tariffs, fewer scandals, and clean, efficient government. As one full-page Liberal newspaper ad explained it: "Win the War With Laurier and Freedom" followed by "Millions for Mackenzie & Mann But A Dollar Ten for the Boys in Khaki."[27]

The Liberals clearly were fighting an uphill battle, hoping to have this broad array of issues resonate with the voters; but for the Unionists all the loose threads of the election could be woven into a single word: conscription. Conscription was the defining issue; if you said "yes" to conscription it meant you supported the war, wanted to do all that you could to see it through to the end, and you were a supporter of the Union government. If you said "no" you were allied with Bourassa and Laurier, the foreigners, the anti-imperialists, the conscientious objectors, the kaiser, the traitors, and all the slackers and cowards. "There is but one issue" announced the *Union Bulletin*. "It is a question of fight under Union or quit under Laurier dominated by Bourassa and a solid Quebec. Canada cannot and will not quit!"[28]

In their struggle — "crusade" was a word often heard — to win both the election and the war the Unionists could also count on the strong support of the Protestant churches. Spokespersons for the Anglican Church frequently issued statements and pastorals calling on the members to back the Union government and support its policies; one bishop in British Columbia raised support for the government into a "sacred" duty, another called on his flock to "close up our ranks and unite the country behind our Union Government for God and country."[29]

The Baptist press had long supported the voluntary method of recruitment, but came out in full support of Borden in the lead-up to the election; similarly the Presbyterian press shifted from voluntarism to compulsion, with the *Presbyterian Witness* declaring in mid-1917 that "compulsory military service is the most equitable and just system of national defence."[30] On December 2, the Rev. T.T. Shields delivered his Sunday morning sermon from the pulpit at Toronto's Jarvis Street Baptist Church and called for Canadians to vote against Laurier. "A vote for a supporter of Laurier," he announced, "is a vote against the men in the trenches, and therefore a vote for the Kaiser."[31]

The Rev. C.W. Gordon, under his pseudonym Ralph Connor, continued to churn out novels and short stories with his characters (now in military dress) exhorting the British Empire, Christianity, and the war effort. The Methodist Church had dropped its critique of war in 1914 and by the time conscription had been introduced had swung squarely behind Borden, his new Union government, the Military Voters Act, and the Military Service Act. Ministers encouraged their men to enlist, their women to knit socks for the soldiers, and their children to donate their pennies to war relief campaigns.[32] For the Rev. S.D. Chown, the general superintendent of the Methodist Church, it was time to enter the political arena. "In my judgment," he wrote, "the elector who votes for the anti-conscription policy, and the repeal of the Military Service Act, forges three links in a fatal chain of personal humiliation, public contempt, and national decay. He degrades the term 'Canadian' from a synonym of glory to a badge of dishonor."[33]

The intensity of support for Union government from the Protestant churches only increased as election day approached. "In the palmiest day of the hierarchy in Quebec," mused O.D. Skelton, "no such fusillade of ecclesiastic advice had ever been fired in Canada."[34]

When it came to the Catholic Church, it was a little more complicated. In Quebec there was no question of the resistance of the Church to conscription and the Union government, although the Church usually advocated compliance with the laws and did not condone violence as a method of protest. In other francophone areas, such as in Acadia and eastern Ontario, the Church was much more supportive of the war effort.[35] English-speaking Catholics, meanwhile, were solidly behind the war effort and had tried to distance themselves from their francophone cousins over education issues like Regulation 17, but they also found themselves regularly suspected, if not accused, of disloyalty by Protestant sources.[36] But in English Canada it was possible — and common — to be both a good Catholic and a supporter of the Union government.

The strongest expression of anti-Catholicism, however, was directed at Quebec, where you could twin Catholicism and the French language with disloyalty and the shirking of duty. For the stern Protestant Newton Rowell, Canadians were faced with a choice between Union government and "a nationalist, clerical, and reactionary movement at work in the province of Quebec" that had a secret plan "to dominate the political situation throughout the Dominion of Canada."[37] Bourassa was not only a *nationaliste* and a francophone, he was also a Catholic, and it was easy, for those inclined, to see the reactionary Catholic clergy lurking behind Quebec's growing opposition to the war. "The average French-Canadian habitant is not educated," concluded Sir William Hearst, the Ontario premier; he "does not read even his own paper, and takes his politics like his religion from his Priest and Laurier."[38] Or, as one official in Government House in Ottawa summed it up in a letter to the Colonial Office, "as I have told you before, the Roman Catholic priests are at the bottom of the whole trouble."[39]

For many English Canadians, belief in the war and the cause was so profound that it was almost unimaginable that any sensible person could have a differing point of view — there had to be some reason or extenuating circumstance to explain it. And in the case of French Canada, it was the Church that had used its insidious influence to warp the minds of an otherwise sensible people. From that premise arose the rather counterintuitive argument that the way to solve the problem of too many priests in Quebec was to bring in *more* priests — this time, ones who would be more supportive of the government's war effort. In June, the prime minister approached the Colonial Office asking the British government to use its influence to encourage a French-speaking cardinal to visit Quebec, or at least issue a message to French Canadians. The British were less than forthcoming; the Foreign Office suggested an appeal to Franco-Americans living in New England — maybe their leaders could make the French Canadians see sense.[40] Neither suggestion was pursued.

In September, on the eve of the election campaign, King George V became involved. The king had a group of Canadian soldiers to dine at Windsor Castle — "strict temperance!" of course — and was shocked at what he heard. The Canadians' "language about the French Canadians had been lurid," Lord Stamfordham reported. Then he quoted what had been said: "When we get back we will shoot Laurier and every d-d. French Canadian — cowards and traitors. We will have Civil War and exterminate the whole lot. Especially the R.C. Bishops and Priests." The king was astonished but his reaction was very much in keeping with the feelings of many of his Anglo-Canadian subjects — he called on the Foreign Office and the Colonial Office "by command of H.M. … to get some influence brought to bear on R.C. Church," and to approach the Vatican with a plea for some French-speaking cardinals to issue an appeal to French Canadians to support the war effort.[41] It was an odd request and the British government rightly did not act on it, arguing that without a direct appeal from the Canadian government (an appeal that would not come so close to an election) its hands were tied.[42] What lingered, however, was the deeply held belief that French Canadians were prevented by their priests from seeing the self-evident truth about the war.

Both parties appealed to female voters, but again the advantage went to the Unionists. Suffrage itself was not a significant election issue because both parties had come out publicly in favour of female suffrage earlier that year. The whole question was debated in Parliament in May 1917, but, while Borden had pledged that his government would extend the franchise, no action was taken before the adjournment of the House.[43] The Liberals criticized the government for not bringing in legislation to give effect to Borden's pledge, and further condemned the Wartime Elections Act as political in nature (because of whom it gave the vote to) and inadequate because it did not extend the vote to *all* Canadian women. Borden countered with the technical argument that you cannot disenfranchise a group of people who had never actually been franchised. More important, the Unionists in Ontario established a Women's Bureau to help provide female speakers and offer other assistance to the ridings;[44] in addition, the government publicized a letter signed by the presidents of the National Council of Women, the Imperial Order Daughters of the Empire, the Women's Christian Temperance Union, and the Equal Suffrage League, accepting, and even justifying, the limited extension of the vote. It was "desirable that a limited franchise" was introduced, the four women argued, so that Canada may do its part in the war. Canadian women, they concluded, "are willing to make any sacrifice for the winning of the war."[45]

Women were a part of Canadian election campaigns before they had the vote; they helped organize and attended rallies and were a part of publicity campaigns. But in 1917 they played a bigger role and were the focus of much more attention, especially those women who had been granted the vote: the relatives of military personnel. It was estimated that there were now from half a million to a million women in this category[46] (the vast majority English-speaking, thanks to the preponderance of English-speaking soldiers in the military), and the Unionists believed that they would vote overwhelmingly for the Union government. In Vancouver some eight hundred women gathered on December 4 to pledge their support for the Unionists, and they displayed widely held views. "Aliens who are in Canada must be held down with an iron heel," one woman said, warning of an Austro-German conspiracy to cripple Canadian industry.[47]

In Winnipeg there were large rallies of "next-of-kin" women and all-female party debates; "Woman met woman on the stage here last night," was how the *Manitoba Free Press* put it.[48] In Toronto, women organized several mass rallies to pledge their support for the war; early in December, Lady Eaton assembled the female Eaton's employees at Massey Hall to hear speeches supporting the Union government. "We can only keep our honor clean and pure by supporting Union Government," she said. "We must pray more than ever we prayed before as we cast our ballots for our men over there."[49] In Halifax, women filled the Masonic Hall to support the war and listen to stirring accounts from France by wounded soldiers.[50] Other prominent women also got involved, many directly as speakers at rallies. Nell Rowell, for example, often accompanied her husband on the campaign trail and at other times addressed rallies on her own.[51]

The Unionist campaign literature directed at women spoke to the same issues as the other literature, although it was often massaged somewhat for Canadian mothers and turned conscription into a women's issue.[52] In a widely promoted open letter to Sir Wilfrid Laurier, a Canadian mother who had lost two sons in the fight called out to the Liberal leader to support those who were left behind. Laurier had "done much for Canada" but in the present crisis he had lost touch and chosen the wrong course. "And you, Sir Wilfrid, an old man, ripe in years, but not ripe in fatherhood, propose to allow these brave men to fight on until exhausted without help from you." The mother then added, "If you fail your 'white plume' will be stained with the blood of your fellow man, and your name will go down to posterity in deserved shame." As for Canadian women, they "will see to it, when the polls are opened, that no man, no matter what his past record may be, shall be sent to Ottawa with power to annul the righteous cry from our men at the front."[53] Another pamphlet called on Canadian women to have "your ammunition ready." These "next-of-kin" women were "fighters, on the front line, and in a fight to the bitter end. Your weapons? They are scraps of paper — little white bullets — VOTES! VOTES! VOTES!"[54] It was an effective strategy and helped coalesce English-speaking women voters into a fairly solid block behind the Union government.

* * *

Another important aspect of the campaign was the effort to attract the military vote. Thanks to the Military Voters Act all members of the armed services regardless of their age were permitted to vote, and that meant the servicemen and servicewomen serving in France, those stationed in Great Britain, those in the naval and air services, those on leave, those in military hospitals, and those at home still in training, or in transit, or who were veterans. Efforts were even made to collect the votes from the few Canadians who were interned in Switzerland, but the Swiss government refused to give the Canadian military representatives access, calling the Canadian request "a violation of Swiss sovereign rights."[55]

The soldiers at home were the easiest to reach; both parties recommended that candidates canvass all the military personnel in their ridings and seek their support; the Union Party sent each candidate the names and addresses of all military personal in each riding, including the men who had been rejected as medically unfit.[56] The military personnel at home

Propaganda for the Dominion Elections of Canada in France, 1917, posted on a salvage company dump.

were also exposed to all the regular campaign publicity; they were just as likely as other Canadians, for example, to see the posters proclaiming "Who would the Kaiser vote for?" that so many Liberals found insulting.[57]

The overseas military vote, however, was large and difficult to get at, and the military was not enthusiastic about being drawn into a political campaign; but that didn't stop the two parties from trying. A Unionist campaign organization was established in London, utilizing a number of veterans and displaced officers as campaign organizers — a fair number of officers received unexpected furloughs that enabled them to embark on political campaigning for the government.[58] Borden turned to Lord Beaverbrook, who assumed the role of chief publicist. Beaverbrook protested throughout the campaign about the lack of information and campaign news and how hard it was to maintain campaign publicity without updated news. "It is impossible to make bricks without straw," he complained.[59] Nevertheless, the Unionists put ads in newspapers, distributed pamphlets, and generally used the government machinery and the acknowledged support of the majority of the Canadian military for conscription to good advantage. Not surprisingly, much of the promotional literature called on the soldiers to vote for the *government* rather than a particular candidate, which would give the Unionists the added advantage of selecting the riding in which to place the vote.[60]

The Liberals turned to Godfroy Langlois and W.T.R. Preston to monitor the vote and promote the Liberal cause among the CEF. Langlois, a former leading Liberal editor and Quebec member of Parliament, was already in Europe as Quebec's representative in Belgium. He tramped through the muddy battlefields in France to visit hundreds of polling stations there.[61] Preston was a colourful and loyal ex-journalist known as "Hug the Machine Preston" because of his earlier use of the phrase in a congratulatory telegram to a winning candidate in a provincial by-election. He opened a Liberal office in London and from there did what he could to publicize the cause. It was a more challenging task for the Liberals, and everywhere Preston went he saw Unionist advantage. Preston met with General Richard Turner of the CEF, who told him that the "King's Regulations practically prevented any campaign being carried on among the soldiers. There could be no public meetings, the men could not be canvassed, literature could not be distributed in the camps nor to the men while they were within the camp areas."[62] But that didn't seem to stop the Unionists, and before long Preston was sensing fraud and corruption. He began flooding Ottawa with multiple conspiracy theories and complaints — charges that would last long after the election was over.[63]

General Arthur Currie, the Canadian commander, had earlier in the year made clear his support for conscription, and in the heightened atmosphere of an election campaign his words inevitably became an issue. The Unionists would have liked more from Currie, and he received several requests urging his involvement.[64] The Liberals wanted less from Currie, and whenever his name was mentioned in support of the government, they counterattacked. Currie tried to stay out of the campaign and refused requests to promote the Union government, but his name and the CEF, of which he was commander, were seen as fair game. Different interpretations of the recent battle of Passchendaele were offered up — for the Unionists, it was a great but costly victory that only served to rededicate Canadians to the fight; to many Liberals, it was a tragic waste that made one question the need for conscription in light of the obvious incompetence of the Canadian military leadership.

Stories appeared that Currie had been removed from command because of the enormous number of casualties at Passchendaele. That was false, and an outraged Currie felt obliged to ask the government to defend his name.[65] "You know how I have striven to keep clear of politics," he wrote Sir George Perley, the high commissioner in London, "but both sides seem determined to mix me up in it. I do not consider that it is fair that in the propaganda issued by the Government my name should appear so prominently. When it does, the Opposition of course consider it good political tactics to throw mud, and some mud always sticks when thrown." It was an unpleasant initiation into politics. After all he had done for Canada, Currie mused, it was hard to bear that "your countrymen should do their best to knife you in the back."[66]

The first phase of battle was now complete. Both sides had staked their claims, each defining its positions and making efforts to inspire its formations to campaign. The party manifestos were uninspired; almost as if everything that had to be said had already been spoken. For Borden, it was the Union that mattered far more than a program. For Laurier, it was a desperate attempt to recapture a sense of promise. Both sides made efforts to customize their appeals to the newly enfranchised women and on that front the Union government had a clear advantage; it had already limited the female voters to those who were eager to help their loved ones at the Front. It was also better prepared financially and, having stacked the vote in its favour, could now focus its attention on demonizing Quebec and French Canada generally. On the Western Front, General Currie had his hands full and enough to keep him busy for the rest of the political campaign; back home, things were just getting started.

7

THE CAMPAIGN: FRENCH CANADA

"Have you read about the rumpus in Canada among the French Canadians? They are having another general election & if Laurier gets in, it looks as though Canada would drop out of the war, anyway they would not send any reinforcements for a good many months. However, I think the present union government will remain in power, it would be a shame if the French Canadians won out against conscription."

— Pte. Frederick J. Milthorp, Katesgrove War Hospital, to Miss M. Beastall, December 4, 1917[1]

Senator Raoul Dandurand, a close friend of Laurier and a major player in Montreal's politics, had little to say in his memoirs about his party's awful year of 1917. He did reveal a story, however, that conveyed his state of mind and something about the political culture of Quebec on the eve of the election campaign. It was September, and he was attending a meeting of the board of directors of the Sun Life Insurance Company at its elegant headquarters in Montreal in front of Dominion Square (now Dorchester Square). As he approached the boardroom, he could hear his colleagues trading heated remarks in English (he was the only francophone on the board). He entered and saw they were all standing, but they abruptly cut off the discussion. "Senator," one said, "We are seeking an elusive answer: How is it that in today's newspaper we read that Franco-Americans are enlisting at the same rate as the rest of the population, while their brothers and cousins in Canada have a completely different attitude?"

"The answer is easy," Dandurand responded, "and I'll give it you. But first, let me ask you a question." Did they think that Canada would have responded to the call to arms in 1914 if it had been an independent country like the United States? He asked. The men hesitated, and one volunteered a "No." Dandurand did not wait for another word. Canada, he said, would have done the same as the United States, the countries of central and South America, and some countries in Europe. Canada would have stayed neutral. "We did not get involved in this war for Canada, we did it for the Empire; or, as you put it, for Great Britain. You got involved for strictly emotional reasons because, as Canadians, you would not have gone to war."

Dandurand paused, then drew himself erect to address his colleagues again. "Now I will answer your question," he continued. "The Franco-American is an American citizen and is responding loyally to the call of his country. The French Canadian, just like his Franco-American cousin, is responding to the duty of his country. You were moved by sentiment — a very understandable and laudable one at that. But the French Canadian is exclusively Canadian and his patriotism does not go beyond its borders." Reflecting on the exchange years later, Dandurand thought he had gone some way toward explaining the difference between English- and French-Canadian attitudes.[2]

As Borden frantically put the finishing touches to his Union cabinet, the tensions in Montreal, which had been rising all summer, reached a boiling point. On September 4, twenty-five hundred people — including many women — attended an anti-conscription rally at the Parc Lafontaine. Paul Lafortune was the keynote speaker, but he was preceded by Alphonse Bernier, a former Tory member of the Quebec legislature who had been defeated in the last provincial election. Bernier appealed to women to fight against forced enrolment because it would mean that men would return disabled. "You want a complete man, I'm sure of it," he exclaimed, "and nothing else will satisfy you."[3] Lafortune eventually took the stage, accompanied by body guards who were there, he said, to protect him from the goons in Mayor Médéric Martin's office who had threatened to kill him. Lafortune tore into Martin, and then declared that English Montrealers had contributed significantly to the tensions in the city with their "denigrations" of French Canadians. In his eyes, they were being treated worse than immigrants.

At another rally the following night, in the Maisonneuve neighbourhood east of Montreal, the entire political class was denounced, including Sir Wilfrid, who, it was argued, should have resigned his seat in Parliament along with every other French Canadian. Another speaker went even further. He declared that he no longer saw himself as French Canadian, but as a "Canadien-Québécois." Mayor Martin was denounced by all the speakers, and young men were urged to resist any attempt at forced enlistment. To cap things off, a petition circulated demanding that the governor general dismiss the Borden government. The following night, a riot broke out in Shawinigan Falls, where anti-conscription demonstrators descended on the business and home of C.H. Flamand, a local businessman who had spoken in favour of conscription. The rioters destroyed both his place of business and his home.

The government and its supporters hit back. Tancrède Marsil, the fiery young *nationaliste* and editor of *Le Réveil,* was mugged by two soldiers on the night of September 12 and wound up in hospital.[4] Pierre-Édouard Blondin, Borden's postmaster general, who had become a lieutenant-colonel to help raise enlistments, tried to appease opinion-leaders in Toronto, predicting that any agitation in Quebec would be over within a month. He reassured journalists that the agitators did not speak on behalf of most Quebeckers.[5] Blondin promised that, with the new enlistments brought on by the Military Service Act, it would soon be possible to form a French-Canadian division, and he promised that the new recruits would be kept together and not spread around to fill vacancies in the other divisions.

The government also pressed charges against several protesters. Fernand Villeneuve, an eighteen-year-old from Prescott, Ontario, and one of the founders of the *Ligue des Constitutionnels,* who had spoken out at the Parc Lafontaine demonstration, was arrested by the Dominion Police on counts of sedition and inciting men to resist the Military Service Act.[6] In fact, most of the Parc Lafontaine speakers that night were eventually brought before the courts on charges of sedition, but Villeneuve was the first person in the country to be charged in such a way: he faced between one to five years in prison. He appeared in court on September 12, but most of the charges were thrown out. He was released the next day.

On September 13, Lionel Groulx, a thirty-nine-year-old priest and professor of Canadian history at the Université de Montréal, gave a much-advertised speech at the Monument National. His aim that night was to reflect on Confederation, both in terms of its origins and its significance. He extolled Louis-Hippolyte Lafontaine, pointedly noting that the Victorian politician had spoken in French in Kingston in favour of the Act of Union in 1841. "It was, for us, an historic moment," said Groulx, "when one of ours, despite the ostracism of our language, spoke in French. It was an act of *'action française'* and from that moment on our future was decided.[7] Groulx drew a parallel between 1841 and 1917 (when a new a *action française* was launched), however imperfectly: "They wanted to make serfs of us," he said. "They wanted to strangle our nationality." For Groulx, Lafontaine showed that it was possible to justify a French fact in British North America, and to insist that French rights be respected. The scholar-priest's choice of subject was not mere coincidence. In the darkest hours of the fight against conscription, he looked to the past not just for guidance, but for a hero who could give hope to French Canada by showing that resistance was possible.[8]

The Ontario schools question reared up again at precisely the same time, as the provincial government tabled bills at Queen's Park authorizing it to spend funds collected on behalf of the Ottawa School Board that had gone unspent since late 1914. Senator Landry again attacked the Borden government for failing to protect the interests of the French-speaking minority in Ontario.[9] He and Belcourt pleaded their case again in the Supreme Court of Canada in early October, basing their argument on the 1916 decision of the Judicial Committee of the Privy Council that had declared the province's takeover of the board unconstitutional. The Ontario schools question simply never left the front pages of Quebec newspapers.

No one could escape the war. In late September, Onésime Nantel-Orsali decided to go to the movies at the Regent theatre and was shocked to see her son Eugène appear on the newsreel that played before the feature — she had not seen him in two and a half years, and he appeared much thinner than when he had left home. Yet there he was, right before

Where Your Money Is Going: A Liberal campaign poster (1917).

her eyes, smiling and posing with four friends, just before the Battle of Vimy Ridge. She screamed his name out loud, surprised at her own visceral reaction; but that did not stop her from returning to the theatre several more times, bringing friends along. "We all came to salute you and applaud you," she wrote to him.[10]

The trial of eleven men accused of stealing dynamite from the Martineau quarry and bombing Lord Atholstan's summer home in Cartierville also dominated the news. Élie Lalumière faced three counts: conspiring to committing crime, robbing a bank, and attempted murder. Joseph Tremblay also faced three charges: stealing dynamite, being in possession of dynamite, and attempted murder. Joseph Paquette was accused of stealing dynamite. Rosario Wisintainer and Aurèle Goyier both faced charges of attempted murder. Henri Arsenault, Louis Bolduc, and Arthur Blackwell, all in their mid-forties, employees of Martineau and thus the "insiders" to the affair, were accused of being in possession of the dynamite. Blackwell, a Boer War veteran, was accused of making the bomb. Jean-Baptiste Cyr was accused of taking part in the bombing. Charles-Auguste Chagnon and Joseph Paquette, the youngest at twenty-one, were accused of theft of dynamite.

In court, Tremblay testified that Lalumière was the ringleader, and that the bomb set off at Atholstan's home was only the first of five planned. The others were to go off at various newspapers (the *Gazette*, *La Patrie*, the *Montreal Star* and *La Presse*) and that attacks were to be carried out against Borden; Joseph Flavelle, the chair of the Imperial Munitions Board; William Mackenzie and Donald Mann, the railway entrepreneurs; and Albert Sévigny and Pierre-Édouard Blondin, the most visible French-Canadian Tories. Tremblay also said that the bomb at Atholstan's house was powerful enough to have levelled the property but that he, with minutes to spare, had placed it in such a way so as to blow off only the balcony.

The unrest, the rioting, and the trials combined to create a toxic atmosphere in Quebec on the eve of the election campaign. "There have continued to be demonstrations in Montreal and other portions of Quebec," John Foster reported to Washington. He added that he had been told that Laurier would support conscription in exchange for the opportunity to name half the Board of Selection for local tribunals that were to be established under the Military Service Act.[11] The consul general's views were informed by his conversations with many people in Ottawa, including members of Borden's government, and he had come to the conclusion that "the Province of Quebec is hopeless from a Conservative standpoint and may therefore be discarded." But, he added, the "Liberal vote will ... be materially curtailed" by the new franchise act. Foster was certain that Laurier would not resign; nor would he be trapped by previous engagements: "I am informed, I think reliably, but very confidentially," he reported, "that he will refuse to give his followers in Quebec any assurances of a repeal of the Conscription Act or of the vacating of any of the measures taken by the present Government under that Act. He may not, however, if returned to power, enforce this measure without a referendum. This last statement, I have assured my informant, would not be any way repeated except for your information."[12]

The American consul general was equally pessimistic about Borden and his new government's ability to win support in Quebec. "The new cabinet represents divergent views on several issues and is only united on conscription as a war issue," Foster informed Washington. The new cabinet was overwhelmingly Protestant and not at all representative of the 40 percent of the population who were Catholic. Moreover, despite that French Canadians were a third of the population, the new Union cabinet had only two French-Canadian representatives. "Under these conditions," noted Foster, "the cleavage between the Province of Quebec and other provinces will be deepened."[13]

Borden was also concerned by that widening gap, and in late October sent Albert Sévigny and Senator L'Espérance to meet with Archbishop Bruchési.[14] The prelate was not impressed. He refused to offer any further support and simply wished them good luck. "They've done us enough harm," he wrote to Mgr. Bégin, the archbishop of Quebec.

> Would they wish to compromise us further? They created the unionist 'Win the war' party. What they want above all is to win the election. They will use all the means available to bring them to their goal. They pose as defenders of our province but they play the game of our enemies. They knocked on a lot of doors to find a French Canadian who would join the hybrid Union government. It was in vain. And here they are coming to us in all humility. For them, this is a significant step. They received nothing, they will receive nothing from me. Let them find on their own the man they need.[15]

Support for the Conservative government in Quebec had been dropping since 1912, when the first francophone ministers had abandoned Borden over his naval policy. By 1917 support was at an all-time low. As one of Borden's correspondents put it, "the riff raff led by demagogues Laurier, Bourassa, Lavergne [*sic*], T. Marcil [*sic*], [labourite leader Alphonse] Verville, [Médéric] Martin," had such influence that a Conservative victory in Quebec was unimaginable. But, even with such open enemies of the Party, there was worse: the "incompetent personnel"[16] of the Conservative Union Committee of Quebec City and its environs.

This was not the first time Borden had received such dire warnings. Months earlier, Rufus H. Pope, who had held the Eastern Townships riding of Compton for fifteen years from 1889 to 1904, had written Borden that "apathy and demoralization" pervaded the party press and the party members. The Department of the Militia had lost the confidence of the people, he added, "we have lost the confidence of the electorate, and defeat is inevitable."[17] Things were not getting better: Compton had elected anglophones since 1867, even though the riding was French Canadian in majority, but now a petition was demanding that a French Canadian be chosen as candidate.[18] (In the end, both party candidates were anglophone and the Liberals retained the riding.)

What support the Conservative Party had inside Quebec increasingly divided along regional lines, but overall the Union government had little impact. In the Quebec City district, for example, complaints had been coming in from political organizers since early in the war that all the patronage decisions were being made in Ottawa. "In the face of all this, should we continue to devote our energies to a government which does not seem to need our services and ignores our sacrifices? The question presents itself: Why should we?" wrote Roméo Langlais, the President of the Conservative Association of the District of Quebec. "The time for concessions cannot last forever," he tried to convince Borden, reflecting on a situation that was similar to the one in Compton. "Why would a few English in Quebec who don't even have the support of their own community want to represent the French Canadians in that district?"[19]

The poor condition of the Conservative Party in Quebec had been revealed in the May 22, 1916, Quebec election, when the party, led by the hapless Philémon Cousineau, lost ten of its sixteen seats and took only 35 percent of the vote. Cousineau lost his own seat and promptly resigned from the leadership. The party in Quebec had little money, and even less organization. "The strong card against us was the bilingual question" wrote Charles Gault, one of the Conservative members in the Quebec legislature, to Borden. Gault was bitter that he had received no help from Ottawa, and he added that the party's woes in the province "were a very serious matter … if we believe that we are right for the country."[20] Alphonse Bernier, the same man who would later appear at the huge

Parc Lafontaine demonstration in September 1917, but who had just lost his seat in the County of Lévis, also protested. He pointed to the federal government's inaction, first on the Ontario schools question, and then in not creating sufficient patronage opportunities. He told Borden, "your minister of my District never took any care of my election during the five weeks which preceded it." Borden was not convinced. "I regret the result in the Province of Quebec," he told Gault, "but I doubt that it proceeded from the causes to which you allude." Borden asked for more detail, but it is not evident that Gault bothered to respond.[21]

Borden, interestingly, asked Frank Cochrane, the minister of railways and canals, for an interpretation of Bernier's complaint. Cochrane, no expert on Quebec, roundly dismissed it.[22] Borden also asked Pierre-Édouard Blondin to go to Quebec to get a sense of what had gone so wrong. Blondin did see problems and recommended that the affairs of the party in the Quebec region be handed over to the quartet of Sir Rodolphe Forget, Albert Sévigny, David L'Espérance, and Joseph Barnard, the editor of *L'Événement*, and that the last be given the lead in the next campaign. He also recommended that the government do a better job in handing out plum patronage, citing one job in particular that had gone to a "red hot Liberal." Borden must have winced.

Sir Rodolphe Forget was another thorn in the government's side. He represented two ridings, and had all the political latitude his enormous wealth could guarantee. He took exception to the favouritism Borden had shown to Thomas Chase-Casgrain in naming him to cabinet, and did not hide his feelings about the government — or about Borden, for that matter. The bitterness was reciprocated. Chase-Casgrain even complained to Borden that Forget had turned *La Patrie* against him. "Every time this paper gets a chance it says something which is damaging to my influence and my prestige," he complained.[23] The prime minister was certainly aware of it. "I have very frequently heard from a great many sources that Sir Rodolphe Forget uses exceedingly abusive language with regard to the Government and its various members including myself," he told a correspondent in January 1917.[24] Such was the disharmony in the Quebec team.

To break through the rancour, Sir Alexandre Lacoste, an old Tory war horse who had once been appointed to the Senate by John A. Macdonald, also convened key thinkers, senators, and activists to craft a strategy to end the erosion of Conservative support in Quebec. The group was unanimous in concluding that Ottawa was not the problem, neither on policy nor in program execution. It was a matter of communication. The group recommended that booklets be produced to counter Henri Bourassa's influence. It also urged that a French-language Conservative newspaper be established in Ottawa to more accurately report the news coming out of Parliament Hill. The idea of creating a strong "fighting newspaper" in Montreal was also popular. Finally, the group hoped to institutionalize itself into an "Advisory Committee" that could help the party during the election campaign. It listed key activists who had experience in the press and politics, not only locally but also in Ottawa and Quebec City, and were likely to provide strong supports to the party.[25]

Nothing came of this. Going into the 1917 election, therefore, the party had some strengths and many weaknesses. On the media front, it had newspapers that were favourable to the Unionist cause, but their support was, in many cases, unreliable. In Quebec City, *L'Événement* was loyal, if a bit stodgy. In Montreal, the weekly *L'Autorité*, run by Dr. Gaston Maillet, was passionately promoting Union and conscription.[26] But the problem was the bigger Montreal dailies. Lord Atholstan's *Montreal Star*, although steadfast in its support for Union government, was seen in some quarters as counterproductive in its support for the war effort, the Empire, and conscription. One Conservative supporter went so far as to call it "evil." "There can be no racial harmony," D.L. McGibbon wrote Borden, "so long as [Atholstan] is left in a position to continue to poison the public mind and to play with the loyalty and patriotism of the people of this province to suit his personal and selfish interest."[27] McGibbon complained that the *Montreal Star* often supported Liberal politicians in Montreal's municipal politics. The Montrealer considered the "English press" in Quebec "a far greater menace to the welfare of the Dominion" than anything being published in other provinces.[28] Brenton Macnab, the founding editor of the *Montreal Daily Mail*, a competing Conservative newspaper launched in 1913 to fortify the "imperial tie," also complained about Atholstan. "He is trying to play something akin to the Bourassa game in this province, *where he is aiming to gain strength!*"[29]

Newspaper troubles also affected *La Patrie*, whose Conservative owners complained that Albert Sévigny had "taken upon himself to throw the paper out of the party." Apparently, an editorial in early September 1917 was not sufficiently friendly to the government; indeed, Sévigny called it a "capital offense." Louis-Joseph Tarte, one of the owners, bitterly responded that *La Patrie* had defended conscription as long as it could but that his life — and that of his newspaper — was now in danger. His wife and children had been insulted publicly several times and he had had to hire private security guards. Tarte also reported to Borden that earlier that summer he had been shot at as he left his office and reminded him that the Atholstan summer home bombers had him and his newspaper on their hit list. "It is true we have not continued to defend the measure that you had brought in parliament [conscription] for the simple reason that had we done so I do not believe we would have ten per cent of our subscribers left," he wrote Borden. By the time the election had been called, *La Patrie* had lost ten thousand subscribers and many advertisers. Tarte blamed his newspaper's sinking fortunes on Bourassa's attacks on *La Patrie*. At the same time, he complained that state censors had done little to suppress *Le Devoir*. In fact, he complained to Borden, he had been told many times by cabinet members "not [to] attack Bourassa."[30] Borden promised to look into the matter, and confirmed to Tarte that any directive to refrain from criticizing the editor of *Le Devoir* was done "entirely without my knowledge."[31]

Disputes and controversies among Conservatives revealed the degree to which Borden's Union government was in disarray in Quebec. In fact, since 1911 the Quebec Conservatives had never been much more than a loose coalition of groups of traditional Conservatives and Bourassa *nationalistes*, united more by their opposition to the Laurier Liberals than by anything uniting them on policy. The Quebec Conservative-Unionists thus went into the election in a gravely weakened position. Even finding candidates to campaign was a challenge. Blondin, hardly the most effective speaker, but one who did vibrate with youthful enthusiasm, was in Britain most of the autumn. Forget dropped out of the election, likely to Borden's delight, but that put two seats on the line. The only other French Canadian who could mount an effective campaign was Albert Sévigny,

Borden's young minister of internal revenue. Ernest Lapointe, a rising star in the Liberal Party, referred to him as "the man whose name no one can speak."[32] When Sévigny tried to campaign in his riding of Dorchester he was subjected to verbal and physical assaults. He and his team were forced to take refuge in a hotel, which was also vandalized.[33] (To hedge his bets, Sévigny also ran in Westmount–St. Henri.)

Borden struggled to understand why the party was not ready for a fight in Quebec in October 1917. "Since the Conservative Government came into power in 1911 it has given not only justice but even generous consideration and attention to the people of [Quebec] and to their needs in the appropriation of public moneys for advancement and consideration," he repeatedly said. "In less than five years we did more for the Province in that way than had been accomplished by Sir Wilfrid Laurier's Government during the fifteen years of his regime."[34]

It was not a widely held view. R.A. Drapeau, an old Quebec French-Canadian Tory, laid the blame at the feet of the Conservative leaders who had shown "negligence" and "inactivity in the face of strong adverse influences on the part of those who should have been their friends." "Because of a culpable inactivity," he continued:

> a press imbued with anti-national sentiments [Drapeau was thinking of Le Devoir] was permitted to carry out a seditious campaign which has had the effect of falsifying the ideas of our people and over-exciting the imagination of the young men who frequent our schools, our colleges, and our universities, and which also penetrated the mind of a far too great a number, unfortunately, of the clergy who, in the Province of Quebec, exercise almost exclusively the control of the education of the young.[35]

For Drapeau and many others, what was lacking was a "Lafontaine" or a "Cartier" to fight the Liberals, a leader who would have denounced the Ontario government's position on French schools during the debates on the Lapointe Resolution and who would have dared to utter, "You are nothing but a band of jokers." Instead, he continued, the Conservatives had Senator Landry — "a cynical politician, [who] start[ed] a stupid campaign which was practically in favour of the Liberal Party. And here we find the same inaction on the part of the Conservative leaders from Quebec and this same culpable negligence which prevented them from enlightening public opinion in this Province." Drapeau also derided all the Quebec Conservatives who "lost their heads" over the issue of conscription. He then called on Borden to mobilize Sir Pierre-Évariste Leblanc, the lieutenant governor of Quebec — who had been placed there by Borden — but nothing came of it.[36] Wilfrid-Bruno Nantel, who had resigned from the cabinet for a position on the Railway Commission, urged Borden to encourage and support his Quebec MPs "so that they may not be discouraged or indisposed to run again." In this election, "I realize that their position is very difficult, but not entirely hopeless," he wrote. It was important that all pro-government candidates stay in the race, and he urged Borden to remind his MPs that the Military Service Act was not to apply to everyone, "especially farmers," which would exempt many French Canadians.[37]

Quebec was Borden's personal "no man's land" and he avoided it. In the seven weeks of the election campaign, the prime minister spent less than three days in Montreal. Borden arrived early on Sunday, November 11, (on his way to the Maritimes) to meet with local party leaders to discuss Henri Bourassa's politics and to deal with the *Montreal Star*'s implacable attitude toward French Canadians. He met with Atholstan in the afternoon and discussed the Union finances, as described in chapter 6. One of Borden's main concerns was also to make sure that cabinet minister Charles Ballantyne secured a riding that would guarantee his election. It was not an easy task, but here, at least, Borden did prevail.[38]

He returned a week later, but stayed only for brief meetings to discuss Quebec conditions. The news was not good. He tried again in late November, hoping to find a friendly audience in Sherbrooke, where two of the leading Conservatives in Quebec, Ballantyne and Charles Doherty, were to hold a rally. He arrived amid the confusion of an anti-government riot and the hall was ransacked. At the same time, Unionist candidate Charles Cahan tried to bring his people together in Maisonneuve (where he was running against Rodolphe Lemieux), but he was pelted with stones and rotten eggs. Borden's last trip to Montreal was on December 12, and limited to meeting privately with party insiders. He was told that the party would be reduced to five seats in Quebec.[39]

Compared to the Unionists, the Liberal Party machine in Quebec seemed nothing less than "a perfect German-like organization,"[40] but Laurier was not without things to worry about in his home province. The first was his health. The dropping of the writ coincided with a bout of flu of some sort that left the near-seventy-six-year-old (he celebrated that birthday on November 20) immobilized in his house in Ottawa, quietly working out his thoughts and strategies. "Conserve your energy — that's essential," advised Rodolphe Lemieux, "no one expects you to be as present as you were in the past."[41] For the Quebec campaign he relied, essentially, on three people: Lemieux, Senator Raoul Dandurand, and Séverin Létourneau, the discreet Quebec MLA and party operative who made his presence felt only in electoral campaigns (as president of the Federation of Liberal Clubs in Quebec, he had his finger on the pulse of the party).

There was no shortage of advice. Lemieux urged him to go after the Wartime Elections Act and denounce it as "the plot of jingoes and plutocrats against electoral freedom." Lemieux argued that "the people don't understand that mystery and will listen to your voice."[42] Senator Paul-Auguste Choquette chimed in with encouragements to prepare for the "rough battle" that was imminent. He prompted Laurier to claim that Borden had categorically refused to hold a referendum on conscription and that Laurier should present the campaign as a vote on the referendum concept.[43]

Laurier was the recipient, not only of advice, but of a great deal of news. Most of it was encouraging.

In Nicolet, the turnout for the Liberal nominating convention was unexpectedly large. Charles Murphy won his candidacy handily in Russell (Ontario), strongly supported by the French Canadians in the riding.

George Graham in Essex South had a much more difficult time in convincing his Franco-Ontarian electors. His pro-conscriptionist stance had caused nothing but consternation in areas around Stoney Point, prompting Emmanuel Desmarais, the vice-president of the riding association, to ask Laurier for an explanation. The Liberal leader responded that he did not agree with Graham on key points of the Liberal platform, but that if Graham did openly declare himself anti-Union, he deserved support.[44] Graham did so, but it was not enough. Desmarais reported that too many French Canadians, as well as English Canadians, did not trust him.[45] The Liberal nomination would go to someone else, regardless of Graham's prominence in the party and of his friendship with Laurier.

By midway through the campaign, Laurier still remained unsure of both his standing and his health. "The years bring nothing that is good," he wrote Archbishop Bruchési, who had just conveyed birthday wishes.[46]

An earlier portrait of Sir Wilfrid Laurier (Charlottetown, P.E.I.).

His health did appear to be improving, but his political problems remained. One of them was how to guard against the wholesale infiltration of *nationalistes* into Liberal ranks; the other was how to resolve disputes between candidates who saw a pro-Liberal wave coming and wished to guarantee seats on the bandwagon. A few *nationalistes* wanted to run for the Liberals but were snubbed. As Lucien Cannon put it in a letter to Laurier, he did not think it was tactical to "allow Bourassa's people to think they can impose their will on our candidates."[47]

The *Gazette* speculated that Laurier even "feared a Bourassa coup."[48] Armand La Vergne, for example, wanted to run in Montmagny, but local party "reds" rebuffed him, forcing him to run as an independent. Albéric Mondou, the *nationaliste* who had won Yamaska in 1911, wanted to keep his seat as a Liberal. Laurier was tempted to say yes, but he liked Oscar Gladu, the Liberal whom Mondou had defeated, and he wanted his loyal friend to get his old seat back.[49] Laurier convinced Mondou not to run at all. Laurier also likely insisted that Honoré Achim, the *nationaliste* MP for Labelle who had crossed the floor and joined the Liberals, not run for the party. A deal was made for a switch so that Achim would run provincially while Adélard Fortier, the provincial MLA, would now present himself as the Liberal candidate for the House of Commons. Laurier also convinced Joseph. A. Barrette, who had won the riding of Berthier in 1911 on a *nationaliste* ticket, not to run again.[50]

A particular problem emerged concerning Tancrède Marsil, who, though recovering from wounds he had suffered a few weeks earlier in a mugging, indicated that he wanted to run for the Liberals and even asserted that he had Laurier's support.[51] Privately, he complained that he felt ostracized, "treated like a leper," by leaders such as Lemieux and "others." Senator David told him that he could hardly expect the Liberal Party to welcome him with open arms. The harsh speeches he had delivered all through 1917 had made him politically "dangerous." Marsil responded that he had been no worse than La Vergne or some of the others. All the same, David warned Laurier that Marsil could "do us harm, if we don't find a way to calm him."[52] Laurier responded that Marsil was his own worst enemy, noting that he had received a letter from him "containing almost eight pages of insults towards Rodolphe Lemieux and almost everyone else." Laurier responded that "it smelled of Greek" to him, implying that he had no time for *nationaliste* candidates hiding in Bourassa's Trojan horse, trying to find a place in the Liberal Party. Marsil had hoped for a candidacy in the new riding of Hochelaga, but Laurier insisted that only the members of the riding association would decide on their candidate.[53] In the end, Marsil did not contest the nomination, and after three rounds of voting in a long nominating meeting chaired by Rodolphe Laflamme, Dr. Edmond Lesage (uncle of the future premier) was chosen the Liberal candidate. Many other *nationalistes*, their political futures cloudy, simply quit trying: Eugène Paquet in L'Islet, J.A. Descarries in Jacques-Cartier, and, last but not least, given his high profile during the previous two years, Paul-Émile Lamarche quit in Nicolet.

A few days after the release of the Liberal manifesto, Laurier felt sufficiently fit to travel. He went first to Quebec City on November 6, and paused for a whistle-stop speech at the railway station in Trois-Rivières. He was handed a bouquet of flowers and — no doubt reflecting on his work of the past few days — poetically declared that all the counties in Quebec were to be as united as the roses he was holding in his hand. His train pulled into Quebec City an hour later to a crowd estimated at fifteen thousand. The former prime minister was then driven through the streets of the city in a parade of no less than three hundred cars, all honking encouragement. He finally arrived at the Château Frontenac, where he took in a succession of meetings and then prepared for a banquet that would be attended by thousands of partisans.

The cacophony behind him, Laurier went over the serious files with his lieutenants. It was decided that Henri Béland, still held by the Germans as a prisoner of war in Belgium, was to keep his candidacy *in absentia*. Charles Power, a wounded veteran, took the Liberal nomination in Quebec South. Andrew Ross MacMaster, Talbot Papineau's friend and partner (Papineau was killed at Passchendaele in late October, as the campaign began), would fight for Sydney Fisher's old seat of Brome. The incumbent Conservative MP, Lt-Col. George Harold Baker, had also been killed at the front, the only active politician to die in action. Charles Marcil, after much hesitation, decided he would again run in Bonaventure. It was confirmed that George Parent would be the

Liberal candidate in Quebec West. Henri-Edgar Lavigueur, the mayor of Quebec, would run against Joseph Barnard, the editor of the Pro-Borden *L'Événement*, in Quebec County while retaining his position in the city. The only bit of bad news was that Wilfrid Lacroix won the nomination for Charlevoix, beating out Pierre-François Casgrain, who had been the Laurier favourite. (Lacroix would sit in the House of Commons until 1958, but would be remembered for his anti-Semitic immigration policy stance and his abandonment of the party over conscription in 1944.)

Laurier then travelled by train to Montreal on November 8 to meet with his organizers. On the same day, Henri Bourassa published the first of his editorials in reaction to Laurier's program. The news was relatively good: Bourassa was favourable to Laurier, but still very critical — it was less a blanket endorsement than an acknowledgement that there was no alternative for the province but to support the Liberals. It was, at best, a lukewarm endorsement, but it was far more welcome than Bourassa's all-out opposition that had cost the Liberal Party dozens of seats in 1911.

Bourassa noted with satisfaction that Laurier was finally espousing positions that *Le Devoir* had advanced years earlier. Bourassa considered the Liberal positions on the necessity of regular elections to be reasonable, but could not help noting that Laurier had fully supported the Borden government in 1915 and 1916 in delaying elections. *Le Devoir* also supported Laurier's denunciation of the Military Voters Act, but was unconvinced by the measures Laurier was proposing to fight inflation. Laurier's slogan of "*La guerre jusqu'au bout*" ("the war until the end") did not square with Bourassa's view — with what money, at what cost? asked *Le Devoir*. Bourassa was also deeply suspicious of Laurier's pledge to hold a referendum. He supported the idea — he had floated a similar one in 1910 during the naval policy debates — but wondered how Laurier could promise to hold a referendum and to suspend the Military Service Act at the same time. Bourassa also pointed out a harsh reality: that the Conservative-dominated Senate was likely to throw a wrench into any Liberal plans. All the same, the Laurier Liberals were more acceptable than a Union government.

Support from Bourassa, however limited, had a negative effect on Laurier's campaign in English Canada. The *Globe* in Toronto on

November 13 declared Bourassa a dictator and speculated that, if the Liberals won, Bourassa would be named to cabinet: "A vote for Laurier is a vote for Bourassa is a vote for the Kaiser," ran the slogan.[54] It became so serious an issue that Laurier had to ask Bourassa, this time via MP Athanase David (the son of his old friend Senator Laurent-Olivier David), to attack the Liberals in *Le Devoir* so as to show that there was no formal association between them.[55]

Laurier, despite his obvious advantages, still had a few Quebec political headaches, and he wrote to a Montreal friend that "an immediate triumph is doubtful."[56] Many ridings in Montreal — Hochelaga, St. Lawrence, St. Antoine — still did not have candidates.[57] The fact that the Unionists were having difficulty finding candidates to run was encouraging, but, in the first week of November, nothing could be taken for granted. Laurier hoped that Lt.-Col. F.W. Hibbard would run in St. Lawrence, but Hibbard could not square his pro-conscriptionist views with Laurier's position.[58] Robert Bickerdike, the long-standing Liberal MP for St. Lawrence in Montreal, also announced that he would not run again — he wanted to devote himself exclusively to the social reforms he favoured.[59] This created a real challenge for the Liberal organization, as Conservative Charles Ballantyne would now have an advantage in the profoundly anglophone — and likely Unionist-leaning — riding. St. Anne was also a problem: Laurier wanted to see Charles Doherty defeated and was likely relieved when John James Guerin, the former mayor of Montreal, finally announced that he would challenge the Unionist in that riding. The situation became more complicated when a rump group of Liberals also nominated Daniel Gallery, an experienced former city councillor and provincial politician who had consistently voted in favour of progressive policies, in the city or in the capital.[60] That could divide the Liberal vote, paving the way for Doherty. More optimistically, Samuel Jacobs, a rare Jewish Liberal candidate, reported in early November that he felt bullish that he could carry the riding of George-Étienne-Cartier.[61]

By November 16, Senator Philippe Casgrain — who had travelled across the province to organize a number of ridings — could report to Laurier that the Liberal list was almost complete. He was particularly happy to have found candidates to oppose Unionist heavyweights

Ballantyne and Herbert Ames in Montreal. "What a change in ten days!" he enthused.[62]

There were still a few holes in the Liberal electoral list, however, and Laurier himself was being pressured to run, in many ridings. "The news from everywhere is good," he wrote Lucien Cannon, "but not as good as you seem to believe. The idea that I would be a candidate where there is no Liberal candidacy does not please me at all, and I don't believe it would be a good tactic."[63] Laurier decided to run in both Quebec-East and Ottawa. Rodolphe Lemieux was nominated in both Maisonneuve and Gaspé.

On nomination day, November 19, twelve Liberals were already elected by acclamation. Two days later, when the Unionist candidates withdrew, Laval–Deux-Montagnes and St-Jacques in Montreal were declared for the Liberals. Within a few more days, Liberals won seventeen seats without contest in all parts of the province, from the Beauce, Kamouraska, and Drummond-Arthabasca on the South Shore, to Trois-Rivières/St-Maurice, Hull, and Labelle on the Western Shore, to Rimouski in the North, and in Montreal. Seven Liberals running for the first time in 1917 were elected by acclamation (Emmanuel D'Anjou in Rimouski, Hermas Deslaurier in St. Mary/Montreal, Joseph-Fernand Fafard in L'Islet, Joseph-Éloi Fontaine in Hull, Adélard Fortier in Labelle, Jules-Édouard Prévost in Terrebonne, and Arthur Trahan in Nicolet). Another, and surely the most bizarre case of a Liberal acclamation, was Louis-Joseph Papineau in Beauharnois. He had first been elected as a Liberal in 1908, but jumped on the Borden bandwagon in 1911 and was then elected. He decided to return to the Liberals in 1917 and was acclaimed. Clearly, the name mattered more than the label in this case.

Deaf to his brother's admonitions and putting aside family traditions, Maréchal Nantel campaigned for the Liberals against Albert Sévigny in the riding of Westmount–St. Henri. "I'm taken more than ever by the election campaign, and I did not need to tell you who I work for," he confessed to his brother. "We differ in opinion on it. It is useless now that you had to vote to try to change the decision, but whatever the position taken on the policy, it does not prevent me to be for you the devoted and loving brother, and I will continue to do for you everything I can to get to your desires and make you happy.[64]

"This is a nationalist cause," Nantel declared publicly, arguing that only Sir Wilfrid could protect French Canada's "traditions, principles and liberty."[65] Nantel was an attractive and eloquent speaker, and was

Eugène Nantel (right) and his sister Alphonsine Nantel (left), Christmas 1917, Paris.

asked to speak in other ridings, including at the Salle Querbes in the Laurier-Outremont riding on December 9.[66]

Neither party leader needed to spend much time in Quebec during the campaign, but for opposite reasons. For Borden, the Unionist cause was lost and there was no compelling reason to devote much attention or spend much time in the province. For Laurier, victory was assured, and for much of the rest of the campaign he was out of the province, focusing on western Canada. He could be confident of success in Quebec and in any ridings where pockets of French Canadians held a balance of power.

In western Canada, francophones were worried. On December 10, at an event designed to blunt Laurier's own giant rally in Winnipeg, the Unionists organized a banquet for the visit of the Duke of Devonshire, the governor general. At that dinner, Archbishop Sinnott of Winnipeg declared that Canada was prepared to send "more men, and still more men" to support the war effort. Mgr. Béliveau, the archbishop of St. Boniface, wrote to Bourassa to relay his disappointment, and sadly noted that there were evidently politics involved. For him, Sinnott's remarks showed how part of the Catholic Church was imperialist. Béliveau's letter arrived in Bourassa's office with the seal of the envelope broken and with the stamp itself upside down. Omer Héroux, Le Devoir's associate editor, wrote a note on the envelope, questioning how such things could have happened. He suspected that the mail had been tampered with by the federal police.

Bourassa responded, two days before the election, that he hesitated to criticize Sinnott's remarks. He was resigned, after years of trying to get Church leaders to stop supporting the war effort, to go no further. He responded to Béliveau that both the Montreal and Toronto archbishops were already angry with him. Bourassa was confident that many bishops supported him; some had even told him that Le Devoir had all their approval. "But all that is secret," he lamented. "What is left for the public is that I deserve to be censored or even denounced in the name of the Church."[67] Bourassa admitted being a little bitter. He had served as stalking horse for a long time, but did not want to run all the risks associated with being branded as hostile to Canadian interests. "I'm starting to understand what I can expect from people who wish to do me harm and also, unfortunately, to start doubting what could be expected from those who say they wish me well."[68]

When the polls opened on the morning of December 17, it was clear that the campaign had hardly changed any minds in French Canada since that day in September when Senator Dandurand had tried to explain his point of view in the boardroom of the Sun Life Company. French Canada would fight only to defend the country, and there was no indication that a Union government was going to convince French Canada that it must go beyond its borders. Judging by the performance of the politicians, French Canada felt isolated, coast to coast. Borden did not speak to it; Laurier's voice was drowned out.

8

THE CAMPAIGN: ENGLISH CANADA

"Those detestable anti-conscriptionists are doing their best to give Canada a bad name. The feeling here is very bitter against Quebec. [I will vote] on the right side, with those who are trying to keep Canada in the proud position in which her army has placed her, and against those traitors who would drag them from that position, and have her dishonoured for all time."

— Lester B. Pearson, December 4, 1917[1]

Any hopes that Sir Robert Borden might have had that the formation of a Union government would prompt the creation of a national Union Party were left unfulfilled. In New Brunswick, Frank Carvell had difficulty, despite his best efforts to be fair, in overcoming the traditional antagonism between the two established parties. In Nova Scotia, the provincial Liberal organization backed the Unionists but was not above making deals with former Liberal associates to ensure Liberal victories in several ridings. Borden himself stepped aside in safe Halifax to give his seat to Liberal-Unionist A.K. Maclean, and another riding was opened for W.S. Fielding. In none of the three Maritime provinces did a full Union organization appear. A similar situation existed in the West, where the Liberal formations went over to the Union cause but did not unite with the Conservatives. While there were efforts in some provinces, such as Saskatchewan, to collaborate, relatively little effective co-operation went beyond an agreement to divide up the seats along fairly equal partisan lines. In British Columbia, where the Conservatives had swept the province in 1911, there was friction between the Liberal- and Conservative-Unionists that continued until election day.[2] This situation had long-term implications for the future of a new party, but did not seriously derail the Union campaign in 1917.

In all cases, the Unionists were helped by widespread public support for their cause, meaning that despite the lack of a united and focused political organization they could still mount a successful campaign. In Toronto, for example, there was an embarrassment of riches in that virtually every candidate — on both sides — supported conscription. There were the Union candidates, who backed the government, of course, and the other candidates, whose opposition was not specifically against conscription but rather the way it was being implemented, or that it needed to be combined with the conscription of wealth. Just about everyone was distancing themselves from Laurier; Liberal E.C. Drury, running outside Toronto in Simcoe North, publicly announced that he had neither asked for nor wanted Laurier's endorsement.[3] Support for conscription was solid; the problem was to remind voters, as the *Mail and Empire* did on election day, that "there is only one Union Government candidate in your riding."[4]

Problems arose almost immediately about the selection of riding candidates, particularly in Ontario. Borden received a steady stream of letters with questions about party policy or requesting his support in a particular riding. The Ontario riding of Kent, Borden was informed, wanted a straight Conservative to run — they claimed they would not accept what they called a "Win-the-war Liberal" as nominee.[5] Another Conservative requested Borden's confirmation that he would be the candidate and not have to go through another selection process as a Unionist.[6] In yet another riding, the Conservative nominee had already resigned and expected to be selected as the Union candidate, but there was also a Liberal-Unionist who expected the same.[7] Who should get the nomination? The Ontario Liberals had their own ideas as well, and insisted that they be allowed to select up to twenty-three or twenty-four Ontario Unionist candidates. Rowell, Frank Carvell, and Fred Pardee pressed their views on J.D. Reid, Borden's trusted minister of railways and the party's manager, and even presented him with a list of the ridings that the Liberals wanted. They also demanded that some Liberal-Unionist candidates be selected at *Liberal* conventions. For Reid, it was all a little too much; at one point the Liberals demanded that a riding be set aside for George Graham. Graham supported conscription but had been sitting on the fence for weeks; he had recently been seen at Laurier gatherings and supporting Laurier's candidates. To find this man a seat, Reid reported to Borden, was "an absolutely ridiculous proposition."[8]

The selection-of-candidates headache would continue through much of the election campaign. It was essential to find good individuals, and imperative that the nomination contests not ruin the Union's election chances in any riding. If the Conservatives and Liberal-Unionists could not agree on a candidate in a particular riding, it might even open up a three-way race, with two pro-conscription candidates running against a Laurier Liberal. That could split the vote and let the Laurier candidate win. To calm things down, Borden issued a statement that sitting MPs of both parties would receive the nomination, provided they demonstrated support for the government and its conscription policy. It was a logical proposition and it gave a great advantage to the Conservatives, thanks to their large parliamentary majority. In other constituencies, government supporters should get together to settle on a suitable candidate. Problems would be dealt with as they arose, and Borden placed Reid and Rowell in charge of Ontario, Meighen and Calder in the West, and himself and Carvell in the Maritimes.[9] Nothing was said about it, but it did not seem necessary to appoint anyone to handle Quebec.

Despite Borden's declaration on the selection of candidates, there were important problems. "The turmoil usual to election is accentuated by the difficulty of adjusting seats between Union Liberals and Conservatives," Sir George Foster wrote in his diary. "The former naturally wish to get as many as possible so as to strengthen the dissidents as against [the] Laurier Liberals. Old Cons. Members who have been true to Union and Conscription do not think it fair to be turned down for new Liberal aspirants."[10]

Newton Rowell had brought much of the provincial Liberal organization with him into the Union government, making him the leading voice for Ontario Liberals there, but, as in the rest of the country there was little unity between the two parties. Rowell and Reid had their differences on the division of the ridings, especially concerning how many Liberal-Unionist seats there should be. Many Conservatives argued that in the present Parliament the Liberals had only twelve of Ontario's eighty-two seats and therefore did not deserve more now, especially if in the process they would be squeezing out a sitting — and faithful — Conservative. Liberal-Unionists were not happy about the situation, either. "It seems almost impossible to get the parties together," Rowell wrote to A.B. Hudson in Winnipeg, "and the overwhelming preponderance of the Conservative representation from Ontario in the last Parliament has made it extremely difficult to get any adequate Liberal-Unionist representation in the new parliament."[11]

Rowell's papers are filled with correspondence from party members and potential candidates involved in candidate selection. Rowell struggled with Reid to secure as many ridings as possible for the Liberal-Unionists, and tried to arrange joint conventions for members of both parties to select the Union candidates. But in many ridings things unfolded in their own ways. In the riding of Wentworth, the joint efforts deteriorated into confusion when the Liberal-Unionists passed a resolution excluding the sitting (Conservative) MP from consideration.[12] In Oxford South, the Conservative-Unionists refused to negotiate with the Liberal-Unionists and renominated the sitting MP. Rowell responded to those complaints by reminding the Liberal-Unionists that it had been agreed that a sitting MP was to be given priority.[13] But in Oxford North it was a different situation; the Liberal MP had not come out strongly in support of the Union government, but as the sitting MP he, too, was granted the Union nomination and this upset some of the Conservatives.[14] Even Rowell had trouble finding a seat. He had hoped to be chosen for a Toronto riding, but "at last had to give it up," wrote one Liberal observer.[15] Every Conservative riding association in Toronto refused him as a candidate and threatened to challenge him with a straight Conservative if he chose to run. Ultimately, he was found a riding in Durham County, but only after the existing Conservative agreed to retire in return for a promise of a Senate appointment.[16]

In the ridings of Brantford and Brant, the situation descended into farce. In Brantford, both groups selected a Unionist candidate, but

Rowell and Reid decided that the Conservative-Unionist — Lt-Col. W.F. Cockshutt — should be the candidate. The Liberal-Unionist candidate withdrew, as expected. Next door, in Brant, it was to be a Liberal-Unionist, but the Conservative-Unionist candidate — Harry Cockshutt (brother of W.F. Cockshutt) — refused to withdraw.

It turned out that Borden had already given Harry his endorsement — but now the party leaders were trying to nominate John Harold.[17] Borden approached W.F. Cockshutt in an effort to have him use his influence on his brother to withdraw. "The Liberal Unionists are exasperated," he wrote, "by their feeling that in Brant the Conservatives are not playing the game fairly."[18] But Harry Cockshutt would not budge. Three days before the election Borden gave up. "I have twice in the strongest terms asked Cockshutt to withdraw but without success. Fear that I cannot do anything further."[19]

An exasperated Rowell became increasingly anxious about the continuing rancour. "The evidence increases every day of the feeling, particularly in rural communities and in Labour centres, against compulsory military service, and the Union Government is fighting for its life," he explained to one colleague. "Under these circumstances it is of the utmost importance that the friends of Union Government should not fight each other, but should work together and unite in support of Union Government candidates."[20]

Borden, Reid, and others shared Rowell's concerns, and near the end of November the prime minister brought Sir Clifford Sifton to Ottawa to discuss the situation. Sifton agreed that the "position in Ontario [was] very dangerous and that there is no effective headquarters organization." In consultation with Rowell, Borden asked Sifton to take charge of the Ontario campaign.[21] In particular, Sifton would be left to handle disputes over candidate duplication in the ridings. Borden's great trust in Sifton's judgment and organizing abilities was not widely shared, and some cabinet ministers, including Sir George Foster, questioned bringing him in. The man was unpopular everywhere in the party, among older Conservatives who still suspected his Liberal sympathies, and with the new Liberal-Unionists, especially those from the West. But Borden had already made up his mind, telling Foster that the government "would be defeated unless active steps taken."[22] Sifton was now in charge, with only a little over three weeks left before election day.

Sifton arrived in Toronto on December 3 and moved into a room on the top floor of the King Edward Hotel. Main Johnson, Rowell's private secretary, was sent to make arrangements for the campaign, meeting Sifton for the first time. His immediate reaction was that Sifton looked just like the German kaiser: "the resemblance was unmistakable, uncanny and inescapable," he wrote. Sifton was sitting alone in the room; "this was a rather queer introduction," Johnson recorded. Sifton, who was practically deaf, "picked up from the table what appeared to be a piece of garden hose: put one end into his ear, and handed the other to me."

Sifton complained of the disorganization in the Union campaign, how there was no direction and no leadership. There had been some thought of Sifton moving into a more public location but Johnson conveyed Rowell's suggestion that, because Sifton was so unpopular, especially in the West — and because there were even charges that the whole Union government "was a Sifton creation" — that he should probably stay holed up in the hotel and maintain a very low profile.[23] There would be no rallies or speeches; only a campaign of advice. Sifton took the suggestion well, and agreed, continuing to work from the hotel for the rest of the campaign.

The Liberals also needed to organize, or to save as much of their organization as possible. For Laurier, keeping the party together became as important as winning the election. In what can only be seen as an act of desperation, he proposed that there could be three kinds of Liberals run in the campaign: those opposed to Union and conscription; those opposed to Union, but in favour of conscription; and a third group of "independent" Liberals who could represent other positions — that were not defined.[24]

It was only partially successful, as English-speaking Liberals continued to drop away over the following weeks. Union government "gave us our only chance of remaining in Public life," one Saskatchewan Liberal wrote Laurier, explaining why he could no longer be a Liberal candidate.[25] Laurier responded that he was disappointed, "but I have seen so many defections about me of late that I must put up with one more disappointment."[26]

The Liberal campaign was hindered by weak organization and difficulties in attracting and holding strong candidates. Special central committees were established to oversee the distribution of information, for finances, et cetera,[27] but on the ground in the individual ridings it was a different story. The organizations in many of the ridings had gone over to the Unionists or were hopelessly divided. One Toronto Liberal offered his assessment of the situation to Laurier; a once strong organization had been "rent asunder" and now it would be extremely difficult "to establish a successful organization, and it looks to me as though we will have to depend more or less upon individual work. If existing organizations, say in Toronto, were called together, it would mean division between the conscription and Laurier Liberals, while under present conditions neither side can make use of the existing organizations."[28]

Mackenzie King agreed, writing from Newmarket that "we are frightfully handicapped through lack of organization and the means wherewith to perfect it."[29] In Toronto, the Reform Association, with Liberal-Unionist Fred Pardee as vice-president, was no longer suitable and the Laurier-Liberals decided to create a new group — the Association of Liberals — to coordinate the Ontario campaign. Sir Allen Aylesworth agreed to be a member and to allow his name to be used on the new association's letterhead.[30]

Aylesworth's re-entry now, while welcomed by Laurier and others, highlighted the difficulties Liberals were facing in attracting high-profile individuals outside Quebec who remained loyal to Sir Wilfrid. There was still Frank Oliver in Alberta, and D.D. McKenzie and Ned Macdonald in Nova Scotia; but beyond that the leadership thinned out. William Pugsley was pro-conscription and defected, but he was so unpopular with New Brunswick Conservatives that he would not find a seat in a Union government. He was appointed lieutenant governor of the province. George Graham dithered so long between his loyalty to Laurier and his support for conscription and a coalition and that he was unable to find a seat under either party. Mackenzie King spoke in coded obscurities and kept close to his riding, refusing requests to accompany Laurier across the country. King was in a difficult position. After all, he had been out of the country for much of the war, he had no seat in Parliament, and he had not been pursued by Borden to join the Union government. But, as a supporter of conscription in a riding (York North) that was leaning toward the Union government, he wondered which way to turn. It was his love for Laurier that made it easier for him to remain a Liberal.

In Toronto West, lawyer Charles W. Kerr complained of the divisions in the riding and called for unity before resigning his position as president of the Liberal Association.[31] A new, rival Liberal organization was created, both camps nominated candidates, and a bitter dispute ensued. One Liberal ultimately agreed to withdraw and the other, Kerr, with Laurier's endorsement, became the Liberal candidate.[32] Laurier was sanguine; "everything will be alright," he wrote Kerr, but such squabbles were not uncommon.[33]

In Waterloo North, the situation was a little different in that the riding association's support for a pro-conscription candidate was challenged by W.D. Euler, an anti-conscriptionist who relied on "the Lutherans and the Catholics" and "the German vote."[34] Euler eventually secured the nomination to challenge the Conservative-Unionist, and sitting MP, William Weichel.

In York North, the Unionists approached the Liberal riding association with an offer to withdraw their candidate if the two groups could agree on a "win-the-war" candidate. But, before any agreement was made, the Conservatives met independently and selected a candidate of their own.[35] The Liberals stayed with Laurier, selecting Mackenzie King as their candidate. King knew he could count on considerable support from the rural areas, but organizing was needed in the towns of Aurora and Newmarket — "it is in these towns that our difficulty lies," he wrote.[36]

In Lincoln, the riding containing St. Catharines, Edwin Lovelace, who had been endorsed by Laurier, faced a stiff challenge from the president of the riding association, who wanted a Liberal-Unionist candidate. Lovelace ultimately secured the nomination.[37] A similar situation appeared in Simcoe North when the majority of the riding executive came out in support of the Union government; E.C. Drury kept the nomination, running as an Independent Liberal, and paid his own campaign expenses.[38] Conversely, the Laurier Liberals were determined to challenge the turncoat and Liberal-Unionist Hugh Guthrie in the riding of South Wellington, but at the last minute J.W. Oakes, the Liberal candidate, withdrew his name from the nomination. Charges of wrongdoing were raised but little action taken and, as a result, the Liberals fielded a candidate who had the approval of the local labour authorities.[39]

Reports from the Maritimes suggested that there were fewer nomination problems, but difficulties persisted. The defection of Frank Carvell, W.S. Fielding, and A.K. Maclean was a serious blow to the party organization, but many riding associations continued to back Laurier. "Straight Liberals" were contesting every seat in New Brunswick, reported A.B. Copp from Sackville. "The whole party are united and working harmoniously."[40]

In Nova Scotia, it was the same. "There is no question as to Nova Scotia's attitude," Ned Macdonald reported to Laurier. "The feeling against Union Government is most intense." He predicted that the Liberals would do well both in Nova Scotia and Prince Edward Island. As for his own seat in Pictou, Macdonald added, "I declared myself as a straight Laurier man with no apologies to offer for my position and received the greatest ovation I ever had here." But he had decided to step aside in favour of Robert MacKay, another Laurier Liberal and member of the provincial legislature. "To run to the end would mean my defeat by a man whom as a Scotchman I would never submit to be defeated by. Reid and Cochrane are after me and between money and soldiers' votes they would do it, so I would not run."[41] It was an enormous blow to Laurier; "you cannot give up public life," he responded. But Macdonald — a good colleague and supporter and another important Maritime Liberal — was out.[42]

The upheaval for the Liberals was perhaps greatest in the West, where the Union government could now boast three heavyweight Liberal-Unionist cabinet members: Crerar, Calder, and Arthur Sifton. Crerar and Calder, joined by Arthur Meighen, staged a huge Union rally in Winnipeg near the end of October (and a second one, days later, in Regina), attracting some five thousand men and women. The Liberals tried to play it down — there was "no enthusiasm" one wrote;[43] another reported that those who attended "came away as puzzled as ever"[44] — but it was hard not to be anxious about Liberal chances in the West. "I can only assure you," one Manitoban Liberal wrote Laurier, "that we are taking care of it to the best advantage."[45]

There was some room for optimism on a riding-by-riding basis, especially in the ones with large francophone and Catholic populations. In some counties, Union supporters were dropped from the riding executives, and in several constituencies the Liberal candidates could expect to face a Liberal-Unionist opponent rather than a "straight" Conservative.[46] "The desire for conscription is strong," reported William Donovan, a Winnipeg lawyer and Liberal organizer, "but coupled with this desire amongst all democratic Liberals is a desire for better co-operation from the wealth of the nation, and grave doubt that the present Fusion Government will be able to accomplish this."[47] In the end the results were mixed. In two ridings, Dauphin and Nelson, the government candidates were acclaimed; in Winnipeg, the Liberals supported two Labour candidates; in the rest of the province they had one doctor, two lawyers, one miller, a soldier, two financial agents, and four farmers as candidates. "I believe that they are uniformly good men," Donovan reported, "and three of the farmers are strong in their own districts."[48]

The situation was even worse further west, where in several ridings no candidates could be found. In both Alberta and Saskatchewan, the provincial governments supported Union government. In Alberta, the fiercely partisan Frank Oliver could count on the support of only a few provincial ministers.[49] In Saskatchewan, there was no organization at all. The government candidates, one Saskatchewan Liberal complained to Oliver, "will have the solid support of the Tories, plus the support of a very substantial number of the other side, and added to this they would reap the benefit of all the nefarious election machinery which the Borden Government recently enacted."[50] To Laurier he was equally gloomy: "So far as organization goes Calder is the whole thing and his going and the acquiescence of the Provincial Government have left us high and dry."[51]

Laurier could offer little advice, responding: "Saskatchewan seems to me the weakest spot from the Liberal point of view between the two oceans."[52]

In British Columbia the Liberals remained hopeful, although in a couple of ridings the candidates had either come out in favour of a win-the-war platform or had decided to run as independent Liberals. "The people at heart are with you," one Liberal reported to Laurier, "and only need a little encouragement to get up their enthusiasm and turn out and work as they will have to return friends from this Province. The lines are gradually being drawn, and, we will have very nearly a straight party fight in each of the B.C. Ridings."[53] The voters will have "a chance of pronouncing judgement," another Liberal explained. Unfortunately, "the other side has all the funds."[54]

There was also a degree of unofficial coexistence between Liberals and many Labour candidates, although the extent of co-operation varied from riding to riding. Organized labour had been hit hard by the war; increased prices had outdistanced wage increases, making it harder for working families to survive. There was also a growing sense that workers had been called upon to make great sacrifices for the war effort, while the business class and their friends in government had reaped most of the rewards. Sir Joseph Flavelle, Borden's friend and supporter and chair of the Imperial Munitions Board (IMB), was a particular target for labour protest, thanks to the IMB's unfriendly labour practices. As the war progressed, labour radicalism increased, and, by 1917, conscription had emerged as a serious point of disagreement. Various labour groups in English Canada began to advocate direct political action.[55] The Trades and Labour Council opposed conscription, and the passage of the Military Service Act was followed by resolutions of protest from labour councils in Victoria, Vancouver, Lethbridge, Calgary, Winnipeg, Ottawa, Toronto, and elsewhere. Independent labour parties appeared in several cities and put forward candidates under various party labels. These labour parties advocated co-operation with other groups, including socialist and farmers' parties.[56]

By November there were labour candidates in some twenty-seven ridings. There was little in the way of a national labour party, but many of these candidates were endorsed by the fledgling Canadian Labour Party. In some cases they turned the campaign into a three-way race; in many other ridings the Labour candidates were supported, or at least unopposed, by the Liberals — in Ontario such ridings included Toronto East, Port Arthur and Kenora, and Fort William. In Hamilton West, Walter Rollo, president of the Hamilton Independent Labour Party, ran as a Labour candidate against a Liberal and a Unionist; next door, however, in Hamilton East, Labour candidate George Halerow ran unopposed by the Liberals. In Timiskaming, Ontario, Arthur Roebuck ran as a Liberal/Labour candidate. One Labour candidate also ran as a Unionist: in Nipissing, Ontario, Charles Harrison was endorsed by the Independent Labour Party but chose to run under the Union banner.[57]

Labour representatives had been invited to the August Liberal Convention in Winnipeg (although none attended) and there were enough planks in the Liberal platform to appeal to Labour voters. Given the weakness of the Liberal campaign in the West, a "marriage of convenience" with the Labour candidates was struck in three western ridings.[58] In Lethbridge, for example, when farmer and labour groups came together to nominate L. Lambert Pack to oppose the Liberal-Unionist William Buchanan, the original Liberal candidate withdrew.[59] Nationally, eight candidates ran under the official "Lib-Lab" banner: two in Alberta, one in Saskatchewan, and five in Ontario. All the Labour and "Lib-Lab" candidates faced an uphill struggle, even to convince their own fellow members to vote for them. To make matters worse, Samuel Gompers, the well-known president of the American Federation of Labor, came to Canada during the campaign and spoke in favour of conscription and the war effort. Of all the Labour candidates selected, only the Unionist Harrison won.

Many of these riding disputes and concerns landed on Laurier's desk, with requests for his help or advice. "On account of the desertion of so many friends," he wrote, "a lot of work has been placed upon my shoulders, work to which I never attended before."[60] The old leader's energy was waning and he wasn't always sure of what to do. "There is some trouble in some ridings in Toronto," he confessed to one supporter, "and I am a little in a quandary as to whom we should endorse. Can you give me any advice on this."[61] On another occasion he wrote: "whom should I support in Brant, Harold or Dore, and North Wellington, Hazlewood or McEwing."[62] He remained optimistic and hopeful, at least in his correspondence, but realistic as well. When one Ontario Liberal wrote that he was confident that many Liberals would be returned to Ottawa on December 17, Laurier agreed. "It is quite possible," he responded, "that there will be a good number of Liberals in next House from Ontario, but I am afraid that most of them will be lined behind the government."[63]

* * *

Sir Robert Borden's campaign was split between the Maritimes and Ontario. In the latter, he shared with Newton Rowell the burden of campaigning; in the former, more of the load fell on his shoulders, as he faced a less united team. The Maritime provinces were a large question mark for Borden and the Union government. Newspaper opinion was more divided than in Toronto or the West. The large Acadian population, especially in New Brunswick, was generally supportive of the war effort but generally cool to conscription, and their numbers were sufficient to ensure close races in several ridings. All three provincial premiers backed the Union government but none was willing to campaign for it vigorously. In Nova Scotia, Liberal premier George Murray had flirted with joining the Union government but got cold feet at the last minute; in New Brunswick, a new Liberal provincial government, under W.E. Forster, was elected earlier that year thanks to wide Acadian support. Only in P.E.I. was there a Conservative government, but it was now with a new premier, Aubin-Edmond Arsenault, who was the first Acadian premier in the island's history.[64]

There were also problems of integrating Liberals and Conservatives into a new party in a region where party loyalties remained strong. Borden was forced to intervene in a couple of riding disputes, in particular to ensure that the Conservatives in Victoria-Carleton did not, as they threatened to do, select a candidate of their own to run against Liberal-Unionist Frank Carvell. He acted in a similar way to ensure that W.S. Fielding was not challenged by a "straight Conservative" in Queen's-Shelburne. Plus, A.K. Maclean was to turn out to be less impressive than expected, at least in Borden's estimation: he was "quite incapable of making up his mind," Borden wrote, and "when he does make it up he soon changes it."[65] A few days later he wrote in his diary: "Fielding acting very badly."[66] Again it was a reminder of just how shallow were the roots of this new Union Party.

His first tour of the Maritimes began with a large meeting in Halifax on November 14. It was considered an enormous success with an estimated four or five thousand men and women gathered at the Market Hall to witness the nomination of Liberal-Unionist A.K. Maclean in Borden's old riding. The *Halifax Herald* called it the "most wonderful meeting in all the 168 years of the history of Halifax."[67]

Borden spoke first and hammered away at the major themes of his campaign: the need for Union government, the need to win the war, and the need for all Canadians to work together. People of different political backgrounds had come together and put aside their differences to work united in a common cause. "What has brought this about," he said, "is a regenerating sense of the national peril, a clear vision of the national destinies involved, a compelling conviction that the future of this Dominion, of the Britannic commonwealth, yes, of the world itself, is at stake."[68]

As a demonstration of the point, he was followed by Maclean, who explained why he had left the Liberal Party and now stood before the people as a member of the Union government. Picking up on this, Borden played on another theme in the campaign — stressing that a Union government could have better prosecuted the war if the Liberals had agreed to an extension but, since they had refused, that it was Laurier who bore the blame for distracting the nation from the war: he had forced this unnecessary election on the Canadian people.

Borden's short tour of the region shifted from Halifax to Sydney, Nova Scotia, where he held another mass meeting on November 16, and then on through the rest of the Maritimes. Each day was a blend of travel, meetings and interviews, and speeches at rallies, usually with the local candidates at his side. The highlight, at least in Borden's diary, came in Sydney when Conservative Senator George Lynch-Staunton rallied the crowd with a fine speech. When he called on all supporters to "render unto Caesar the things that are Caesar's," before he could finish the quotation he was interrupted by a drunken Union supporter who yelled out "and unto Borden the things that are Borden's."[69] By November 18, Borden was back in Ottawa, preparing to launch his Ontario campaign.[70]

In the West, oversight of the campaign fell to Meighen, Crerar, Calder, and Sifton. Meighen and Calder were responsible for dividing up the constituencies, and they agreed to an even split between Liberal and Conservative-Unionists (in fact, the Conservatives wound up with a majority of the ridings). Following the large rallies in Winnipeg and

Regina in late October, Meighen went alone further west to Saskatoon, Edmonton, Calgary, and Vancouver. He returned to Manitoba in early November and toured the province with Premier T.C. Norris. He then left for a second tour of the West and, in fact, was in Vancouver on election day.[71] Like Meighen, Crerar had a relatively safe Manitoba seat, which enabled him to travel to help the campaign in other provinces, including Ontario. For Crerar, however, the "great danger in the Constituency is overconfidence. It is not sufficient to have a majority. We want the verdict as unmistakably emphatic as it is possible to make it."[72]

The western Unionists could count on the strong support of the western press and, in particular, found a steadfast ally in J.W. Dafoe and the *Manitoba Free Press*, the most influential newspaper in western Canada. Throughout the campaign, the *Free Press* published endless articles supporting Union, playing up and reprinting speeches by prominent Unionists, giving wide coverage to their meetings and rallies. At the same time, there was critical coverage of Laurier and the Liberals, of Bourassa and Quebec generally, and articles refuting the arguments made by opposition candidates.[73]

One candidate that Borden did not have in the West was R.B. Bennett. Bennett had been the only Conservative elected in Alberta in 1911, but, as we saw in chapter 5, his relationship with Borden had soured. Late in the summer of 1917, Bennett met with the prime minister and told him that he had decided not to run in the approaching election, but that he hoped he would be appointed to the Senate. The two Senate appointments for Alberta were unfilled and Bennett was a logical choice, and he left the meeting believing that he had Borden's support and promise. But Bennett could not keep his distaste for the Union government to himself and his blistering attack on the coalition just prior to the dissolution of Parliament likely destroyed whatever chance he had of a senatorship.[74] He returned to Calgary and campaigned for the Union government, but then wandered in a political wilderness until the late 1920s. "Bonfire Bennett" was one candidate Borden didn't seem to miss.

Another future western prime minister, John Diefenbaker, made his federal political debut in Saskatchewan. Diefenbaker had enlisted in the CEF and made it to England as a lieutenant in the 1st Canadian

Mounted Rifles, but, under somewhat mysterious circumstances, was declared medically unfit to serve and returned to Canada early in 1917. He restarted his law career and actively campaigned for J.R. Wilson, the Union candidate in Saskatoon, even though the young Diefenbaker reportedly opposed the Wartime Elections Act and was later quite critical of Arthur Meighen for his manipulation of the soldier vote. His campaign speeches were short, Diefenbaker recalled in his memoirs. "I tried to memorize what I was to say. Not having anything approaching a photographic memory, I failed."[75]

In Ontario, the Union campaign kicked off in Hamilton on November 2, with a big rally sponsored by the Win-the-War League. Frank Carvell travelled up from New Brunswick to stand with Newton Rowell and General Mewburn in a show of solidarity with his fellow Liberal-Unionists. The auditorium of the Royal Connaught Hotel was filled with men — and with "ladies busily engaged on patriotic knitting." Rowell spoke last and "appealed to Ontario Liberalism to be big and manly and patriotic in the existing crisis." He called on those who had come from all across the province to "surrender your party prejudices, but not your principles, for the sake of our boys at the front."[76] Similar rallies followed in other parts of the province, and Rowell, in particular, was a frequent speaker. He toured northern Ontario with Premier Hearst and accompanied the prime minister on most of his campaign stops. But the Union campaign sometimes made for strange bedfellows. In Temiskaming, for example, he found himself in an awkward situation sharing the stage with fellow Unionist Frank Cochrane, a former opponent with whom he had often clashed. At the same time, Cochrane's opponent was the "Lib-Lab" candidate Arthur Roebuck, who had been a vigorous Rowell supporter in the previous provincial election and a man whose views were similar to Rowell's on many of the pressing issues.[77] But these were unusual times.

Borden arrived in Toronto to launch the Ontario leg of his campaign with a giant rally at Massey Hall on November 22. From Toronto he travelled to ridings in London, Kitchener, Renfrew, and Milton, and to Mackenzie King's riding of York North. He spoke with Rowell and various other candidates at his side, including such Liberal-Unionists as T.A.

Crerar and Charles Ballantyne. He also shared the stage on one occasion with Sir Sam Hughes, but only after his former minister of militia finally declared his support for the Union government. Borden rose to cries of "Borden's the man for us!"[78] In all locations the message was the same: the choice for Canadians was between fighting to the end and quitting. "This makes 19 meetings in one week," an exhilarated Borden wrote in his diary, "but not greatly fatigued."[79]

Only in Kitchener did trouble erupt. Borden was scheduled to speak at the town's skating rink, which could hold some six thousand people, on November 24. Kitchener had changed its name from Berlin only the year before, and anti-conscription feelings ran high. An anti-conscription mob (young men, "many of them German descent and military age" according to the *Globe*) paraded through the streets in the early evening and, after clashing with a few returned soldiers, descended on the packed arena to disrupt the proceedings. Borden took the stage escorted by a group of wounded veterans and had received a bouquet of flowers from "a lassie in Highland dress," when the mob began chanting "Down with conscription!" and "We want Laurier!"

Union supporters responded with their own taunts of "O, you yellow-backs!" and "Slackers!"

W.G. Weichel, the sitting MP and Unionist candidate, pointed to all the reporters in attendance and shouted: "this will go from Atlantic to Pacific — that you have insulted the Prime Minister of Canada." But that didn't help, and with yells, chants, whistles, and foot stomping the crowd refused to let Borden speak. For many who read about the event in their newspapers the following day it likely only confirmed their views about anti-conscriptionist slackers and traitors. The *Halifax Herald*, for example, asked if this was "another deliberate plot to murder" Borden?[80] To make matters worse, the Kitchener town council debated, and at first refused to apologize for the mob's action.[81]

The uproar in Kitchener only added to the growing concern shared by Borden, Rowell, Sifton, Reid, and others that the campaign in Ontario was not going as smoothly as they had hoped. There were many causes for this concern. There were the problems that arose from the weak organization in Ontario and the lingering debates over the

Are the Slackers in Quebec to rule Canada?

A vote against
the Government
means—   **YES**

A vote for
the Government
means—   **NO**

Printed and Published by THE HAYCOCK-CADLE CO., Neate Street, Camberwell, London, S.E. 5

Are the Slackers in Quebec to Rule Canada? A Union campaign poster (1917).

selection of candidates, and there was considerable public consternation over the apparent failure in implementing the Military Service Act
with all the requests for exemptions. And while those at home seemed
unwilling to fight, the newspaper lists containing the names of the
fallen at Passchendaele were growing longer by the day.[82] There were,
as well, questions about the strength of the opposition to conscription
— if hundreds of thousands of young people were trying to stay out
of the army and were willing to demonstrate against it, how would
they vote on the issue? Combining these factors with the continuing
personal popularity of Laurier in English Canada, the soft support for
Union government in the Maritimes, and the solid block of opposition
in Quebec, the Unionists believed they had reason to worry.

The greatest worry, however, was in rural Ontario, where anti-
conscription feelings mixed with fears over depopulation and the growing
demands to increase food production. The rural vote was over-represented
in Ontario, so, although the population was split fairly evenly between
rural and urban, some fifty of the eighty-two Ontario ridings were still
considered rural.[83] And the farmers of Ontario (and many in the West,
too) balked at allowing their sons to be conscripted; better for them to do
their patriotic duty at home — growing the food to feed the Empire. Even
though under the Military Service Act a farmer's son could be granted
an exemption as an essential worker, it did not always turn out that way;
and there were complaints that, while the Quebec tribunals were granting
exemptions to almost everyone, the ones in Ontario were much stricter.
It didn't seem fair. The Union government was going to lose the election, one Toronto supporter wrote, because the Military Service Act was
allowing more Quebeckers to shirk their duty while forcing the sons of
Ontario farmers into military service. "You cannot fool our shrewd hard
headed present-day farming community," he warned.[84]

On November 19, Borden wrote in his diary that Reid informed him
"as to situation in Ontario. He says Laurierites have large funds and are
putting up big fight."[85]

The evening before the Kitchener fiasco Borden added: "Difficulty
reported as to sentiment of farmers re conscription. They want to retain
their sons, increase their production and get good prices."[86]

The Unionists felt something needed to be done. Sifton, for one, insisted that Borden take action to calm this rural unrest.[87] On November 24, in Dundas, Ontario, General Mewburn, the minister of militia and defence, announced that all farmers' sons would be exempted from conscription. "Mewburn's pledge," as it came to be known, was made official by Order-in-Council on December 2. All farmers called up in the first group "who are actually employed on a farm in the production of foodstuffs and whose services are necessary in the work of such farm" would be released from military service, provided they continued to work on their farms.[88] It was a popular move within the rural communities. With one stroke the Unionists had swept aside the biggest obstacle to complete victory in Ontario.

In hindsight, the Order-in-Council appears as another political manipulation by Borden's government to ensure its victory; the charge was even made at the time, and was hardly denied by the government. What is striking is how precarious the Unionists believed their position to be, when all indications suggested that they were heading for success even without such manipulation. Winning the election was everything — an absolute necessity. It is hard to believe that Newton Rowell was referring to a Canadian election when he wrote two days after the issuance of the Order-in-Council that "the interests of civilization are hanging in the balance." In extreme times extreme measures were justifiable. "I have no hesitation in saying that I believe the defeat of the Union Government would be a national calamity," he added, while a "return to power of a party pledged to suspend the operation of the Military Service Act would mean Canada's dropping out of the war."[89] It may not have saved civilization, but the measure made it easier for rural Ontarians to vote Union, and Borden could draw some satisfaction from that as he wound up his Ontario tour and returned to Ottawa.

Laurier spent most of the early campaign in Quebec and the Ottawa area, making relatively few speeches. At a big rally at Ottawa's Russell Theatre on November 27 he spoke to a packed house alongside Charles Murphy and Hartley Dewart. Laurier repeated what had become his standard campaign speech, focusing on the war and explaining his position on conscription. He condemned the Wartime Elections Act, stated that conscription was unnecessary, and promised that the voluntary method of recruitment could still work. Being opposed to conscription did not make one anti-British, he argued; after all, Canada's sister Dominion Australia — an "all-British" country — had rejected conscription. He also claimed that there was no difference between the new Union government and the old Conservative one and went on to attack the government's record on its railway and agriculture policies, on corruption and patronage, and for weakening national unity. Laurier also took a moment to address the outbreak of violence in Kitchener a few days earlier. He always believed in free speech, he said, and therefore the prime minister should have been permitted to speak. But then he turned the argument around: "the gag is the gag," he pronounced, "whether applied by a mob at a public meeting or in Parliament by a cold-blooded Government." The *Globe* reported the audience's enthusiastic response. There was little heckling or interruption of Laurier, the story ran, but then added that, when Laurier spoke a few words in French, "the applause which he then received testified to the considerable number of his own fellow-countrymen in the audience."[90]

Laurier and Liberals everywhere could attack the government on its record, but their campaign would succeed or fail on the issue of conscription. "If the Government want to confine the issue in this election to conscription," Laurier told a large crowd in the Arnprior town hall on December 3, "I am here ready to meet them upon the ground chosen by themselves. Premier Borden has changed his mind on conscription. I have not changed mine." That line of reasoning was also used to fend off accusations of disloyalty. Liberals were quick to point out that Borden was opposed to conscription only a year earlier, and no one called him a traitor. That the Unionists were using the word now only showed that conscription was little more than a political ploy to win the election, not the war. When that didn't work Laurier could always fall back on the old "sunny ways" which never failed to please a crowd. "I stand here a Canadian," he told the people of South Renfrew, "and my platform is Canada, and if I cannot win on that platform I do not want to win on any platform."[91]

Laurier and his party knew they were fighting an uphill battle in English Canada. Most of the riding associations were gone or weakened, accessing the military vote was difficult everywhere, the female vote was clearly with the Unionists, the loss of the "enemy alien" vote was a major blow, especially in the West, and editorial opinion and all the "big interests" were stacked against them. The feeling in the rural areas was with the Liberals, Laurier believed, and in the cities it was divided. "The defeat of the government by a large majority would be certain but for one fact: the iniquities of the Franchise Act."[92]

Sir Allen Aylesworth blamed the Military Voters Act for the problems facing the party in Ontario. He would be "very hopeful" about Liberal prospects in the province "if it were not for the infamous floating vote of 30,000 or 40,000 men in uniform overseas, who don't know one County in Canada from another." It was an "unspeakable outrage," he wrote.[93]

From London, U.K., W.T.R. Preston reported numerous irregularities in arranging the soldier vote. There were also complaints about the use of enumerators to prepare the voter lists and charges of partisanship and manipulation. "The whole machinery of the election is in the hands of the Government's own officials, both here and across the seas," wrote an angry Mackenzie King. "They have appointed their own enumerators to revise the lists and there is no appeal to any court, but only to the enumerators themselves against injustice."[94] There was lack of funds and raising money was difficult, leaving many candidates to complain about having to pay their own election expenses.

"One thing, however, I am sure of," Laurier concluded, "it is that if money can defeat us, we will be defeated."[95]

Liberal candidates, for the most part, were left to fend for themselves in their ridings. Overall, the Liberals held fewer mass rallies, those that were held were less well attended, and Liberal candidates had greater trouble bringing in prominent supporters to speak. In most cities and towns, the Liberal newspapers threw their support behind the Unionists, which meant the domination of pro-Union news stories, a solid block of editorial support for Union, and more difficulty for Liberals to get their message out. In some places, the Liberals were forced to produce their own papers; in Kitchener, for example, W.D. Euler's campaign printed its own paper, the *Voice of the People*.[96] And the Union campaign message was clearer and stronger. The Union poster "Who would the Kaiser vote for?" resonated well and was almost impossible to counter. In Regina, some Liberal and Labour supporters tried their own version: "How would the Big Interests and the war profiteers vote?" but it just wasn't as sharp and likely failed to sway many votes in a pro-conscription city.[97] In Ottawa, Charles Murphy tried to make the case that the kaiser would, in fact, vote for the Union government because it was Borden — a "menace to democracy" — who let the voluntary recruitment fail and permitted Sir Joseph Flavelle to reap huge profits selling tainted bacon.[98] But he probably convinced no one.

Aylesworth crisscrossed the province, giving speeches in support of local candidates in Orillia, London, Renfrew, Perth, Windsor, and elsewhere. Hartley Dewart did likewise and accompanied Laurier on his final campaign swing through the West. Neither was running for a seat in the House of Commons, but they campaigned for Laurier, for national unity, and for democracy in the face of autocracy.[99]

In York North, Mackenzie King campaigned in isolation, on the slogan "The purpose of the Union Government is to win the election, not the War."[100] He received little support from old friends; even Sir William Mulock, a former cabinet colleague who had held the riding under Laurier for five elections, went missing. And he was criticized for being too close to, on the one hand, Henri Bourassa, and, on the other, J.D. Rockefeller. His biographer uses the words "short and vicious" to describe the campaign;[101] at one point a Liberal rally in Newmarket was broken up by a group of men in uniform who refused to let the candidates speak. It was a "deliberately organized attempt to break up the meeting," King complained, by soldiers from Toronto who came in Department of Militia trucks. "I cannot believe that the Government would knowingly sanction for political ends conduct which constitutes an abuse of both military and civil authority," he wrote to General Mewburn.[102]

There had been reason for hope in the rural areas of Ontario, at least until the announcement of the Order-in-Council exempting farmers' sons from conscription. In late November, five hundred citizens paraded in the streets of Perth protesting conscription,[103] but by early December protests like these were a thing of the past. The Unionists had accommodated the demands of Ontario farmers; Liberals were now on the defensive in rural Ontario and more likely to hear charges of treason and slander than cheers of support.[104]

Things were not much better in the West. In Vancouver, a Liberal meeting of three thousand at the Horse Show Building was broken up by a group of returned soldiers who refused to let the Liberal candidates speak. The three Liberals were themselves returned soldiers, but the members of the Great War Veterans' Association said that they did not speak for them. At one point, some soldiers in the audience grabbed the legs of one of the speakers on the stage, and he fell back over the speakers' table, smashing the water pitcher and glasses.

"Umbrellas and crutches were brandished," the *Daily Sun* reported, "by returned soldiers and their wives."[105]

Wilson MacDonald, poet and member of the Liberal Association, recorded the events in his diary:

> A great crowd was present and as I made my way with the other speakers of the evening to the platform I heard such a medley of mingled cheers and groans as I never before listened to. The cheers came from the Canadians in the building — the groans were the presentation of the scum of Whitechapel and Billingsgate. On our platform were a number of returned soldiers who were billed to speak but the liberty loving riff-raff of Mile End Road refused to allow them a free-man's privilege. The soldiers in the audience demanded that the Unionist candidates also be allowed to speak, but as soon as they had finished their insulting diatribes they struck anew the evil chorus and before 3,000 witnesses tore up the scrap of paper given a few minutes before.[106]

For some in the Liberal campaign, the country was teetering on the brink of catastrophe. If the Unionists won, Mackenzie King lamented, it would produce a government in which there would be no, or few, French

Canadians or Catholics. "Can you imagine anything calculated to do more harm to Canada, and through Canada to the British Empire, in this present crisis?" He knew where the responsibility lay. "The Government has deliberately sought to make this election one of prejudice against Sir Wilfrid on account of his race and religion. They have gone too far."[107] On the brighter side, he took comfort in the knowledge that his grandfather had resisted Upper Canada's Family Compact in the same riding ninety years earlier. And, if nothing else, election day, December 17, was his birthday.

The final leg of the election campaign in English Canada saw the national leaders going in different directions: Borden travelled east again to tour the Maritimes while Laurier embarked on his one great campaign swing through the West. Meighen and Crerar promoted Union government in the West; Rowell, Hearst, and a few others toured Ontario. Sir Clifford Sifton observed from his hotel room in Toronto and Sir George Foster was active, until he broke his collar bone in a collision with a train in Toronto's Union Station. "It was really a miracle that I was not wiped off the map," he later wrote.[108] Foster was meant to close the campaign in Waterloo North, helping the Unionist candidate there,[109] but now was forced to direct the rest of his campaign from a hospital bed.

Borden arrived in Saint John, New Brunswick, on December 3 and visited St. Andrews, and then went on to Sackville and Amherst, Nova Scotia, before crossing to P.E.I. Along the way he was accompanied by Frank Carvell, who told him that the "Nova Scotia Liberals were not doing their part, Fielding being partisan and Murray timid."[110] Again his days were filled with train rides, official dinners, meetings, and speeches, the latter usually in the company of the local Unionist candidates and other notables.

On December 6, during short visits to Summerside and Charlottetown, he was informed that an explosion had occurred in Halifax, and it was worse than anything ever before. Two ships — the Norwegian steamer *Imo*, which was carrying Belgian relief supplies, and the French steamship *Mont-Blanc* — collided in the harbour around eight in the morning. The ensuing fire on the *Mont-Blanc* spread to its munitions cargo and set off the greatest human-made explosion to that time, causing unimaginable destruction in the city. The blast completely destroyed the *Mont-Blanc*; one of its cannons landed in Dartmouth, parts of its anchor were found some two miles away. It could have been even worse, because a third ship, the steamer *Pictou*, was nearby and also carrying munitions, but its captain stayed on board at great personal risk and managed to avoid the fire.

Borden crossed back to Nova Scotia, cancelled his visits to Pictou and Antigonish, and immediately travelled to Halifax. A.K. Maclean and Frank Carvell suspended their campaigns and did likewise. They found a city in ruins. Some two thousand Haligonians were killed; another six to eight thousand were wounded, many with gruesome injuries from the millions of pieces of flying glass, and thousands more were homeless. The blast completely demolished the Richmond district, shattered all the windows for miles, and was felt and heard some sixty miles away. Virtually every home in Halifax was damaged to some extent, and an estimated four thousand were destroyed.

"The disaster had indeed been appalling," Borden wrote in his memoirs. "All this happened in the twinkling of an eye; and in its suddenness and extent the disaster surpassed anything experienced in France or Belgium."[111]

Rumours spread immediately that this was the work of German saboteurs, and the fourteen German residents of Halifax were arrested at once. One of the crew of the *Imo* was turned over to the military authorities as a suspected German spy because of his post-explosion behaviour. He was in hospital for injuries but the nurse attending him "noticed that the patient was acting queerly, and that he did not seem to be wounded."[112] Investigations began within days, but no evidence of enemy sabotage was ever found.

Borden immediately wired Reid in Ottawa for the cabinet to issue an Order-in-Council authorizing $500,000 in aid. Other aid for Halifax began to pour in immediately, from all across the Maritimes, from Toronto, Hamilton, Winnipeg, and Calgary, from the governments of Ontario, British Columbia, and Saskatchewan, from many parts of the United States, from the British government, and from as far away as New Zealand. Boston sent a complete medical unit; other cities and organizations collected money or sent supplies. A Halifax Relief Commission was set up to oversee the rebuilding of the city, but that was a task that would take months, if not years. Within a few days it was agreed that staging an election under these conditions was impossible and a second Order-in-Council was issued postponing the Halifax vote until January 28, the same day as polling in Yukon. Ultimately, the two Halifax seats were won by Unionists, by acclamation.

The Halifax explosion removed the election campaign from Canadian newspapers, at least for a few days. Stories of campaign meetings and speeches were replaced by stories of the disaster, the anguish of the survivors, tales of loss, of families torn asunder, and of the difficulties facing relief workers. Right up to the day before the election, the *Ottawa Citizen* filled its first three pages with Halifax stories.[113] Before long, however, the election reasserted itself, integrating the disaster into the campaign. Newton Rowell at the Toronto Armories asked a crowd of supporters if Canadians needed a referendum to decide whether or not to help the people of Halifax. The crowd yelled out "No!" Then why have a referendum on sending relief to our boys overseas?[114]

Others did the same. In Halifax, the *Morning Chronicle* called for all Canadians to "draw rational instruction from misfortune," and to not let partisan politics obscure the necessity of Union government. The *Toronto Daily News* reported the arrest of the sixteen Halifax Germans; and announced that "the Hun is at our gate," and that Germany was ultimately responsible for the explosion. As a result, the need to see the war through to the end was greater than ever, and the way to do that was to vote Union.[115]

Borden visited his riding in Kings, and then, on December 12, left for Ottawa, where he spent the rest of the campaign. The governor general found him "hopeful" for the election; Borden recorded in his diary "how extreme was my exhaustion."[116]

But the campaigning continued in high gear; in Toronto, Frank Cochrane denounced Laurier and all French Canadians. "The country realizes that it must face and settle once and for all the question of Quebec domination," he said. "That province has to be put into its place."[117] Premier Hearst repeated a similar line in Georgetown.[118] Another report suggested that many of the officers in the CEF would resign if Laurier were to be elected; the source remained unnamed.[119] A campaign ad in the *Daily Star* expressed it in a cartoon, picturing Bourassa sitting at a desk with his feet up, smoking a cigar, and saying "*Parlez-vous Français!!*" Underneath, in large type, the caption read: "Quebec must not rule all Canada."[120]

Laurier must have known, somewhere deep inside, that he was unlikely to be ruling any part of Canada after December 17. But he made one last effort. He had not planned a western trip, at least one that went further west than Winnipeg, but he could not resist the calls for his presence to help save the flagging campaign. Laurier arrived in Winnipeg on December 10 and spoke to western Liberals about 1911, reciprocity, the tariff, and British preference, and denied that he had made any alliance with Bourassa and the *nationalistes*.[121] He continued west, making several unscheduled speeches at train stations along the way, and repeated his message the following day in Regina, stating that "neither Bourassa nor anyone else will dominate Laurier." In Regina he appeared at the city hall and three local churches and blamed the low recruitment figures on the Borden government — if only they had tried harder in Quebec they could have found the needed men without resorting to conscription, he argued. He met some hecklers: "Put him out," someone cried, and Laurier replied "I am here to stay."[122] He arrived in Calgary five hours late because of bad weather and began his speech at the Grand Theatre at 11:15 p.m. He promised that a Liberal government would hold the conscription referendum within sixty days of the election.[123]

Laurier's final stop was in Vancouver on December 14. He arrived at 11:30 a.m., made five appearances, and left at 8 p.m. He was met by an adoring Liberal crowd at the train station, and by the end of the day had been heard by an estimated eight thousand people; many others lined the streets to catch a glimpse of him as he passed. One of those who met Laurier was Wilson MacDonald, who, after speaking with the former prime minister, gave him a copy of his poem and sketch, entitled *France*. MacDonald, who was young enough to be conscripted, worried about the outcome of the election. "Truly, as Tolstoi [*sic*] says, Militarism and Truth cannot crowd into the same soul," he wrote in his diary after meeting Laurier. "For days I have feared the 'press gang' and although I am not in the 'first draft' still I know that the military authorities the other day on the streets of Vancouver kidnapped a youth of 18 to show their love of freedom. What is to prevent them from pursuing this policy?"[124]

The Liberal gathering in the ballroom of the Hotel Vancouver was for women only, but at all his stops Laurier repeated his campaign message of persuasion over coercion when it came to recruitment, and he responded once again to the accusations of treason. He reminded everyone how he had been called traitor before; as a traitor to his race by *nationalistes* and a traitor to the Empire by imperialists, but that he stood "upon the broad principle of Canadian nationality. I am not appealing to any creed or any race, but simply on our common nationality and Canadian citizenship." The *Daily Sun*, despite its support for conscription and Union government, gave his visit wide and positive coverage; for many there was the realization that, whatever the outcome of the election, this was likely Laurier's last visit to the West Coast.[125]

It is doubtful that his words changed many minds. That same day in Toronto the *Globe* displayed an editorial cartoon with Laurier standing next to a large mangy dog sporting a collar that read: "the property of Bourassa." The dog was filled with large spots and each spot contained words such as "treason," "anti-enlist," "sedition," "anti-British," and "pro-Germanism." Laurier says: "My friends, don't be afraid! This animal is so attached to me, that if I win the Election, he will automatically change his spots."[126] In Calgary, the *Daily Herald* took a similar approach, with Laurier pictured as a snail moving slowly in one direction in front of a "Win the War Road" sign pointing in the other. Behind them is the kaiser, who says: "Well, that just suits me."[127] And probably the most memorable of all editorial cartoons was displayed in the *Toronto Daily News*: a map of Canada with each province in white except Quebec, which was all in black. The caption underneath read: "The Foul Blot on Canada."[128] On election day the *Globe* summed it all up with a full banner front page headline: "Cast Your Vote To-day for Union Government."[129]

It was all a little too late for Laurier and the Liberal campaign. The crowds were still there, and there was enthusiasm — he knew he was still speaking to thousands of Liberals; it was just that for now they were supporting the war effort and conscription, and therefore voting with

The Kaiser is pleased: A Union campaign poster (1917).

the Unionists. He left Winnipeg for home instead of staying and waiting for the election returns. He heard the first reports as he crossed northern Ontario, and was later recorded saying, surely with a hint of resignation: "They cheered for me but they didn't vote for me."[130]

The campaign in English Canada was revealing. The Unionists were clearly better organized than the Liberals. In many ways, it was a campaign with an embarrassment of riches — there was no shortage of Union candidates vying for nominations and there was enough cash to keep the operation humming. Borden focused his first energies on the Maritimes, perhaps sensing his weakness in his home province, but quickly swung back to concentrate on Ontario, while his Union colleagues conducted the campaign in the West. The press was onside; the rallies were well attended and mostly went off without a hitch. The Union campaign promised much, but at first something was still amiss: the rural areas were unconvinced. The mid-campaign promise to exempt farmers from conscription was nothing short of a bombshell — and, as it turned out, a winning strategy for Union. It caught the Liberals flatfooted, and they were unable to respond coherently to what was essentially a cynical promise.

The Liberals were less prepared. Laurier and his lieutenants faced a chronic shortage of money and were forced to rely on a weak and confused ground organization, which often left them scrambling for nominations. The campaign itself was haphazard. The Liberal manifesto offered nothing new, and pledges of "Canada" as a platform failed to resonate with most Canadians as strongly as they had in past elections. The aging Laurier did not even visit the Maritimes, focusing on Ontario and Quebec, while his tour in the West came late, almost as an afterthought. In this election there were two campaigns, moving in opposite directions across a much-divided country. The election results would show just how stark those divisions were.

9

THE RESULTS

"Do you really think that there will be trouble in Montreal with the French over the conscription law, Alice? Well, let them hop to it. They will find all the trouble they want when they get the length of this country. But by that time, I guess they will have some of the nonsense knocked out of them or else I am much mistaken."

— Pte. Robert Hale to Alice, September 23, 1917[1]

Monday, December 17, was brisk and clear practically everywhere in the country. Christmas was in the air — already the fourth since the war began. Not unexpectedly, it was cold, but there were few weather-related complaints about voting. In the eastern part of the continent, severe snowstorms had complicated the final days of the campaign but by the morning of election day a large high-pressure system had settled in. It was cold and snowy in the Maritimes, and voting turnout was high, except in Halifax where the election was postponed as the city was still coping with the catastrophic explosion of December 6. It was bright and crisp in Montreal and Toronto, though both cities had received heavy snowfalls over the weekend that made it harder to get around. In the surrounding rural areas, even the use of automobiles was problematic and many people reverted to sleighs for transportation to the polling booths. There were good conditions all across the Prairies; after a severe cold snap the temperature finally had risen to the freezing point.[2] The good weather contributed to the record turnout.

There were relatively few incidents, although there was a report of a sixty-three-year-old man in Leamington, Ontario (in the tightly contested Essex South riding), who, after a heated political debate, collapsed on his way home and died.[3] One defeated Toronto candidate complained of "grave irregularities" in his riding, claiming that the returned soldiers who worked as scrutineers in one polling station questioned all "foreigners" who showed up to vote. If they claimed to support the Military Service Act they were allowed to vote; if not, they were refused a ballot and ordered out. In the tight race of Waterloo North that saw a Unionist incumbent defeated by the Liberal, a fight broke out between the two camps as the Liberals stormed the Unionist office.[4] Some women who showed up, on the other hand, were given ballots even if their names were not on the voters list. In Montreal, Onésime Nantel-Orsali complained of "English ladies voting in five different polls."[5] Such reports were rare, and none were formally contested or proven, but there is evidence that such events did happen.

The big story on election day for many Canadians was the female vote. Newspapers were filled with stories of women voting and how there were long lines of both men and women waiting before the opening of the polling stations. For some newspapers, it was the novelty and the new angles; how, for example, in some ridings the Union committees had organized to send women into the homes to look after the young children so their mothers could go vote.[6] Or how women approached their first vote; one report had a "Scottish" woman walking into a polling station: "I'm for the candidate that's for conscription," she called out. "What's his name?" Another woman who had lost her husband in France also proclaimed her support for conscription, but asked for the name of the Labour candidate. When told that the Labour candidate did not support conscription she replied, "Well, the old man always voted for the Labour candidate, a' so'll I, for he'd turn over in his grave if I voted for a Tory or a Grit, conscription or no conscription."[7]

The Independent Labour candidate in South York (Toronto) told reporters that he attributed his defeat "to the fact that many female voters decided to support Union government. Whether that choice was a wise one remains to be seen."[8] In East York, the opposite happened.

Major Ross Cockburn, who ran for the Liberals, complained that many women in his riding had been denied the vote, even though they were qualified to do so.[9] Even more important, for many it was the example of women doing their patriotic duty for their country and their families. In Montreal, the *Gazette* reported on a sixty-five-year-old woman who was carried to the polls in her bed, accompanied by her twice-wounded returned soldier son. "Warnings against exposure could not deter her," noted the *Gazette*, "as she believed that people at home should be willing to make whatever sacrifices they could in order to help the soldiers whose lives were continually exposed."[10]

Everyone agreed that women were voting in significant numbers. "During the day we heard rumours of the large vote which was coming out in Toronto — and especially among the women," wrote Main Johnson. "This phenomenon was particularly marked at Rosedale polls in North Toronto, where long lines of women were waiting for their turn to cast their ballots."[11] For the *Toronto Daily Star* the message was clear: "[E]verywhere the women were giving the lie to the age-long contention that women wouldn't use the ballot if they had it."[12] Those who felt the sting of the largely Unionist female vote were less generous; "[T]he triumph of the fires of evil was complete," complained Wilson MacDonald in his diary. "The Women's vote has elected Robert Borden."[13] Whatever one felt about women voting, quipped one election agent, it was clear that "the women were voting to the man."[14]

Borden, his wife, and a few friends gathered in the improvised Senate chamber for most of the evening and by midnight, when the outcome was determined, he left for home. There was relatively little celebration, although Borden was immensely pleased. On their way home, the Bordens were met by a group of cheering returned soldiers. Borden stopped to give them a short speech before going inside; but as he closed his door "their cheers could be heard all over town."[15] Laurier was still returning to Ottawa in his private train car from his late campaign swing through the West, and he learned of the early results as he arrived in Fort William (now Thunder Bay) in western Ontario. He took the news in stride, but did not linger and continued on his way. He had clung to the hope that his message might have been heard and that he would again receive the support of Canadians, but he knew deep down that his hour had passed. Arthur Meighen, who had spent relatively little time in his riding of Portage La Prairie, remained in Vancouver to hear the results. For Mackenzie King, defeat was twinned with tragedy as his mother died the day after the election and he was obliged to leave for Ottawa to prepare for the funeral. Sir George Foster was still in hospital in Toronto after his train accident, and it was there that he learned he had won the biggest majority of his career. Most of the Liberal-Unionists in the Maritimes stayed near their ridings, as did the western Liberal-Unionists.

In Montreal there were reports of a record turnout at the polls, while the fears of civil unrest proved unjustified. As a precaution, the offices of

Wartime portrait of Sir George Foster, G.C.M.G.

the *Montreal Star*, the *Gazette*, and *La Patrie* were boarded up and police stationed outside, but at the end of the day there was little trouble.[16] There had been stories of small groups of women being blocked from voting in a few Montreal-area ridings, and the police were called, but the "rowdies" stepped aside and everyone got their chance to cast their ballots.[17]

Ten thousand people gathered at Yonge and King to watch the returns as they were projected outside a window of the *Toronto Daily Star*. The crowds were subdued, though they were large. There was some jostling here and there, and sometimes angry words were exchanged, "but nothing happened," noted a *Star* reporter. "There was ... no wild enthusiasm such as has often characterized victories on even trivial issues. The matter at stake this time was serious, and the crowds realized it."[18] But not all the attention that night in Toronto was devoted to the election results. William Gillette, the actor who had become famous for playing Sherlock Holmes, on both stage and screen, performed the leading role in *A Successful Calamity* at the Royal Alexandra Theatre.

A few blocks away, the stage again gave way to the election. Massey Hall was filled to capacity to hear the election returns, while the 48th Highlanders band played patriotic tunes and several victorious candidates appeared and spoke.[19] "Poor old Laurier," announced one former Laurier admirer after casting his vote; "I little thought I'd see the day when I'd plant a ballot like a brick on his famous plume."[20] In the east end, jubilant crowds filled the streets along Broadview, Queen, and Gerrard, and overfilled the Odd Fellows' Hall on Broadview to hear the results. It all went well, until the chair of the meeting announced the results from Quebec and one older man yelled out in protest against the "Chairman giving them French Canadians so much publicity."[21] Overall, the *Toronto Daily News* was impressed by the turnout; "it was really surprising the interest taken in the election by foreigners in Toronto," it concluded, adding an odd twist: "the Jews evinced keen interest in the result."[22]

Newton Rowell could not stay in his office to hear the results, and ventured across downtown Toronto accompanied by Main Johnson. "Until the very end," Johnson wrote in his diary, "in spite of the improved conditions of the last ten days, we were still under the shadow of the pessimism and the fear which had filled the Unionist cause all over the country, and which for a long time seemed quite justified." In front of the *Globe* office, Rowell waded through a deep snowbank to read the results on a large bulletin board and "gave an astonished exclamation" when he saw that Laurier had lost his race in Ottawa East.[23] Rowell entered the *Globe* building, climbed the stairs, and after a few formalities decided to give an impromptu speech from the office fire escape on Melinda Street. Unfortunately, some in the crowd were "die-hards" — or Liberals — and soon after he started speaking the catcalls began. Someone yelled out "Renegade Rowell!" and the mood turned sour. Rowell retreated and, with Johnson, walked along Yonge Street to the offices of the *Toronto Daily Star* on King, and lost himself in the immense crowd.[24] He eventually made his way into the building and spoke from a window to "a much larger and also a friendlier audience than at the *Globe*."[25]

In Kitchener, where commotions a few weeks before had prevented Borden from speaking, there was considerable tension on election day. In Waterloo North, the victory parade for Liberal William Euler was led by an empty coffin, and the symbolism was too much for many observers. Some fighting was reported and several days of protest followed. One soldier complained to the Unionist headquarters that he had been spat upon, and he suggested that British Canadians leave the riding and let the soldiers take care of the unpatriotic citizens who remained behind. William Weichel, the sitting MP (but losing Unionist candidate), was outraged at what he believed to be an insult to the flag; later, after hearing the results, he concluded that "you cannot beat the Kaiser in North Waterloo."[26]

In Winnipeg, the *Free Press* erected nine bulletin boards in the front of its office to display results from all across the country, and the paper was thrilled to announce the use of an "ingenious electrical device, first time shown in Winnipeg, [that] will throw work of *Free Press* cartoonists upon [the] screen as they draw." On the building's roof they placed a huge whistle that would announce the results: one long ten-minute blast for a Union victory; a ten-minute series of one-minute blasts with thirty-second intervals if the Liberals won.[27] In Vancouver, Liberals met at their headquarters for a subdued meeting and short speeches from the defeated candidates; across town, the Unionists gathered at the Union headquarters on Hastings Street and then mounted an impromptu parade to the Hotel Vancouver. Led by the band of the Great War Veterans' Association, and followed by a line of automobiles along streets lined with hundreds of supporters, the group ultimately ended up at the hotel, where the local victorious candidates addressed the triumphant crowd.[28]

Wilson MacDonald, however, cast his vote this time "for freedom and Laurier," and was less jubilant. He wrote in his diary:

> [A]fter dinner I crossed on the ferry to North Vancouver … and sought the silent places along the Grouse Mountain Trail. When I reached a point one thousand feet above the sea I looked back over Vancouver and far out to the lovely islands of the Gulf. How peaceful all the world seemed! How beautiful were the paths I trod! The great hills to the north and the west were snow covered and their silent beauty was like a song too exquisite for sound.

But all was not well in this oasis of tranquility. "Vancouver was covered with a canopy of smoke to hide her shame — for every vote she records for that law of evil, Conscription, will be like a new nail driven into the bleeding hands of the Master."[29] He awoke the following morning to the unhappy truth: "the morning papers brought no consolation," he sadly wrote.[30]

The returns from the Maritimes started coming in by late afternoon, and the *Toronto Daily Star*'s election extra edition appeared at 6 p.m., proclaiming a Unionist victory based on what it was hearing from Halifax, Fredericton, Charlottetown, and, especially, Toronto — which was again voting massively for Borden. By 9 p.m., the government had secured a majority of at least thirty seats. In North Toronto, the support for Sir George Foster was so pronounced that one supporter was quoted in the *Toronto Daily Star* as saying that "this isn't an election, it's a crime." The newsboys that night sold an extra seventy-five thousand copies.

MacDonald was not alone in rushing for newspapers on that Tuesday morning. For most Canadians the voting was over, but explaining what had happened had only begun. The early editions across the country easily called it a Union majority and Borden felt justified in issuing a statement to the press expressing his satisfaction with the results, predicting a sixty-seat majority once all the votes — including the soldier vote — were counted. "It was not a partisan victory in any sense," he said. "If party lines are to be taken it is a triumph as much for Liberals as for Conservatives."[31]

By the time the final editions rolled out, the Borden forces were leading by a fifty-one-seat majority and Canada's electoral map had changed dramatically. Many of the ballot boxes would have to wait five or six more weeks before being counted: they were still making their way from the mud tunnels of France and Belgium. For soldiers, voting day had actually started more than two weeks before, on December 1, managed by an overseas team charged with ensuring that the process of campaigning and voting was fair. Sir Edward Kemp, Borden's reliable fixer of all things Ontarian, was named the Canadian Union cabinet's representative in London, and was responsible for ensuring that the vote took place. Borden named W.F. O'Connor as general returning officer. Both parties also named three scrutineers.

The soldiers were presented with a ballot that would have seemed strange to those back home. It involved a particular process. First, an

Nursing Sisters at a Canadian hospital voting in the Canadian federal election, France, December 1917.

envelope had to be filled out. The soldier was to write on it his name, rank, number, and branch of service. He had to indicate if he was a British subject, whether he had voted before, and whether he had enlisted in Canada. He then had to write his Canadian address, and the name of his riding. For those unable to remember the name of their electoral constituency, a place on the ballot was reserved to pick one.

Once the envelope was certified, the soldier was handed a ballot that simply gave four choices: Government, Opposition, Labour, or Independent. If he chose, the soldier could also write in the name of a candidate. In Kings, for instance, "Sir R.L. Borden" received twenty votes in addition to the "Government" tally. "James Sealy" also received votes this way. In Quebec East, "Sir Wilfrid Laurier" received the equivalent of 50 percent of the votes cast for "Opposition." Some soldiers wanted no confusion about which candidate they supported.[32]

Once filled out, the ballot was placed in the envelope and the thin package was slipped into a ballot bag. The bag would be sent to London if its contents had been cast in Europe, and to Ottawa if the votes had been pledged in North America. Each ballot would be applied to the electoral district written on the envelope. A tally was then kept until all the votes were counted. If the soldier wrote in a name on the ballot, that would be counted.

For W.T.R. Preston, one of the Liberal scrutineers, each of these steps seemed to be an opportunity for government cheating. A good number of the young soldiers could not remember the name of their riding. It seemed that others were more than willing to whisper the names of particular constituencies where Union support needed help. Sometimes, entire ballot bags seemed destined to one riding. The riding of Cumberland, for instance, seemed to be the destination for all the votes cast by the soldiers working at the ordnance depot in Ashworth (in the riding of Kent). According to Preston, a Major Burke was responsible for this alleged fraud, but no proof of this act was ever produced.[33] Godfroy Langlois, the Liberal scrutineer who travelled to the Front, observed, or might have heard, that a surprising number of ballots were destined for Temiskaming, the Ontario riding where Frank Cochrane was running in what was expected to be a fairly tight race (Cochrane did win the civilian vote by more than 5 percent), and the Quebec riding of Gaspé, where Rodolphe Lemieux was running (although his command over the civilian vote made the soldier vote irrelevant). Such revelations threatened to impair the entire affair, so the government changed course. It was decided that any ballot where the soldier's address and riding were blank would be discarded. That amounted to about 12 percent of the entire soldiers vote. The entire process would take a great deal of time; it would be months before all the soldier votes were verified, counted, checked, and allotted to their constituencies.[34]

Back home, things were much quieter. Like most of the elections in Canada since 1867, the outcome of this election was anticipated well in advance of election day. The feelings in the streets, and in the kitchens and parlours of Canadian homes, presaged the reality that there would be few ballot box "conversions." The question was not whether the Union government would win; it was more of a question of how well the Liberal opposition would do.

Nevertheless, people had rushed to the polls — more than ever before. As the *Toronto Daily Star* put it, "the voters went at it … in much the same way as their sons over Vimy Ridge, or tore their way over Passchendaele."[35] The disenfranchisement of recent immigrants from enemy countries notwithstanding, the voters list had inflated by 577,788 names. There were now 2,093,826 electors eligible (out of a population of 7,591,971), 27.6 percent of the population. Of that number, 1,805,888 actually voted, an astounding turnout of 86.2 percent. It was even higher than in Laurier's triumphal re-election in 1900, which was 77.4 percent. The record set in 1917 has never been beaten.[36]

Many reasons may explain the growth in the eligible numbers. The first was the massive increase contributed by women who were related to enlisted men; the second was a natural growth in the number of eligible male voters. Third, and not least, was the cause. There was much at stake in Canada in the last few days of the cruel year of 1917 that made people particularly eager to exercise their franchise. Finally, the high turnout rate could also be explained by the possibility that enumerators, who hastened to create the eligibility lists, unwittingly omitted many women whose sons, husbands, or fathers were now in the army. Those women would have turned up on polling day insisting that they had earned the right to vote. If the original eligibility lists were not revised in light of this new wave of voters, then the apparent participation rate would be considerably elevated. It is impossible to be sure, because it remains unclear whether the official list of registered voters in 1917 includes all those who presented themselves on December 17 to vote.

In that light, it is a little surprising that participation among soldiers was not higher. Trapped in the wartime trenches and camps, they now had the opportunity to vote: the ballot box came to them. According to the official history of Canada's army in the First World War, there were 307,129 men in uniform on election day. The ballot count was 224,430, producing a turnout of 73 percent among the military.[37]

The electoral map of 1917, as a result of the 1911 census, had changed slightly in Canada's eastern half since the previous election. Nova Scotia and New Brunswick each lost two seats; Ontario lost four. The seat allocation for Quebec (sixty-five), Prince Edward Island (four in three ridings) and Yukon (one) were maintained at 1911 levels. In the West, the map changed considerably as fourteen seats had been added to the total. Manitoba's number of seats leaped by 50 percent, going from ten to fifteen. Saskatchewan went from ten to sixteen seats. Alberta more than doubled, from seven to fifteen seats. British Columbia almost doubled, going from seven to thirteen seats. The West's allocation of seats had thus gone from 15.8 percent of the seats in the House of Commons in 1911 to 23.3 percent in 1917. That would work in favour of Union.

For many incumbents, survivors of the 12th Parliament, which had sat since 1911, politics had taken too much of a toll. Thirty-one percent of them (61 of the 196 still sitting in October 1917) had decided to retire. This was almost twice the 17 percent average recorded over the ten previous elections (the only election to come close was that of 1896, when 24 percent had chosen to step away). Of the sixty-one retirees, forty-four had sat as Conservatives. R.B. Bennett, for example, had had enough. He had been a member of Parliament since 1900 (representing a seat in the Northwest Territories, as Alberta had not yet been officially created).

Frustrated by Borden, by Ottawa, by all of it, he slammed the door on the capital. He was forty-seven-years old now, and decided to focus even more on making his fortune. Bennett would have had a nodding acquaintance with Honoré Achim, a thirty-six-year-old lawyer who also decided to leave federal politics, and ran successfully for a seat in the Quebec legislature. Achim had been elected as a *nationaliste* in the Conservative Party fold in the Bourassa stronghold of Labelle. Another was Ésioff-Léon Patenaude, forty-four, who had been brought into cabinet by Borden in 1915, following a by-election in Hochelaga. He also had had enough. He returned to practice law, his two-year adventure in politics over. He would never re-enter the house, though he tried twice in the mid-1920s. David Neely, who had represented Humbolt, Saskatchewan, for the Liberals since 1908, had read the writing on the wall. The forty-four-year-old doctor returned to his practice. Edmond Fortier, a sixty-seven-year-old teacher who had represented Lotbinière since 1900, no longer had the stomach for politics. He simply retired. There were dozens more stories like this. Parliament was destined to be transformed on December 17, 1917.

NOVA SCOTIA

On December 17 Nova Scotians were among the first to have their votes counted, as usual. The turnout rate in Nova Scotia was 75.1 percent overall (by far the lowest in the country), with the soldier vote constituting 10.2 percent of the entire vote (third-lowest in the country). A total of 118,756 votes were eventually counted in that province (voters had two ballots in the riding of Cape Breton South-Richmond), an increase of 6.8 percent over the number who had cast their ballots in 1911. The increase was low in comparison with other provinces, because a remarkable four seats — one-quarter of the Nova Scotian catch — were won by acclamation. In the end, all the acclamations were for Union incumbents, including the two-seat riding in bomb-devastated Halifax. Former Liberals W.S. Fielding, in Shelburne-Queen's, and A.K. Maclean, in Halifax, returned to Ottawa this way. Peter Martin (Halifax), running for the first time, was acclaimed, as was Fleming McCurdy (Colchester), who had won as a Conservative in 1911 in Shelburne and Queen's.

The Union government collected 47.7 percent of the total vote in the province — practically the same result the Tories had in 1911 — while the Liberals took 46.2 percent, a drop of more than 4 percent. The high proportion of acclamations had a distorting effect on the calculation of the civilian vote. On paper, the Liberals won the civilian vote, taking 49.8 percent of the ballots, while the Union took 43.9 percent. Third parties took 6.1 percent of the vote, the highest rate in the country (tied with British Columbia). The difference between 1911 and 1917 was the unusual rise of third parties in the province and, of course, the soldier vote.

The number of acclamations raises a question about the soldier vote that remains unresolved. Many of the soldiers would have cast a ballot in their riding before the acclamation date. It is not clear if their vote was thus eliminated, or redirected. In the seven ridings won by the Unionists, the soldier vote averaged 88.6 percent support for Union; in the four ridings taken by the Liberals, the support among soldiers for the winners was 17 percent — a result that indicates that, even in Liberal ridings, military support for Union was extremely high, at 83 percent. Overall, the military vote in Nova Scotia was 89 percent in support of Union. No military vote recorded for Nova Scotia was in favour of a third party.

The civilian contest was comparatively tight in the prime minister's home province, where sixteen seats were up for grabs in fourteen ridings. There were two seats less in the province in 1917, the result of a relative decline in the province's population, and it hurt the Liberals. In 1911 they had split the seats evenly with the Conservatives at nine each. Six years later, the Liberals only took four. Their support in Cape Breton, in the area of New Glasgow and on the southern tip, had been wiped out. Every seat, with the exception of Cape Breton South and Richmond was taken by Unionists with majority support, and three were won with over 60 percent of the vote. Robert Borden ran in Kings, winning 61 percent of the vote. He won the civilian vote in his riding by more than 15 percentage points. The Union government took two other seats from the Liberals: Pictou went for Union, with a plurality of about 6 percent. In Yarmouth-Clare, the southernmost seat, the voters flipped decidedly and abandoned the Liberals in favour of the Union government.

Third parties cost the Liberals some support. Collectively, they earned the highest rate in the country. The coal mining–dominated riding of Cape Breton South and Richmond was a surprise because six candidates vied for the two seats. In 1911, only a few hundred votes had been cast for "others" — one of the lowest rates in the country. Six years later, the Labour Party ran two candidates, collectively earning almost 20 percent of the vote, while the two Liberal candidates won 43.1 percent of the civilian vote, and the Unionists took 37 percent. What made the difference in this case was indeed the soldier vote. An overwhelming 87.8 percent of 4,376 votes from the military went to the Union. The Union candidates both won seats, collecting 43 percent of the votes — just 1 percent more than the Liberals — by far the smallest plurality in the province. Still, they did take the seats from the Liberals. The reverse happened in North Cape Breton-Victoria, where 83 percent of the soldier vote went to the Unionist camp; but it was not enough to beat the Liberals, who had a commanding lead among the civilian vote, a good part of which was Acadian.

The Liberals won the civilian vote, but lost the race, in three ridings: Cumberland, Pictou, and Hants. They also narrowly lost Digby-Annapolis, even though they had 49 percent of the civilian vote. In Cumberland, Edgar Rhodes, the Unionist speaker of the House of Commons, was initially considered defeated, narrowly, as he had taken only 49.6 percent of the civilian vote. He was declared victor when the military vote was counted: 94 percent of it was Unionist (1,454 votes against 92 for the Liberals). This brought his support to 54.9 percent of the final vote, allowing him to defeat his opponent by ten points. There is no doubt that if the military vote had been distributed similarly to the civilian vote, Rhodes would have lost. But the soldiers voted in a manner that was consistent with their brothers-in-arms in other ridings, and so Rhodes won his re-election fair and square. The same thing happened in Pictou, where the Unionist Alexander McGregor took the seat from the Liberals on the strength of 49.4 percent of the civilian vote, but 89 percent of the soldier vote. Hants was another tight race that was won without a majority of the civilian vote. Conservative Hadley Tremain kept his seat as a Unionist with 2,989 civilian votes, giving him an edge over the Liberal

Lewis Martell's 2,696 votes. The soldier vote gave him a much larger plurality, with 514 votes (Martell earned only 55 votes). Soldiers who called Hants home had voted over 90 percent in favour of the Union candidate. In Digby-Annapolis, the Union narrowly won the civilian vote and the Liberals were crushed by the military vote.

The Liberals easily retained North Cape Breton–Victoria, Inverness, and Antigonish-Guysborough with commanding pluralities in the civilian vote. They took one seat from the Conservatives. It was, surprisingly, in Lunenburg, and it was won by shipowner William Duff, who took almost 10 percent more votes than the Unionist. Duff won by taking 58 percent of the civilian vote, but less than 4 percent of the military vote (seventy soldiers voted for him — the best result among the Liberals in the province).

NEW BRUNSWICK

The Union government triumphed in New Brunswick. There were 94,456 voters (a rate of 80.5 percent), about the same as in 1911, but 95,261 votes were cast (as a result of the double representation in the riding of St. John–Albert). There were 10,853 military votes recorded in New Brunswick, 11.4 percent of the total ballots cast, and therefore not out of the ordinary. It was the fourth-lowest rate in the country. There were no third parties running in New Brunswick, and all the races were decided by majorities. In the end, Unionists took 61.2 percent of the vote, a jump of a full ten percentage points over the Conservative results in 1911. The Unionists also won a resounding majority of the civilian vote, at 57.2 percent, and 91.8 percent of the military vote. New Brunswick, like Nova Scotia, had lost two seats as a result of the 1911 census and now had a total of eleven in ten ridings. Of those, the Union government took six, including two new wins: former Liberal Frank Carvell won by acclamation in Victoria-Carleton, and in Northumberland, merchant William Loggie beat his Liberal adversary by almost 13 percent. Some of the biggest wins were taken by the Union side: Harry McLeod took York-Sunbury by almost 70 percent of the vote and Hugh McLean took Royal by almost 68 percent, doubling his rival. The double-seated riding of St. John–Albert also went to the Union, which took 71 percent of the votes.

The Liberals were elected in four seats (including one by acclamation); four fewer than in 1911. All four wins were in the coastal areas with significant Acadian populations (about 25 percent of New Brunswick's population was French-speaking, according to the 1911 census). Gloucester, overwhelmingly francophone, was won by acclamation by Onésiphore Turgeon, who had represented the riding since 1900. Auguste Léger took Kent, dominated by the villages of Richibucto and Bouctouche, with almost 73 percent of the vote as the riding switched its choice radically. Pius Michaud, running for the first time, retained Restigouche-Madawaska by almost 70 percent. Westmoreland was also retained by the Liberals. In two of the three Liberal victories, the soldier vote was strongly in favour of Union. Only in the riding of Westmoreland was a majority (54.8 percent) of the soldier vote recorded in favour of Laurier's party. The Liberals were strong in the towns; they took 48 percent of the civilian vote in Charlotte and 49 percent of the civilian vote in Northhumberland. But it was not enough; they still lost to the Unionists.

PRINCE EDWARD ISLAND

The island was split, as in 1911, right down the middle. There were 35,460 votes cast on the island — 7,000 more than in the three preceding elections, an increase of 23.8 percent over 1911 alone. As in New Brunswick, the number of votes cast dwarfed the number of people on the voters list: 28, 221, a distortion brought about by the two-seat riding of Queen's. When finally tallied, 3,211 soldier-ballots were cast, representing 9.1 percent of the total vote, the second-lowest rate in the country. The participation rate on the island was 87.6 percent.

The government and the Liberals took two seats each, based on a virtual tie in the popular vote: 50 percent for the government and 49.8 for the Laurier candidates. In the civilian vote, the Liberals won, 53.8 to 46.2 percent. The Union took Kings (on the eastern side) from the Liberals with 47.7 percent of the civilian vote, but secured the win by taking 85.5 percent of the soldier vote. The Liberals retained Prince (on the west side of the island, where Acadians constituted about 27 percent of the population) with 55 percent of the civilian vote, and less than 15 percent of the soldier vote. In the end, Joseph Read won by taking 51.7 percent of the combined vote. The even split among islanders was more dramatic in Queen's (the riding in the middle, around Charlottetown), where the two seats were divided almost exactly four ways. The Liberals, John Sinclair and Alexander Warburton, both won the civilian vote but the Unionists, Donald Nicholson and Alexander Martin, overwhelmingly took the soldier vote. In the end, Nicholson (Union) came in first with 25.3 percent of the vote while Sinclair (Liberal) came in second. They both would go to Ottawa. The Unionist Martin, who came third, received three votes fewer than Sinclair. Warburton, the Liberal who came in last, received only 159 votes fewer than Nicholson.

The result in Prince Edward Island was thus the same as in 1911: two seats on either side of the aisle in the House of Commons. Prince Edward Island was the only province outside Quebec that granted a win to the Liberals in terms of the civilian vote. What made the difference here was that the islanders in the military voted 88.6 percent in favour of Union — the lowest rate outside Quebec. Even though more people voted for the Laurier party than in 1911, it was not enough. The Borden team could claim majority support on the island.

QUEBEC

Eugène Nantel asked his family to vote for conscription and to stay loyal to the Conservative Party. Instead, his brother tirelessly worked for the Liberals and his mother Onésime had to disappoint him. "No, my dear Eugène, I did not vote for conscription," she wrote to him a few weeks after the election. "First, I think it's unfair to the *Canadiens*. They have largely paid their debts, their people, and their blood to England. Conscription was so important among the women, not least the upper-class ladies. I was disgusted and I feared to demean myself by voting. For me the duty of a woman, above all, is at home with her husband and children."[38]

The Union government walked into Quebec with every handicap. In 1911, the Conservatives had taken fourteen seats on their own ticket, but had entered the 12th Parliament fortified by thirteen more under the banner of Bourassa's *nationalistes*. Six years later, the Union list of candidates could not have been more different. Fewer people actually voted in the 1917 election than in 1911. In 1917, some 319,081 people cast their vote in the province, compared to 324,039 in 1911, a drop of 1.5 percent — the only federal jurisdiction to drop along with Yukon. The military proportion of the vote in Quebec was the smallest recorded in any province: 5.5 percent. The general turnout rate was 80.4 percent, the lowest in the country.

As in Nova Scotia, much of the drop was because seventeen of the sixty-five seats (over a quarter) were taken by the Laurier Liberals by acclamation (no Unionist was acclaimed). In the end, the Liberals took sixty-two of the sixty-five seats, and 72.8 percent of the provincial vote (and 75.9 of the civilian vote). The actual result in terms of seats, of course, proved a massive distortion of the voting intentions. The Union won 27 percent of the vote, but had practically nothing to show for it. In 1911, fortified by the Bourassa *nationalistes*, they had taken almost 49 percent of the vote. In 1917, they were left with three seats in English-speaking ridings, the barest bones of the Conservative vote. The Liberals took twenty-six seats from the Conservatives and *nationalistes* of 1911. The Unionist-Conservatives took St. Lawrence–St. George in Montreal from the Liberals.

The Union government had thrown in the towel, not even running candidates in six of the forty-eight ridings remaining. In two, the Liberals faced local independent candidates. The protest vote against the two major parties amounted to just over 8,300 across the province, scattered among a very small Labour party, one stubborn *nationaliste* candidate, and a smattering of independent candidates, fifteen all told. The most successful independent was Armand La Vergne, who ran on his personal brand of *nationaliste* ticket in Montmagny. He came in second with over 35 percent of the vote, far behind the Liberal candidate's 63 percent. In George-Étienne-Cartier, the Labour Party ran Michael Buhay, the courageous socialist who was just starting his long career in leftist politics. He took over 8 percent of the vote (an independent also took over 7 percent of the vote — their combination was the largest non-traditional party vote in the province). Gédéon Martel also ran for Labour, in Hochelaga.

The sixth Liberal win capped a most unusual race in Joliette, where two Laurier Liberals fought it out for the privilege of representing the town and its environs.

The thirteen *nationalistes* winners of 1911 who had chosen to sit on the government side all but disappeared. Only four — in spite of having won in 1911 in open opposition to involvement in any British wars — had the audacity to run as Unionist candidates. They were Joseph Rainville (Chambly-Verchères), Joseph Girard (Chicoutimi-Saguenay), Albert Sévigny (Dorchester), and Louis-Philippe Gauthier (Gaspé): each was humiliated at the polls. Two proved a bit more adroit, though their political integrity was shredded. Louis-Joseph Papineau, the political turncoat extraordinaire who had won as a Liberal in 1908 and turned *nationaliste* in 1911, changed his colours back to red, and was acclaimed as a Liberal. In Montreal's St. James riding, Louis-Audet Lapointe, another who had won as a *nationaliste* in 1911, was also acclaimed as a Liberal in 1917.

The military vote in Quebec was not as supportive of Union as elsewhere in the country. Soldiers from Quebec gave 82.3 percent of their vote to Borden, a reflection that a majority of the Quebec soldiers were anglophones, and that many francophones — like Eugène Nantel — also supported Union. In Yamaska and Montmagny, only a few soldiers voted, but they all voted against conscription. In the Montreal riding of Hochelaga, for instance, 252 of the 254 soldiers rejected Union. In George-Étienne-Cartier, almost 96 percent of the voters expressed themselves against the Union.

Results in all the other ridings were more consistent with the broader Canadian pattern. In Jacques-Cartier, for example, the Liberal David Lafortune won the civil vote handily, but over 90 percent of the soldiers were against him and supported Union. He still won the seat. In the three ridings that went Union (St. Antoine, St. Anne, and St. Lawrence–St. George in Montreal) over 93 percent of the vote by soldiers was Union. But, in the small riding of Yamaska, the eight soldiers who voted abroad were unanimously for Laurier. The tightest races in terms of the military vote were Témiscouata, where 47.4 percent voted for the Opposition; L'Assomption-Montcalm (52.6 in favour of Laurier); Charlevoix-Montmorency, where 46.7 voted for the Opposition; and

Chicoutimi-Saguenay, where the Liberals took 45.3 percent of the vote. In all cases, the Liberals triumphed.

Quebec was thus a lopsided triumph for the Liberals. Some of the results were practically obscene. Bagot, Bellechasse, Charlevoix-Montmorency, l'Assomption-Montcalm, and Lotbinière, were won with over 95 percent of the vote. Another eighteen seats were taken with more than 80 percent. Overall, the Liberals took 72.7 percent of the vote. Rodolphe Lemieux, Laurier's staunch lieutenant, was elected in two ridings, Gaspé and Maisonneuve (and would serve for the duration of the Parliament for both ridings). In comparison with 1911, there were few close battles in Quebec. The tightest race was in Westmount–St. Henri, where Albert Sévigny ran on the Union ticket. Albert Leduc, who had trained as a butcher in his father's store, but who would rise to become the president of the Butcher's Association and a vice-president of the Montreal Livestock Exchange, ran for the Liberal team. With no political experience, he ran against the prestigious Sévigny and defeated him by a thousand votes, 6.8 percentage points more than his adversary. Emmanuel Devlin won the riding of Wright by winning 52 percent of the civil vote, but took 85 percent of the military. He beat his adversary by taking more than two-thirds of the vote overall. In all, sixteen other ridings were won by the Liberals with more than 90 percent of the civilian vote and another seven were won with more than 80 percent. In the Quebec City region, the highest civilian vote was 96.6 percent in favour of the Liberals, where Charles "Chubby" Power won Quebec South. Laurier himself took 92.5 percent of the vote in Quebec East. The "tightest" races were only barely so.

The Union government was denied any legitimacy in the province, being left with only three seats, won by anglophone ministers in the stalwart Montreal districts of St. Anne (Charles Doherty) and St. Lawrence–St. George (Charles Ballantyne); and by Sir Herbert Ames, new to national politics, in St. Antoine. All three were carried by important majorities. W.T.R. Preston's claim that Ballantyne, for one, had particularly benefitted from a tampering with the military vote, proved baseless. Ballantyne won 62 percent of the civilian vote, more than enough to win, though he also did take 94 percent of the military vote, which was 12 percent more than the provincial average.

ONTARIO

Ontario lost four seats as a result of the census and the redistricting of 1914, but that did not dampen the turnout — 89.9 percent. In 1917, 811,812 votes were cast, a dramatic 68.9 percent increase over the 480,572 ballots counted in 1911. If the Union was defeated in Quebec, its fortunes were reversed in the sister province. Borden's government took 62.7 percent of the total vote, 58.3 percent of the civil vote, 95 percent of the soldier vote, and 90 percent of the seats: seventy-four of the eighty-two ridings.

For Laurier, the Ontario news was devastating. The Liberals were routed almost everywhere. They took only eight ridings, and in only three other ridings were they even close. In twenty ridings, they took over 40 percent of the civilian vote, and posted clear majorities in Essex South and Perth South. They won in Middlesex West, Prescott, Renfrew South, Russell, Waterloo North, Bruce South, Essex North, and Kent. In Prescott and Russell, the majority of electors were French-speaking. In Essex North, French Canadians constituted 40 percent of the population. The other five ridings supported Liberalism and Laurier for particular reasons.

In Nipissing, a Conservative seat where 43 percent of the population was Franco-Ontarian, Edmond Lapierre, the Liberal candidate, won 56 percent of the civilian vote, but only nine military votes went his way. He lost the election by forty-four votes. In Perth South, the Liberals again narrowly won the civilian vote, surpassing the Union vote by two percentage points, but lost massively once the soldiers' tally was included. Perth South had been Conservative going into the election, and stayed Unionist — despite the civilian population's voting 52.7 percent in favour of the Liberal. The soldier vote made the difference.

In Essex North and Essex South, the two parties battled hard. In Essex North, Liberal William Kennedy took the seat by a few hundred votes despite massive soldier opposition. The riding was 22 percent French Canadian according to the 1911 census, and 10 percent German Canadian. Essex South, with almost 24 percent of its population French Canadian, had been a Liberal seat — the George Graham stronghold. Graham, now pro-conscription, clearly read the political mood and knew that he was unlikely to be returned to the House of Commons, given his views. He dropped out, the Laurierites took 50.9 percent of the civil vote, and Unionist John Brien took the seat by 169 votes on the strength of the 314 votes cast in his favour in Europe (he earned 49.1 percent of the civilian vote and 92.4 percent of the soldier vote). There was some hope that perhaps the seat of London might return to the Liberals, given the support of the *London Advertiser*, the only English-language newspaper in the province to support Laurier, but Hume Cronyn, the Unionist candidate (and father of the actor) and a former soldier (he had fought at the Battle of Cut Knife during the North-West Rebellion of 1885), won handily.

Laurier, who had been easily re-elected in Quebec East, was trounced in the double-seat riding of Ottawa, losing to Union incumbents Ernest Fripp and John Chabot by 16.6 percentage points. His party's seats in Ontario were scattered across the southern and eastern tips of the province — most won with relatively small pluralities of less than 10 percent. In all eight wins, the Liberals won an average of 53 percent of the civilian vote. In Bruce South, Ruben Truax (who was seen in some quarters as a Unionist disguised as a Liberal)[39] took over 56 percent of the civilian vote and won for the Liberals, but just barely: he collected only twenty-three soldier votes. His Unionist opponent had taken fewer civilian votes, but received 96 percent of the soldier votes. That, however, was not quite enough for a Unionist win.

The most decisive victories for the Liberals were in Franco-Ontarian–rich Prescott (with 74.1 percent of the civilian vote) and Russell (with 63.4 percent of the civilian vote). William Euler won Waterloo North for the Liberals on the strength of the German vote (over 78 percent of the population in that riding was considered "German," according to the 1911 census). Most of this population had been established long before 1902, the cutoff date fixed by the Wartime Elections Act. Euler won with an imposing twenty-point margin (he won 63.1 percent of the civilian vote, but only 4.6 percent of the soldier vote). Fourteen ridings were contested by more than the two main parties: ten by Labour, and four by independents. Altogether, the third parties took 3.6 percent of the votes, nine times more than in 1911.

A total of 101,723 military votes were recorded in Ontario, 12.5 percent of the total. This was in line with most jurisdictions, and in practically all the districts the pro-Unionist vote averaged 95 percent. But it really did not matter, as most of the ridings would have gone Union on the civilian vote alone. Only in five ridings did the winners (all Unionists) fail to win a plurality of the civil vote. In Brant, the soldiers more than made up the difference with 96.8 percent going in favour of the Unionists. In Essex South, 92.4 percent of soldiers voted the same way. In Hamilton West, it was 96.7 percent; Nipissing, 91.1 percent; and Perth South, 96.3 percent. In fact, the only ridings in Ontario where military support for the Borden government was relatively weak were Kent, where only 65 percent of soldiers voted Union, Prescott (85.9 percent), and Welland (74.3 percent). Those relatively weak results were likely because of strong Franco-Ontarian presence in Prescott and, in Kent (centred by the town of Chatham) and Welland (in the Niagara peninsula), because of the strong presence of farmers. In Kent, no Union candidate was presented. Archibald McCoig, the Laurier candidate (who many considered a Unionist),[40] took 54 percent of the votes, running against an "Independent Liberal." In Welland, the Liberals came close to taking a ninth seat. Labour ran a candidate and picked up 14.6 percent of the vote, dividing the opposition against the Union candidate. Evan Fraser took the seat for the Unionists with less than a majority. Welland was the only seat the opposition lost by being divided against itself.

Only one riding was won by acclamation — Liberal John McMartin was re-elected in Glengarry-Stormont, this time running as a Unionist.

For the Liberals, the humiliations kept on coming through election night. In Hamilton East, Major-General Sydney Mewburn, the minister of militia and defence, won 100 percent of the vote, completely shutting out his Liberal opponent, though he was not acclaimed. Mewburn had volunteered (at age fifty) for overseas duty, but instead had been offered a posting in home defence. According to official records, Liberal candidate George Halcrow won no votes at all.

Three seats were won by Unionists with more than 80 percent of the vote: Dufferin, Toronto North, and Durham. Another ten seats were taken with more than 70 percent of the vote. In Toronto, Union won solid support across the city, averaging 77.6 percent in the five ridings.

The effect of third parties was felt in a number of ridings. As chronicled in chapter 8, Harry Cockshutt had assumed that he would be given the Union government candidacy in Brant, but Borden had already made a commitment to John Harold, so Cockshutt ran as an independent, instead.[41] Cockshutt took 37.27 percent of the vote, eighty-three votes less than Harold, the Union candidate. For the Liberals, it made little difference: their candidate picked up only 24 percent of the vote — in line with the provincial average. Cockshutt's brother, William, ran and won in Brantford for the Union government, with almost 60 percent of the vote. His main opposition came from a Labour candidate, who managed to pick up over 17 percent.

MANITOBA

Canada's fifth province continued its march toward Conservatism in this khaki election. Long forgotten were the results of the election in 1904, when Manitobans had voted for the Liberals, giving them seven of the ten seats in the province. They had soured on Liberalism over the next few years, inspired by Conservative premier Rodmond Roblin, who constantly railed against Laurier and his compromises that favoured French-language rights in the West. Liberal support had eroded rapidly, and in 1908 and 1911 the Liberals took only two of the ten seats. No other province was as strongly Unionist as Manitoba. The number of voters boomed in this province, going from 77,696 to 134,034, a 72.5 percent increase, and the turnout was extraordinary: 97.1 percent. There were no third parties running in 1917, and the Union simply crushed its opposition, winning 79.7 percent of the total vote — the highest proportion, by far — with 76 percent of the civilian vote and 95.5 percent of the soldier vote. Union results were the largest pluralities recorded in the country. The soldier vote represented 18.3 percent of all the votes cast.

The Union harvest was plentiful in Manitoba: fourteen of the fifteen seats. Three of those fifteen seats were won by acclamation. John Campbell, running for the first time as a Unionist, won by no-contest in

Nelson. Albert Finney did the same in Souris. Robert Cruise, a former Laurier Liberal, was acclaimed this time as a Unionist in Dauphin.

The Unionists took the majority of the civilian vote in all the ridings except Provencher, the riding once held by Louis Riel, where a good portion of Franco-Manitobans lived. In the end, Liberal John Patrick Malloy beat his Unionist adversary with 52 percent of the vote. Luckily for him, there were fewer soldiers voting in that riding, though they did constitute a full 10 percent of the votes, the highest proportion of any district in the province. That riding also generated the lowest level of support for the Union government among soldiers: 90 percent.

The next smallest plurality was in Springfield, where Robert Lorne Richardson won as a Unionist. He took over 60 percent of the vote. He had sat on all sides of the House of Commons since being first elected in 1896 on the Liberal tide that brought Laurier to power. Richardson, owner and editor of the *Winnipeg Tribune,* had then fallen out with his leader, unable to accept the compromise Laurier and Sifton crafted on the schools question in his province. He ran and won as an independent in 1902, but was defeated in 1904. The stubborn journalist continued to run in various ridings — first as an independent in 1904, then as an independent Conservative in 1908, and then again as a Liberal in a 1912 by-election. In all of these he was defeated. Victory was finally his again in 1917. In Winnipeg Centre and Winnipeg South, both Unionists won with at least 85 percent of the vote. Winnipeg North lagged a little, relatively speaking, giving the Unionist Matthew Blake only 74 percent of the ballots. Arthur Meighen won his seat in Portage La Prairie with over 82 percent of the vote and Ferris Bolton won Lisgar with 86 percent.

SASKATCHEWAN

Once a Laurier stronghold — and continuing to elect Liberal governments provincially — Saskatchewan experienced a dramatic reversal. Support for the federal Liberals collapsed, going from almost 60 percent of the votes in 1911 to a quarter of the votes in 1917. Where it had given nine of ten seats to the Laurier Liberals in 1911, it now gave all its sixteen seats, including four by acclamation, to Borden's Union. Many more people voted in Saskatchewan in 1917 than in 1911. In the first Borden victory, 89,043 people voted. Six years later, the number had jumped by 25,880 (almost 30 percent) to 114, 931, and the turnout was 85.9 percent, which was all the more remarkable because four ridings were taken without active voting. John Johnston in Last Mountain, John Maharg in Maple Creek, and Richard Thompson in Weyburn were all running for the first time and won by acclamation on the Union ticket. Levi Thomson, who had represented Qu'Appelle as a Liberal since 1911, was also acclaimed as a Unionist. The number of acclamations could be considered higher if the riding of Mackenzie, where both candidates ran on the Union ticket, was included. The rest were equally humiliating for the Liberals, as they suffered in each riding, barely eking out the support of one in four voters.

In the end, 72 percent of Saskatchewan voters chose Union. The civilian support for the Union was strong at 68.9 percent of recorded votes. The soldiers in Saskatchewan voted almost unanimously for Union: 95 percent on average, in each riding. In Saskatoon and Moose Jaw, the rate was 97 percent. The soldiers represented 13.6 percent of all votes cast. The Borden coalition won a crushing majority in all ridings. The smallest win was with 56.2 percent in Mackenzie, the product of a most unusual military vote: the Union, in this riding, was massively unpopular among the soldiers — they gave it only 2.9 percent. Perhaps the next closest race was in North Battleford, where the Unionist Charles Long, a farmer, took only 41 percent of the civilian vote. He still beat his Liberal opponent by a 20 percent plurality because of a massive military support. Saskatchewan was behind only Manitoba in its support for Union.

ALBERTA

Alberta was a stunning win for the Unionists, and a bitter defeat for the Liberals, who lost six seats. Voters turned out en masse: 90.8 percent of those on the voters list recorded their vote. Among the civilians, the Unionists collected 54.4 percent of the vote. Some 94.9 percent of soldiers (who represented 16.1 percent of the total vote) voted Union. The province had changed. With its 127,818 voters — 58,043 more than in 1911, a staggering increase of 97.1 percent — Alberta was now the fourth-largest province in the country and packed a powerful political punch. Like Saskatchewan, Alberta also switched hard, giving eleven of its twelve seats to the Union Party, as well as 61 percent of the combined votes — an increase of 50 percent compared to the result in 1911, when Borden's Tories had won the support of only 42.5 percent of voters and taken just one seat.

In 1911, the province sent six of its seven MPs to the Liberal side of the House, with more than 53 percent of its votes. Things were different in 1917. The Liberals lost two ridings when their incumbents (Dr. Michael Clark in Red Deer and James Douglas in Strathcona) turned Unionist in October. The only jewel the Liberals could pocket was the riding of Victoria, which included parts of Edmonton and the town of Strathcona. Henry White, the Liberal incumbent, had voted in favour of conscription, thus retaining much of his previous support. He won the seat by taking 51.7 percent of the civilian vote, but was fortunate that very few soldiers called this riding home. Even though White took only 5.4 percent of the soldier vote, it was enough for him to squeak by: he won by 254 votes. An independent candidate (John W. Leedy, the former governor of Kansas) took enough votes from the Union to allow White to squeak in with an advantage of only 4 percent of the total vote.

The Union strategy worked remarkably well in Alberta. All the seats that went Union were won with at least 54 percent of the civilian vote and 62 percent of the combined vote. Two of the ridings were won with less than a majority: Edmonton West and Bow River. In Edmonton West, Frank Oliver, the former minister of the interior, who had survived the 1911 election and who had stayed loyal to Laurier, thought he had won. He did beat Antrobus Griesbach, a brigadier-general and commander of the 1st Brigade, in terms of the civilian vote, but ultimately lost because 94.8 percent of the soldiers in the riding voted against him. In eleven of the ridings, over 94 percent of the military vote was given to the Borden forces.

The Bow River contest was far more controversial. The Unionist, Howard Halladay, won by taking only 44.1 percent of the general vote (38.5 percent of the civilian vote and 94.1 percent of the military vote).

The Liberal support had been siphoned off, partly by the candidate running for the Non-Partisan League, who gathered over 17 percent of the vote, and partly by the Labour Party, which earned 3.6 percent. The Liberal loss in this new riding was directly attributed to the presence of the two protest parties; its candidate, Elmer Gouge, had been gouged.

The presence of third and sometimes fourth parties made a difference for the Liberals in Bow River only. The Non-Partisan League ran four candidates in Alberta, and its efforts in the ridings of Bow River, Red Deer, Victoria, and Macleod were respectable. All told, the candidates garnered only about three thousand votes, not enough to defeat the Union forces. Two Labour candidates also ran, in Red Deer and Bow River, but collected only a thousand votes between the two of them.

BRITISH COLUMBIA AND YUKON

British Columbia's growth in voters dwarfed even the remarkable growth of Alberta's. In total, 126,429 people voted in the Pacific province, a whopping 190.2 percent increase over the 43,559 who had voted in 1911. The turnout was an impossible 103.6 percent: according to the official report, there were more votes cast (126,429) than electors on the voting list (122,071). Clearly, a good many soldiers identified themselves as living in British Columbia, and their proportion of the total votes cast — 22.5 percent — was the largest recorded in any province. The results for British Columbia would give more than one Liberal partisan cause to be suspicious.

British Columbia was a Union triumph. Although the Union government garnered a very important majority of the vote among civilians, and 93.5 percent of the soldier vote, considerably less than in the other western provinces, all thirteen seats went Union. The 68.4 percent of the total vote garnered was more than enough to claim the province. Only one seat was taken by acclamation: that of Martin Burrell, who had sat as a Conservative since 1908.

Three of the seats were taken with more than 70 percent of the vote and eight more were won with more than 60 percent. The result was not entirely surprising, as British Columbia had been progressively turning its back on the Liberals. Much like Manitoba, it had supported Laurier in the 1904 election, but had not seen a way clear to do so after that. In 1908, the Conservatives had taken almost half the vote, and five of the seven seats. The Liberals were even more in freefall in 1911, when all seven seats were taken by the Conservatives, with almost 60 percent of the vote.

In 1917, things went from bad to worse, and magnified by the almost-doubling of electoral districts. The tightest race was the new riding of Skeena, where the Liberals earned almost 43 percent of the total ballots cast — still 14 percent less than the Unionists. Skeena's soldiers were hardened Unionists: 95 percent in favour of the government.

The Labour Party was active in the province, running in six districts and earning 6.1 percent of the vote, possibly robbing the Laurier Liberals of a decent showing in a few ridings. Its best results were achieved in the Kootenays. Kootenay West gave Labour 16.4 percent of its vote, while Kootenay East awarded it just a bit more than 8 percent. In Vancouver South, another pronounced working-class neigbourhood, Labour won 11 percent of the vote. In Nanaimo, 10.8 percent of the vote went Labour. Collectively, Labour's vote was not concentrated enough to take a win. In all cases, however, the Labour Party scored well only among the civilian population. The soldiers had no time for it.

In Yukon, the Union held the seat the Conservatives had taken from the Liberals in 1911, but only with the military vote, which at 18.4 percent was among the highest proportion in Canada. The Liberals actually won the civilian vote, taking 53.8 percent, but the Union won 90.2 percent of the military. In the end, the Liberals took 45.7 percent of the vote, but Unionist Alfred Thompson was re-elected with a comfortable overall total of 54.3 percent. Frostbitten Yukon produced 1,767 voters, a drop of 16.4 percent from the 1911 turnout (the official results for the Territory were not officially released until April 1918).

The Union's "great gerrymander" had worked, but it had not been necessary. A majority of Canadians supported the Borden government's platform and gave it a resounding mandate to introduce conscription and to continue with the war effort as it intended to do. If the 1911 election had been a nail-biter, dominated by countless ridings won by small margins (less than 5 percent of the vote), the 1917 khaki election was completely different. Only thirteen races were really close, and, of those, six were won by the Liberals and seven by the Unionists. The argument that the soldier vote made the difference is not supported by the evidence.[42] The results of giving the right to vote to some women, however, defies speculation. The records simply do not indicate how many females voted, and say nothing of how they voted, though it is clear that adding them to the franchise boosted the Union government's electoral results. From that angle, Borden's gambit may well have made a difference.

The victory of the Union Government was undeniable — even if the soldier vote would not be fully counted until late January, 1918. It took 153 of the 235 seats, 65 percent of the total, on the strength of a 57.1 percent share of all votes; 53.3 percent of the civilian vote and, eventually, 93.1 percent of the military vote. The Union took thirty seats from the Liberals, all outside Quebec except one (St. Lawrence–St. George, in Montreal). It won a plurality of votes in every province save Quebec, collecting nearly 80 percent of the vote in Manitoba on the high end, and almost 48 percent of the count in Nova Scotia on the low end. Even if the military vote had been apportioned to the same degree as the civilian vote, the Unionists would still have collected over 53 percent of the total vote and won a resounding victory. It won more votes than in 1911 in every province save Quebec.

For the old Conservatives, that was twenty-one more seats than in 1911. The Union government won 1,077,569 votes; 411,495 more than the Tories' 666,074 of 1911. That was 61.7 percent more votes in 1917 than six years before, and represented an increase of 6.6 percent more in popular votes than in 1911. For Borden, the exercise had been "a notable test of democracy." For him, this was an affirmation of his mandate, given that Canadians had been provided with the opportunity "to say whether Canada's effort in the war should be maintained."[43] Borden also believed that the large pro-Union vote sent a message to those on the battlefront. "Canada now sends them the message for which they have longed; and it will bring joy and comfort to every heart among them."[44]

Overseas, 232,952 soldier votes made their way to the counting tables in London (for fear that they would be lost at sea en route to Canada, victims of German U-boats), and almost all of them supported the Unionists and their promise for more men, more support, and more effort in helping defeat the kaiser. The day-after predictions of total victory for the Unionists proved correct, but the soldier vote merely reinforced the statement made by the civilians.

The Union cabinet won an almost complete victory. All the former Conservative cabinet ministers were triumphant, save for Albert Sévigny, who was humiliated at the polls. Burrell was acclaimed in Yale (British Columbia), the only former Conservative to return uncontested. Borden took Kings (Nova Scotia) with almost 61 percent. White took Leeds with 64 percent. Meighen crushed his opponent in Portage La Prairie (Manitoba) with 82.5 percent of the vote. Foster took North Toronto with almost 88 percent of the vote. Charles Doherty, running in Montreal's St. Anne district against John James Guerin, a former mayor, and Daniel Gallery a long-time Liberal activist in the city, easily rode to victory with 63.8 percent of the total vote, including 58 percent of the civilian vote and 92 percent of the military. Kemp took Toronto East with almost 79 percent. Reid took Grenville (Ontario) with close to 64 percent of the riding.

The seven Liberal members of the House of Commons who had joined the Union government were all elected — most with even larger pluralities than those recorded by the former Conservatives. Carvell took Victoria-Carleton in New Brunswick by acclamation. Though not officially acclaimed, Mewburn in Hamilton East (Ontario) nevertheless took 100 percent of the vote. Crerar won in Marquette (Manitoba) with more than 88 percent of the vote. Rowell captured Durham (Ontario) with 80 percent. Calder took Moose Jaw (Saskatchewan) with 75 percent, and Sifton took Medicine Hat (Alberta) with 63 percent. Ballantyne took 70.7 percent in St. Lawrence–St. George (Montreal). They had been vindicated.

Herbert Ames in Montreal declared on the night of the victory that the country's verdict had been clear and that Laurier had to "keep his promise" and cease his opposition to conscription now that the people had voted for it. "The worst thing that could possibly happen would be for Laurier and his followers to assume an attitude of opposition to what is undoubtedly the verdict of the people of Canada as a whole," he declared. "That would isolate our Province with a vengeance."[45]

In Toronto, W.L. Grant was installed as the principal of Upper Canada College on the day after the election and he used his introductory speech to say that Laurier should be proud of Canada. "Misguided he may think her if he will, but he must be glad to belong to any nation which so proudly takes up so great a burden."[46] The newspapers across the country were correct in predicting a landslide victory for Borden and his new government, almost from the moment the polls closed. The results in the Maritime provinces and the early returns in central Canada were the only difficult terrain for the Unionists. Few people expected many gains for the Liberals in the West. The golden age of Laurier's western Canada power base was over.

Outside Quebec, the Liberal opposition took five seats that had previously been held by Conservatives (Kent in New Brunswick; Lunenberg in Nova Scotia; Bruce South, Essex North, and Waterloo North in Ontario), and they recaptured twenty-six seats inside Quebec. The Laurier team won eighty-two seats on the strength of just about 35 percent of the vote. In terms of vote counts, it was a catastrophe for the Liberals. Having taken 623,554 ballots (47.7 percent of the vote) in 1911, they only took 548,611 in 1917. It was, for them, the worst result since Confederation.

The impact of the gerrymander has been discussed ever since, but it will never be possible to measure its impact with certainty. Giving the vote to soldiers was the proper thing to do. They were citizens, for the most part, and the argument that their military involvement should disqualify them made no sense. The few foreigners enlisted in the Canadian forces who may have exercised their right to vote did not have a significant impact. Even if the ballots with no riding destination were eliminated, it is doubtful that those who knew so little of Canada's political geography had much impact on the final tally. Whatever their impact might have been, there was much room to justify giving men who were fighting in the trenches for king and country the right to have a say in an election. As Talbot

Papineau put it the year before, "We should not look upon the soldier as a non-combatant or in a class by himself, he is merely a militant citizen."[47]

Giving the right to some women and not others was blatantly wrong. This gift to Unionist forces could have made a difference in a few ridings; but, then again, given the overwhelming victories among the civilian voters, it is doubtful that in English Canada giving the vote to all women would have changed much. In Quebec, and perhaps in a few ridings in Ontario, the fact that fewer women were able to vote simply because fewer men had enrolled could have been a factor. It could have accentuated the Liberal, anti-conscriptionist vote. All the same, such effects would have been localized. The Unionists would have won anyway.

The civilian vote demonstrated strong tendencies. Union was strongest in the West. Manitoba, giving 80 percent of its civilian vote to the Union, was the most supportive. In British Columbia and Saskatchewan, around 70 percent of the civilians swung toward Union, a gigantic shift from the 1911 results. Alberta and Ontario's civilians were slightly less enthusiastic — around 61 percent supported the Union in those provinces. In Quebec and the Maritimes, it was a different story. Only 23 percent of Quebec civilian voters favoured Union, as did a minority in Nova Scotia and Prince Edward Island.

The general vote, on a province-by-province basis, reflected the consensus. Except in Quebec, the Unionists won the election. The switchers — those who had supported Laurier in the past, including in the crucial 1911 vote — often simply voted for the Liberal candidate who had also switched his allegiance.

Whereas in English Canada the soldier vote on the provincial level ranged between 88 and 95 percent in favour of Unionists (lower in the East and highest in the West), in Quebec the soldier vote in favour of the Union government averaged 82.3 percent across the ridings.

The military vote was remarkably consistent. Overall, it constituted 13 percent of the entire vote, not an insignificant number, but, given the overwhelmingly strong civilian support for Union, not particularly impactful on local ridings. If the soldiers had voted in the same proportions as their civilian counterparts, the results would not have changed at all.

The 1917 election saw a massive increase in votes for third parties and independents of all sorts: 51,728 votes, 2.7 percent of ballots, more than double what had been attained in 1911. Most of the votes were for the twenty-two candidates that were informally endorsed by the Canadian Labour Party (CLP). Five years earlier, the support for Labour in English Canada had amounted to less than 1 percent of total votes cast. The new CLP functioned without a coherent, national leadership, but clearly responded to local needs. In French Canada, Bourassa's *nationalistes* had taken 26.7 percent of the protest vote in 1911.

A big factor in this election was the number of acclamations. Since 1867, there had never been more than a handful, typically because of a remarkably popular incumbent from either party. In the fall of 1917, however, more often the riding consensus was so strong that no one individual felt sufficiently confident to represent the "other side." On the morning of election day, December 17, fourteen candidates had already been elected by acclamation for the Union Party, and eighteen had similarly won by default on the Liberal side. The Union acclamations were sprinkled across the country, except Quebec. From east to west, four Unionists had already won in Nova Scotia, and one in each of New Brunswick, Ontario, and British Columbia. Three candidates so won in Manitoba, and no less than four in Saskatchewan. Quebec supplied the greatest number of acclamations: seventeen out of sixty-five seats, all Liberal. The eighteenth seat the Liberals won by acclamation was Gloucester, in New Brunswick.

The 1917 election brought 110 new men to Parliament Hill, 47 percent of the 235 elected, including Samuel William Jacobs, who won the George-Étienne-Cartier riding in Montreal, the first Jewish person elected to the House of Commons. The cohort of MPs from Manitoba, Saskatchewan, and Alberta were almost all newcomers and close to half of the delegations from Ontario and Quebec had been changed. In addition, the government side had twenty-six veterans who had served at the Front or in the military hierarchy since 1914; another eighteen of them had served in some sort of military function previously. In comparison, only two Liberals had been to the Front, and, of the pair, Henri Béland had spent four years in a German prison. Only four others on the

Opposition benches had served in the military in the past. The outlook of the two parties could not have been more fundamentally different. Parliament had been changed.

The vote for Union could have been called utilitarian. It was not so much a vote for Borden or for the Unionists as it was for a cause. Canadians outside Quebec were willing to run the risk of completely alienating Quebec, at least for a while, and to support a united party that was committed to helping the soldiers; who, in turn, were helping Britain, Belgium, and France. It was nothing more than that. The war finished, the voters turned against the Conservatives massively in the election of 1921 and the three-party system was born.

Most Canadians, once the election campaign was over, hoped to forget about the war and politics, if only for a few days. Two days after the election, the first season of the National Hockey League started. Christmas poultry advertising now replaced political news. Department stores in the big cities remained open until ten in the evening to accommodate the Christmas rush. They cheerily beckoned shoppers looking for ties, military-style trench coats, special china, books and toys for children, satin hats for women, and, most of all, the gramophones, Victrolas, phonographs, and Grafonolas that promised to play Christmas records that "will make this day a source of great enjoyment and a day to always remember."[48] "Make this a Christmas to be remembered for years to come," the Toronto music store Heintzman and Co. urged in its newspaper advertisement. That Christmas would not be forgotten for a long time, but for reasons that had little to do with music.[49]

10

THE AFTERMATH: UNION WITHOUT UNITY

"I could tell you everything that happened. It was especially the English who did this. Here, it was not either red
or blue, but English against the *Canadien*. It was a race
struggle that took place in the Dominion, and it seems
now that the English are in power."

— Onésime Nantel-Orsali to Eugène Nantel,
January 1918[1]

Everyone might agree that the election had been about Union government and conscription, but it quickly appeared that the aftermath
of the election would be about Quebec. But it was not at all clear just
in what way. The *Globe*'s headline screamed that "Dominion Rejects
Quebec Domination."[2] For its part, the *Toronto Daily Star* editorialized
that "Quebec for the present is isolated, and the task of restoring unity
will be one of great difficulty. Perhaps we should say of creating unity, for
the war has revealed rather than caused a deplorable lack of sympathy,
knowledge, and insight. The two communities have drifted apart and the
wisest statesmanship will be required to bring them together."[3]

"It is early to forecast the effect of this election and of the new group-
ings of parties on the Dominion," the governor general wrote to Walter
Long, the British colonial secretary, a few days after the election. "On
the whole, the result was received very quietly in the Province of Quebec
and there was no trouble anywhere. I do not anticipate any trouble in the
Province, although the result was undoubtedly a great surprise and a great
shock to Sir Wilfrid and his followers."[4] In Toronto, several friends and

advisers of Newton Rowell met in his house the day after the election and the one topic of discussion was "What to do about Quebec?"[5] Across town at Queen's Park, Conservative premier Sir William Hearst was thinking in a similar fashion. "What the result of the election on the future of Canada will be it is hard to say," he wrote his son who was serving in France. His first thought was that the result would be good for Canada, in that Quebec no longer held the balance of power. In the new Union government Quebec had "isolated herself. She may now as never before see the folly of the policy she has pursued."[6] In Ottawa, the prime minister was equally uncertain but was quick to realize that a triumphalist Ontario could only inflame a delicate situation. "During the next two or three weeks," he wrote Rowell, "members of the Government should make no public utterances with respect to conditions in that Province [Quebec]." And he asked Rowell to put the word out that it would also be a good idea if the English press remained calm and, above all, silent on the issue of Quebec.[7]

Postmortems filled the mail bags, and dominated discussions at large meetings and in small kitchens. Borden's office was flooded with dozens of letters celebrating the great Union triumph and especially highlighting his role in that victory; in return he sent out multiple letters of thanks to his supporters for the role they played. Victory meant that the war would be prosecuted to the end; that the Canadian soldiers would not be let down or dishonoured. For most, the only snag was, again, Quebec, and here opinion varied, with a mixture of regret and concern combined with frustration and some anger that Quebec had not come to its senses and joined the Union government and the war effort.

"It looks to me as though a firm but conciliatory stand should be taken with regard to the Province of Quebec," the victorious one of the Cockshutt brothers wrote the prime minister from Brantford, Ontario. "The feeling in this section is that they have not up to date at all realized the war sacrifices that are necessary in a crisis such as this, and our people will not be satisfied unless a strong effort is made in this direction."[8]

Not surprisingly, many newspapers reported that former American president Theodore Roosevelt — who had ceaselessly pushed to see the United States involved in fighting the war — pronounced himself "delighted" by the Borden victory.[9]

In Winnipeg, John Dafoe was feeling anything but magnanimous or conciliatory. The day after the election he wrote that he had warned Sir Wilfrid that his course of action would mean certain defeat at the polls and the ultimate destruction of the Liberal Party, and that now French Canadians found themselves in Parliament as a bloc with no power other than obstruction. "I have always been clear in my mind that a solid Quebec was bound to mean a solid English Canada against Quebec," he wrote Thomas Côté, a long-time Liberal organizer in Quebec. "I do not think the situation, which is full of peril to Canada, can be changed, except upon the initiative of Quebec herself."

An incredulous Côté responded that Quebec had been accused of disloyalty because its people had opposed conscription, while the English press had systematically insulted Quebec and made "racial" appeals to anglophones; and now Dafoe was suggesting that it was up to Quebec to reconcile with the rest of the country? "It takes a man of no ordinary gall to utter such a declaration," he concluded sharply.

Dafoe responded angrily and with racial emphasis: "[T]he trouble between the English and the French Canadians has become acute, because the French Canadians have refused to play their part in the war — being the only known race of white men to quit." The French Canadian offers only excuses about domestic linguistic grievances, he continued. "Do not flatter yourself with the idea that the English-Canadians are disturbed by your attitude of injured innocence or your threats of reprisals. You can do precisely as you please; and we shall do whatever may be necessary. When we demonstrate, as we shall, that a solid Quebec is without power, there may be a return to reason along the banks of the St. Lawrence."[10]

Everyone seemed to have an idea about what went wrong with the Liberal campaign, and for every letter of congratulations received by Borden there was one of condolence for Laurier. "The dice were so loaded that it was an impossibility," wrote friend and Liberal benefactor Peter Larkin.[11] For some, it was "race and religion" that were used against the Liberals; others pointed to unscrupulous enumerators who worked mischief for the Tories; still others blamed the impact of having any women voting, not just the women who voted. "Husbands voted with their wives, not wives with their husbands," complained one Liberal in an odd misogynist outburst. "Daughters voted with their mothers. When woman suffers from hysteria man placates her by agreeing with her. The election was distinctly of the emotional type and in no way suggested an occasion of reasoning."[12]

From Nova Scotia there was some satisfaction that the Liberals had remained united in the face of the harmful defections of Premier Murray and W.S. Fielding. From Ontario the conclusion was that the last-minute exemption for farmers pulled the rug out from under the Liberal campaign. In Alberta, Liberals blamed the Wartime Elections Act and the disenfranchisement of so many Liberal voters. From Winnipeg, one supporter concluded that the election was not really about conscription; the sole issue was "the desire to in some way coerce Quebec, or as the man on the street puts it to 'show Quebec where it gets off.'"[13]

Laurier received these words with a mixture of understanding, acknowledgement, and grace; but not resignation. "It would be of no use to cry over spilled milk," he wrote an Alberta MLA; if there were voting irregularities either at home or overseas, Laurier wanted the facts compiled from all the ridings so that a serious case could be made.[14] He asked the defeated Frank Oliver for evidence of Unionist vote tampering, adding that "we should instruct our candidates to get facts and affidavits substantiating every instance of wrong doing."[15] A month after the election, Laurier was still encouraging W.T.R. Preston to continue his investigations of fraud with the military vote: "persist to the end against … counting ballots which never went legally in the boxes. You may be overcome, but we must prepare a strong case for the public," he wrote in a private letter. "We have been defeated by the same methods on this side of the Atlantic," he continued, "the 'War Times Elections Act' did the trick. With the ordinary Franchise and under the ordinary law of election we would have won, not overwhelmingly, but surely. I say not overwhelmingly, because the defection of the Liberal-Unionists, was in itself a heavy blow."[16] "At present we are defeated," he responded to one sympathetic Manitoban, "and so long as the war lasts the loyalty cry will cover a multitude of sins. It behooves us, however, to prepare for the next fight."[17]

Le Clairon in Saint-Hyacinthe argued that Quebec had lost because of its lack of leadership in supporting voluntary enlistment. It was a small paper, but Laurier clipped the editorial and kept it in his files. "How many French-Canadian public men dared to speak the language of common sense and public interest on this issue of volunteer enlistment?" it asked. "They are counted on the fingers of one hand those who held meetings to enlighten public opinion on voluntary enlistment that would have saved us from conscription if it had yielded the results which we were entitled to expect in the province of Quebec." *Le Clairon* railed against those who said nothing or little on the issue, or who simply argued against "*les anglais*."[18] For the editorialist of *Le Clairon*, the Liberals who had done nothing but support Laurier — who had spoken eloquently in favour of a vigorous enlistment campaign — were only guaranteeing their electoral seats. They should have declared themselves foursquare in favour of the war and in favour of enlistment. Victorious though they were in their ridings, on the morrow after the election, they had won nothing. Quebec had only given Laurier a "fatal gift." "There is one grand lesson to be drawn from this defeat," the editorial concluded:

> The politics of intransigence will always be fatal for French Canadians. A politics of compromise will save our race, in the end. Laurier put it into practice, and it gave marvellous results. In this case, voluntary enlistment was a noble compromise between the non-participation in the war and the conscription of men; it was a middle-road policy that would have ensured peace between the diverse races in this country, but the influence of near-sighted and narrow-minded people who want everything without conceding to others prevailed and the direct result of Bourassa by name or by ideas has given us conscription and the defeat of the great French Canadian, defeat that comes of our hypocrites who must, in the recesses of their perverted souls, salute with joy because it was they who prepared it so willingly. Here is hoping that this defeat will open the eyes of our race, and that it will not be the prelude of our greatest national misfortunes.[19]

To George Graham, now in Montreal, Laurier was more open, regretting that his former close colleague had not run as a Liberal in North Renfrew, where he might have won. "We have still some good men in the ranks of the Opposition," he added, "but our fighting strength has been very much reduced."

Laurier had delayed his planned visit to Montreal; "I suffer now from a reaction, and feel a little depressed." But his biggest concern was still the reaction of Quebec to the election results and the government's move ahead with conscription. "What worries me now is the application of Conscription in Quebec. I am afraid of passive resistance to the application of the Act."[20]

If English Canadians were convinced that this was "Canada's war" and that the war was a "national opportunity" that needed to be pursued to the fullest extent, French Canadians were shaken, angry, and resentful at what had happened. "What fanaticism among the English populations of Ontario and the western provinces," wrote Quebec Minister of Agriculture J.E. Caron to Laurier the day after the election. "What has happened is a misfortune for Canada, in general, and for Quebec in particular. All of us are very anxious." Has Borden lost his head? Caron asked in a second letter; "if he knew the deplorable effect of the actions which he is taking he would immediately stop the application of the conscription law."[21]

The sense of isolation within Canada was complete and it led almost immediately to the introduction of a motion in the Quebec Legislative Assembly by Joseph-Napoléon Francoeur on January 17, 1918, stating: "This House is of the opinion that the province of Quebec would be disposed to accept the breaking of the Confederation Pact of 1867 if, in the other provinces, it is believed that she is an obstacle to the union, progress and development of Canada." The debate on the "Francoeur Motion" was lively and diverse, with many members venting their anger, frustration, and outrage over the attacks on French Canadians during the election campaign, over conscription, Regulation 17, and other issues, but there was also overwhelming opposition to the motion. Premier Gouin rose and gave a spirited defence of Confederation, and the motion was withdrawn without a vote. All the same, it was the first time Quebec separation was debated in the legislature. The symbolism of the motion would not be soon forgotten.

"There is no [secession] movement at all," Laurier wrote, "this is simply an answer to the vicious campaign of abuse of Quebec which has been carried on by the [T]ories during the last contest."[22] If anything, the debate over the motion helped clear the air somewhat both in Quebec and across the rest of the country. The wisdom of Borden's call for calm was evident. Gouin's speech was welcomed in Quebec as a clear statement of the wrongs inflicted on French Canada during the war; it was also praised in English Canada for its support of Confederation and for its appeal to Quebeckers to remain calm and obey the law. Fears that Quebec would rise in armed resistance were quieted; Quebec's place in Canada was reaffirmed. As one historian later wrote, the "abscess of Quebec's discontent burst."[23]

Borden wrote privately that "a French Canadian said to me a few days ago that the [election] result was due to Bourassa's teachings coupled with Laurier's [l]eadership."[24] This was the second time he had profited from that combination, he could have thought. Happy with the results, he left for a brief holiday in Virginia soon after the election and returned to Ottawa — much refreshed — at the start of the new year.

Given that collecting and counting the votes would continue for several weeks, Parliament was not scheduled to sit until March 1918. In the meantime, the reformed Union government resumed its operations. It comprised essentially the same individuals as before the election, with a few minor changes. The largest gap remained in the representation from Quebec, except that now things were even worse. Albert Sévigny, defeated in the election, stayed on as minister of inland revenue until he finally resigned in March 1918. Pierre-Édouard Blondin, who was defeated in Laurier-Outremont, was retained as postmaster general, even though he was posted as a lieutenant-colonel in London, far from Ottawa. He lobbied for a diplomatic post, convincing himself between Christmas and New Year's that the Borden government should do nothing to include French Canadians in the cabinet.[25] Borden, eager to find a replacement for Sévigny, chose to make Blondin a senator in April 1918, and he was sworn in to the upper chamber that July. He would continue to serve Borden until the end of the government in 1921.[26] There were no elected French Canadians in the Union government, and Blondin was one of the two Catholics in cabinet (Charles Doherty was the other).

Borden was later quite positive about the Union government. "From first to last," he wrote in his memoirs, "not once was there any division upon former party lines. On many occasions there was keen divergence of opinion, warm and even heated discussion, but always there were former Liberals and former Conservatives on each side."[27] Nevertheless, there were problems from the very start. Newton Rowell, for example, immediately complained about the overrepresentation of former Conservatives in the government and demanded more Liberal-Unionist ministers. J.D. Reid, who had clashed with Rowell over the distribution of ridings before the election, was critical of Rowell's argument and complained that the Liberal-Unionist press, especially the *Toronto Globe* and *Toronto Daily Star*, had returned to their partisan Liberal viewpoints and had been unfairly targeting Borden and the Conservative-Unionists.[28]

Nevertheless, during the election Borden had promised decisive action, and the Union government was fairly active in 1918 delivering on its promises, including civil service reform, nationalization of the railways, the introduction of prohibition (at least briefly), legislation extending the federal vote to most women, and the establishment of a Canadian War Mission in Washington. Taxes were raised and more attention was paid to veterans and resettlement; daylight saving time was introduced, and the Dominion Bureau of Statistics was created; and, in response to the new tenor of the times, hereditary titles for Canadians were abolished.[29] Since the "anti-alien" feelings that had been whipped up during the election campaign had not faded, new, tougher, immigration regulations were introduced, as well.

Throughout, the opposition Liberals attacked the Military Service Act and complained about the election results. Laurier "looked lonely and ill supported," wrote Sir George Foster. "He constituted a pathetic figure in his old age and party weakness."[30] Borden, on the other hand, could claim the leadership of an activist government with a progressive edge that included state management and social reconstruction.

For much of the winter and early spring the Liberals tried to over-turn the election results. There had already been complaints during the election campaign about what was considered to be the unfair activities of the Unionists and the military establishment overseas, and concerning the work of enumerators at home. There were clear irregularities in the soldier vote. The soldiers did not need much persuasion to support con-scription and the Union government, but there were allegations that the government used its advantage to encourage the men to vote Union and to leave their choice of constituency open, and had then placed some of those floating votes in ridings of the government's choosing.[31]

W.T.R. Preston, the Liberal scrutineer in Europe, had, since before the election, been making allegations of fraud, perjury, and other illegal activities, going so far as to allege murder, in that some soldiers were reportedly shipped unexpectedly to the Front — and their possible deaths — because they had shown Liberal sympathies. There was little hope for a commission of inquiry he reported, because "there were rea-sonable chances for the greater part of the evidence to be lying in graves in Flanders."[32] Preston alleged that "fraud of the most shocking char-acter"[33] had occurred in the stuffing of ballot boxes and the casting of fraudulent votes, and he flooded Laurier with letters detailing his accus-ations. He later wrote about the experience in his memoirs, in a chapter entitled "The Election Frauds of 1917." Several individuals were named as perpetrators of this "travesty," but Borden and Meighen were singled out as the "worst offenders."[34] Preston's more outlandish allegations were denied at the time, seriously questioned by later historians,[35] and shown in the previous chapter here to be baseless.

There were also complaints about the way the vote was conducted at home. There were a number of voting irregularities reported to Laurier: cases of people voting in ridings where they did not live or having their names improperly placed on the voting lists, of individuals being barred from voting when they were legally entitled to, of ridings where "for-eigners" were turned away even though their names were on the voting lists; and cases of men and women voting multiple times and in different ridings. Edmonton East was given special attention because it was a very close contest and the riding of Liberal stalwart Frank Oliver. One report declared that thirty-six "Scandinavians" were turned away at the polls even though entitled to vote, while others were allowed to vote twenty times in the same riding. "The more I think of this thing," wrote one Alberta Liberal MLA, "the more convinced I am that it was a wholesale steal."[36]

Laurier and many Liberals were convinced that there had been widespread electoral fraud, but what to do about it was a different matter. There were calls for a judicial inquiry; Oliver was prompted to make an official protest; others suggested suing the government for its actions, or introducing a petition in Parliament. Everyone had an opinion, including Ned Macdonald in Nova Scotia, Oliver in Alberta, and Sir Allen Aylesworth in Ontario, but the evidence just was not there. Laurier repeatedly asked his sources for evidence — letters or documents to support the allegations — but does not appear to have received much concrete proof of wrongdoing. There were enough reports from across the country to leave little doubt that some electoral chicanery occurred. But fraud was very hard to prove and, while Borden and his government clearly manipulated the voters through legislation and Orders-in-Council before the election, there is no evidence to suggest that his government had a hand in rigging the vote at home.

Time began to run out as Parliament opened in March 1918: it proved difficult to sustain public interest in the issue for very long. Oliver decided against an official protest, believing that it likely would not make much difference in any event.[37] Senator Dandurand persisted in calling the election a fraud to his dying day; for him it had been stolen by the government's manipulations of the franchise, not because the idea of Canada had failed.[38] Preston tried to revive interest in the alleged election fraud in 1919 with new charges directed against Arthur Meighen. That led to a bitter debate in Parliament; but it all produced more smoke than fire and soon faded. By then the war was over and Liberal attention had become more focused on reuniting a divided party. Liberals were more interested in preparing for the next election than in re-fighting the last one.[39]

There was still a war to be fought, and Canada's war effort remained the Borden government's main concern. Laurier may not have gotten his plebiscite, but the election vote was seen as the closest thing possible to a national referendum on conscription, and the verdict of the Canadian people was clear: the Union success was a victory for conscription and the war effort. Canada's war effort would not be allowed to falter. "On December 17 the people of Canada, with no uncertain voice, spoke their determination to back this Corps with all the resources at their disposal," wrote General Currie from the Canadian Corps's overseas headquarters, "and this Corps today is, on that account, more than ever determined to do its duty to Canada and the Empire."[40]

The election may have been interpreted as giving legitimacy to the policy of conscription, but its implementation was anything but smooth, and the problems continued. The goal of the Military Service Act was to raise approximately 100,000 men. A Military Service Council was established to oversee implementation and local tribunals to adjudicate exemptions, which were given for those involved in essential work, those with special qualifications, serious hardship, or a physical disability, and for conscientious objectors and clergymen. The first group was called up to register in October 1917. It was clear before the election that very few eligible Canadians were eager to join the CEF, and by the end of 1917 no less than 93.7 percent of the 400,000 men called to serve had applied for exemptions. Criticism arose immediately that the tribunals in Quebec were granting a high percentage of exemption requests, but they were high everywhere. And still no man had been ordered to report for duty, in keeping with Borden's promise not to enforce conscription until after the election. When finally ordered to report for training at the beginning of January 1918, barely twenty thousand men showed up and very few of them were from Quebec.[41] "The M[ilitary] S[ervice] A[ct] is not working out satisfactorily," Foster complained in his diary in early February. "The heart is sick and that is the whole trouble. Quebec is badly led but alas does not resent the leading."[42] For Laurier the ongoing debacle over conscription only confirmed him in his view that the Military Service Act had been more about winning the election than about winning the war.[43]

In light of the resistance to enlist, the 5th Division, already stationed in England, was broken up in February to provide the necessary reinforcements for the CEF. But things only got worse; in March the

Germans launched one last desperate offensive on the Western Front and pushed the allied forces to their limits. Russia's exit from the war early in 1918 with the Treaty of Brest-Litovsk meant the Germans could focus all their energies on the West, in an effort to smash the British lines and force them back to the sea. The CEF was not at the heart of the fighting, but for many Canadians this offensive appeared to be the defining moment of the war, with victory or defeat hanging in the balance. "Titanic Fight Goes On" announced the *Calgary Daily Herald*, while the *Montreal Gazette* informed its readers that this battle "rivalled in ferocity any that has preceded it during three and a half years of warfare."[44] Canadians, like their British cousins, now realized the "momentousness of the battle."[45]

With each passing day the news from Europe got worse, and the demands for more reinforcements louder. The Borden government, under intense pressure, promised to do all it could, and that would include increased efforts to enforce the Military Service Act. Near the end of March anti-conscription rioting again erupted in Quebec City, this time brutal as never before: four protesters died, five soldiers were wounded, and thousands were jailed, before peace returned to the city on April 1. "Blood Flows in Quebec," proclaimed the *Vancouver Daily Sun*, as morning "dawned with the spirit of mob rule and battle in the air."[46] Borden responded quickly and severely: an army battalion was sent in to protect government and military installations; an Order-in-Council was issued that made it possible to draft into the military anyone who participated in the rioting; and another Order-in-Council put limits on free speech by cracking down on any speech or publication considered "seditious."[47] "What a pity," Foster wrote in his diary during the riots, "that just now when our very existence as a nation and Empire is swaying in the balance this trouble at home should develop."[48]

The sense of emergency continued well into April. The demand came from England that fifteen thousand men were needed by the end of the month; Ottawa could deliver only five thousand. It would take only a few ships to transport the limited number of recruits from Quebec, complained Sir Edward Kemp, from London. At the same time, the troops who "voted practically that they should come over and take a hand in this fight, will be exasperated beyond measure unless something is done."[49]

As Borden's biographer put it, the "manpower crisis, delayed over the winter, was at hand."[50]

On April 19, in a rare secret session of Parliament, the Union government cancelled almost all exemptions on men from twenty to twenty-two years of age, including the exemption to farmers' sons granted during the election campaign. The move was defended as a necessary response to the war crisis and as something unforeseen during the election — not as a backtracking on an election promise. But that was how it was seen, especially by thousands of farmers across the country. The outbursts of condemnation were loud, and several farmers' delegations from Ontario and Quebec descended on Ottawa in protest in May. Angry words were exchanged; farmers warned of the loss of agricultural production; Borden warned of defeat and the loss of the Channel Ports, after which agricultural production wouldn't matter.[51] In the end, he stood firm and the protests petered out; but the anger remained, and a new political movement was born; it would soon manifest itself in political action.

The various Orders-in-Council, the tightening of the exemptions, and a more assertive application of the policy helped increase the number of reinforcements through the summer of 1918, but the concerns over finding enough men remained. Only with the ending of the war in November did the situation resolve itself. By Armistice Day, conscription had produced 99,651 men, of which only 24,132 made it to France. As the German offensive in the summer of 1918 took its toll, more and more French Canadian men were marched to war. In the end, 27,557 would be drafted (about 23 percent of the conscripted corps).[52] That most of the conscripts were English Canadians was not lost on anyone, while the whole experience left a bitter taste in French Canada. The goal of 100,000 men was reached, but few Canadians rejoiced, or called the policy a success. On the contrary, conscription became the symbol of a bad and terrible war; it was forever linked to the Union government and it became Borden's most enduring legacy.

In November 1918, less than a year after the election, the First World War finally ended, and, in many ways, the end of the war marked the beginning of the end for the Union government and party. Despite the apparent sweeping victory in December 1917, the great weaknesses of Union government became evident almost immediately. The Conservative- and Liberal-Unionists never really fused into a single party; they continued to meet in their own caucuses and often viewed one another with suspicion. The war was the glue holding the two groups together, and once that was removed the government's cohesion began to deteriorate.

The Union government — although technically elected for the first time in 1917 — was already a mature government, especially within the Conservative ranks. Sir Thomas White, Sir George Foster, Sir Edward Kemp, J.D. Reid, Charles Doherty, Frank Cochrane, and, of course, Sir Robert Borden, had been in office since 1911 and were worn to the bone by the war administration. Several longed for retirement or were looking for other ways to get out. For their part, the Liberal-Unionists proved to be more inexperienced in politics and less committed to the Union than Borden may have hoped for, and few of the new ministers emerged as potential leaders. Frank Carvell had always been too much a Liberal partisan to attract much support from the Conservative wing of the party; similarly, Newton Rowell, perhaps the leading Liberal-Unionist before the election, never overcame his lack of personal popularity among Conservatives. Others, such as Charles Ballantyne and A.K. Maclean were either too inexperienced or too unreliable to attract much support, while General Mewburn and James Calder announced that they wanted to retire from political life.[53] Only T.A. Crerar emerged as a leader, but, as it turned out, just not as a leader within the Union government.

To make matters worse, the prime minister was out of the country for much of 1918 and 1919, first to attend another meeting of the Imperial War Cabinet, and then again for the Paris Peace Conference. On both occasions he was accompanied by a delegation of cabinet ministers, meaning that others, including Foster, Doherty, Sifton, and Kemp (who as minister of overseas military forces was stationed in the United Kingdom) also were away from Ottawa for months at a time. Ill health and exhaustion also dogged the prime minister and affected him for much of the rest of 1919. He appeared increasingly indecisive and distracted. Stories circulated that he had fallen out of touch, that he never got to know all the members of the Union Party and, in one case, mistook a new MP for an errand-boy and asked him to deliver a message to another colleague.[54] In the meantime, the economy sank into a deep depression, organized labour rose up in revolt, and farmers organized politically, posing the greatest challenge ever seen to the two old parties.

Provincial support for Union government also dissolved. In the Maritimes, what little support there was evaporated relatively quickly as old political lines reasserted themselves. By the end of 1919, even Nova Scotia premier George Murray, who had publicly supported Union in the election, found himself back in the federal Liberal family. Quebec had voted against Borden in 1917, and there was no indication that the province was warming up to Union government. The provincial Liberals won a convincing mandate in Quebec in 1919, leaving the Conservative opposition decimated. In Ontario, anger over the cancellation of the exemption for farmers' sons, anxiety arising from rural depopulation and the dislocation caused by the war, and lingering annoyance with Laurier's Quebec tarnished both the Union and the Liberal brands, and produced the surprise third-party victory of the United Farmers of Ontario in October 1919. Facing similar problems in the West, the Liberal provincial governments turned their backs on the Union once the war came to an end and as older more traditional issues — such as the tariff — re-emerged. There were no Conservative governments in Canada by 1920.

Within a year, the Union government began to fall apart. One of the first to defect was W.S. Fielding. Borden had provided him a safe seat in Nova Scotia but kept him out of the Union cabinet, and Fielding soon found himself adrift, between the two parties. Before long he rekindled his dormant Liberalism. Sir George Foster looked on with some disdain. Fielding "took his devious way to a back bench on the Opposition side" he observed in his diary. "Granted by grace only an acclamation on ground of being a unionist he at once proceeded to work in a way against the union forces. He now dodges around the shadows of the back opposition benches."[55]

The backtracking on the election promise to exempt farmers' sons from conscription fed into the rising sense of western grievance and made it a little uncomfortable for the western Liberal-Unionists. But

Calder, Sifton, and Crerar remained in the government, at least at first, even as Union support on the Prairies faded. With the introduction of the 1919 budget, which contained few significant tariff reductions, Crerar resigned from the cabinet and, along with eight other western Unionists, bolted to form the new, agrarian-based Progressive Party.[56] Crerar's defection was soon followed by the resignation of Frank Carvell, who left for the Board of Railway Commissioners, and of Sir Thomas White who, after repeated attempts, finally resigned as minister of finance in August 1919 and retired from politics.[57]

Even Borden vacillated. Exhausted and with his health declining, the prime minister late in 1919 decided he would retire, but agreed to postpone his departure until after several months of vacation. As his biographer points out, this was a bad decision in that it only delayed the inevitable; and in the interim the Union government continued to drift.[58] "So now we are launched on a troubled sea," wrote Sir George Foster, "without Chart, Compass or Captain. We shall see."[59] In the spring of 1920 Borden returned to Ottawa and to his role as prime minister, but things did not improve. In July, he announced his retirement. Arthur Meighen was selected as the new leader and, on July 7, became prime minister.

Meighen faced an almost impossible task. He was the obvious choice to follow Borden (Sir Thomas White was the only other possibility as he was favoured by the caucus, but he rejected the idea), but brought considerable electoral baggage to the prime minister's office. As the architect of conscription and the Military Service Act, he was a marked man in Quebec and French Canada generally; as the main defender of the Wartime Elections Act, he had earned the hostility of tens of thousands of non-British Canadians; as a staunch economic protectionist, he could count on little support from rural and western Canada; and as the government's point man during the Winnipeg General Strike, he won few friends in organized labour. Moreover, in the next election campaign the government would have few of the advantages that it had in 1917. The Wartime Elections Act and Military Voters Act had lapsed with the ending of the war, meaning that all those "enemy aliens" who were disenfranchised in 1917 would now have their votes back, and they would be unlikely to throw their support to Meighen or the Union government.

In addition, giving the vote to most women over the age of twenty-one was a progressive action that Borden could claim credit for, but that in no way meant that the Unionists could count on the support of Canadian women in the next election — certainly not in the way they could under the Military Voters Act. Likewise, in the next election there would be no soldier vote to rely on. It was hard to be optimistic for Meighen's chances; as historian John English concluded, "[I]n 1917 manipulation of the franchise was unnecessary, but it was possible; in the next election it might well be necessary, but it would most certainly be impossible."[60] To guard against any retaliatory manipulations of the voters list, the Borden government created the Office of the Chief Electoral Officer in 1920 by passing the Dominion Elections Act. This new office was designed to de-politicize the administration of federal elections: it would be more professional; more thorough in keeping the voters list; and would report to the members of the House of Commons, instead of to the prime minister and cabinet.

By the time of the 1921 election, the Union had disappeared, and most of the Unionists with it. Frank Cochrane died of a stroke in April 1920; Sir Sam Hughes died in August 1921; Arthur Sifton, who had stayed in the government and served as minister of public works, also died in 1921. For those who survived, the Senate became the refuge of choice: J.D. Reid and Sir Edward Kemp declined to run in 1921 and, along with Sir George Foster, were appointed to the Senate by Meighen. Fred Pardee returned to the Liberal Party, but lost in his bid for re-election and was appointed to the Senate in 1922 by Mackenzie King. Charles Ballantyne tried to remain in politics but was defeated in 1921, and was appointed to the Senate by R.B. Bennett in 1932. General Mewburn resigned in 1920, but bucked the senatorial trend. He remained in politics and was re-elected as a Conservative in 1921 and 1925. Newton Rowell — estranged from the Liberal Party and unpopular with Conservatives — left politics in 1920 and went on to a distinguished career in business. He served as a Canadian delegate to the League of Nations, and ultimately was named chief justice of Ontario. In the late 1930s, he was co-chair of the Royal Commission on Dominion-Provincial Relations. One consequence of this dissolution of the Union was that there were few

Unionist-Conservatives remaining to serve in future Conservative governments under either Meighen or Bennett.

Union supporters outside the party also went their separate ways. Sir Clifford Sifton left Canada for Britain just days after the 1917 election, and never returned to active political life. John Dafoe's party allegiances shifted from Liberal to Conservative to Unionist in 1917, then to the Progressives and back to the Liberals again, but throughout he remained constant as editor of the *Manitoba Free Press* until his death in 1944. J.S. Willison continued his career in journalism and wrote for the *London Times* until he died in 1927; his political life was over, however, and he never received the Senate appointment he hoped for. Sir Joseph Flavelle fended off profiteering charges for his wartime business dealings and, once the war ended and the Imperial Munitions Board folded, he returned to his business and philanthropic pursuits. His political influence waned under the new Liberal government.

Sir Wilfrid Laurier died in February 1919, only fourteen months after the election. His death sparked a leadership contest, and a Liberal convention — something completely new — was held in August. Four candidates vied for the leadership, including George Graham and D.D. McKenzie, the interim Liberal leader, but the frontrunners were Fielding and Mackenzie King. The election of 1917 framed the leadership race in 1919. In 1917, King had stood with Laurier and went down to defeat with him. In 1919, that loyalty won him the overwhelming support of the Quebec wing of the party. Fielding, unforgiven by Nova Scotia Liberals for deserting the party before the election, could not hold the Nova Scotian votes.[61] King won on the fourth ballot and began the long process of reuniting the party. That one decision to stand and fall with Laurier in 1917 had a profound impact on the evolution of Canadian politics for the next thirty years.

Fielding and Graham stayed in politics despite losing their leadership bids, and served in King's first administration. Following that, Graham was appointed to the Senate in 1926. Likewise, Rodolphe Lemieux, who stayed loyal to Mackenzie King, was re-elected and served as speaker of the House of Commons for much of the 1920s, and was appointed to the Senate in 1930. Some other colleagues from 1917 moved on, including Frank Oliver, who never returned to active political life, and William

Sir Wilfrid Laurier lying in state in the Victoria Museum Building, Ottawa, February 1919.

Pugsley, who finished his career as lieutenant governor of New Brunswick. In Quebec, Armand La Vergne ran again as an independent in 1921 and lost, but returned to the House of Commons as a Conservative in 1925.

For many of the other central figures, the election of 1917 proved to be only one stop in a longer journey. Mackenzie King and Meighen continued sparring through the interwar years and into the Second World War; Lapointe, Crerar, Macdonald, and a few others went on to serve in various ways in future governments. Belcourt never abandoned the crusade against Regulation 17, and continued to argue that the right to schooling was tied to the right of free speech. As for Henri Bourassa, he continued on his own personal odyssey as editor of *Le Devoir* and as a politician (he returned to the House of Commons for ten years between 1925 and 1935), but the election signalled the end of the *nationalistes*, and his popularity and his brand of French-Canadian nationalism was never again as influential in Quebec as it was in 1917. Nor was he ever again demonized as he had been in 1917, even when he opposed conscription a second time, in 1942.

HRH The Prince of Wales laying the cornerstone of the Peace Tower, Ottawa, September 1, 1919. Borden is cheering, second from the right.

* * *

In 1920 the House of Commons formally reopened in the new Centre Block on Parliament Hill. Furniture was brought over from the Victoria Museum Building and construction continued all around the MPs for several more years, even beyond the official opening of the Peace Tower in 1927, a full ten years after the searing election of 1917. The new structures were larger and stronger and reflected a more developed and independent nation. Many carvings and stained glass windows recalled Canada's war effort, and a Memorial Chamber in the Peace Tower was established in memory of those who served. The burned-out Parliament Buildings, the bitter wartime election, and even the war itself were now safely in the past. Some of the faces in the audience or participating in the opening ceremonies were familiar, but a new generation had emerged to lead postwar Canada into its uncertain future.

11

CONCLUSION

The election of 1917 was fought on the issue of conscription, but it was decided on the basis of identity. Never has an election so divided the country. Never before or after did the country come so close to the brink of destruction. Never had it endured a moment so marked by rancour and violence. That Canada survived its fiftieth anniversary is a testament to the strong bonds that had been created over the previous fifty years: links of economics, culture, and civil society that were able to withstand a divisive vote on the very legitimacy of the country.

A hundred years later, it is still difficult to grasp the urgency English Canadians felt in wanting to help "the boys" who were serving in the trenches for a cause few people understood or really cared for. The 1917 contest was the last victory for the idea of a "British Canada." Borden and his supporters were fundamentally committed to the war effort, and in their desire to see it through became convinced that conscription and a coalition government were required. When it became necessary to hold the election, they were determined to win at any cost and prepared to rally all British Canadians — both men and women — against French Canadians, "foreigners," slackers, and anyone else in the name of the war effort. The election had to be won or the war could be lost, and in that they found the justification for manipulating the franchise to include and exclude potential supporters and opponents. They won the election, and, emboldened by a sweeping victory delivered by the majority ethnic group of English Canadians, pushed through conscription over the opposition of the "non-British" population.

In the process, the politicians of the age drove Canada to the edge of disaster. Sir Robert Borden has to shoulder much of the responsibility, by not addressing the factors that underpinned this extraordinary crisis. By refusing to get involved in defusing the schools question in Ontario, he allowed it to fester endlessly, providing the best excuse imaginable for French Canada not to get involved in the global struggle. How could English Canada expect francophones to risk their lives in a fight that had nothing to do with the country's security interests, while at the same time standing idly by as the Ontario government suffocated the educational rights of its French-speaking minority? Even a hundred years later, the query is unanswerable. Borden was correct in saying that it was a provincial issue, but that was no excuse. Laurier had involved the federal government in brokering a deal with Manitoba in 1896 and again found a compromise in Alberta and Saskatchewan in 1905. A gesture of support — perhaps even a few motions of support for his colleague Senator Philippe Landry — might have made a difference.

But Borden did not understand French Canada. It was willing to send volunteers to fight, but resisted conscription. He was equally deaf to the demands to make the military more accommodating to the French fact in Canada. Countless opportunities to raise the profile of French-Canadian officers were lost, and the failure to create and support French-Canadian formations simply betrayed a spirit that had no time, let alone sensitivity, for the possibilities of what might have been. The opportunity to associate his government with visiting French prime minister René Viviani and French General Joffre on the eve of the introduction of conscription was entirely missed: the Canadian government could handle the prime minister's schedule no better than it managed the war effort. One hundred years later, it still befuddles. Such political incompetence begged for disaster.

Borden had sensed by Christmas 1916 — even in his own province — that Canada was divided and that his government's re-election was far from assured. By early 1917 he realized that he needed either an extension to the life of Parliament or a coalition with at least some Liberals (something like that accomplished by Lloyd George in the United Kingdom), to remain in office and to implement conscription — even if that meant pitting one part of Canada against another. The Borden government's recourse was electoral manipulation by giving the vote to some women and removing it from people held in suspicion of maintaining an allegiance to their homelands. Worse, it allowed appeals to be based on prejudice. To cap the cynicism, a last-minute promise was made during the election campaign to exempt from conscription farmers working on family property: it was revoked a few months later. Never has a government so failed its people.

Laurier was hardly better. He was also slow in responding to the crisis in Ontario. The *bons mots* were not enough. Laurier let four years of political erosion pass on this toxic issue before finally getting involved in the winter of 1916, when children were literally begging at his door on Parliament Hill. His vision for the country as a hopeful alliance of French and English, of Protestant and Catholic, of westerner and easterner, needed endless repeating. In his mid-seventies as the war raged, he was no longer up for the strenuous fight, and he did nothing to train his lieutenants or to seek new ones to echo his views. His party organization on the ground continued to languish, as it had in 1911. Convinced that Borden wanted conscription, he wisely refused to join the Union government; but his idea of putting the issue of conscription to a referendum was disingenuous. The election campaign had turned into one. What more did he wish for? Canadians saw it for what it was: a ruse. Laurier wanted power and then the discretion to deal with the issues as he wished. In 1917, when war deaths of local boys regularly made headlines, when tears and sacrifice were the pain of every day, his views were nothing more than a luxury that a country in crisis could not abide. He did not understand, or respond to, English Canada. His election manifesto was as tired as he was. There was no fresh, inspiring vision there for an embattled Canada.

It would be too easy to suggest that the election of 1917 signalled Canada's "loss of innocence," but there have been few elections in Canada's history that were so focused on one central issue of such significance to the whole country, an issue that literally had implications of life and death on both the national and individual levels. Politics was different after that, and if a more mature country did not emerge, the nation that the war and the 1917 election did produce was at least less naïve about politics and the lengths to which people will go when they feel their nation is threatened.

The election of 1917 overturned the old political order in Canada, in large part, because the founding parties had failed. It marked the end of the first fifty years of Confederation, an era dominated by two nation-builders — Macdonald and Laurier — the masterful politicians who had assembled Confederation in 1867 and consolidated the country. It was also, as John Dafoe wrote, the ending of the "era of the Great Parties," a period marked by the remarkable ability of Macdonald and Laurier to inspire deep personal loyalty among their followers.[1] Sir Robert Borden never inspired such allegiance from his followers, nor could he be considered a true nation-builder. Although he tried to create the conditions for more efficient, better organized, and less corrupt government, and to forge a new national identity from the searing experience of the war, his legacy was mostly rejected.

Exhausted by the conflict and the difficult years that followed it, Canadians turned against the Conservatives in the 1921 election, giving the party led by Arthur Meighen barely 30 percent of the vote and only fifty seats. Conservatives were wiped out completely in Nova Scotia, Prince Edward Island, Quebec, Manitoba, Saskatchewan, and Alberta. In Saskatchewan, the party received less than 17 percent of the vote. Quebec turned a very cold shoulder, giving the Meighen Tories 18.4 percent. It gave the Liberals over 70 percent of the vote, and all of its sixty-five seats. That made the difference, giving the Liberals a two-seat edge in the House of Commons. The Liberals had bounced back, winning government, but with only 40 percent of the total vote. The West had turned against both parties, choosing instead a third party, the Progressives, now led by T.A. Crerar, which took 22.9 percent of the vote nationally, but over 50 percent of the vote in Alberta and Saskatchewan.

The anger against the Tories in English Canada proved to be short-lived, however. By 1925, the Conservatives had largely recovered under Meighen's leadership and earned over 46 percent of the vote (more than the Liberals, who managed to hang on to power only with the support of the Progressive Party). By the 1926 election, the Progressive Party had been wiped off the political map by the resurgent Conservatives. Quebec, however, was never as forgiving. In 1925 and 1926, the Tories took over 34 percent of the vote, an improvement on the 1921 result for sure, but still their third-worst showing since Confederation. In 1926, the Liberals were awarded a victory, re-elected under Mackenzie King with 52 percent of the seats in the House of Commons, edging out the Tories with only 46.1 percent of the votes. What made the difference, again, was Quebec. It gave the Liberals sixty seats — almost half of the party's harvest of 128 seats across Canada. Quebec would never again be friendly to the Conservatives, except for extraordinary (and temporary) occasions such as the 1958 Diefenbaker and 1984 Mulroney landslides. The 1917 election relegated the Conservative Party to the furthest reaches of Quebec's political culture.

Writing at the end of the war, Dafoe was pessimistic about the future of Canada. He was not alone. In Toronto, a new movement rose from the ashes of the *Bonne Entente* movement that had sprung up in 1916 and 1917 as a motley group of Torontonians sought to repair the damage between the two language groups. Arthur Hawkes and lawyers such as John Godfrey and William Henry Moore joined forces with university professors Charles B. Sissons, George W. Wrong, and O.D. Skelton to announce that reconciliation was possible. In the wake of the 1917 election, some writers went to work. Moore published *The Clash: A Study in Nationalities* (1918), while Hawkes wrote *The Birthright*, and Percival Fellman Morley penned *Bridging the Chasm: A Study of the Ontario-Quebec Question* (both came out in 1919). This group was renamed the Unity League of Ontario and, in the early 1920s, attained a membership of some 150 key opinion-leaders. One of the central members was Senator Belcourt, who worked closely with the group to seek justice; if the courts could not work in favour of Franco-Ontarians, perhaps political pressure could.[2] Through their lectures, publications, and personal efforts in lobbying the government, the league made it acceptable again to speak of bilingual rights in Ontario, and in Canada generally. Their efforts bore fruit, and the Ontario government finally abandoned Regulation 17 in 1927 (and apologized for it in 2016).

The 1917 election brought Laurier's career to an end, and Borden's soon after that. It is somewhat ironic, if not tragic, that both leaders had devoted so much of their political lives to the concept of national unity, however different their perspectives may have been, only to have the culmination of their careers arrive at the moment in Canada's history that posed the greatest threat to that national unity. Laurier, especially, tried to remain positive about the future. "I still have faith," he wrote soon after the election, "in the sound sense of the Canadian people and in the broad forces that make for national unity on a basis of fair and respecting partnership. Once the war is over, no election, no dozen elections, no unscrupulous propaganda, can prevent Canadians more and more becoming Canadians first, and when they are so, we shall hear less and less of Ontario and Quebec."[3] But, given his experience during the election campaign, at the moment of his last breath he could not have been so optimistic about the future.

The election of 1917 was inexorably linked to conscription. As Loring Christie, an official in the small Department of External Affairs and a close adviser to Prime Minister Borden, wrote a few years after the war, "[E]veryone knows that even the Union Government could not have gone ahead with conscription throughout Canada without that election."[4] But if the election made conscription possible, conscription made the election of 1917 necessary. And the consequences of conscription scarred the Canadian political landscape for decades. It became a defining issue in Canadian political life, and was compounded by a second war and a second round of acrimonious debate. Several of those who lived through the first round were there for the second, including Mackenzie King, Arthur Meighen, Ernest Lapointe, J.L. Ralston, T.A. Crerar, Ned Macdonald, Henri Bourassa, and a few others.[5]

The conscription debate in the Second World War was familiar to these individuals, and the roles they played might have been scripted in 1917, but there were also lessons learned. For one, Mackenzie King, remembering the destructive impact of the 1917 election on his party and his leader, promised not to introduce conscription. He wisely called an election in 1940, soon after the outbreak of the war, thereby avoiding the disruption of another wartime election later. He also brought Louis St-Laurent into cabinet and, remembering Laurier's 1917 platform, called for a plebiscite in 1942, asking Canadians to relieve the government of its anti-conscription pledge. Quebec voted massively against it; the wounds exposed in 1917 still had not healed. That being said, Quebec voters also respected the gesture. In the 1945 election, there was a massive vote for the *Bloc Canadien*, a third party born in the same mold as the *nationalistes* of 1911, but the Liberals were easily re-elected, earning more than 50 percent of the vote in Quebec. But not all the lessons of Canada's First World War experience were retained; in the Second World War Canadians found a new "enemy alien" in Japanese Canadians, and responded with even greater hostility. Appeals to race die hard.

French Canada was as much changed by the politics of 1914–1918 as English Canada was, but in a different way. After the war, two clearly competing visions of French Canada emerged. The first was a notion that the French fact outside Quebec was a reality under siege, and that

Maréchal Nantel, circa 1917.

new action had to be taken to preserve the vitality of those minorities. The second was that Quebec was isolated in the face of English Canada's growing sense of power. The debates took on a new immediacy with the events of the war: no longer could positions be defended by invoking the events of the distant past. French Canada emerged from the war in factions and, after Laurier's death in 1919, without a uniting figure.

The Union government has been described as the "culmination of ideas and impulses at work in Canadian society for more than a decade," while the First World War became the "great patriotic challenge which would purge Canada of petty politics, materialism, and corruption."[6] It was an era of social reform, the Social Gospel, moral regeneration, and political purification, espoused especially, but not exclusively, by middle-class Anglo-Protestants. The war gave a great boost to several causes, including prohibition and suffrage, and gave considerable hope to many Canadians for the better world that might emerge when the war came to an end. The election of 1917 occurred in this context, but what is notable is the degree to which the causes of social reform and moral regeneration faded into the background during the campaign.

The alternatives facing the electorate were stark and the divisions in the country were clear. The election brought together all the elements of the war — its conduct, its tragedy, its meaning, the call to duty, and the sense of shared sacrifice — and condensed them into a single ballot question for Canadians to decide. The election issues were reduced into basic alternatives between apparent opposites: win/lose; pro-war/anti-war; loyalty/treason. The many causes of the era remained — as ends to be achieved — but for one moment in 1917 what it meant to be Canadian was distilled into a simple choice. Making that choice placed an enormous stress on the worn fabric of national unity and threatened permanently to damage it.

Canada — the embattled nation — not fully prepared for the political contest that it faced, was pushed to its limits. The results of the election of 1917 were decided on identity, and the legitimacy of the Canadian project was put to the test as never before, or since. Canada would bear the scars of the crisis for generations to come. The country bent under the strain but, remarkably, did not break.

APPENDIX 1

RESULTS OF THE 1917 ELECTION

	Seats	Candidates			Elected				Popular Votes							Total
		U	L	O	U	%	L	%	U	%	L	%	O	%	Turnout	
Nova Scotia	16	16	12	2	12	75.0	4	25.0	56,617	47.7	54,857	46.2	7,282	6.1	75.1	118,756
New Brunswick	11	10	10	0	7	63.6	4	36.4	58,256	61.2	37,005	38.8	0	0.0	80.5	95,261
Prince Edward Island	4	4	4	0	2	50.0	2	50.0	17,672	49.9	17,778	50.1	0	0.0	87.6	35,460
Quebec	65	41	65	15	3	4.6	62	95.4	80,823	25.3	231,970	72.6	6,608	2.1	80.5	319,401
Ontario	86	82	81	15	74	90.2	8	9.8	509,316	62.7	277,153	34.1	25,343	3.1	89.8	811,812
Manitoba	15	15	12	0	14	93.3	1	6.7	106,858	79.7	27,176	20.3	0	0.0	97.1	134,034
Saskatchewan	16	16	11	1	16	100.0	0	0.0	82,741	72.0	32,182	28	8	0.06	85.9	114,931
Alberta	12	12	12	6	11	91.7	1	8.3	77,912	61.0	45,428	35.5	4,478	3.8	90.8	127,818
British Columbia	13	13	12	8	13	100.0	0	0.0	86,415	68.4	32,324	25.6	7690	6.1	103.6	126,429
Yukon	1	1	1	0	1	100.0	0	0.0	959	54.3	808	45.7	0	0.0	98.8	1,767
Total	235	210	220	47	153	65.1	82	34.9	1,077,569	57.1	756,691	40.1	51,409	2.7	86.2	1,885,669

Elected by acclamation:
Union (14): Nova Scotia (4); New Brunswick (1); Ontario (1); Manitoba (3); Saskatchewan (4); British Columbia (1)
Liberal (18): New Brunswick (1); Quebec (17)
"Other" candidates:
Nova Scotia (2): Labour (2)
Quebec (19): Nationalist (1); Labour (2); Independent Labour (4); Independent Conservative (4), Ind. Liberal (4), Independent (4)
Ontario (15): Labour (10); Independent Conservative (1); Independent (4)
Saskatchewan (1): Independent (1)
Alberta (6): Non-Partisan League (3); Labour (2); Independent (1)
British Columbia (8): Labour (6); Independent (2)
Adapted from J. Murray Beck, *Pendulum of Power* (Toronto: Prentice Hall, 1968), 148.

APPENDIX 2

WINNERS OF THE 1917 ELECTION

		NAME OF RIDING	WINNER	PARTY
ALBERTA	1	Battle River	BLAIR, William John	Union
	2	Calgary East	REDMAN, Daniel Lee	Union
	3	Calgary West	TWEEDIE, Thomas M.	Union
	4	Edmonton East	MACKIE, Henry Arthur	Union
	5	Lethbridge	BUCHANAN, William A.	Union
	6	Macleod	SHAW, Hugh Murray	Union
	7	Medicine Hat	SIFTON, Hon. Arthur Lewis	Union
	8	Victoria	WHITE, William Henry	Opp.
	9	Red Deer	CLARK, Michae	Union
	10	Strathcona	DOUGLAS, James McCrie	Union
	11	Edmonton West	GRIESBACH, W.A.	Union
	12	Bow River	HALLADAY, Howard H.	Union
BRITISH	13	Cariboo	FULTON, Frederick John	Union
COLUMBIA	14	Comox-Alberni	CLEMENTS, Herbert S.	Union
	15	Kootenay East	BONNELL, Saul	Union
	16	Kootenay West	GREEN, Robert Francis	Union
	17	Nanaimo	MCINTOSH, John Charles	Union
	18	New Westminster	MCQUARRIE, William G.	Union
	19	Skeena	PECK, Cyrus Wesley	Union
	20	Vancouver Centre	STEVENS, Henry Herber	Union
	21	Yale	BURRELL, Hon. Martin	Union
	22	Westminster	STACEY, Frank Bainard	Union
	23	Victoria City	TOLMIE, Simon Fraser	Union
	24	Vancouver South	COOPER, Richard Clive	Union
	25	Burrard	CROWE, Sanford Johnston	Union

		NAME OF RIDING	WINNER	PARTY
MANITOBA	26	Dauphin	CRUISE, Robert	Union
	27	Lisgar	BOLTON, Ferris	Union
	28	Brandon	WHIDDEN, Howard P.	Union
	29	Macdonald	HENDERS, Richard Coe	Union
	30	Marquette	CRERAR, Hon. Thomas	Union
	31	Neepawa	DAVIS, Fred Langdon	Union
	32	Nelson	CAMPBELL, John A.	Union
	33	Portage La Prairie	MEIGHEN, Hon. Arthur	Union
	34	Provencher	MOLLOY, John Patrick	Opp.
	35	Selkirk	HAY, Thomas	Union
	36	Souris	FINLEY, Albert Ernest	Union
	37	Springfield	RICHARDSON, Robert L.	Union
	38	Winnipeg Centre	ANDREWS, George William	Union
	39	Winnipeg North	BLAKE, Matthew Robert	Union
	40	Winnipeg South	ALLAN, George William	Union
NEW BRUNSWICK	41	Charlotte	HARTT, Thomas Aaron	Union
	42	Gloucester	TURGEON, Onésiphore	Opp.
	43	Kent	LÉGER, Auguste Théophile	Opp.
	44	Northumberland	LOGGIE, William Stewart	Union
	45	Restigouche-Madawaska	MICHAUD, Pius	Opp.
	46	Royal	MCLEAN, Hugh Havelock	Union
	47	St. John–Albert	WIGMORE, R.W. and ELKIN, S.E.	Union
	48	Victoria-Carleton	CARVELL, Frank B.	Union
	49	Westmorland	COPP, Arthur Bliss	Opp.
	50	York-Sunbury	MCLEOD, Harry Fulton	Union
NOVA SCOTIA	51	Antigonish-Guysborough	SINCLAIR, John Howard	Opp.
	52	Cape Breton South and Richmond	DOUGLAS, John Carey BUTTS, Robert Hamilton	Union

		NAME OF RIDING	WINNER	PARTY
	53	North Cape Breton and Victoria	MCKENZIE, Daniel D.	Opp.
	54	Colchester	MCCURDY, Fleming B.	Union
	55	Cumberland	RHODES, Hon. Edgar N.	Union
	56	Digby and Annapolis	DAVIDSON, Avard L.	Union
	57	Halifax	MACLEAN, Alexander K.	Union
			MARTIN, Peter Francis	Union
	58	Hants	TREMAIN, Hadley Brown	Union
	59	Inverness	CHISHOLM, Alexander W.	Opp.
	60	Kings	BORDEN, Rt. Hon. Sir Robert L.	Union
	61	Lunenburg	DUFF, William	Opp.
	62	Pictou	MCGREGOR, Alexander	Union
	63	Shelburne and Queen's	FIELDING, Hon. William Stevens	Union
	64	Yarmouth and Clare	SPINNEY, Edgar Keith	Union
ONTARIO	65	Algoma West	SIMPSON, Thomas Edward	Union
	66	Brant	HAROLD, John	Union
	67	Bruce North	CLARK, Hugh	Union
	68	Bruce South	TRUAX, Reuben Eldridge	Opp.
	69	Carleton	BOYCE, George	Opp.
	70	Dufferin	BEST, John	Union
	71	Dundas	CASSELMAN, Orren D.	Union
	72	Elgin East	MARSHALL, David	Union
	73	Elgin West	CROTHERS, Hon. Thomas	Union
	74	Essex North	KENNEDY, William C.	Opp.
	75	Essex South	BRIEN, John Wesley	Union
	76	Frontenac	EDWARDS, John Wesley	Union
	77	Glengarry and Stormont	MCMARTIN, John	Union
	78	Grenville	REID, Hon. John Dowsley	Union
	79	Grey North	MIDDLEBRO, William S.	Union

	NAME OF RIDING	WINNER	PARTY
80	Grey Southeast	BALL, Robert James	Union
81	Halton	ANDERSON, Robert King	Union
82	Huron North	BOWMAN, James	Union
83	Huron South	MERNER, Jonathan Joseph	Union
84	Kent	MCCOIG, Archibald Blake	Opp.
85	Kingston	NICKLE, William Folger	Union
86	Lambton East	ARMSTRONG, Joseph E.	Union
87	Lambton West	PARDEE, Frederick Forsyth	Union
88	Hamilton East	MEWBURN, Hon. Sydney	Union
89	Hamilton West	STEWART, Thomas Joseph	Union
90	Lanark	HANNA, Adelbert Edward	Union
91	Leeds	WHITE, William Thomas	Union
92	Lincoln	CHAPLIN, James Dew	Union
93	London	CRONYN, Hume	Union
94	Middlesex East	GLASS, Samuel Francis	Union
95	Middlesex West	ROSS, Duncan Campbell	Opp.
96	Nipissing	HARRISON, Charles Rober	Union
97	Norfolk	CHARLTON, William A.	Union
98	Haldimand	LALOR, Francis Ramsey	Union
99	Northumberland	MUNSON, Charles Arthur	Union
100	Ottawa (City of)	FRIPP, Alfred Ernest CHABOT, John Léo	Union
101	Muskoka	MCGIBBON, Peter	Union
102	Ontario North	SHARPE, Samuel Simpson	Union
103	Ontario South	SMITH, William	Union
104	Oxford North	NESBITT, Edward Walter	Union
105	Oxford South	SUTHERLAND, Donald	Union
106	Parkdale	MOWAT, Herbert M.	Union
107	Parry Sound	ARTHURS, James	Union
108	Peel	CHARTERS, Samuel	Union
109	Perth North	MORPHY, Hugh Boulton	Union
110	Perth South	STEELE, Michael	Union

	NAME OF RIDING	WINNER	PARTY
111	Peterborough East	SEXSMITH, John Albert	Union
112	Peterborough West	BURNHAM, John Hampden	Union
113	Prescott	PROULX, Edmond	Opp.
114	Prince Edward	HEPBURN, Bernard R.	Union
115	Renfrew South	PEDLOW, Isaac Ellis	Opp.
116	Renfrew North	MACKIE, Herbert John	Union
117	Russell	MURPHY, Hon. Charles	Opp.
118	Simcoe East	TUDHOPE, James Brockett	Union
119	Simcoe South	BOYS, William Alves	Union
120	Simcoe North	CURRIE, John Allister	Union
121	Timiskaming	COCHRANE, Hon. Francis	Union
122	Algoma East	NICHOLSON, George B.	Union
123	Toronto Centre	BRISTOL, Edmund	Union
124	Toronto East	KEMP, Hon. Sir Albert E.	Union
125	Toronto North	FOSTER, Rt. Hon. Sir George	Union
126	Toronto South	SHEARD, Charles	Union
127	Toronto West	HOCKEN, Horatio Clarence	Union
128	Victoria	HUGHES, Hon. Sir Sam	Union
129	Waterloo North	EULER, William Daum	Opp.
130	Waterloo South	SCOTT, Frank Stewart	Union
131	Welland	FRASER, Evan Eugene	Union
132	Wellington North	CLARKE, William Aurelius	Union
133	Wellington South	GUTHRIE, Hon. Hugh	Union
134	York North	ARMSTRONG, John A.M.	Union
135	York West	WALLACE, Thomas G.	Union
136	York East	FOSTER, Thomas	Union
137	York South	MACLEAN, William F.	Union
138	Port Arthur and Kenora	KEEFER, Francis Henry	Union
139	Brantford	COCKSHUTT, William F.	Union
140	Fort William and Rainy River	MANION, Robert James	Union
141	Lennox and Addington	PAUL, William James	Union

		NAME OF RIDING	WINNER	PARTY
	142	Hastings East	THOMPSON, Thomas H.	Union
	143	Hastings West	PORTER, Edward Guss	Union
	144	Durham	ROWELL, Newton Wesley	Union
	145	Wentworth	WILSON, Gordon Crooks	Union
PRINCE	146	King's	MCISAAC, James	Union
EDWARD	147	Prince	READ, Joseph	Opp.
ISLAND	148	Queen's	NICHOLSON, Donald	Union
			SINCLAIR, John Ewen	Opp.
QUEBEC	149	Argenteuil	MCGIBBON, Peter Robert	Opp.
	150	Bagot	MARCILE, Joseph Edmond	Opp.
	151	Beauce	BÉLAND, Hon. Henri S.	Opp.
	152	Bellechasse	FOURNIER, Charles Alphonse	Opp.
	153	Beauharnois	PAPINEAU, Louis-Joseph	Opp.
	154	Bonaventure	MARCIL, Hon. Charles	Opp.
	155	Brome	MCMASTER, Andrew Ross	Opp.
	156	Chambly-Verchères	ARCHAMBAULT, Joseph	Opp.
	157	Charlevoix-Montmorency	CASGRAIN, Pierre-François	Opp.
	158	Châteauguay-Huntingdon	ROBB, James Alexander	Opp.
	159	Chicoutimi-Saguenay	SAVARD, Edmond	Opp.
	160	Compton	HUNT, Aylmer Byron	Opp.
	161	Dorchester	CANNON, Lucien	Opp.
	162	Drummond-Arthabaska	BROUILLARD, Joseph Ovide	Opp.
	163	Gaspé	LEMIEUX, Hon. Rodolphe	Opp.
	164	Hull	FONTAINE, Joseph-Éloi	Opp.
	165	Jacques-Cartier	LAFORTUNE, David A..	Opp.
	166	Joliette	DENIS, Jean-Joseph	Opp.
	167	Kamouraska	LAPOINTE, Ernest	Opp
	168	Labelle	FORTIER, Hyacinthe-Adélard	Opp

NAME OF RIDING	WINNER	PARTY
169	Laprairie-Napierville	LANCTÔT, Roch	Opp.
170	Terrebonne	PRÉVOST, Jules-Édouard	Opp.
171	L'assomption-Montcalm	SÉGUIN, Paul-Arthur	Opp.
172	Laurier-Outremont	DU TREMBLAY, Pamphile	Opp.
173	Laval-Two Mountains	ÉTHIER, Joseph Arthur Calixte	Opp.
174	Lévi	BOURASSA, J.B.	Opp.
175	L'Islet	FAFARD, Joseph-Fernand	Opp.
176	Lotbinière	VIEN, Thomas	Opp.
177	Maisonneuve	LEMIEUX, Hon. Rodolphe	Opp.
178	Matane	PELLETIER, François-Jean	Opp.
179	Mégantic	PACAUD, Lucien Turcotte	Opp.
180	Missisquoi	KAY, William Frederic	Opp.
181	Montmagny	DÉCHÊNE, Aimé Miville	Opp.
182	Nicolet	TRAHAN, Arthur	Opp.
183	Portneuf	DELISLE, Michel-Siméon	Opp.
184	Quebec County	LAVIGUEUR, Henri-Edgar	Opp.
185	Quebec East	LAURIER, Rt. Hon. Sir Wilfrid	Opp.
186	Quebec South	POWER, Charles Gavan	Opp.
187	Quebec West	PARENT, Georges	Opp.
188	Richelieu	CARDIN, Pierre-Joseph-Arthur	Opp.
189	Richmond-Wolfe	TOBIN, Edmund William	Opp.
190	Rimouski	D'ANJOU, Émmanuel	Opp.
191	Montreal St. Anne	DOHERTY, Hon. Charles	Union
192	Montreal St. Antoine	AMES, Sir Herbert Brown	Union
193	George-Étienne Cartier	JACOBS, Samuel William	Opp.
194	Hochelaga	LESAGE, Joseph-Edmond	Opp.
195	Montreal St. Denis	VERVILLE, Alphonse	Opp.
196	St. Hyacinthe-Rouville	GAUTHIER, Louis-Joseph	Opp.
197	Montreal St. James	LAPOINTE, Louis-Audet	Opp.

		NAME OF RIDING	WINNER	PARTY
	198	St. Johns–Iberville	DEMERS, Marie Joseph	Opp.
	199	Montreal St. Lawrence–St. George	BALLANTYNE, Hon. Charles C.	Union
	200	Montreal St. Mary	DESLAURIERS, Hermas	Opp.
	201	Sherbrooke (Town of)	MCCREA, Francis "N."	Opp.
	202	Shefford	BOIVIN, Georges Henri	Opp.
	203	Stanstead	BALDWIN, Willis Keith	Opp.
	204	Témiscouata	GAUVREAU, Charles Arthur	Opp.
	205	Vaudreuil-Soulanges	BOYER, Gustave	Opp.
	206	Yamaska	GLADU, Joseph Ernest Oscar	Opp.
	207	Maskinongé	MAYRAND, Hormidas	Opp.
	208	Berthier	GERVAIS, Théodore	Opp.
	209	Champlain	DESAULNIERS, Arthur L.	Opp.
	210	Three Rivers and St. Maurice	BUREAU, Jacques	Opp.
	211	Wright	DEVLIN, Emmanuel B.	Opp.
	212	Pontiac	CAHILL, Frank S.	Opp.
	213	Westmount–St. Henri	LEDUC, Hon. Joseph Alfred	Opp.
SASKATCHEWAN	214	Assiniboia	TURRIFF, John Gillanders	Union
	215	Battleford	WRIGHT, Henry Oswald	Union
	216	Humboldt	LANG, Norman	Union
	217	Kindersley	MYERS, E.T.W.	Union
	218	Last Mountain	JOHNSTON, John Frederick	Union
	219	Mackenzie	REID, John Flaws	Union
	220	Maple Creek	MAHARG, John Archibald	Union
	221	Moose Jaw	CALDER, Hon. James A	Union
	222	North Battleford	LONG, Charles Edwin	Union
	223	Prince Albert	KNOX, Andrew	Union
	224	Qu'Appelle	THOMSON, Levi	Union
	225	Regina	COWAN, Walter Davy	Union

		NAME OF RIDING	WINNER	PARTY
	226	Saltcoats	MACNUTT, Thomas	Union
	227	Saskatoon	WILSON, James Robert	Union
	228	Swift Current	ARGUE, Ira Eugene	Union
	229	Weyburn	THOMPSON, Richard F.	Union
YUKON	230	Yukon	THOMPSON, Alfred	Union

APPENDIX 3

ELECTORAL MAPS

Atlantic Canada: Voting Results

Atlantic Canada: Changes in Ridings

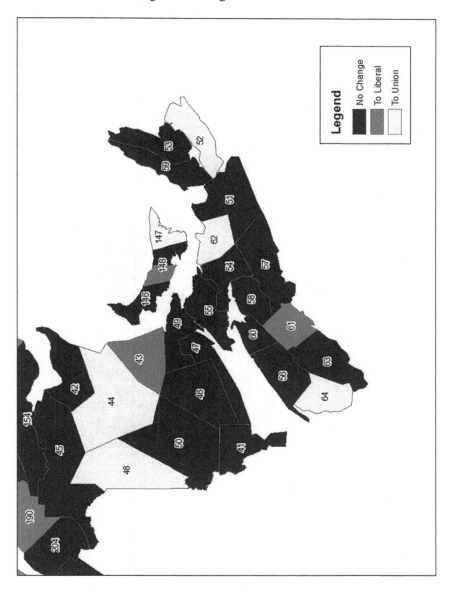

Quebec: Voting Results Canada: Changes in Ridings

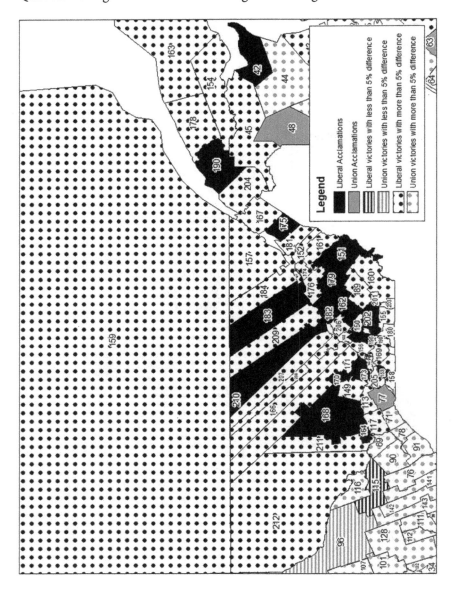

Quebec: Changes in Ridings

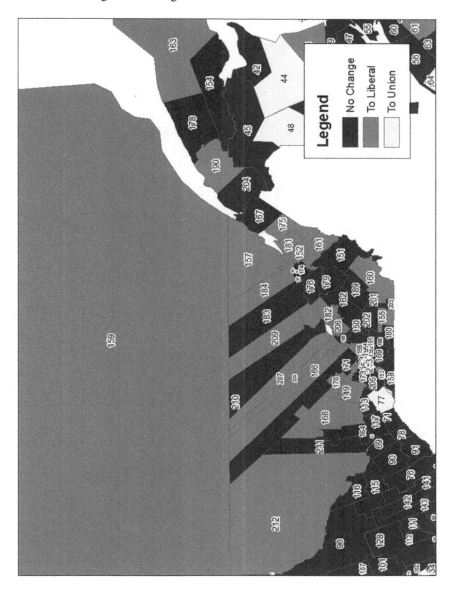

EMBATTLED NATION

Southern Ontario: Voting Results

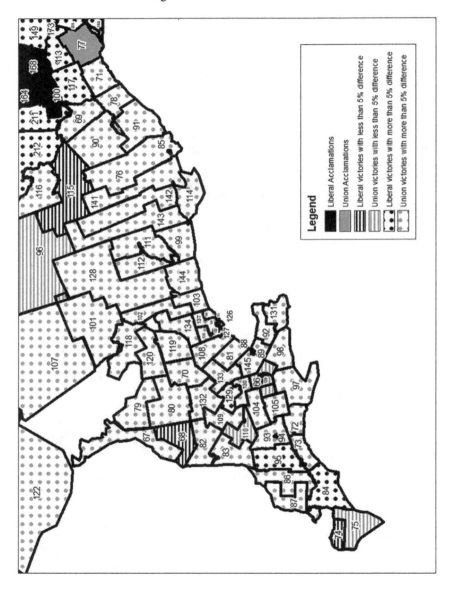

Southern Ontario: Changes in Ridings

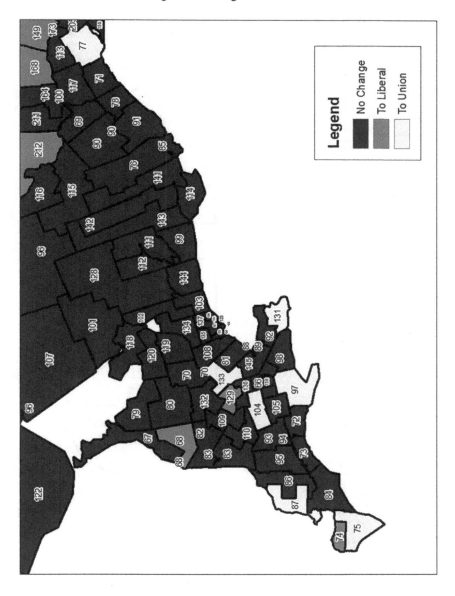

Western Canada: Voting Results

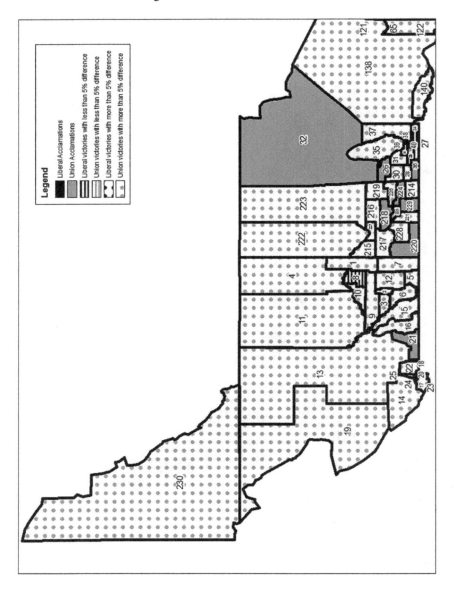

Western Canada: Changes in Ridings

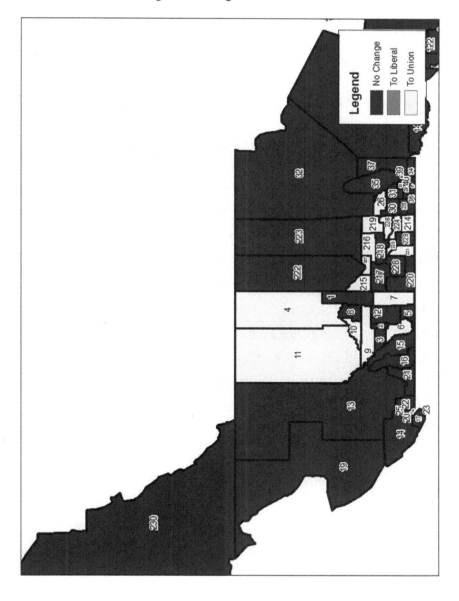

ABBREVIATIONS

ACAM	Archives de la Chancellerie de l'Archevêché de Montréal
BANQ-VM	Bibliothèque et Archives nationales du Québec–Vieux-Montréal
CAR	*Canadian Annual Review of Public Affairs*
CEF	Canadian Expeditionary Force
LAC	Library and Archives Canada (Ottawa)
NAUK	National Archives, U.K. (London)
NAUS	National Archives of the United States (Washington)
OA	Ontario Archives (Toronto)
PA	Parliamentary Archives, House of Lords, U.K. (London)
QUA	Queen's University Archives (Kingston)
TRL	Toronto Reference Library
UTA	University of Toronto Archives

NOTES

PREFACE

1. Borden's reputation has been tarnished, according to polls of historians and political scientists conducted by *Maclean's* magazine. He placed seventh in 1997, eighth in 2011, and ninth in 2016. See *Maclean's*, April 21, 1997, June 11, 2011, and October 17, 2016.
2. Laurier has ranged within the top three, trading places with Mackenzie King and Sir John A. Macdonald. The 2011 poll of historians and political scientists conducted by Norman Hillmer and Stephen Azzi ranked him first. See *Maclean's*, June 11, 2011. The 2016 poll placed him second. See *Maclean's*, October 17, 2016. The 1997 poll ranked him in third place. See *Maclean's*, April 21, 1997.

CHAPTER 1: THE CONUNDRUM

1. See Henry Borden, ed., *Robert Laird Borden: His Memoirs*, vol. 1 (Toronto: Macmillan, 1938), 450–51. See Gordon Martel, *The Month that Changed the World* (London: Oxford University Press, 2014).
2. The following material on the election and naval debate is taken from Patrice Dutil and David MacKenzie, *Canada 1911: The Decisive Election that Shaped the Country* (Toronto: Dundurn Press, 2011); William Johnston et al., *The Seabound Coast: The Official History of the Royal Canadian Navy, 1867–1939* (Toronto: Dundurn Press, 2010), 187–210; and Martin Thornton, *Churchill,*

Borden and Anglo-Canadian Naval Relations, 1911–1914 (Houndmills, UK: Palgrave Macmillan, 2013).

3. House of Commons, *Debates*, 12th Parliament, 4th Session, vol. 1, August 19, 1914, 1. The Throne Speech is available online: www.lop.parl.gc.ca/ParlInfo/Documents/ThroneSpeech/12-04-e.pdf.

4. Philippe Landry to Amélie Landry, 19 August 1914, dossier P155, S4, SS3, SSS2, D6, Fonds Famille Landry, BANQ–Vieux-Montréal.

5. Amélie Landry to Philippe Landry, 20 August 1914, dossier P155, S4, SS3, SSS2, D6, Fonds Famille Landry, BANQ–Vieux-Montréal.

6. Cited in Borden, ed., *Robert Laird Borden: His Memoirs*, 1:461.

7. Ibid., 459.

8. See Elizabeth Armstrong, *The Crisis of Quebec, 1914–19* (Toronto: McClelland & Stewart, 1974), 57.

9. *La Patrie*, August 5, 1914. Cited in Armstrong, *The Crisis of Quebec, 1914–19*, 68.

10. *Montreal Gazette*, August 6, 1914.

11. Desmond Morton, "Entente Cordiale? La section montréalaise du fonds patriotique canadien, 1914–1923: Le bénévolat de guerre à Montréal," *Revue d'histoire de l'Amérique française* 53, no. 2 (1999), 215.

12. *Montreal Gazette*, August 8, 1914.

13. *Lettre pastorale de NN. SS. Les archevêques et évêques des provinces ecclésiastiques de Québec, Montréal et Ottawa, sur les devoirs des Catholiques dans la guerre actuelle*, 1914, no. 86.

14. Ibid.

15. Armstrong, *The Crisis of Quebec, 1914–19*, 85.

16. "Discours, Parc Sohmer Octobre 1914," N.A. Belcourt Papers, 1, Archives Deschâtelets, Université St-Paul.

17. Ibid., 3.

18. CAR, *1914*, 142.

19. Rodolphe Lemieux to Bruchési, 13 November 1914, Paul Bruchési Fonds, Archives de la Chancellerie de l'Archevêché à Montréal.

20. Ibid.

21. Robert Craig Brown, *Robert Laird Borden: A Biography, 1854–1914*, vol. 1 (Toronto: Macmillan of Canada, 1975), 256.

22. Robert Craig Brown, *Robert Laird Borden: A Biography, 1914–1937*, vol. 2 (Toronto: Macmillan of Canada, 1978), 19.

23. Borden, ed., *Robert Laird Borden: His Memoirs*, 1:462.

24. Brown, *Robert Laird Borden: A Biography*, 2:21.

25. K.A.H. Buckley and M.C. Urquhart, "Estimates of Gross National Product and Gross Income Produced, 1870 to 1920," in *Historical Statistics of Canada* (Cambridge: Cambridge University Press, 1965), 141.

26. See Richard Roberts, *Saving the City: The Great Financial Crisis of 1914* (London: Oxford University Press, 2013).

27. Borden, ed., *Robert Laird Borden: His Memoirs*, 1:471.

28. Buckley and Urquhart, "Federal Government Budgetary Revenue by Major Source, 1867 to 1960," in *Historical Statistics of Canada*, 191.

29. See J.J. Deutsch, "War Finance and the Canadian Economy, 1914–1928," *Canadian Journal of Economics and Political Science* 6, no. 4 (1940), 526.

30. See E.M. Macdonald, *Recollections: Personal and Political* (Toronto: Ryerson Press, 1938), 279.

31. Borden, ed., *Robert Laird Borden: His Memoirs*, 1:471.

32. Macdonald, *Recollections*, 279.

33. See Brown, *Robert Laird Borden: A Biography*, vol. 1, chapter 9.

34. For an effective overview of the railway policy issue, see Joseph Martin, "'Irrational Exuberance': The Creation of the CNR," in *Relentless Change: A Case Book for the Study of Business History* (Toronto: University of Toronto Press, 2009).

35. See Patrice Dutil, *The Origins of Prime Ministerial Power: Its Origins Under Macdonald, Laurier and Borden* (Vancouver: University of British Columbia Press, 2017), 188.

36. Andrew McMaster to Wilfrid Laurier, 13 November 1916, 193755, Laurier Papers, LAC.

37. Borden, "Diary," March 18, 1915.

38. Ibid., March 26, 1915.

39. "Memorandum for the Minister of Justice," 27 March 1915, 13969, Robert L. Borden Papers, LAC.

40. Borden to Connaught, 3 May 1915, 13514, Robert L. Borden Papers, LAC. Cited in Brown, *Robert Laird Borden: A Biography*, 2:40.

41. Borden, "Diary," March 8, 1915. Cited in Brown, *Robert Laird Borden: A Biography*, 2:41.

42. Borden, ed., *Robert Laird Borden: His Memoirs*, 1:514–22.

43. Andrew McMaster to Talbot Papineau, 13 November 1916, 193760–64, Laurier Papers, LAC.

44. "Address by Sir Robert Borden to the Halifax Canadian Club, 18 December 1914," 34672, Borden Papers, LAC.

45. Brown, *Robert Laird Borden: A Biography*, 2:32.

46. Ibid., 33.

47. Ibid.

CHAPTER 2: THE RESPONSE OF FRENCH CANADA

1. "Wilcox, Charles Letter: 1916 January 27th," *Canadian Letters and Images Project*, www.canadianletters.ca/content/document-7816. Wilcox was wounded at Passchendaele in October 1917, but survived and returned to Canada in 1919.

2. Brown, *Robert Laird Borden: A Biography*, 1:246.

3. Brown, *Robert Laird Borden: A Biography*, 2:53.

4. On the importance of the issue, see Michel Bock and François Charbonneau, "Introduction: Le Siècle du règlement 18," and Michel Bock, "Le germe d'un divorce: La langue, la foi et le règlement 17," both in *Le Siècle du règlement 17 : Regards sur une crise scolaire et nationale*, eds. Michel Bock and François Charbonneau (Sudbury, ON: Éditions Prise de parole, 2015). For Elizabeth Armstrong, Regulation 17 was the single greatest factor that slowed the war effort in Canada: see *The Crisis of Quebec*. H.B. Neatby called Regulation 17 "the most important factor" in undermining the French-Canadian participation in the war effort: see *Laurier and a Liberal Quebec* (Toronto: McClelland & Stewart, 1973), 222. John Dafoe suggested that the "movement against Ontario was Nationalist in its spirit, its inspiration, and its direction. Side by side with it went a Nationalist agitation of ever-increasing boldness against the war." See J.W.

Dafoe, *Laurier: A Study in Canadian Politics* (Toronto: McClelland & Stewart, 1968), 95. The grip of regulation 17 was obvious to following generations of historians. Fernand Dumont brings it up in his introduction to Jean Provencher's book about the deaths of Quebeckers who dared to protest conscription: see *Québec sous la loi des mesures de guerre, 1918* (Montréal: Les éditions du Boréal Express, 1971). J.L. Granatstein and J.M. Hitsman agreed that "with great force and great effect, Bourassa carried the attack against the Ontario government policy on bilingual schools and linked this issue to the war": see their discussion in *Broken Promises: A History of Conscription in Canada* (Toronto: Oxford University Press, 1977), 31. A more recent observer has dissented from this position: see René Castonguay, *Le chevalier du roi : Rodolphe Lemieux et le parti libéral, 1866–1937* (Quebec: Presse de l'Université Laval, 2000), 155.

5. On Irish Catholic motivations, see Jean-Philippe Croteau, "Pourquoi le règlement 17 paraissait-il nécessaire aux Irlandais," in *Le Siècle du Règlement 17*, eds. Bock and Charbonneau.

6. Regulation 17 can be found online: "Regulation 17," *SLMC, University of Ottawa*, https://slmc.uottawa.ca/?q=leg_regulation_17.

7. See Charles W. Humphries, *"Honest Enough to Be Bold": The Life and Times of Sir James Pliny Whitney* (Toronto: University of Toronto Press, 1985), 202.

8. Marilyn Barber, "The Ontario Bilingual Schools Issue," in *Minorities, Schools, and Politics*, ed. R. Craig Brown, (Toronto: University of Toronto Press, 1969), 66. Historians have examined the "creation" of the Franco-Ontarian "nation" and support Belcourt's notion that Franco-Ontarians constituted a people. See Chad Gaffield, *Language, Schooling, and Cultural Conflict: The Origins of the French-Language Controversy in Ontario* (Montreal: McGill-Queen's University Press, 1987), and Gaétan Gervais, "L'Ontario français (1821–1910)," in *Les Franco-ontariens*, ed. Cornelius Jaenen (Ottawa: Presses de l'Université d'Ottawa, 1993), 113. See also David Welch, "The Social Construction of Franco-Ontarian Interests Towards French Language Schooling" (Ph.D. thesis, University of Toronto, 1988).

9. On Belcourt, see Patrice Dutil, "Against Isolationism: Napoléon

Belcourt, French Canada and 'la grande guerre,'" in *Canada and the First World War*, ed. David MacKenzie (Toronto: University of Toronto Press, 2005); Geneviève Richer, "'L'apôtre infatigable de l'irrédentisme français : la lutte de Napoléon-Antoine Belcourt en faveur de la langue française en Ontario durant les années 1910 et 1920," *Francophonies d'Amérique* 31 (spring 2011).

10. Belcourt to Omer Héroux, 16 April 1920, HH6017B42M39, Belcourt Papers.

11. Historian Pierre Anctil calculates that from 1910 to 1920, Henri Bourassa's *Le Devoir* devoted almost as much editorial space to the Ontario crisis as it did to Quebec's social and political scene. He counts 241 editorials on the Ontario situation and 297 on Quebec. See Pierre Anctil, "Le Journal *Le Devoir* et la crise des écoles ontariennes," in *Le Siècle du Règlement 17*, eds. Bock and Charbonneau.

12. Bourassa to Tierney, 21 September 1916, File P65/C2,4, Fonds Famille Bourassa, BANQ.

13. *Ottawa Citizen*, December 18, 1912.

14. *Ottawa Witness*, December 19, 1912.

15. "Aux électeurs de la division électorale de Labelle, May 1, 1896," dossier P65/C4,1, Fonds Famille Bourassa, BANQ.

16. See Patrice Dutil and David MacKenzie, *Canada, 1911: The Decisive Election that Shaped the Country* (Toronto: Dundurn Press, 2011).

17. *Le Devoir*, September 8, 1914, trans. Elizabeth Armstrong, 78.

18. See Robert Rumilly, *Henri Bourassa : La vie publique d'un grand canadien* (Montreal: Éditions Chantecler, 1953), 502, 507; Bourassa to J.A. Charlebois, 4 November 1914, dossier P65/C5,15, Fonds Famille Bourassa, BANQ.

19. Rodolphe Lemieux to Bruchési, 13 November 1914, Paul-Napoléon Bruchési Fonds, ACAM.

20. Bourassa to J.A. Charlebois, 4 November 1914, dossier P65/C5, 15, Paul-Napoléon Bruchési Fonds, ACAM; see also Bourassa to P.H. Gagné, 21 November 1914 and 10 December 1914; L.A. Paquet to Arthur Letellier, 13 October 1914, dossier P65/C5,15.

21. Henri Bourassa, "The Duty of Canada at the Present Hour: An Address Meant to be Delivered at Ottawa, in November and

December, 1914, but Twice Suppressed in the Name of 'Loyalty and Patriotism,'" *Le Devoir, Internet Archive*, https://archive.org/stream/dutyofcanadaatpr00bouriala/dutyofcanadaatpr00bouriala_djvu.txt

22. *Le Devoir*, October 31, 1914, cited in Rumilly, *Henri Bourassa*, 517.
23. *Ottawa Citizen*, December 17, 1914, 10.
24. In nearby Rockland, the school board had just sent a letter of protest to Ontario premier Hearst, pointing out that Canada's military mission in Europe in support of various minorities was incompatible with the province's own educational laws. For more on this episode see Dutil, "Against Isolationism," 96–97.
25. Rumilly, *Henri Bourassa*, 518.
26. Dossier P65-C6.41, Fonds Famille Bourassa.
27. Henri Bourassa, "La langue française au Canada. Ses durées, sa nécessité, ses avantages. 19 mars 1915." The notes for the speech are available online: http://crccf.uottawa.ca/reglement17/archive/la-langue-francaise-au-canada-ses-droits-sa-necessite-ses-avantages-plan-dun-discours.
28. Fonds Famille Bourassa, Bourassa to Béliveau, 7 June 1916, P65/C7,18.
29. *Le Devoir et la guerre : Discours prononcé au banquet des amis du « Devoir »*, January 12, 1916.
30. Amélie Landry to Philippe Landry, 11 February 1916, dossier P155, S4, SS3, SSS2, Fonds Famille Landry, D6 BANQ–Vieux-Montréal.
31. Robert Rumilly, *Histoire de la province de Quebec*, vol. 22 (Montreal: Montréal Editions, n.d.), 33.
32. "La lutte pour l'existence nationale" notes, dossier P65, C6, 71, Fonds Famille Bourassa.
33. Ibid.
34. See Paul Bernier, "Ernest Lapointe. Député de Kamouraska 1904–1919," *Revue d'histoire de l'Amérique française* 33, no. 3 (1979), 122–33. See also François Charbonneau, "Le débat sur le règlement 17 au parlement canadien," in *Le Siècle du Règlement 17*, eds. Bock and Charbonneau.
35. See Nelson Michaud, *L'énigme du Sphinx : regards sur la vie politique d'un nationaliste : 1910–1926* (Sainte-Foy: Presse de l'Université Laval, 1998), 48–51; Brown, *Robert Laird Borden: A Biography*, 2:52.

36. See dossier P155, S4, SS5, d77, Fonds Famille Landry, BANQ–Vieux-Montréal. Landry, as a Quebec Conservative, stood out — his views were not widely shared. See Nelson Michaud, "Les écoles d'Ontario ou le dilemme des conservateurs Québécois : confrontation des principes nationalistes et de la réalité politique," *Revue d'histoire de l'Amérique française* 49, no. 1 (1996), and Damien-Claude Bélanger, "Thomas Chapais et le règlement 17," in *Le Siècle du Règlement 17*, eds. Bock and Charbonneau.

37. For background on Rome's decision, and Mgr Stagni's report, see John Zucchi, ed., *The View from Rome: Archbishop Stagni's 1915 Reports on the Ontario School Question* (Montreal: McGill-Queen's University Press, 2002). See also Michel Bock, "Le Vatican et l'ACFÉO au moment du Règlement 17," in *Le Saint-Siège, le Québec et l'Amérique française*, eds. Martin Pâquet, Matteo Sanfilippo, and Jean-Philippe Warren (Quebec: Presses de l'Université Laval, 2013).

38. See P. Whitney Lackenbauer, "Soldiers Behaving Badly: CEF Soldier 'Rioting' in Canada during the First World War" in *The Apathetic and the Defiant: Case Studies of Canadian Mutiny and Disobedience, 1812 to 1919*, ed. Craig Leslie Mantle (Toronto: Dundurn Press, 2007), 195–260.

39. Granatstein and Hitsman, *Broken Promises*, 123.

40. Eugène Nantel to Maréchal Nantel, 14 March 1915, Fonds Bergeron-Nantel.

41. Ibid.

42. Eugène Nantel to Maréchal Nantel, 17 March 1915, Fonds Bergeron-Nantel. Nantel met Sam Hughes that spring, and the latter made the connection between the young officer and his former colleague in cabinet. See Eugène Nantel to Maréchal Nantel, 29 March 1915, Fonds Bergeron-Nantel.

43. Eugène Nantel to Maréchal Nantel, 10 April 1915, Fonds Bergeron-Nantel. Eugène Nantel's service file does not reflect this. See "Files of the Canadian Expeditionary Force (CEF): Soldiers, Nurses and Chaplains (RG150)," 1992–93\166, box 7232 – 51, file number: 332-64-15.

44. C.A. Sharpe, "Enlistment in the Canadian Expeditionary Force 1914–1918: A Regional Analysis," *Journal of Canadian Studies* 18,

no. 4 (1983–84): 20. Sharpe's "revised data" makes clear distinctions of eligibility.

45. Granatstein and Hitsman, *Broken Promises*, 62. The authors cite cabinet documents.

46. See R. Matthew Bray, "'Fighting as an Ally': The English-Canadian Patriotic Response to the Great War," *Canadian Historical Review* 41, no. 2 (1980): 152.

47. CAR, 1915, 276.

48. Maréchal Nantel to Eugène Nantel, 20 July 1915, Fonds Bergeron-Nantel.

49. Maréchal Nantel to Eugène Nantel, 2 September, 1915, Fonds Bergeron-Nantel.

50. Maréchal Nantel to Eugène Nantel, 24 September 1915, Fonds Bergeron-Nantel.

51. Douglas Delaney, "The Corps Nervous System in Action: Commanders, Staffs, and Battle Procedure" in *Capturing Hill 70: Canada's Forgotten Battle of the First World War*, eds. Douglas E. Delaney and Serge Marc Durflinger (Vancouver: University of British Columbia Press, 2016), 54–56.

52. Landry was the highest-ranking militia officer before the war. He had volunteered to serve in Europe in 1912 and assisted in war games organized by England and France, and accompanied General Ian Hamilton. In August 1914, Sam Hughes offered Landry a brigade. Landry accepted on the spot, but the commission was not formalized.

53. The Landry Family Papers contain a complete file on this story. See Landry to Chase-Casgrain, 1 December 1914, P155, S7, SS7, SSS2, D6; see entire file P155, S7, SS7, SSS2, D10; P155, S4, SS3, SSS1, D8; Senator Landry to J.P. Landry, 23 August 1915, P155, S7, SS3, D1; Senator Landry to J.P. Landry, 6 September 1915, P155, S7, SS3, D1; P. Landry to J.P. Landry, 5 July 1915, P155, S7, SS3, D1; Deputy Minister Eugène Fiset blamed Hughes. See Senator Landry to J.P. Landry, 30 August 1915, P155, S7, SS3, D1. P. Landry to Robert Borden, 18 September 1915; P. Landry to J.P. Landry, 24 September 1915, P155, S7, SS3, D1; Landry to Borden, 1 February 1916, P155,

S4, SS3, SSS1, D8; Landry to J.P. Landry, 24 September 1915, P155, S7, SS3, D1. See also Desmond Morton, "Limits of Loyalty: French Canadian Officers in the First World War" in *The Limits of Loyalty*, ed. Edgar Denton (Waterloo, ON: Wilfrid Laurier University Press), 90.

54. See *Le Devoir*, January 22, 1916.

55. Fonds Bergeron-Nantel, Maréchal Nantel to Eugène Nantel, December 1, 1915.

56. See Pierre Vennat, *Les poilus québécois de 1914–18 : histoire des militaires canadiens-français de la première guerre mondiale* (Montreal: Éditions du Méridien), 297–305.

57. Onésime Nantel-Orsali to Eugène Nantel, 20 June 1916, Fonds Bergeron-Nantel.

58. Ibid., 27 September 1916, Fonds Bergeron-Nantel.

59. For more detail on Talbot Papineau, see Geoff Keelan, "Canada's Cultural Mobilization during the First World War and a Case for Canadian War Culture" *Canadian Historical Review* 97, no. 3 (2015); Sandra Gwyn, *Tapestry of War: A Private View of Canadians in the First World War* (Toronto: HarperCollins, 1994).

60. Henri Bourassa to Andrew McMaster, 12 August 1916, Talbot Papineau Papers, BANQ. For the commentary on the issue, see the *Montreal Gazette* July 28 and August 7, 1916; *L'Événement*, August 12, 1916; *La Patrie*, August 7, 1916; *Le Canada*, August 8, 1916.

61. Talbot Papineau to Andrew McMaster, 10 November 1916, 193757, Laurier Papers, LAC.

62. Ibid.

63. Laurier to Andrew McMaster, 14 November 1916, 193765, Laurier Papers.

64. See McKim's *Directory of Canadian Publications* (Montreal: A. McKim, 1917).

65. *Le Devoir*, August 25, 1916.

66. See Durocher for a description of Bourassa's evolution on the issue. See also Béatrice Richard, "Henri Bourassa et la conscription : Traître ou sauveur," *Revue militaire canadienne* 7, no. 4 (Winter 2006–2007), 75–83.

67. Among them were *The Foreign Policy of Great Britain* (1914), *The Duty of Canada at the Present Hour* (1914), *Canadian Nationalism and the War* (1916), and *Independence or Imperial Partnerships?* (1916).

68. Rumilly, *Histoire de la province de Québec*, 22:14.

69. Ibid., 12.

70. Dale C. Thomson, *Louis St. Laurent: Canadian* (Toronto: Macmillan of Canada, 1967), 80–81. St-Laurent was thirty-four years old at the time, was married, and had five children.

71. Rumilly, *Histoire de la province de Québec*, 22:15.

72. Ibid., 16.

73. Ibid., 21.

74. Ibid., 23.

75. See Maréchal Nantel to Eugène Nantel, 13 February 1917 and 29 March 1917, Nantel-Bergeron Papers.

76. Borden, "Diary," February 4, 1917.

CHAPTER 3: THE ISSUE

1. "Brown, Robert Gordon Letter: 1917 June 2nd," *Canadian Letters and Images Project*, www.canadianletters.ca/content/document-13257.

2. Brown, *Robert Laird Borden: A Biography*, 2:74. It should be noted that Borden asked the U.K. government for its opinion on the matter and was informed by the Colonial Office that London would acquiesce to Borden's wishes one way or the other. See Walter Long to Sir George Perley, 1 January 1917, CO 42/1002, Colonial Office, NAUK.

3. Philip G. Wigley, *Canada and the Transition to Commonwealth: British-Canadian relations 1917–1926* (Cambridge: Cambridge University Press, 1977), 39.

4. Brown, *Robert Laird Borden: A Biography*, 2:75.

5. See Robert Craig Brown and Robert Bothwell, "The 'Canadian Resolution,'" in *Policy by Other Means: Essays in Honour of C. P. Stacey*, eds. Michael Cross and Robert Bothwell (Toronto: Clarke, Irwin, 1972), 163–78.

6. Borden, "Diary," April 10, 1917.

7. See A.M. Willms, "Conscription 1917: A Brief for the Defence," *Canadian Historical Review* 37 (1956), 338–56.

8. Henry Borden, ed., *Robert Laird Borden: His Memoirs*, vol. 2 (Toronto: Macmillan of Canada, 1938), 697.

9. Diaries, May 17, 1917, reel A-653, Devonshire Papers, LAC.

10. Rumilly, *Histoire de la Province de Québec*, 22:73.

11. Borden, "Diary," May 17, 1917.

12. See Nelson Michaud's book on Ésioff-Léon Patenaude, *L'Énigme du sphinx : Regards sur la vie politique d'un nationaliste (1910–1926)* (Quebec: Les presses de l'Université Laval, 1998), 93.

13. The exchange is described in Rumilly, *Histoire de la Province de Québec*, 22:74. Borden and Meighen thought, for a while, anyway, that Patenaude would support conscription. Nelson Michaud discusses these impressions, but finds them difficult to justify. He does not rely on Rumilly's account, but comes to the same conclusion: Patenaude, like Sévigny, considered conscription suicidal for the party.

14. House of Commons speech, printed in Borden, ed., *Robert Laird Borden: His Memoirs*, 2:698–99.

15. Borden, "Diary," May 18, 1917.

16. For a survey of opinion see "Press Comment on Conscription," *Toronto Globe*, May 19, 1917.

17. "The Government Will Enforce Selective Draft," *Toronto Daily Star*, May 19, 1917, 1.

18. Cited in Rumilly, *Histoire de la Province de Québec*, 22:78.

19. Ibid.

20. Ramsay Cook, *The Politics of John W. Dafoe and the Free Press* (Toronto: University of Toronto Press, 1963), 76.

21. Dorothy Smith to Borden, 22 May 1917, 44004–05, reel C-4323, Borden Papers, LAC.

22. "Conscript Wealth and Food as well as Men," *Toronto Globe*, May 19, 1917, 2.

23. See the correspondence in 43986–44274, reel C-4323, Borden Papers, LAC.

24. Skelton to Laurier, 30 May 1917, 195816, reel C-913, Laurier Papers, LAC.

25. Ian Hugh Maclean Miller, *Our Glory and Our Grief: Torontonians and the Great War* (Toronto: University of Toronto Press, 2002), 137.

26. Memorandum from J.G. Foster, "Political Situation in Canada," 28 May 1917, Consular Correspondence, General Records of the Department of State, NAUS.

27. Rumilly, *Histoire de la Province de Québec*, 22:41.

28. Ibid., 52.

29. Ibid.

30. *Le Soleil*, cited in Rumilly, *Histoire de la Province de Québec*, 22:69.

31. Ibid., 82.

32. The rate of enlistment among French Canadians may have been higher than assumed. Jean Martin calculates it at upwards of 70,000, almost double what is commonly thought. See Jean Martin, "Francophone Enlistment in the Canadian Expeditionary Force, 1914–1918: The Evidence" *Canadian Military History* 25, no. 1 (2016), 1–12.

33. *La Patrie*, May 8, 1917; Rumilly, *Histoire de la Province de Québec*, 22:63.

34. Macdonald, *Recollections*, 322.

35. Onésime Nantel to Eugène Nantel, May 15, 1917, Fonds Nantel-Bergeron Papers.

36. *Le Devoir*, May 1, 1917.

37. *Le Soleil*, cited in Rumilly, *Histoire de la Province de Québec*, 22:62.

38. "Quebec's Young Men Against Equal Service," *Montreal Gazette*, May 22, 1917, 1.

39. "Conscription is Condemned by Big Rally of Young Men, *Montreal Gazette*, May 24, 1917, 4; "Anti-Conscription Meeting in Montreal," *Toronto Globe*, May 24, 1917, 2.

40. Lamarche died of influenza in 1918 at the age of 36. See Réal Bélanger, *Paul-Émile Lamarche : Le Pays avant le parti (1904–1918)* (Sainte-Foy, Quebec: Les Presses de l'Université Laval, 1984), 388.

41. Bruchési to Borden, 22 May 1917, 123399-401, Borden Papers, LAC. Translated by Serge Durflinger, who cites it in "Vimy's Consequence?: The Montreal Anti-Conscription Disturbances, May-September 1917," in *Turning Point Year 1917: The British Empire at War*, eds. Douglas E. Delaney and Nikolas Gardner (Vancouver: UBC Press, 2017).

42. Rumilly, *Histoire de la Province de Québec*, 22:87–88.

43. Ibid., 102.

44. Ibid., 92.

45. Fonds Nantel-Bergeron, Onésime Nantel-Orsali to Eugène Nantel, June 4, 1917.

46. Ibid., Eugène Nantel to Onésime Nantel-Orsali, June 5, 1917.

47. Fonds Famille Bourassa, Paquet to Bourassa, May 5, 1917, P65/C2,5.

48. Ibid., Bourassa to Pâquet, June 1, 1917 P65/C2,5.

49. *Le Devoir*, June 6, 1917, trans. Tonu Onu, cited in Pierre Anctil, ed., *'Do What You Must': Selected Editorials from* Le Devoir *under Henri Bourassa, 1910–1932* (Toronto: Champlain Society, 2017).

50. Rumilly, *Histoire de la Province de Québec*, 22:175.

51. J.E. Caron to Laurier, 22 May 1917, 195686, reel C-913, Laurier Papers, LAC.

52. Laurier to Aylesworth, May 15, 1917, cited in O.D. Skelton, *Life and Letters of Sir Wilfrid Laurier*, vol. 2 (Toronto: Oxford University Press, 1921), 510.

53. Laurier to Dewart, May 29, 1917, 195738–40, reel C-913, Laurier Papers, LAC.

54. Foster to Robert Lansing, 14 June 1917, Consular Correspondence, General Records of the Department of State, NAUS.

55. Foster to Robert Lansing, 20 June 1017, Consular Correspondence, General Records of the Department of State, NAUS.

56. "Bind by Conscription Pledge to Trenches," *Toronto Globe*, June 11, 1917, 1.

57. "Leaders Join Hands to Back Conscription," *Toronto Globe*, June 12, 1917, 1.

58. Prang, *N.W. Rowell, Ontario Nationalist*, 177.

59. For a survey of opinion, see CAR, 1917, 339–41; "Owen Sound Meeting Calls for Conscription," *Toronto Globe*, June 11, 1917, 5.

60. Fielding to Laurier, 31 May 1917, 195844–49, reel C-913, Laurier Papers, LAC.

61. Borden, "Diary," May 24, 1917.

62. For a list of the dates, see CAR, 1917, 328.

63. For a review of the debate on the Military Service Act, see CAR,

1917, 340–47, and Roger Graham, *Arthur Meighen: A Biography*, vol. 1 (Toronto: Macmillan of Canada, 1960), 126–44.

64. John English, *The Decline of Politics: The Conservatives and the Party System 1901–20* (Toronto: University of Toronto Press, 1977), 139.

65. Diaries, 5 July 1917, vol. 5, Sir George Foster Papers, LAC. The "man" referred to was the Liberal Frank Oliver, "who obstinately sat."

66. *Le Canada*, June 15, 26, and July 13, 1917; *La Presse*, July 6, 1917.

67. *Montreal Gazette*, June 16, 1917, cited in Durflinger, op. cit.

68. *Montreal Gazette*, June 22, 1917, and *Le Devoir*, June 22, 1917.

69. Rumilly, *Histoire de la Province de Québec*, 22:104.

70. *La Presse*, July 16, 1917.

71. Rumilly, *Histoire de la Province de Québec*, 22:130.

72. Maréchal Nantel to Eugène Nantel, 28 June 1917, Fonds Nantel-Bergeron.

73. Ibid., 20 August 1917, Fonds Nantel-Bergeron.

74. Onésime Nantel-Orsali to Eugène Nantel, 29 August 1917, Fonds Nantel-Bergeron.

75. Maréchal Nantel to Eugène Nantel, 23 October 1917, Fonds Nantel-Bergeron.

76. Foster, "Political Situation in Canada."

77. On the growing support for a coalition government, see the letters, et cetera, in 32134–67, reel C-4310, Borden Papers, LAC. See also the correspondence in Series 3 – B2003–0005 / Box 13 and Box 14, George Wrong Family Papers, UTA; J.W. Dafoe to Clifford Sifton, 27 February 1917, reel M-73, Dafoe Papers, LAC; and George Wrong to Dafoe, 19 December 1917, reel M-73, Dafoe Papers, LAC; and CAR, 1917, 554–60.

78. "Borden and Sir Wilfrid Were in Conference," *Montreal Gazette*, May 30, 1917, 1.

79. Murray Donnelly, *Dafoe of the Free Press* (Toronto: Macmillan, 1968), 78.

80. Dafoe to Wrong, 12 December 1917, Series 3 –Acc. B2003–0005 / Box 14, George Wrong Family Papers, UTA. See also Cook, *Politics of John W. Dafoe*, 71–73.

81. Flavelle to Borden, 13 December 1916, 32149–50, reel C-4310, Borden Papers, LAC. On Flavelle, see Michael Bliss, *A Canadian Millionaire: The Life and Business Times of Sir Joseph Flavelle, Bart. 1858–1939* (Toronto: Macmillan, 1978).

82. Flavelle to Borden, 13 December 1916, 32149–50, reel C-4310, Borden Papers, LAC.

83. For a survey of some newspaper opinion, see CAR, 1917, 555.

84. Blount to Borden, 28 March 1917, A.E. Blount Papers, vol. 1, LAC.

85. A.E. Blount memo for Borden, 13 December 1916, 32151, reel C-4310, Borden Papers, LAC.

86. Borden to F.B. Fetherstonhaugh, 2 February 1917, 32179, reel C-4310, Borden Papers, LAC.

87. Ibid., Meighen to Borden, 12 May 1915, 13540, reel C-4227, Borden Papers, LAC.

88. Borden, "Diary," May 17, 1917.

89. Borden, ed., *Robert Laird Borden: His Memoirs*, 2:720.

90. Diaries, 6 June 1917, vol. 5, Sir George Foster Papers, LAC.

91. Laurier to Rowell, 23 January 1917, reel C-931, Newton Rowell Papers, LAC.

92. Dafoe to Laurier, 26 April 1917, reel M-73, Dafoe Papers, LAC.

93. Laurier to Dafoe, 10 April 1917, reel M-73, Dafoe Papers, LAC.

94. Borden to Governor General, 2 June 1917, 40041, reel C-4318, Borden Papers, LAC.

95. Borden to Governor General, 2 June 1917, 40042, reel C-4318, Borden Papers, LAC.

96. Borden draft memo, 6 June 1917, 195982, reel C-913, Laurier Papers, LAC. See also Laurier to Borden, 6 June 1917, reel C-4319, Borden Papers, LAC.

97. See Macdonald, *Recollections*, 323. Rumilly writes that his account is drawn from an even more direct source, 95.

98. Rumilly, *Histoire de la Province de Québec*, 22:93.

99. Rodolphe Lemieux to Laurier, 3 June 1917, 195934–37, reel C-913, Laurier Papers, LAC. The original in French is reproduced in Réal Castonguay, *Rodolphe Lemieux et le Parti libéral, 1866–1937 : Le Chevalier du roi* (Quebec: Presses de l'Université Laval, 2000), 158.

100. Carvell to Laurier, 4 June 1917, 195944–47, reel C-913, Laurier Papers, LAC.

101. Howard Cane to King, 29 May 1917, 31369, reel C-1929, Mackenzie King Papers, LAC.

102. Laurier to Rowell, 2 June 1917, reel C-931, Rowell Papers, LAC.

103. Laurier to Skelton, 5 June 1917, 195817, reel C-913, Laurier Papers, LAC.

104. "Coalition Is All Off: Election Looms Up Near," *Toronto Globe*, June 7, 1917, 1. For more on Laurier's objections see Skelton, *Life and Letters of Sir Wilfrid Laurier*, 2:513–24.

105. Borden to Governor General, 7 June 1917, 40056–57, reel C-4318, Borden Papers, LAC. The letters are reprinted in Borden, ed., *Robert Laird Borden: His Memoirs*, 2:724–26.

106. "Coalition or Dissolution Within Forty-Eight Hours," *Toronto Globe*, June 6, 1917, 1.

107. For the debate, see CAR, 1917, 329–30; "Extension Resolution will be Dropped," *Halifax Herald*, July 19, 1917, 1.

CHAPTER 4: THE LIBERALS IN OPPOSITION

1. "Scherer, George Leslie MM Letter: 1917 June 20th," *Canadian Letters and Images Project*, www.canadianletters.ca/content/document-10374.

2. Maclean to Borden, 13 June 1917, 39749, reel C-4318, Borden Papers, LAC.

3. King to Howard Cane, June 11, 1917, 31372, reel C-1929, King Papers, LAC.

4. Quoted in Skelton, *Life and Letters of Sir Wilfrid Laurier*, 2:518.

5. Diaries, 21 June 1917, vol. 5, Foster Papers, LAC.

6. "Confidential Memorandum of Mr. Rowell," 23 June 1917, Correspondence 1917, vol. 89, Rowell Papers, LAC.

7. Richard Clippingdale, *The Power of the Pen: The Politics, Nationalism, and Influence of Sir John Willison* (Toronto: Dundurn Press, 2012), 310–19. For more on Willison see A.H.U. Colquhoun, *Press, Politics and People: The Life and Letters of Sir John Willison* (Toronto: Macmillan, 1935).

8. "Confidential Memorandum of Mr. Rowell," 18 June 1917, Correspondence 1917, vol. 89, Rowell Papers, LAC.

9. Rowell to Borden, July 6, 1917, 40064–67, reel C-4318, Borden Papers, LAC.

10. "Confidential Memorandum of Mr. Rowell," 23 June 1917, Correspondence 1917, vol. 89, Rowell Papers, LAC.

11. Ibid.

12. Borden to Willison, 23 August 1917, 40074, reel C-4318, Borden Papers, LAC.

13. Laurier to Rowell, 4 July 1917, reel C-931, Rowell Papers, LAC.

14. Laurier to Rowell, 14 July 1917, reel C-931, Rowell Papers, LAC.

15. Rowell to Laurier, 20 July 1917, 196312–17, reel C-913, Laurier Papers, LAC.

16. Ibid.

17. Laurier to Rowell, 23 July 1917, reel C-931, Rowell Papers, LAC. For more on the Laurier-Rowell correspondence see Prang, *N.W. Rowell, Ontario Nationalist*, 194–96.

18. For the Win-the-War Convention, see CAR, 1917, 567–68; see also Miller, *Our Glory and Our Grief*, 140.

19. See Pardee to King, 14 July 1917, 32638, reel C-1930, King Papers, LAC.

20. See the minutes of the meeting in "Chronological Correspondence June-July 1917," private report, 20 July 1917, Box 35, T.A. Crerar Papers, QUA. Mackenzie King also left his account; see King, "Diary," July 20, 1917.

21. Graham to Rowell, 21 July 1917, reel C-931, Rowell Papers, LAC.

22. See "Ontario Liberals Oppose Conscription, Stand by Laurier," *Ottawa Citizen*, July 21, 1917, 2; "To Campaign With Laurier as Leader," *Montreal Gazette*, July 21, 1917, 1.

23. Graham to Rowell, 21 July 1917, reel C-931, Rowell Papers, LAC.

24. See the unsigned memo in "13795–885," 13817–18, vol. 32/34, Charles Murphy Papers, LAC; and Dafoe to Rowell, 25 July 1917, reel M-73, Dafoe Papers, LAC.

25. CAR, 1917, 567; "Stinging Condemnation by Liberal Newspapers," *Halifax Herald*, July 23, 1917, 1.

26. Rowell to Dafoe, 21 July 1917, reel M-73, Dafoe Papers, LAC.

27. Borden, "Diary," July 10, 1917.

28. Ibid., July 21, 1917.

29. Willison to Borden, 12 June 1917, 40504, reel C-4319, Borden Papers, LAC.

30. Willison to Borden, 22 July 1917, 2512, vol. 4, Willison Papers, LAC.

31. Sifton to W.M. Southam, 28 July 1917, reel C-595, Clifford Sifton Papers, LAC; see also Dafoe to Rowell, 25 July 1917, reel M-73, Dafoe Papers, LAC.

32. Borden, "Diary," July 30, 1917.

33. "Four Factions at the Western Convention," *Montreal Gazette*, August 6, 1917, 1.

34. "Main Johnson's notes of Winnipeg Western Liberal Convention, August 1917," vol. "1917," William Main Johnson Papers, TRL.

35. Ibid.

36. CAR, 1917, 575.

37. Hearst to William Hearst, 10 August 1917, B253647, Box MU 1317, Heart Papers, AO.

38. "Diaries," 10 August 1917, vol. 5, Foster Papers, LAC.

39. Quoted in CAR, 1917, 577.

40. See John Herd Thompson, *The Harvests of War: The Prairie West, 1914–1918* (Toronto: McClelland & Stewart, 1978), 125.

41. "Main Johnson's notes," vol. "1917," William Main Johnson Papers, TRL.

42. Borden, "Diary," August 6, 1917.

43. For the Convention resolutions, see CAR, 1917, 572–75.

44. "The Winnipeg Convention," case 8, Norman Lambert Papers, QUA.

45. "Issues Are Too Big For Party Politics," *Toronto Daily Star*, August 27, 1917, 1.

46. Foster to Robert Lansing, 10 August 1917, Consular Correspondence, General Records of the Department of State, NAUS.

47. Devonshire to Borden, 26 July 1917, 40340–41, reel C-4319, Borden Papers, LAC.

48. Ibid.

49. "Diaries," 9 August 1917, reel A-653, Devonshire Papers, LAC.

50. Borden, ed., *Robert Laird Borden: His Memoirs*, 2:740.

51. Diaries, 9 August 1917, reel A-653, Devonshire Papers, LAC; see also Diaries, 9 August 1917, vol. 5, Foster Papers, LAC.

52. King to J.M. Walton, 8 August 1917, 33294, reel C-1930, King Papers, LAC.

53. See Dutil and MacKenzie, *Canada 1911*.

54. "Liberals of Manitoba Are Anti-Laurier," *Montreal Gazette*, August 22, 1917, 1; Joseph Schull, *Laurier: The First Canadian* (Toronto: Macmillan, 1965), 589.

55. W.L. Morton, *The Progressive Party in Canada* (Toronto: University of Toronto Press, 1950), 56.

56. L.G. Thomas, *The Liberal Party in Alberta: A History of Politics in the Province of Alberta, 1905–1921* (Toronto: University of Toronto Press, 1959), 170–71.

57. Ibid., 180.

58. David E. Smith, *Prairie Liberalism: The Liberal Party in Saskatchewan, 1905–71* (Toronto: University of Toronto Press, 1975), 40.

59. See CAR, 1917, 577.

60. See English, *The Decline of Politics*, 141–47.

61. Hughes to Borden, 27 July 1917, 40563–68, reel C-4913, Borden Papers, LAC.

62. Hughes to Borden, 28 August 1917, 40711, reel C-4913, Borden Papers, LAC. Interestingly, Hughes had met Sir Clifford Sifton earlier with the hope of getting the westerner to form a Union government. Sifton declined, citing his poor hearing. Hughes then asked if Sifton would support *him* at the head of a government. "No," was the answer. "He is a queer fellow," Sifton said. See Macdonald, *Recollections*, 323–24; Rumilly, *Histoire de la Province de Québec*, 22:101.

63. James H. Gray, *R.B. Bennett: The Calgary Years* (Toronto: University of Toronto Press, 1991), 187.

64. Bennett quoted in John Boyko, *Bennett: The Rebel Who Challenged and Changed a Nation* (Fredericton: Goose Lane, 2010), 107.

65. Borden, "Diary," August 15, 1917.

66. Borden, ed., *Robert Laird Borden: His Memoirs*, 2:719.
67. See English, *The Decline of Politics*, 147–48.
68. For the details on the scandal, see CAR, 1917, 318–20.
69. Borden, "Diary," August 3, 1917.
70. Ibid., August 17, 1917.
71. Rogers to Borden, 18 August 1917, 40895–97, reel C-4913, Borden Papers, LAC; "The Hon. Robert Rogers Is No Longer Minister of the Borden Cabinet," *Halifax Herald*, August 21, 1917, 1.
72. Devonshire to Walter Long, 30 August 1917, CO 42/1001, Colonial Office, NAUK; English, *The Decline of Politics*, 149–51.
73. English, *The Decline of Politics*, 133–35.

CHAPTER 5: CREATING DIVISIONS, CHOOSING SIDES

1. "Thorburn, Howard Beverley Letter: 1917 June 28th," *Canadian Letters and Images Project*, www.canadianletters.ca/content/document-4552.
2. Diaries, 31 August 1917, vol. 6, Wilson MacDonald Papers, LAC.
3. See Dutil and MacKenzie, *Canada 1911*, 245–46.
4. Diaries, 21 October 1917, vol. 7, Wilson MacDonald Papers, LAC.
5. Foster to Robert Lansing, 10 August 1917, Consular Correspondence, General Records of the Department of State, NAUS.
6. Blondin to Borden, 21 August 1917, 188, vol. 65, A.E. Kemp Papers, LAC.
7. On the riots, see "Montreal Riots Are Discussed in Parliament," *Montreal Gazette*, September 1, 1917; "Lalumiere up in Court at Montreal," *Toronto Globe*, September 1, 1917, 2.
8. Rumilly, *Histoire de la Province de Québec*, 22:137.
9. Jean Provencher, *Québec sous la loi des mesures de guerre 1918* (Montreal: Boréal, 1971), 32–3. The author draws on original documents in this more detailed account.
10. CAR, 1917, 328.
11. Granatstein and Hitsman, *Broken Promises*, 72.
12. For a review of the legislation, see CAR, 1917, 327–35.
13. Richard Krever, "The Origin of Federal Income Taxation in Canada," *Canadian Taxation* 3, no. 4 (1981), 170–88.

14. For background on the railway situation, see Robert C. Brown and Ramsay Cook, *Canada 1896–1921: A Nation Transformed* (Toronto: McClelland & Stewart, 1974), 243–47.

15. See R.B. Fleming, *The Railway King of Canada: Sir William Mackenzie, 1849–1923* (Vancouver: UBC Press, 1991), 217–26; and G.R. Stevens, *History of the Canadian National Railways* (New York: Macmillan, 1973), 274–80.

16. Mackenzie King, "Diary," October 3, 1917.

17. Ibid., October 9, 1917.

18. See John A. Eagle, "Sir Robert Borden, Union Government and Railway Nationalization," *Journal of Canadian Studies* 10, no. 4 (1975), 59–66, and Skelton, *Life and Letters of Sir Wilfrid Laurier*, vol. 2; 517.

19. For example, see Sergeant B.M. Stitt to J.D. Reid, 12 September 1917, 40597, reel C-4913, Borden Papers, LAC.

20. Foster to Lansing, 30 August 1917, Consular Correspondence, General Records of the Department of State, NAUS.

21. See Desmond Morton, "Polling the Soldier Vote: The Overseas Campaign in the Canadian General Election of 1917," *Journal of Canadian Studies* 10, no. 4 (1975), 43–45.

22. W.T.R. Preston to Laurier, September 1917, reel C-914, Laurier Papers, LAC.

23. Quoted in Morton, "Polling the Soldier Vote," 39.

24. Quoted in Graham, *Arthur Meighen: A Biography*, 1:165.

25. Ibid.

26. Borden had written of the main aspects of the bill as early as April. See Borden to Meighen, 20 April 1917, 35517, reel C-4314, Borden Papers, LAC.

27. CAR, 1917, 332.

28. See Amy Shaw, *Crisis of Conscience: Conscientious Objection in Canada During the First World War* (Vancouver: UBC Press, 2009).

29. CAR, 1917, 332.

30. Quoted in Brown, *Robert Laird Borden: A Biography*, 2:101.

31. Alison Prentice et al., *Canadian Women: A History* (Toronto: Harcourt Brace Jovanovich, 1988), 208.

32. LAC, Laurier Papers, reel C-914, Laurier to Preston, 25 September 1917.

33. King to Carruthers, 8 October 1917, 32460, reel C-1930, King Papers, LAC. Newton Rowell similarly saw the bill as a purely political action. See Prang, *N.W. Rowell, Ontario Nationalist*, 204. For more on the "election stealing bill," see "Carvell's Stinging Criticism of Borden's Prussian Measure Makes the Premier Wince," *Morning Chronicle*, September 13, 1917, 1.

34. Quoted in Graham, *Arthur Meighen: A Biography*, 1:169.

35. Brown, *Borden*, 100.

36. Skelton, *Life and Letters of Sir Wilfrid Laurier*, 529.

37. Graham, *Arthur Meighen: A Biography*, 1:166.

38. NAUS, General Records of the Department of State, Consular Correspondence, Foster Memorandum, "Prorogation of Parliament," September 21, 1917.

39. See Graham, *Arthur Meighen: A Biography*, 1:168; John W. Dafoe, *Clifford Sifton in Relation to his Times*. (Toronto: Macmillan, 1931), 435–36.

40. Crerar to J.B. Parker, 3 October 1917, "Chronological Correspondence, Oct. 1917," box 37, Crerar Papers, QUA.

41. Crerar to J.A. Glen, 6 September 1917, "Chronological Correspondence, Aug.-Sept. 1917," box 36, Crerar Papers, QUA.

42. Crerar to H.B. Cowan, 27 August 1917, "Chronological Correspondence, Aug.-Sept. 1917," box 36, Crerar Papers, QUA.

43. Crerar to J.A. Glen, 6 September 1917, "Chronological Correspondence, Aug.-Sept. 1917," box 36, Crerar Papers, QUA.

44. Borden to Willison, 31 August 1917, file 32, vol. 4, Willison Papers, LAC.

45. Henry Borden, ed., *Sir Robert Borden, Letters to Limbo* (Toronto: University of Toronto Press, 1971), 71.

46. Quoted in English, *The Decline of Politics*, 151.

47. Diaries, 27 August 1917, vol. 6, Foster Papers, LAC.

48. Borden, ed., *Robert Laird Borden: His Memoirs*, 1:743.

49. Borden to Willison, 31 August 1917, file 32, vol. 4, Willison Papers, LAC; H.F. Gadsby, "Cheers and Tears at the Tory Caucus," *Halifax Morning Chronicle*, September 7, 1917, 1.

50. Borden, "Diary," September 7, 1917.
51. See Graham, *Arthur Meighen: A Biography*, 1:175.
52. Reid to Borden, September 1917, 3545, reel C-4205, Borden Papers, LAC.
53. Sifton to Dafoe, 9 October 1917, reel M-73, Dafoe Papers, LAC.
54. Borden, "Diary," September 19, 1917.
55. Reid to Borden, 20 September 1917, 3549, reel C-4205, Borden Papers, LAC.
56. Crerar to T.A. Springmann, 4 October 1917, "Chronological Correspondence, Oct. 1917," box 37, Crerar Papers, QUA.
57. John T. Haig to Meighen, 21 September 1917, 3560, reel C-4205, Borden Papers, LAC.
58. Borden, ed., *Robert Laird Borden: His Memoirs*, 1:748.
59. Borden, "Diary," September 25, 1917.
60. Borden, ed., *Robert Laird Borden: His Memoirs*, 1:751.
61. Ibid., 755–59; English, *The Decline of Politics*, 156–58.
62. English, *The Decline of Politics*, 165–66.
63. Sifton to Willison, 12 October 1917, folder 286, vol. 37, Willison Papers, LAC.
64. Mackenzie King, "Diary," October 6, 1917.
65. Arthur R. Ford, "Some Notes on the Formation of the Union Government in 1917," *Canadian Historical Review* 19, no. 4 (1938), 362. See the more detailed version in Arthur R. Ford, *As the World Wags On* (Toronto: Ryerson Press, 1950), 95–96; see also "Sir Wilfrid Laurier Tenders Resignation of Leadership," *Halifax Herald*, October 4, 1917, 1.
66. Laurier to A.B. MacKay, 12 October 1917, 197311, reel C-914, Laurier Papers, LAC.
67. For the expressions of support for Laurier and newspaper coverage, see CAR, 1917, 582–83.
68. Laurier to D.D. McKenzie, 13 October 1917, 197497, reel C-914, Laurier Papers, LAC.
69. *Le Devoir*, June 30, 1917.
70. Eustache Santerre to Bourassa, 5 June 1917, P65/C2, 5, Fonds Famille Bourassa, BANQ–Vieux-Montréal.

71. Bourassa to Santerre, 13 June 1917, P65/C2, 5, Fonds Famille Bourassa, BANQ–Vieux-Montréal.

72. Schull, *Laurier: The First Canadian*, 592.

73. Pardee to Laurier, 22 October 1917, 197692, reel C-914, Laurier Papers, LAC.

74. Prang, *N.W. Rowell, Ontario Nationalist*, 214–15.

75. Rumilly, *Histoire de la Province de Québec*, 22:165.

76. Sifton to Willison, 24 October 1917, folder 286, vol. 37, Willison Papers, LAC.

77. Sifton to Willison, 16 October 1917, folder 286, vol. 37, Willison Papers, LAC.

78. For a review of opinion, see "How Canadian Newspapers View Formation of Union Government," *Toronto Daily Star*, October 13, 1917, 2. For Godfrey's reaction, see "Unity Is Now Assured with New War Cabinet," 12.

79. "The Union Government," *Toronto Daily Star*, October 13, 1917, 10.

80. Charles M. Johnston, *E.C. Drury: Agrarian Idealist* (Toronto: University of Toronto Press, 1986), 48.

81. "Sam Hughes Raps Union Govt. Says It Was Not Necessary," *Toronto Daily Star*, October 16, 1917, 11.

82. See Graham, *Arthur Meighen: A Biography*, 1:176–77; and English, *The Decline of Politics*, 157–58.

83. Diary, 12 October 1917, file: Diaries, vol. 6, Foster Papers, LAC.

84. Crerar to J.A. Glen, 6 September 1917, "Chronological Correspondence, Aug.–Sept. 1917," Box 36, Crerar Papers, QUA.

85. Ford, "Some Notes on the Formation of the Union Government," 363.

86. Macdonald, *Recollections*, 328.

87. Reid to Borden, 24 October 1917, 40914, reel C-4319, Borden Papers, LAC.

88. Mackenzie King, "Diary," October 12, 1917.

89. Borden, ed., *Robert Laird Borden: His Memoirs*, 1:757–59.

90. "Partyism Is Dying in West," *Toronto Globe*, October 26, 1917, 1; Schull, *Laurier: The First Canadian*, 591–92.

91. Quoted in Prang, *N.W. Rowell, Ontario Nationalist*, 208.

92. Diary, 15 October 1917, L33, vol. "1918," Main Johnson Papers, TRL.

93. For Borden's announcement and the Union government manifesto, see CAR, 1917, 587–90.

94. Dafoe to H.J. Chisholm, 14 October 1917, reel M-73, Dafoe Papers, LAC.

95. Laurier to Aylesworth, 16 October 1917, 197669, reel C-914, Laurier Papers, LAC.

CHAPTER 6: FRAMING THE CAMPAIGN

1. "Mayse, Amos William (Will) Letter: 1917 May 25th," *Canadian Letters and Images Project*, www.canadianletters.ca/content/document-9809.

2. On the battle see Tim Cook, *Shock Troops: Canadians Fighting the Great War 1917–1918* (Toronto: Penguin, 2008), 314–66.

3. Quoted in Cook, *Shock Troops*, 339.

4. Diaries, 5 November 1917, vol. 6, Foster Papers, LAC.

5. CAR, 1917, 597–99.

6. Ibid., 597.

7. Ibid.

8. Ibid., 598.

9. Ibid., 599.

10. Ibid., 589.

11. Ibid.

12. Ibid., 590.

13. See Thompson, *The Harvests of War*, 130–31.

14. CAR, 1917, 590.

15. Hankey to Bonar Law, 27 November 1917, LG/F/23/1/29, Lloyd George Papers, PA.

16. Ibid.

17. Beaverbrook to Peacock, 20 December 1917, BBK /E/1/34, Beaverbrook Papers, PA.

18. Beaverbrook to Peacock, 29 December 1917, BBK /H/328, Beaverbrook Papers, PA.

19. See, for example, "Bourassa Rules if Laurier Wins," *Manitoba Free Press*, December 5, 1917, 2; "Shall Quebec, Which Will Neither Fight Nor Pay, Rule?" *Manitoba Free Press*, December 11, 1917, 2; "Is

the One Disloyal Province to Dominate the Eight Loyal Provinces?" *Toronto Daily News*, December 15, 1917, 3.

20. "Union Government: The Reason for Its Formation; Its Policy and Aims and a Discussion of the Political Issue," 74781, reel C-4358, Borden Papers, LAC.

21. "Plain Facts for English-Speaking Electors," file 15, box 161, T.A. Crerar Papers, QUA.

22. "Fate of English in Quebec Province Hangs on Result of Election," *Manitoba Free Press*, December 3, 1917, 1.

23. "Laurier-Bourassa Reign of Terror," *Halifax Herald*, November 26, 1917, 1.

24. Granatstein and Hitsman, *Broken Promises*, 84–85.

25. Borden, "Diary," November 26, 1917; Brown, *Robert Laird Borden: A Biography*, 2:114.

26. R. Haycock, "The 1917 Federal Election in Victoria-Haliburton: A Case Study," *Ontario History* (June 1975): 113.

27. *Vancouver Daily Sun*, December 5, 1917, 8.

28. *Union Bulletin* 1, no. 8 (December 13, 1917), 1.

29. Quoted in CAR, 1917, 629.

30. Gordon Heath, "The Protestant Denominational Press and the Conscription Crisis in Canada, 1917–1918," *CCHA Historical Studies* 78 (2012): 35–36.

31. Quoted in "Bourassa a Traitor, Allied to Laurier," *Toronto Daily Star*, December 3, 1917, 5.

32. J.M. Bliss, "The Methodist Church and World War I," *Canadian Historical Review* 44, no. 3 (1968): 219.

33. Quoted in "Dr. Chown and General Currie," *Toronto Daily Star*, December 4, 1917, 2.

34. Skelton, *Life and Letters of Sir Wilfrid Laurier*, 2: 536.

35. Gordon Heath, "The Protestant Denominational Press and the Conscription Crisis in Canada, 1917–1918," CCHA *Historical Studies* 78 (2012): 39.

36. Philip Currie, "Reluctant Britons: The Toronto Irish, Home Rule, and the Great War," *Ontario History* 87, no. 1 (1995): 70–71.

37. Kevin Anderson, "'The Cockroaches of Canada': French-Canada,

Immigration and Nationalism, Anti-Catholicism in English-Canada, 1905–1929," *Journal of Religious History* 39, no. 1 (2015): 112.

38. Hearst to William Hearst, 23 December 1917, B253647, box MU1317, F6, Hearst Papers, AO.

39. E.A. Stanton to Davidson, 26 June 1916, DAV/42, J.C.C. Davidson Papers, PA.

40. Unsigned telegram to Sir Cecil Spring Rice, 21 June 1917, CO 537/1158, Colonial Office, NAUK; Foreign Office to A.J. Balfour, 21 June 1917.

41. Walter Long to Devonshire, 18 September 1917, CO 537/158, Colonial Office, NAUK.

42. Handwritten note by Long, 10 September 1917, CO 537/158, Colonial Office, NAUK.

43. Catherine Cleverdon, *The Woman Suffrage Movement in Canada* (Toronto: University of Toronto Press, 1974) 118–22; see also, more generally, Brian Tennyson, "Premier Hearst, the War and Votes for Women," *Ontario History* 57, no. 3 (1965): 115–21.

44. A. Plumptre to Foster, 3 December 1917, file 3636, vol. 24, Foster Papers, LAC.

45. "Women of Canada and the War Franchise Act," 74783, reel C-4358, Borden Papers, LAC. See also Gloria Geller, "The Wartime Elections Act of 1917 and the Canadian Women's Movement," *Atlantis* 2, no. 1 (1976): 103.

46. Sarah Glassford and Amy Shaw, eds., *A Sisterhood of Suffering and Service: Women and Girls of Canada and Newfoundland during the First World War* (Vancouver: UBC Press, 2012), 16.

47. "Women Unionists Hold Big Meeting," *Vancouver Daily Sun*, December 4, 1917, 5.

48. "Women Earnestly Support Union," *Manitoba Free Press*, December 5, 1917, 2; "Women Clash in Debate at Teulon," *Manitoba Free Press*, December 13, 1917, 7.

49. "Lady Eaton's Earnest Appeal," *Toronto Globe*, December 12, 1917, 8; see also Miller, *Our Glory and Our Grief*, 158.

50. "Women Pledge Support to Union," *Morning Chronicle*, November 27, 1917, 1.

51. See Daniel Byers, "The Conscription Election of 1917 and Its Aftermath in Orillia, Ontario," *Ontario History* 83, no. 4 (1991): 283.

52. Tarah Brookfield, "Divided by the Ballot Box: The Montreal Council of Women and the 1917 Election," *Canadian Historical Review* 89, no. 4 (2008): 475.

53. "An Open Letter from a Winnipeg Mother to Sir Wilfrid Laurier," 74753, reel C-4358, Borden Papers, LAC.

54. "To the Women of Canada — 'Next-of-Kin' — Who May Vote," 74766, reel C-4358, Borden Papers, LAC.

55. Borden to Devonshire, 12 January 1918, CO 42/1007, Colonial Office, NAUK. See also Devonshire to Long, 19 January 1918, CO 42/1007, Colonial Office, NAUK.

56. See Union Government Special Organizer for Soldier Vote to Crerar, file 15, box 161, T.A. Crerar Papers, QUA.

57. See C.M. Goddard to King, 16 November 1917, 31767, reel C-1929, King Papers, LAC.

58. English, *The Decline of Politics*, 183.

59. Beaverbrook to Sir George Perley, 28 November 1917, BBK/E/1/34, Beaverbrook Papers, PA.

60. See the literature in BBK/E/1/37, Beaverbrook Papers, PA.

61. Patrice Dutil, *Devil's Advocate: Godfroy Langlois and the Politics of Liberal Progressivism in Laurier's Quebec* (Montreal: Robert Davies, 1994), 327–29.

62. "Memorandum re General Turner," 13325–395, vol. 32/34, Charles Murphy Papers, LAC.

63. On the military vote see Morton, "Polling the Soldier Vote," 44–48; on Preston, see English, *The Decline of Politics*, 193–94.

64. See Daniel G. Dancocks, *Sir Arthur Currie: A Biography* (Toronto: University of Toronto Press, 1985), 124.

65. See A.M.J. Hyatt, *General Sir Arthur Currie: A Military Biography* (Toronto: University of Toronto Press, 1987), 91–96.

66. Currie to Perley, 10 December 1917, file A, vol. 1, H. Daly Papers, LAC.

CHAPTER 7: THE CAMPAIGN: FRENCH CANADA

1. "Milthorp, Frederick John Letter: 1917 December 4th," *Canadian Letters and Images Project* www.canadianletters.ca/content/document-3939. Milthorp was born in England and arrived in Canada in 1912. He enrolled in Winnipeg in 1915 and served in France until he was discharged in 1919.

2. Marcel Hamelin, ed., *Mémoires du Sénateur Raoul Dandurand (1861–1942)* (Quebec: Presses de l'Université Laval, 1967), 210–11.

3. *La Presse*, "Le maire Martin est de nouveau pris à partie," September 4, 1917.

4. *Montreal Gazette*, September 13, 1917.

5. *La Presse*, "Les troubles ont pris fin dans Québec," September 4, 1917.

6. *La Presse*, September 13, 1917.

7. *La Presse*, September 14, 1917.

8. Ibid.

9. *La Presse*, editorial, September 4, 1917.

10. Onésime Nantel-Orsali to Eugène Nantel, 27 September 1917, Fonds Bergeron-Nantel. Nantel's bravery at Vimy was noted by the press months earlier. See "22nd Battalion Should Be Proud of These Two Men," *Montreal Star*, March 17, 1917.

11. John G. Foster to Robert Lansing, 30 August 1917, Consular Correspondence, General Records of the Department of State, NAUS.

12. John G. Foster to Robert Lansing, October 5, 1917, Consular Correspondence, General Records of the Department of State, NAUS.

13. Ibid.

14. Borden to Bruchési, 25 October 1917, ACAM.

15. Bruchési to Mgr Bégin, 3 November 1917, ACAM.

16. Fred. C. Wurtele to Borden, 19 December 1917, 127893, reel C-4314, Borden Papers, LAC.

17. R.H. Pope to Borden, 14 October 1916, 11216, reel C-4314, Borden Papers, LAC.

18. "Aux électeurs du comté de Compton," 197867, reel C-915, Laurier Papers, LAC.

19. Langlais to R. Borden, 4 December 1915, 11167–11170, reel C-4312, Borden Papers, LAC. The letter was translated and a copy retained in the Borden papers, see 11174–76. The first passage is quoted as it was translated. The second passage was translated by the authors so as to better convey the raw anger of the message.

20. C.E. Gault to Borden, 23 May 1916, 11192–93, reel C-4313, Borden Papers, LAC.

21. Borden to C.E. Gault, 2 June 1916, 11196, reel C-4313, Borden Papers, LAC.

22. Cochrane to Borden, 3 June 1916, 11197, reel C-4313, Borden Papers, LAC.

23. Chase-Casgrain to Borden, 6 November 1916, 11226, reel C-4313, Borden Papers, LAC.

24. Borden to E.A.O. Morgan, January 15, 1917, 11232, reel C-4314, Borden Papers, LAC.

25. P.E. Blondin to Borden, June 30, 1916, 11202–03, reel C-4313, Borden Papers, LAC.

26. Maillet's hatred of the Liberals and *nationalistes* had prompted him to move his newspaper in this direction. Though a long-time associate of Godfroy Langlois and his brand of progressive Liberalism, Maillet had switched in the war. See his letters to Borden vaunting his newspaper's efforts in 1917: Maillet to Borden, 15 January 1918, 54856–57, Borden Papers, LAC; Borden to Maillet, 17 January 1918, 54858, Borden Papers, LAC; see also P.E. Blondin to Borden, 12 February 1918, 1298268, Borden Papers, LAC. Fernande Roy treats *L'Autorité* as an artefact of Liberal radicalism in the First World War, but bypasses the paper's pro-Unionist and pro-conscriptionist stance in "Le journal *L'Autorité* dans le cadre de la presse libérale montréalaise," in *Combats Libéraux au tournant du XXe siècle*, ed. Yvan Lamonde (Montreal: Fides, 1995).

27. D. Lorne McGibbon to Borden, 8 January 1918, 54839–41, reel C-4314, Borden Papers, LAC.

28. Ibid.

29. B.A. Macnab to Ernest Blount, 22 March 1916, reel C-4313, Borden Papers, LAC. Emphasis in original.

30. L.J. Tarte to Borden, 10 September 1917, 11250–53, reel C-4314, Borden Papers, LAC.

31. Borden to L.J. Tarte, 14 September 1917, 11254, reel C-4314, Borden Papers, LAC.

32. Rumilly, *Histoire de la Province de Québec*, 22:185.

33. Ibid.

34. Borden to Blondin, 17 January 1918, 129820, reel C-4314, Borden Papers, LAC.

35. R.A. Drapeau to Borden, 4 August 1917, 11242–47, reel C-4314, Borden Papers, LAC.

36. Ibid.

37. W.B. Nantel to Borden, 14 September 1917, 11255, reel C-4314, Borden Papers, LAC.

38. Borden to C.H. Cahan, 17 October 1917, 11273, reel C-4314, Borden Papers, LAC.

39. Borden, "Diary," December 12, 1917.

40. Blondin to Borden, 12 February 1918, 129825–26, reel C-4314, Borden Papers, LAC.

41. Rodolphe Lemieux to Laurier, 30 October 1917, 197888–89, reel C-915, Laurier Papers, LAC.

42. Ibid.

43. P.A. Choquette to Laurier, 31 October 1917, 197921–22, reel C-915, Laurier Papers, LAC.

44. See Emmanuel Desmarais to Laurier, 9 November 1917, 198175–56, reel C-915, Laurier Papers, LAC; Laurier to Desmarais, 13 November 1917, 198176, reel C-915, Laurier Papers, LAC.

45. Emmanuel Desmarais to Laurier, 21 November 1917, 198177, reel C-915, Laurier Papers, LAC.

46. Laurier to Bruchési, 22 November 1917, ACAM, trans. by authors.

47. L.A. Cannon to Laurier, 14 November 1917, 1983311–12, reel C-915, Laurier Papers, LAC.

48. *Montreal Gazette*, October 24, 1917.

49. Rumilly, *Histoire de la Province de Québec*, 22:181.

50. Laurier to J.A. Barrette, 17 November 1917, 198420, reel C-915, Laurier Papers, LAC.

51. Rodolphe Lemieux to Wilfrid Laurier, 14 November 1917, 198332–33, reel C-915, Laurier Papers, LAC.

52. L.O. David to Laurier, October 1917, 197961–62, reel C-915, Laurier Papers, LAC.

53. Laurier to L.O. David, 1 November 1917, 197964, reel C-915, Laurier Papers, LAC. The letter in question from Marsil has not been retained. See also Laurier to Séverin Létourneau, 17 November 1917, 198422, reel C-915, Laurier Papers, LAC.

54. Rumilly, *Histoire de la Province de Québec*, 22:193–95.

55. Ibid., 191.

56. Laurier to John Boyd, 6 November 1917, 198085, reel C-915, Laurier Papers, LAC.

57. S. Létourneau to Laurier, 7 November 1917, 198155–56, reel C-915, Laurier Papers, LAC.

58. F.W. Hibbard to Laurier, 16 November 1917, 198371–73, reel C-915, Laurier Papers, LAC.

59. Robert Bickerdike to Laurier, 30 October 1917, 197872–73, reel C-915, Laurier Papers, LAC.

60. On Daniel Gallery, see Dutil, *Devil's Advocate*.

61. S.W. Jacobs to C.M. Goddard, 5 November 1917, 198315, reel C-915, Laurier Papers, LAC.

62. Casgrain to Laurier, 16 November 1917, 198387–90, reel C-915, Laurier Papers, LAC.

63. Laurier to L.A. Cannon, 17 November 1917, 198313, reel C-915, Laurier Papers, LAC.

64. Maréchal Nantel to Eugène, December 7, 1917, Bergeron-Nantel Papers.

65. *L'Avenir du Nord*, November 30, 1917.

66. *Le Nationaliste*, December 9, 1917, 4.

67. Bourassa to Mgr Arthur Béliveau, 15 December 1917, P65/C2,5, Famille Bourassa Papers.

68. Ibid.

CHAPTER 8: THE CAMPAIGN: ENGLISH CANADA

1. Lester Pearson to his parents, 4 December 1917, Lester Pearson Papers, LAC. Cited in Antony Anderson, *The Diplomat: Lester Pearson and the Suez Crisis* (Fredericton, NB: Goose Lane, 2015), 51.

2. For a thorough examination of the party organization see English, *The Decline of Politics*, 167–78.

3. "Drury Cannot Follow Laurier," *Toronto Globe*, December 11, 1917, 15.

4. Quoted in Miller, *Our Glory and Our Grief*, 157. On the Toronto ridings, see ibid., 152–58.

5. A.H. Birmingham to Frank Cochrane, 20 September 1917, 3555–56, reel C-4205, Borden Papers, LAC.

6. W.F. Cockshutt to Borden, 15 October 1917, 40901, reel C-4319, Borden Papers, LAC.

7. George Lynch-Staunton to Borden, 23 October 1917, 40912–13, reel C-4319, Borden Papers, LAC.

8. Reid to Borden, 24 October 1917, 40914–19, reel C-4319, Borden Papers, LAC; and the unsigned memo, 19 October 1917, 40903–04, reel C-4319, Borden Papers, LAC.

9. Brown, *Robert Laird Borden: A Biography*, 2:118; see also Borden, ed., *Robert Laird Borden: His Memoirs*, 760–61; Rowell to David Williams, 27 October 1917, reel C-932, Rowell Papers, LAC.

10. Diaries, 4 November 1917, vol. 6, Foster Papers, LAC.

11. Rowell to Hudson, 23 November 1917, 2283, reel C-932, Rowell Papers, LAC.

12. Rowell to Lawrason, 12 November 1917, 2211, reel C-932, Rowell Papers.

13. Unknown to Rowell, 14 November 1917, 2228, reel C-932, Rowell Papers; Rowell to Brown, 15 November 1917, 2231, reel C-932, Rowell Papers.

14. John Ross Shaw to Rowell, 17 November 1917, 2250, reel C-932, Rowell Papers.

15. P.C. Larkin to Laurier, 23 October 1917, 197703, reel C-914, Laurier Papers, LAC.

16. Prang, *N.W. Rowell, Ontario Nationalist*, 218.

17. John Harold to Rowell, 14 November 1917, 2224, reel C-932, Rowell Papers, LAC.
18. Borden to W.F. Cockshutt, 20 November 1917, 40987, reel C-4319, Borden Papers, LAC.
19. Borden to G.A. Warburton, 14 December 1917, 41018, reel C-4319, Borden Papers.
20. Rowell to J.R. Shaw, November 16, 1917, 2244, reel C-932, Rowell Papers, LAC.
21. Borden, "Diary," November 30, 1917.
22. Ibid., December 2, 1917.
23. Confidential Notes on Federal Election Campaign, 22–23, vol. "1918," L33, Main Johnson Papers, TRL.
24. Laurier to G.W. Kyte, 30 October 1917, 198037, reel C-915, Laurier Papers, LAC.
25. D.B. Neely to Laurier, 20 October 1917, 197679, reel C-914, Laurier Papers.
26. Laurier to D.B. Neely, 26 October 1917, 197680, reel C-914, Laurier Papers.
27. See the list of names in 197210–12, reel C-914, Laurier Papers.
28. A.H. Beaton to Laurier, 6 November 1917, 197955–56, reel C-915, Laurier Papers.
29. King to Laurier, 16 November 1917, 198376, reel C-915, Laurier Papers.
30. P.C. Larkin to Laurier, 27 October 1917, 197705, reel C-914, Laurier Papers.
31. C.W. Kerr to Laurier, 8 November 1917, 198215, reel C-915, Laurier Papers.
32. H.H. Dewart to Laurier, 16 November 1917, 198407, reel C-915, Laurier Papers; and Kerr to Laurier, 19 November 1917, 198486, reel C-915, Laurier Papers.
33. Laurier to Kerr, 14 November 1917, 198216, reel C-915, Laurier Papers.
34. H.J. Sims to Mackenzie King, 5 November 1917, 33113–14, reel C-1930, King Papers, LAC.
35. John Godfrey to Borden, 1 November 1917, 40955, reel C-4319, Borden Papers, LAC.

36. King to Laurier, 7 November 1917, 198160, reel C-915, Laurier Papers, LAC.

37. R.T. Harding to Laurier, 24 November 1917, 198658–60, Laurier Papers.

38. His campaign cost about $800. See Charles M. Johnston, *E.C. Drury: Agrarian Idealist* (Toronto: University of Toronto Press, 1986), 49–50.

39. James E. Day to Laurier, 19 November 1917, 198489–92, reel C-915, Laurier Papers, LAC.

40. Copp to Laurier, 20 November 1917, 198520, reel C-915, Laurier Papers.

41. Macdonald to Laurier, 16 November 1917, 198410–11, reel C-915, Laurier Papers.

42. Laurier to Macdonald, 19 November 1917, 198413, reel C-915, Laurier Papers.

43. Knott to Laurier, 26 October 1917, 197766, reel C-914, Laurier Papers.

44. Donovan to Laurier, 24 October 1917, 197544, reel C-915, Laurier Papers; see also "Western Govt Men Open Campaign for 'Carry On' Policy," *Saskatoon Phoenix*, October 23, 1917, 1.

45. Knott to Laurier, 26 October 1917, 197766, reel C-914, Laurier Papers, LAC.

46. W.J. Donovan to Laurier, 26 October 1917, 197753–55, reel C-914, Laurier Papers.

47. W.J. Donovan to Laurier, 1 November 1917, 197940, reel C-914, Laurier Papers.

48. W.J. Donovan to Laurier, 16 November 1917, 198355, reel C-915, Laurier Papers.

49. Skelton, *Life and Letters of Sir Wilfrid Laurier*, 540.

50. William Knowles to Frank Oliver, 24 October 1917, 198105, reel C-915, Laurier Papers, LAC.

51. Knowles to Laurier, 6 November 1917, 198103, reel C-915, Laurier Papers.

52. Laurier to Knowles, 27 November 1917, 198651, reel C-914, Laurier Papers.

53. F.R. Russell to Laurier, 14 November 1917, 198324, reel C-915, Laurier Papers.

54. David Douglas to Laurier, 5 November 1917, 198080, reel C-914, Laurier Papers. On the western candidates see Thompson, *The Harvests of War*, 137–38.

55. Desmond Morton, with Terry Copp, *Working People* (Toronto: Deneau, 1980), 103–12.

56. Martin Robin, "Registration, Conscription, and Independent Labour Politics, 1916–1917," *Canadian Historical Review* 47, no. 2 (1966): 106–07.

57. Ibid., 114–18.

58. A. Ross McCormack, *Reformers, Rebels, and Revolutionaries: The Western Canadian Radical Movement, 1899–1919* (Toronto: University of Toronto Press, 1977), 133.

59. Robert Rutherdale, *Hometown Horizons: Local Responses to Canada's Great War* (Vancouver: UBC Press, 2004), 172.

60. Laurier to R.T. Harding, 26 November 1917, 198660, reel C-915, Laurier Papers, LAC.

61. Laurier to R.T. Harding, 22 November 1917, 198501, reel C-915, Laurier Papers.

62. Laurier to G.S. Gibbons, 20 November 1917, 198505, reel C-915, Laurier Papers.

63. Laurier to A.H. Beaton, 3 November 1917, 197953, reel C-915, Laurier Papers.

64. See David MacKenzie, "Maritime Canada and Newfoundland," in *Canada and the First World War*, 364–65; Philippe Doucet, "Politics and the Acadians," in *The Acadians of the Maritimes: Thematic Studies*, ed. Jean Daigle (Moncton: Centre d'études acadiennes, 1982), 252–57.

65. Borden, "Diary," November 13, 1917.

66. Ibid., December 7, 1917.

67. "The Most Wonderful Meeting in All the 168 Years of the History of Halifax," *Halifax Herald*, November 15, 1917, 1. See also "Premier Borden Opened His Campaign for Union Government," *Morning Chronicle*, November 15, 1917, 1.

68. Quoted in "Year's Delay in Referendum," *Toronto Daily Star*, November 15, 1917, 1.

69. Borden, "Diary," November 16, 1917.

70. CAR, 1917, 591.

71. For Meighen's campaign, see Graham, *Arthur Meighen: A Biography*, 1:185–87.

72. "Chronological Correspondence Nov. 1917," 17 November 1917, box 38, Crerar Papers, QUA.

73. See, for example, "Laurier's Stand on Recreiting [*sic*] Unchanged," December 10, 1917, 2; "Sir Thomas White Denies Statements Made by Dewart," December 10, 1917, 3; "Laurier Fails to Convince Electors," December 13, 1917, 2.

74. See John Boyko, *Bennett: The Rebel Who Challenged and Changed a Nation* (Fredericton, Goose Lane, 2010), 108–10; P.B. Waite, *In Search of R.B. Bennett* (Montreal: McGill-Queen's University Press, 2012), 20.

75. John G. Diefenbaker, *One Canada: Memoirs of the Right Honourable John G. Diefenbaker, the Crusading Years 1895–1956* (Toronto: Macmillan, 1975), 91; Denis Smith, *Rogue Tory: The Life and Legend of John G. Diefenbaker* (Toronto: Macfarlane Walter & Ross, 1995), 42. On his military career, see Smith, *Rogue Tory*, 18–31.

76. "Conscription Liberals' Convention Pledge Support to Fusionists," *Toronto Globe*, November 3, 1917, 1.

77. Prang, *N.W. Rowell, Ontario Nationalist*, 223.

78. "Sir Sam Makes Suggestion to Borden," *Toronto Daily Star*, December 1, 1917, 6.

79. Borden, "Diary," December 1, 1917.

80. "Was This Another Deliberate Plot to Murder Prime Minister Sir Robert Borden?" *Halifax Herald*, November 29, 1917, 1.

81. "Kitchener Anti-Conscriptionists Howl Down Sir Robert Borden," *Toronto Globe*, November 26, 1917, 1; W.H. Heick, "'If We Lose the War, Nothing Else Matters': The 1917 Federal Election in North Waterloo," *Ontario History* 72 (June 1980): 75–77.

82. See, for example, Daniel Byers, "The Conscription Election of 1917 and Its Aftermath in Orillia, Ontario," *Ontario History* 83 (December 1991): 285–86.

83. English, *The Decline of Politics*, 196.

84. W. Gillespie to Edward Kemp, 20 November 1917, reel C-4323, Borden Papers, LAC.

85. Borden, "Diary," November 19, 1917.

86. Ibid., November 23, 1917.

87. D.J. Hall, *Clifford Sifton*, vol. 2 (Vancouver: UBC Press, 1985), 290.

88. See W.R. Young, "Conscription, Rural Depopulation, and the Farmers of Ontario," *Canadian Historical Review* 53, no. 3 (1972): 305–06; Byers, "The Conscription Election of 1917," 285; and the *Union Bulletin* 1, no. 7 (December 10, 1917). For the text of "Mewburn's Pledge," see "The Draft and Farmers' Sons," *Manitoba Free Press*, December 3, 1917, 3.

89. Rowell to J.W. Taylor, 4 December 1917, reel C-932, Rowell Papers, LAC.

90. "Sir Wilfrid to Ottawans," *Toronto Globe*, November 28, 1917, 1.

91. "Appeal to Soul, Says Sir Wilfrid," *Toronto Globe*, December 4, 1917, 1.

92. Laurier to W.C. Edwards, 28 November 1917, 198720, reel C-915, Laurier Papers, LAC.

93. Aylesworth to Laurier, 4 December 1917, 198835, reel C-915, Laurier Papers.

94. King to Violet Carruthers, 28 November 1917, 32479–80, reel C-1930, King Papers, LAC.

95. Laurier to R.R. Cromarty, 23 November 1917, 198625, reel C-915, Laurier Papers, LAC.

96. Heick, "If We Lose the War," 84.

97. James Pitsula, *For All We Have and Are: Regina and the Experience of the Great War* (Winnipeg: University of Manitoba Press, 2008), 178.

98. Quoted in "Sir Wilfrid to Ottawans," *Toronto Globe*, November 28, 1917, 3.

99. For the Liberal campaign stops, see CAR, 1917, 618–19; "Says Only Laurier Can Avert Strife," *Toronto Globe*, December 12, 1917, 2.

100. H.S. Ferns and Bernard Ostry, "Mackenzie King and the First World War," *Canadian Historical Review* 36, no. 2 (1955): 111.

101. R. MacGregor Dawson, *William Lyon Mackenzie King: A Political Biography, 1874–1923* (Toronto: University of Toronto Press, 1958), 267–69.

102. King to Mewburn, 4 December 1917, 32519, reel C-1930, King Papers, LAC.
103. CAR, 1917, 621.
104. See Adam Crerar, "Ontario and the Great War," in *Canada and the First World War*, 239–40.
105. "Returned Soldiers Turn Liberal Meeting into Pandemonium," *Vancouver Daily Sun*, December 4, 1917, 1.
106. Diaries, 1 December 1917, vol. 7, Wilson MacDonald Papers, LAC.
107. King to Violet Carruthers, 28 November 1917, 32479, reel C-1930, King Papers, LAC.
108. Foster to Borden, 19 December 1917, 78864, reel C-4362, Borden Papers, LAC.
109. See Heick, "If We Lose the War," 74.
110. Borden, ed., *Robert Laird Borden: His Memoirs*, 2:764.
111. Ibid.; on the explosion see *CAR 1917*, 467–69.
112. "Suspected German Spy Detained at Halifax," *Toronto Globe*, December 14, 1917, 1. See also "Practically All the Germans in Halifax Are to Be Arrested," *Halifax Herald*, December 10, 1917, 1; "Imo Helmsman Believed to Be German Spy," *Manitoba Free Press*, December 14, 1917, 1.
113. See *Ottawa Citizen*, December 16, 1917, 1–3.
114. "Rowell Flays His Critics, Calls Them Reactionaries," *Toronto Daily Star*, December 11, 1917, 16.
115. "A Direful Warning," *Morning Chronicle*, December 15, 1917, 6; "Fate of Halifax Warns All the Rest of Canada," *Toronto Daily News*, December 15, 1917, 1.
116. Borden, ed., *Robert Laird Borden: His Memoirs*, 2:765; Diary, 14 December 1917, reel A-653, Devonshire Papers, LAC.
117. "Cochrane Says Union Will Win by 40 Majority," *Toronto Daily Star*, December 15, 1917, 1.
118. "Shall Quebec Rule Canada?" *Toronto Globe*, December 13, 1917, 4.
119. "Officers Will Resign Posts If Laurier Wins," *Toronto Daily Star*, December 13, 1917, 1.
120. *Toronto Daily Star*, December 12, 1917, 11.

121. "Laurier Says He Is Loyal," *Toronto Globe*, December 11, 1917, 1; "Monster Crowd Hears Laurier on Political Issues," *Manitoba Free Press*, December 11, 1917, 11.

122. "Sir Wilfrid at Regina," *Toronto Globe*, December 12, 1917, 2.

123. "Referendum in Sixty Days," *Toronto Globe*, December 13, 1917, 2.

124. Diary, December 14, 1917, vol. 7, Wilson MacDonald Papers, LAC.

125. "Laurier's Triumphal Tour Across Canada Ends Here with Remarkable Ovation," *Vancouver Daily Sun*, December 17, 1917, 1; "Laurier Heard by Big Crowds in Vancouver City," *Saskatoon Phoenix*, December 15, 1917, 1.

126. *Toronto Globe*, December 14, 1917, 6.

127. *Calgary Daily Herald*, December 13, 1917, 1.

128. *Toronto Daily News*, December 14, 1917, 13.

129. *Toronto Globe*, December 17, 1917, 1.

130. Skelton, *Life and Letters of Sir Wilfrid Laurier*, 542.

CHAPTER 9: THE RESULTS

1. "Hale, Robert Letter: 1917 September 23rd," *Canadian Letters and Images Project*, www.canadianletters.ca/content/document-1546.

2. "Great Rush of Voters to Polls Today," *Calgary Daily Herald*, December 17, 1917, 1; "Rising Temperature," *Montreal Gazette*, December 17, 1917, 5.

3. "Over-Excitement Causes Man's Death," *Toronto Globe*, December 18, 1917, 5.

4. *Toronto Daily Star*, December 18, 1917, 25.

5. Onésime Nantel to Eugène Nantel, January 1918, Fonds Nantel-Bergeron Papers.

6. "Electors Are Urged to Go to the Polls," *Saskatoon Phoenix*, December 17, 1917, 3.

7. "Billy Really Was for Conscription," *Vancouver Daily Sun*, December 18, 1917, 6.

8. *Toronto Daily Star*, December 18, 1917, 13.

9. "Foster Beats Maj. Cockburn," *Toronto Globe*, December 18, 1917, 3.

10. "Carried to Polls in Bed," *Montreal Gazette*, December 19, 1917, 6.

11. Diary, 17 December 1917, vol. "1918," L33, William Main Johnson Papers, TPL.

12. "Women Vote with Their Men," *Toronto Daily Star*, December 18, 1917, 4.

13. Diary, 17 December 1917, vol. 7, Wilson MacDonald Papers, LAC.

14. "Rush of Votes to the Polls," *Toronto Globe*, December 18, 1917, 5.

15. Brown, *Robert Laird Borden: A Biography*, 2:122–23.

16. "Montreal Fears Weren't Realized, Night Was Quiet," *Toronto Daily Star*, December 18, 1917, 1.

17. "Rush of Votes to the Polls," *Toronto Globe*, December 18, 1917, 5.

18. *Toronto Daily Star*, December 18, 1917, 1

19. "Toronto and York Speak Positively for Union," *Toronto Globe*, December 18, 1917, 8.

20. "Snapshots on Election Day," *Toronto Daily News*, December 18, 1917, 5.

21. "Good News Is Sent to Kemp," *Toronto Globe*, December 18, 1917, 9.

22. "Snapshots on Election Day," *Toronto Daily News*, December 18, 1917, 5.

23. Diary, December 17, 1917, Johnson Papers.

24. Miller, *Our Glory and Our Grief*, 158.

25. Diary, 17 December 1917, Johnson Papers. See also Prang, *N.W. Rowell, Ontario Nationalist*, 225–27.

26. Heick, "'If We Lose the War, Nothing Else Matters,'" 85–86.

27. "Election Returns," *Manitoba Free Press*, December 17, 1917, 11.

28. "Local Ridings Overwhelming for Unionists," *Vancouver Daily Sun*, December 18, 1917, 1.

29. Diary, 17 December 1917, E.M. Macdonald Papers, LAC.

30. Diary, 18 December 1917, E.M. Macdonald Papers.

31. *Toronto Daily Star*, December 18, 1917, 1.

32. Returning Officers Reports on Military Voting, North America, vol. 7, O'Connor Papers, LAC.

33. W.T.R. Preston, *My Generation of Politics and Politicians* (Toronto: Rose, 1927), 368.

34. The cost of the election on the Front has not been found. The election in Canada cost $714,071: "Report of the General Elections 1917," vol. 9, O'Connor Papers, LAC.
35. *Toronto Daily Star*, December 18, 1917, 9.
36. Figures provided for this election by writers have varied widely, and for this reason, we had to go back to the official source. Our study is based on the figures provided by the official report of the results, the *Return of the Thirteenth General Election for the House of Commons of Canada*. All the figures were imported into an Excel sheet and recalculated. Our numbers differ slightly from the official record. The number of voters on the Voter's List is the same, but, while the writers of the Return recorded "votes," we recorded "voters" to determine the rate of participation. The disparity is the result of the three ridings that had two MPs, so voters were thus given two ballots (and thus voted twice). (A fourth riding, Halifax, acclaimed two Union candidates.) The record of participation for the 1917 election is typically listed as 75 percent.

    The government report itself did not report a turnout rate, so the origin of that figure seems to be Howard Scarrow who, in his *Canada Votes: A Handbook of Federal and Provincial Election Data*, listed pre-1920 Elections Act figures in a separate note, indicating a figure of 75 percent turnout for civilians only. How this figure was calculated is not clear. The official government report listed 2,093,799 eligible voters and 1,885,329 recorded votes — including military votes. That would indicate a turnout rate of 90.04 percent. The Government of Canada to this day also officially lists the participation rate at 75 percent, even though it offers 2,093,799 voters listed and 1,892,741 ballots cast (inexplicably, 7412 more voters than the official government report): a 90.4 percent turnout. See www.elections.ca/content.aspx?section=res&dir=his&document=appx& lang=e. The easiest reference for electoral statistics is Elections Canada. See www.elections.ca/content.aspx?section=ele&dir=turn &document=index&lang=e.

    If the 235,003 recorded military votes are withdrawn from the listed vote, the participation rate would still be calculated at

79 percent. The recorded votes, it is important to remember, do not include the ballots that were discarded as spoiled. It also does not include soldier ballots that were rejected because they did not list ridings. Desmond Morton reports (See "Polling the Soldier Vote," 52) that O'Connor believed that 12.5 percent of the military vote might have been rejected. Others gave higher and lower figures; it is, in fact, impossible to know. What is clear, however, is that the turnout was dramatically higher than recorded. See Howard A. Scarrow, *Canada Votes: A Handbook of Federal and Provincial Election Data* (New Orleans: Hauser Press, 1962), 238. J. Murray Beck gives slightly different figures. See *Pendulum of Power* (Toronto: Prentice Hall, 1968), 148. Desmond Morton gives still another version of numbers but does not attribute a source. See Morton, "Polling the Soldier Vote," 55.

37. G.W.L. Nicholson, *Official History of the Canadian Army in the First World War: Canadian Expeditionary Force, 1914–1919* (Ottawa: Queen's Printer and Controller of Stationery, 1964), Appendix C, Table 2, 547. It is worth noting, again, that an estimated 12 percent of soldier ballots were discarded because no riding was indicated on the envelope. As such, the turnout would have been over 80 percent, close to the civilian average.

38. Onésime Nantel to Eugène Nantel, January 1918, Fonds Nantel-Bergeron Papers.

39. *Toronto Daily Star*, December 18, 1917, 1.

40. Ibid.

41. See Gary Muir, "Bits and Pieces of Brantford's History: The History of the Cockshutt Family" (unpublished manuscript, 1977), *Brantford Public Library*, http://brantford.library.on.ca/files/pdfs/localhistory/cockshuttfamily.pdf.

42. J. Murray Beck, in *Pendulum of Power*, asserts that Unionists won fourteen ridings as a result of the soldier vote: five in Nova Scotia, four in Ontario, two in Prince Edward Island, one in Alberta, and one in British Columbia and Yukon. Only one riding is named: Cumberland in Nova Scotia (p. 146). No evidence is shown to sustain Beck's charge that "there were other kinds of villainy."

43. *Toronto Daily Star*, December 18, 1917, 1.

44. Ibid.
45. *Toronto Daily Star*, December 18, 1917, 2.
46. Ibid., 7.
47. Talbot Papineau to Andrew McMaster, 10 November 1916, 193757, reel C-115, Laurier Papers, LAC.
48. See the ad for Burroughes in the *Toronto Daily Star*, December 18, 1917, 3.
49. *Toronto Daily Star*, December 18, 1917, 15.

CHAPTER 10: THE AFTERMATH

1. Onésime Nantel-Orsali to Eugène Nantel, January 1918, Fonds Nantel-Bergeron Papers.
2. *Toronto Globe*, December 18, 1917, 1.
3. Ibid., 9.
4. Devonshire to Long, 20 December 1917, CO 42/1001, Colonial Office, NAUK.
5. Prang, *N.W. Rowell, Ontario Nationalist*, 231.
6. Hearst to William Hearst, 23 December 1917, B253647, box MU1317, F6, A.O. Hearst Papers.
7. Borden to Rowell, 22 December 1917, 54835, reel C-4332, Borden Papers, LAC.
8. W.F. Cockshutt to Borden, 19 December 1917, 127074, reel C-4406, Borden Papers.
9. *Toronto Daily Star*, December 18, 1917, 25.
10. Dafoe to Côté, 18 December 1917, reel M-73, Dafoe Papers, LAC; Côté to Dafoe, 27 December 1917, reel M-73, Dafoe Papers; Dafoe to Côté, 1 January 1918, reel M-73, Dafoe Papers.
11. Larkin to Laurier, 18 December 1917, 198966, reel C-915, Laurier Papers, LAC.
12. Frank Denton to Laurier, 24 December 1917, 199118–19, reel C-916, Laurier Papers; see also A.J. Young to Laurier, 19 December 1917, 199014–15, reel C-916, Laurier Papers.
13. W.J. Donovan to Laurier, 21 December 1917, 199088, reel C-916, Laurier Papers; see also W.D. Gregory to Laurier, 24 December 1917,

199414, reel C-916, Laurier Papers; A.G. MacKay to Laurier, 31 December 1917, 199215, reel C-916, Laurier Papers; and D.C. Cameron to Laurier, 18 December 1917, 198968–69, reel C-915, Laurier Papers.

14. Laurier to A.G. MacKay, 5 January 1918, 199224, reel C-916, Laurier Papers.

15. Laurier to Oliver, 20 December 1917, 198956, reel C-915, Laurier Papers.

16. Letter from Laurier to Preston, 18 January 1918, cited in Preston, *My Generation of Politics and Politicians*, 374.

17. Laurier to A. McLeod, 10 January 1918, 199302, reel C-916, Laurier Papers, LAC.

18. *Le Clairon* (St-Hyacinthe), December 21, 1917, found in reel C-117 8, Laurier Papers, LAC.

19. Ibid.

20. Laurier to Graham, 20 December 1917, 198983, reel C-915, Laurier Papers.

21. Caron to Laurier, 18 December 1917, 198072, reel C-915, Laurier Papers; Caron to Laurier, 24 December 1917, 199140, reel C-916, Laurier Papers.

22. Laurier to L. Power, 26 December 1917, 199112, reel C-916, Laurier Papers.

23. Armstrong, *The Crisis of Quebec*, 225; see also Paul-André Linteau et al., *Quebec: A History 1867–1929*, trans. Robert Chodos (Toronto: Lorimer, 1983), 509.

24. Borden to Blondin, 17 January 1918, 129820, reel C-4406, Borden Papers, LAC.

25. See Blondin to Borden, 22 December 1917, 129811, reel C-4406, Borden Papers.

26. Sévigny to Borden, 7 March 1918, 41425–28, reel C-4320, Borden Papers; Perley to Borden, 7 January 1918, 54810, reel C-4332, Borden Papers.

27. Borden, ed., *Robert Laird Borden: His Memoirs*, 2:753.

28. "Confidential Memorandum for Borden," 1918, 40583–86, reel C-491 3, Borden Papers, LAC.

29. Brown, *Robert Laird Borden: A Biography*, 2:133–34.

30. Diary, 19 March 1918, vol. 6, Foster Papers, LAC.

31. See, for example, Joseph Hayes to F.B. McCurdy, 21 December 1917, 411800, reel C-4320, Borden Papers, LAC.

32. Preston to Laurier, 21 December 1917, 199080, reel C-916, Laurier Papers, LAC.

33. Preston to Sergeant Wood, 16 March 1918, 41242–44, reel C-4320, Borden Papers, LAC.

34. Preston, *My Generation of Politics and Politicians*, 378, 368.

35. For examples and an assessment of the fraud see English, *The Decline of Politics*, 193–94; Morton, "Polling the Soldier Vote," 49–56; Graham, *Arthur Meighen: A Biography*, 1:255–60; and Granatstein and Hitsman, *Broken Promises*, 80–81.

36. A.G. MacKay to Laurier, 23 January 1918, 199515–21, reel C-916, Laurier Papers, LAC.

37. Oliver to Laurier, 6 March 1918, 199916–17, reel C-916, Laurier Papers; see also Macdonald to Laurier, 28 January 1918, 199551, reel C-916, Laurier Papers.

38. Hamelin, ed., *Mémoires du Sénateur Raoul Dandurand*, 214.

39. Graham, *Arthur Meighen: A Biography*, 1:255–60.

40. Currie to Daly, 27 January 1918, vol. 1, Harold Daly Papers, LAC.

41. See Granatstein and Hitsman, *Broken Promises*, 83–86.

42. Diary, 12 February 1918, vol. 6, Foster Papers, LAC.

43. Skelton, *Life and Letters of Sir Wilfrid Laurier*, 2:545.

44. "Titanic Fight Goes On," March 23, 1918, *Calgary Daily Herald*, 1; "British Line Bent Back 2 Miles," March 23, 1918, *Montreal Gazette*, 1.

45. "Most Anxious Week-End Since Mons Retreat," March 25, 1918, *Montreal Gazette*, 1.

46. "Blood Flows in Quebec — Troops Rushed to City," April 1, 1918, *Vancouver Daily Sun*, 1. On the riots, see Martin Auger, "On the Brink of Civil War: The Canadian Government and the Suppression of the 1918 Quebec Easter Riots," *Canadian Historical Review* 89, no. 4 (2008): 503–40.

47. Brown, *Robert Laird Borden: A Biography*, 2:128–29; Granatstein and Hitsman, *Broken Promises*, 88–90; Borden, ed., *Robert Laird Borden: His Memoirs*, 2:786–91.

48. LAC, Foster Papers, vol. 6, Diary, March 30, 1918.
49. LAC, Kemp Papers, vol. 164, file: W-6, Kemp to J.S. Willison, April 2, 1918.
50. Brown, *Robert Laird Borden: A Biography*, 2:132.
51. Borden, ed., *Robert Laird Borden: His Memoirs*, 2:801–02; Thompson, *The Harvests of War*, 149–51.
52. Granatstein and Hitsman, *Broken Promises*, 96–98.
53. English, *The Decline of Politics*, 212.
54. Ford, *As the World Wags On*, 141.
55. Diary, 18 March 1918, vol. 6, Foster Papers, LAC.
56. Morton, *The Progressive Party in Canada*, 68–70.
57. Brown, *Robert Laird Borden: A Biography*, 2:167–70.
58. Ibid., 178–79.
59. Diary, 20 January 1920, vol. 9, Foster Papers, LAC.
60. English, *The Decline of Politics*, 205.
61. Dawson, *William Lyon Mackenzie King: A Political Biography*, 298–302.

CHAPTER 11: CONCLUSION

1. John W. Dafoe, *Laurier: A Study in Canadian Politics* (Toronto: Thomas Allen, 1922), 176.
2. See Geneviève Richer, "Napoléon-Antoine Belcourt et l'élite anglo-ontarienne" and Hans-Jürgen Lusebrink; "Un Anglophone contre le Règlement 17: William Henry Moore," in *Le Siècle du Règlement 17*, eds. Bock and Charbonneau; and Peter Oliver "The Resolution of the Ontario Bilingual Schools Crisis, 1919–1929," *Journal of Canadian Studies* 7, no. 1 (1972).
3. Quoted in Skelton, *Life and Letters of Sir Wilfrid Laurier*, 543.
4. Christie to Kerr, 14 December 1925, 10590, reel C-3883, Christie Papers, LAC.
5. See Frances V. Harbour, "Conscription and Socialization: Four Canadian Ministers," *Armed Forces and Society* 15, no. 2 (1989): 227–47.
6. Robert Craig Brown and Ramsay Cook, *Canada 1896–1921: A Nation Transformed* (Toronto: McClelland & Stewart, 1974), 294–95.

BIBLIOGRAPHY

PRIMARY SOURCES

ARCHIVES DE LA CHANCELLERIE DE L'ARCHEVÊCHÉ DE MONTRÉAL

Fonds Paul-Napoléon Bruchési

ARCHIVES DESCHÂTELETS, UNIVERSITÉ ST-PAUL (UNIVERSITY OF OTTAWA)

Fonds Napoléon-Antoine Belcourt

ARCHIVES OF ONTARIO (TORONTO)

Sir William Hearst Papers

BIBLIOTHÈQUE ET ARCHIVES NATIONALES DU QUÉBEC—VIEUX-MONTRÉAL

Fonds Famille Bourassa
Fonds Famille Landry
Fonds Talbot Mercer Papineau

LIBRARY AND ARCHIVES CANADA (OTTAWA)

A.E. Blount Papers
A.E. Kemp Papers
Charles Murphy Papers
Clifford Sifton Papers

George Foster Papers
Harold Daly Papers
John W. Dafoe Papers
J.S. Willison Papers
Lord Devonshire Papers
Loring Christie Papers
Mackenzie King Papers
Newton Rowell Papers
Robert Borden Papers
Wilfrid Laurier Papers
Wilson MacDonald Papers

MME DOMINIQUE BERGERON NANTEL (MONTREAL)

Fonds Nantel-Bergeron

NATIONAL ARCHIVES (LONDON, U.K.)

Colonial Office, CO 537
Colonial Office Records, CO 42

NATIONAL ARCHIVES OF THE UNITED STATES (COLLEGE STATION, MARYLAND, U.S.)

General Records of the Department of State, Consular Correspondence

PARLIAMENTARY ARCHIVES (LONDON, U.K.)

Beaverbrook Papers, BBK
J.C.C. Davidson Papers, DAV
Lloyd George Papers, LG

QUEEN'S UNIVERSITY ARCHIVES (KINGSTON)

Norman Lambert Papers
T.A. Crerar Papers

TORONTO REFERENCE LIBRARY
William Main Johnson Papers

UNIVERSITY OF TORONTO ARCHIVES
George Wrong Family Papers

ONLINE SOURCES
Mackenzie King Diary
Sir Robert Borden Diary

NEWSPAPERS
Calgary Daily Herald
Halifax Herald
Halifax Morning Chronicle
La Presse (Montreal)
Le Canada (Montreal)
Le Devoir (Montreal)
L'Événement (Quebec City)
Manitoba Free Press
Montreal Gazette
Ottawa Citizen
Saskatoon Phoenix
Toronto Daily Star
Toronto Globe
Vancouver Daily Sun

IMAGE CREDITS

177 William James Topley/Library and Archives Canada/PA-012299.

183 Mme Dominique Bergeron-Nantel (Montréal), Fonds Nantel-Bergeron.

203 Library and Archives Canada, 1983-28-3445.

215 Library and Archives Canada, Acc. No. 1983-28-738, C-093224.

220 Dept. of National Defence/Library and Archives Canada/PA-007173.

224 William Rider-Rider/Canada. Dept. of National Defence/Library and Archives Canada/PA-002279.

270 Secretary of State/Library and Archives Canada/C-022355.

271 Canada. Dept. of Public Works/Library and Archives Canada/PA-057515.

278 Mme Dominique Bergeron-Nantel (Montréal), Fonds Nantel-Bergeron.

INDEX